CRIMINOLOGICAL
RESEARCH

Sara Miller McCune founded SAGE Publishing in 1965 to support the dissemination of usable knowledge and educate a global community. SAGE publishes more than 1000 journals and over 800 new books each year, spanning a wide range of subject areas. Our growing selection of library products includes archives, data, case studies and video. SAGE remains majority owned by our founder and after her lifetime will become owned by a charitable trust that secures the company's continued independence.

Los Angeles | London | New Delhi | Singapore | Washington DC | Melbourne

Jamie Harding

CRIMINOLOGICAL RESEARCH

A Student's Guide

$SAGE

Los Angeles | London | New Delhi
Singapore | Washington DC | Melbourne

Los Angeles | London | New Delhi
Singapore | Washington DC | Melbourne

SAGE Publications Ltd
1 Oliver's Yard
55 City Road
London EC1Y 1SP

SAGE Publications Inc.
2455 Teller Road
Thousand Oaks, California 91320

SAGE Publications India Pvt Ltd
B 1/I 1 Mohan Cooperative Industrial Area
Mathura Road
New Delhi 110 044

SAGE Publications Asia-Pacific Pte Ltd
3 Church Street
#10-04 Samsung Hub
Singapore 049483

Editor: Alana Clogan
Assistant editor: Rhoda OlaSaid
Production editor: Manmeet Kaur Tura
Copyeditor: Sarah Bury
Proofreader: Sharon Cawood
Indexer: David Rudeforth
Marketing manager: Ruslana Khatagova
Cover design: Francis Kenney
Typeset by: C&M Digitals (P) Ltd, Chennai, India
Printed in the UK

Library of Congress Control Number: 2021945168

British Library Cataloguing in Publication data

A catalogue record for this book is available from the British Library

ISBN 978-1-5264-2088-6
ISBN 978-1-5264-2089-3 (pbk)

At SAGE we take sustainability seriously. Most of our products are printed in the UK using responsibly sourced papers and boards. When we print overseas we ensure sustainable papers are used as measured by the PREPS grading system. We undertake an annual audit to monitor our sustainability

This book is dedicated to my grandchildren, Callan and Corryn, whose ability to invent games is such a joy and distraction. I took particular encouragement from the one where Professor R. G. Davidson earned £1,000,000 from writing an academic book.

CONTENTS

ACKNOWLEDGEMENTS

I am extremely grateful to a large number of people without whose help this book would not exist, or at least not in its current form:

The police officers who very kindly gave up their time to be interviewed and provided excellent data.

My colleagues who took part in such a lively discussion in the online focus group.

Libbie Thrower and Emily Hindmarch who did a fabulous job of proofreading the draft, making comments and finding/checking references.

Louise Riccalton, Ian Cook, Thomas Raymen, Mary Laing, Adele Irving, Mike Rowe and other colleagues who either provided, or pointed me to, helpful examples.

Professor Kurt Barling who provided me with such informative feedback on my analysis of the Who Killed PC Blakelock? documentary.

The ever-patient staff at Sage who supported me so well: Natalie Aguilera, Eve Williams, John Nightingale, Ozlem Merakli and Alana Clogan. It has taken so long that I can only apologise if I have forgotten the contribution that someone made!

The anonymous reviewers who gave helpful and constructive feedback on the draft chapters.

Everybody who gave me encouragement when I was finding writing hard going, particularly my wife Allison.

Lucy the Labrador for keeping me grounded with her constant reminders that the need for food is even more fundamental than the need for good research methods.

ABOUT THE AUTHOR

Jamie Harding received his PhD from the Department of Sociology and Social Policy at the University of Newcastle upon Tyne. He has been employed at Northumbria University since 1995, first as a lecturer in Housing Studies and more recently as a Senior Lecturer in Research Methods in the Department of Social Sciences. Before moving into higher education, he worked for a number of social housing organisations.

Jamie's main area of interest is qualitative and quantitative research methods, which he teaches at undergraduate, postgraduate and doctoral level. He also lectures on criminal justice – an area in which he has co-edited the SAGE textbook, *An Introduction to Criminal Justice* with Pamela Davies and George Mair – and homelessness, a subject on which he has written two monographs. He is programme leader for the Police Constable Degree Apprenticeship, which is run in partnership with Northumbria Police.

Jamie is married with two adult children and two grandchildren. He enjoys running and was delighted to win the highly prestigious Claremont Road Runners summer club handicap race in 2021.

ABOUT THE AUTHOR

DISCOVER THE ONLINE RESOURCES

Criminological Research is accompanied by online resources to support your teaching. Find them at: **https://study.sagepub.com/crimresearch**

Lecturers can log in to access the following:

Podcasts

- Four podcasts in which academic colleagues discuss some of the methodological questions that they faced when undertaking research. I am very grateful to my colleagues for giving up their time to provide these.
- Seven podcasts in which undergraduate students are interviewed shortly after they finished their dissertations. All achieved a very high mark. I am extremely grateful to the students for giving up their time to talk to me so that others can benefit from their experience and good practice.

Essay Questions, Multiple Choice Questions, Helpful Learning Resources and Tips for Lecturers

Each chapter is accompanied by:

- Two essay questions and four multiple choice questions, which can be used by lecturers in teaching and exams.
- Links to the most relevant SAGE Research Methods and Criminology videos, which can also be shared with students.
- Links to any other learning resources that are relevant.
- Key tips for lecturers on presenting the topic.

PowerPoint Slides

Approximately five PowerPoint slides accompany each chapter highlighting key points.

Dissertation Questions

Dissertation questions are provided, including a selection for everyone as well as for students who used empirical data.

Students can access the following:

Dataset

The dataset that readers will need for the analysis in the second part of Chapter 11 is provided here.

1

INTRODUCTION

──What you will learn in this chapter──

By the end of this chapter, you will:

- Understand the purpose of the book
- Be aware of the damage that can be caused by using research methods incorrectly
- Understand the contribution that research methods can make to the study of Criminology when they are used correctly
- Begin to read criminological research findings critically, thinking about the methods that have been used
- Be able to identify the types of criminological research that are most likely to be feasible for an undergraduate student

Purpose of the Book

There were three reasons for writing this book, beyond my enthusiasm for the use of research in the Social Sciences in general and Criminology in particular:

1   To demonstrate how the knowledge and skills that are needed to conduct methodologically sound research have been, and can be, applied to research into the area of crime.
2   To enable you to conduct your own research into criminological issues, should you wish to. This will involve an assessment of the forms of research that are most likely to be feasible for you as a student. More substantially, it will require you to become aware of the issues to consider at each stage of the research process and to develop a range of skills in areas such as sampling, data collection and data analysis.

3   To enable you to evaluate published research and to identify its most appropriate application to issues surrounding crime and criminal justice. You will be encouraged to look for key factors that can determine the quality and value of research into criminological issues. In addition, you will be equipped to critically evaluate the use that is made of research by public bodies and politicians.

Why Research is Important

Research can increase our understanding both of crime and of criminal justice. To take one example, domestic violence (or intimate partner violence) was a crime that, before the groundbreaking research of Dobash and Dobash (1979), was regarded as being of little significance, and one that required a minimal police response. This study demonstrated that women were most at risk of violence from their partner, that the violence was linked to assumptions about marriage that focused on male needs and male control, and that the sources of 'help' that women turned to often left them alienated and victimised. It was one of several factors that gave a far higher profile to domestic violence as a crime and led to a transformation in the way the police and other agencies responded to the issue. The extent of change was demonstrated when the government launched a specific strategy to end violence against women and girls in 2016 (HM Government, 2016).

More recent research has provided a more detailed understanding of the issue. It has demonstrated that, while domestic violence is predominantly committed by men against women, the issue can also arise in same-sex relationships and women can be perpetrators of domestic violence against men. The areas that have been explored by research have included the motivations of male and female perpetrators of domestic violence (Elmquist et al., 2014), the long-term impact on children of growing up in a family where domestic violence is happening (Ryan et al., 2015), the factors that influence police response (Stith, 1990) and the training needs of professionals working with victims and survivors (Murray et al., 2016). However, despite all the advances in knowledge and improvements in services, the Crime Survey of England and Wales provides a sobering reminder that the problem has not been eliminated or even significantly reduced. Figures for 2017–18 were largely unchanged from previous years, suggesting that 2 million adults aged 16 to 59 years had been subjected to domestic violence in the period – 1.3 million women and 695,000 men (Office for National Statistics, 2018).

Agencies of criminal justice are increasingly depending on research findings to direct their work. For example, the College of Policing was established in 2012 to determine 'what works' in policing in England and Wales, supported by the What Works Centre for Crime Reduction, which was founded in 2013. Modern policing makes use of data to establish patterns of crime, to determine how resources can best be used and to evaluate the strategies that are employed by police forces (Telep and Somers, 2019: 172).

The Dangers of Bad Research Methods

The dangers of using research methods incorrectly were perhaps most starkly illustrated by the wrongful convictions that arose from the 'expert' testimony provided to criminal trials by senior paediatrician Professor Sir Roy Meadow. Meadow made incorrect use of statistics to identify the risk of two children in the same family dying from sudden infant death syndrome (SIDS), popularly known as cot death.

In November 1998, Donna Anthony was convicted of murdering her two children, one year apart, after Meadow and another expert testified that the chances of two occurrences of SIDS incidents in a case like hers were one in 1 million. One year later, Sally Clark was convicted for murdering her two baby sons after Meadow gave evidence that the likelihood of two cot deaths in her case was one in 73 million. In fact, the likelihood was one in 77, but Sally Clark spent over three years in prison before her conviction was quashed. Donna Anthony waited even longer for her conviction to be overturned, and a third woman, Angela Cannings, was also wrongfully convicted of murdering her two sons in a case where Meadow gave evidence (*The Guardian*, 15.07.2005, www.theguardian.com/society/2005/jul/15/NHS.uknews1). The possible consequences of bad research were tragically demonstrated by Sally Clark's death in 2007: the coroner ruled that she had accidentally died from drinking too much alcohol as she struggled to deal with the traumatic experience of being wrongly convicted (Pallister, 2007).

Of course, such cases are extreme, but there are numerous other examples of research being discredited because of the methods used. Although Cesare Lombroso can perhaps be excused on the grounds that his was one of the first pieces of criminological research, nobody today would take seriously his claim to have demonstrated that criminals could be identified by physical characteristics such as thick and close eyebrows or broad cheekbones (Case et al., 2017: 347). So, poorly conducted research can have major negative implications for both criminological knowledge and practical decisions in criminal justice.

Being Critical of Research

It is because research is not always conducted or reported in a methodologically sound manner that you should be critical when reading and citing research findings. Being critical does not necessarily mean criticising but it does involve considering whether the claims that writers make are justified and supported by appropriate data.

A further reason for being critical is that there is not necessarily one 'correct' interpretation of research findings. For example, Ranasinghe (2017) re-examined four classic policing ethnographies (see Chapter 5 for a discussion of ethnography) that many subsequent writers had interpreted as meaning that police officers spent little time on patrol dealing with crime. The four ethnographies include data that was collected between the late 1940s and early 1980s, and Ranasinghe (2017: 871) acknowledges that definitions of crime have changed with time – for example, as discussed above, domestic violence is now viewed as a crime where it was once seen as a private matter. However, even when allowing for this factor, Ranasinghe (2017: 881–882) argues that the evidence presented in these classic works suggests that crime was a bigger part of patrol work than previous interpretations had acknowledged.

Research in academic journals, for example, has already been through a process of academic review – a point that is discussed further in Chapter 3. However, you should still reach your own view of the quality of the study or studies that you are reading.

Criminological Research and Students

A great frustration for many undergraduate students I have spoken to is the limited options that are available to them for conducting their own research. There are several reasons for this: we have all become more aware of the risks associated with some forms of research and so decisions about ethical approval are much more cautious than they used to be; people are increasingly sceptical when asked to fill in a questionnaire (for example); and professionals such as police and probation officers face huge pressures on their time so are unlikely to be available to take part in interviews or focus groups. In addition, crime is a particularly difficult area in which to conduct research for a number of reasons: victims of crime are often vulnerable and may be unwilling to discuss their experience; perpetrators may be vulnerable and/or dangerous people; and there is a major ethical question as to what to do if, in the course of your research, you discover information about a crime that the police may not be aware of. In addition, undergraduate students usually have a limited time period in which to conduct their research and prisons are one of the most difficult environments of all to access for research purposes. So it is important to consider the forms of research that are most likely to be realistic options:

- If you know a professional (a relative or friend) who works in the criminal justice sector, they may well be willing to take time to provide you with data (by being interviewed, filling in a questionnaire, etc.) and/or persuade some of their colleagues to do so. This is an approach that is far more likely to be successful than approaching a youth offending service, police force, etc., where you do not know anyone.

- Alternatively, you may be involved in some paid or voluntary work that brings you into contact with offenders, victims and/or the professionals who work with them. For example, while it is certainly not true that all people who use homeless hostels are offenders, these hostels usually accommodate some people with recent experience of prison. Of course, there will still be major practical and ethical issues to consider – including concerns around your own role as an 'insider', as discussed in Chapter 5 – but an environment in which you are already involved is often one where it is easier to gain access to data.

- It is almost always more feasible to investigate attitudes to, rather than experience of, crime and criminal justice. People are far less likely to be sensitive about discussing their attitudes and opinions than about recounting their experience of crime. Of course, attitudes may not be what you would ideally like to research but this broadens your options considerably in terms of the people that you can talk to and the issues that you can ask them about. Vignettes can assist in exploring opinions and attitudes, as will be discussed in Chapter 5.

- There are increasing numbers of documents that provide a rich source of data for analysis, many of them available online. This data can be subjected to content analysis, as discussed in Chapter 10. To take a very simple example, you could compare two newspapers for the words that they use to describe prisoners (offenders, inmates, etc.).

- Alternatively, if you are interested in studying the manner in which crime is portrayed in the media, there is a huge amount of material to choose from, such as documentaries, television dramas and films. The analysis of sources such as these is also discussed in Chapter 10.

- Finally, there is the option to consider analysis of 'traces' of crime. You could look round a city centre early one weekend morning and seek to measure the level and types of crime and anti-social behaviour that have occurred the night before through traces such as vandalised buildings or street furniture, litter left behind, traffic cones moved to places that someone thought amusing, and so on. Again, Chapter 10 includes more discussion of this option.

Key points for your own research

- No matter how interesting your plan for your research, think carefully about whether it is feasible.
- Think particularly about the people who are most likely to agree to take part in your research.
- Consider the option of using forms of data that do not need to be collected directly from people (e.g. documents, television programmes).

Key points when reading other people's research

- Do not quote or cite research without reading it critically.
- Be critical when reading the information that is provided about the methods used, and even more critical if this information is missing.

Further reading

For more explanations of the mistakes made by Professor Sir Roy Meadow, as well as other mathematical errors that have affected criminal justice issues, see Chapter 3 of:

Yates, K. (2019) *The Maths of Life and Death*. London: Quercus Editions Ltd.

PART I

PLANNING AND EARLY STEPS

Introduction to Part I

Part 1 of this book covers all the issues that you should consider, and decisions that you should make, before beginning your research – except for decisions about data collection, which is such a large topic that it merits a section of its own. As with most areas of life, careful planning and preparation of research can help to avoid difficulties and ensure that the best possible outcome is achieved. Many students only think about how they are going to collect their data, but each of the chapters in this section deals with another important issue that should be considered carefully.

Chapter 2 deals with issues of methodology. Qualitative research arose from a very different way of thinking about social sciences compared to the more traditional, quantitative approach. While many decisions about which of these methodologies to use are made on pragmatic grounds – and mixed methods can combine features of both approaches – it is important to understand that the underlying philosophy of qualitative research is fundamentally different to the one that underpins quantitative studies. A choice between a primarily inductive and a primarily deductive approach is another important decision that you must make; this chapter explains the difference between the two.

Chapter 3 discusses the literature review and the steps that you should take to find and select the most relevant literature. It is crucial that the outcome of this review is to show how your research fits with what is already known about your topic.

Chapter 4 assumes that a deductive approach is being taken (as is the case for the large majority of student research projects) and focuses on the research question or questions that you set yourself. Many projects are doomed from the start because they set questions which are fascinating but are impossible to answer through a piece of research. This chapter will discuss how you can set yourself a question or questions that you have a realistic prospect of answering.

Chapter 5 considers the plan or design that you put in place for your research. This is an issue that many students do not give much thought to, but there are a range of ways that research can be planned, and you should consider which one is most likely to answer your research question(s) or achieve your research objectives. The value that is placed on your research will be determined partly by whether you have chosen an appropriate research design.

Chapter 6 considers ethical issues. No research project avoids ethical scrutiny today, nor should it. Putting together a plan for your research in which the relevant ethical issues have been identified and dealt with is crucial to ensuring that you receive approval to go ahead.

Chapter 7 discusses populations and samples. The nature of the data that you collect will inevitably be affected by who it is collected from and how they are selected. Various methods of selection, and the situations in which they are most appropriate, will be considered.

If you make well-informed choices in all these areas, you will be in an excellent position to collect data that makes a valuable contribution to understanding your chosen topic.

2

KEY METHODOLOGICAL APPROACHES

What you will learn in this chapter

By the end of this chapter, you will:

- Understand the distinction between deductive and inductive approaches to research
- Be able to apply the distinction between positivism and interpretivism to practical questions such as the accuracy of crime statistics
- Understand the part played in the research process by theory, research questions and research objectives
- Be able to identify the thinking behind quantitative, qualitative, mixed methods and critical methodologies

Introduction

This chapter will consider the major questions around methodology. It is important to distinguish between methodology and methods. As Clough and Nutbrown (2012: 36) note, these are difficult concepts to define, with different writers often providing different definitions. Sapsford (2006: 175) argues that 'Methodology is the philosophy of methods'. Clough and Nutbrown (2012: 31) suggest that methodology is the purpose of the study, while methods are the tools by which this purpose is achieved.

I suggest that, under the heading of methodology, there are two crucial questions, involving terms that I will explain in the sections below. The first question is whether the research will be primarily inductive or primarily deductive. The second is whether it takes a quantitative, qualitative or mixed methods approach. Once these questions are determined, you can move on to the more practical issues that come under the heading of methods, such as who to collect the data from, how to collect it (e.g. whether to use questionnaires) and how to analyse it.

Induction and Deduction

The first distinction is one that many students find it difficult to grasp. Deductive methodology is often presented as the 'standard' approach and is the easier one to understand. However, you should also be aware of the inductive approach and the differences that it can make to the way that research is conducted.

Deductive Research and Research Questions

A deductive approach moves from the general to the particular. In practical terms, this is likely to mean that you undertake a thorough search of a broad range of the general literature in your area of interest before choosing your own particular topic of study. Deductive research is sometimes characterised as testing theory by creating specific hypotheses and then using research to determine whether they are correct (a process described by De Vaus, 2002: 13–15). However, in the case of the major criminological theories, it would be unrealistic to suggest that (for example) a piece of research could be completed that would test whether labelling theory was accurate. Instead, deductive pieces of criminological research often examine whether theories or concepts can be applied to particular situations or types of crime.

For example, Murphy and Harris (2007) took as their starting point the theory that John Braithwaite put forward in 1989 that shaming, when used in a reintegrative rather than a destructive fashion, can help to reduce re-offending. The theory specified that when disapproval of an offender's crime was expressed in a respectful manner, and followed by rituals of forgiveness or reconciliation, the impact could be positive, in contrast to an approach that gave an offender a label (e.g. thief). A number of pieces of research had tested this theory in relation to young people and manual workers, with far fewer studies examining its applicability in relation to white-collar crime (Murphy and Harris, 2007: 901–902). Murphy and Harris applied the theory to tax offenders in Australia and sought to test a very specific feature of it – namely that the interaction between the disapproval of others and the shame-related emotions of offenders influenced the level of re-offending. The applicability of reintegrative shaming theory to tax offenders was tested using a number of hypotheses, two of which were:

1   Offenders who experienced enforcement activities as reintegrative were less likely to re-offend than those who perceived them to be stigmatising.
2   Offenders who experienced greater feelings of shame were less likely to re-offend (Murphy and Harris, 2007: 903–904).

The findings clearly supported the first hypothesis because offenders who regarded the manner in which they were treated by the Australian Tax Office (ATO) as reintegrative were less likely to re-offend than those who found that it was stigmatising. However, the second hypothesis was not supported because feelings of shame had little impact on re-offending and a 'desire to put things right' was the feeling that had most impact on whether offenders complied with tax laws in the future (Murphy and Harris, 2007: 910–911). The conclusion to the research was that reintegrative shaming theory was broadly applicable to this type of white-collar crime, but that the theory needed to be developed further in terms of the types of emotions that affected re-offending (Murphy and Harris, 2007: 913).

However, in many cases a slightly modified version of the deductive approach is adopted – rather than forming a hypothesis based on a theory, the researcher seeks to answer a research question that is based on the existing literature. So, for example, Maguire et al. (2019) undertook research to answer the question: 'Did the implementation of community policing in Gonzales, a distressed Caribbean community, reduce fear of crime and increase perceptions of safety?' The answer to the question that the authors reached was that, in the initial stages, fear seemed to increase under community policing and people did not feel safer. However, as the community policing approach developed and became more effective, fear decreased and the people of Gonzales experienced greater feelings of safety. This study demonstrates that, no matter how much we long for a simple and straightforward answer to our question, the answer is usually less definitive and more complex than we had hoped!

Research questions are considered further in Chapter 4.

Inductive Research

In contrast, an inductive approach begins with the particular and moves to the general; the researcher does not start with what is already known about a subject but instead with data collection and analysis. It is only at a later point that efforts are made to build more general truths, by considering the relationship of the findings to existing knowledge (Moses and Knutsen, 2007: 22). So a substantial reading of the literature usually takes place after the researcher has reached findings based on their data.

Vollum and Longmire's (2007) research around the execution of murderers – focusing particularly on the reaction of family and friends of the victim (referred to as covictims) – is an example of a predominantly inductive study. The material they analysed was the statements of covictims reported in *The Huntsville Item* in Texas. In discussing the approach taken, Vollum and Longmire suggest that all the earlier pieces of work in this field had been journalistic; the lack of previous academic research in this area made an inductive approach the obvious one to take.

The key themes that Vollum and Longmire identified in the comments of family and friends that were reported in the newspaper were: just desserts, justice for the victim, justice for society, comparisons of the suffering of the victim and the condemned, a belief that execution was not harsh enough and a desire to see or inflict suffering or harm. Their first key finding was that family and friends largely believed that the death penalty had provided justice for the loss of their friend or relative. The second was that, although they had hoped that the execution of the murderer would being them closure in relation to their loss, many reported that they found little comfort from the execution.

Vollum and Longmire's study did not entirely fit with the model of inductive research described above because there was no substantial consideration of links with existing theory – the authors concentrated instead in their discussion and conclusion on the lack of research into the needs of covictims and how this difficulty could be tackled by further research. One part of their conclusion could have provided a link to existing theory, that is:

> Covictims' voices are generally obscured in the death penalty process. From the early stages, the victims and covictims of capital murder are removed as meaningful subjects in the justice process. (Vollum and Longmire, 2007: 615)

This point could have been developed to consider how their work contributed to existing theory on the 'ideal victim' (Cook and Davies, 2017: 391–392) or the role of criminal justice systems in creating secondary victimisation (Cook and Davies, 2017: 399–400). If this had been done, the study would have fitted more closely with the standard model of inductive research.

Grounded theory

Grounded theory is a particular form of inductive research which has gained importance within the methodology literature, with quite large numbers of studies in the social sciences claiming to use it – although this claim is often inaccurate in my opinion. It was introduced by Glaser and Strauss (1967), who rejected the idea of allowing theory to dictate the nature of research and instead advocated the use of an inductive approach. They argued that there was an 'embarrassing gap between theory and empirical research' (Glaser and Strauss, 1967: vii) and suggested that researchers should approach a subject without pre-determined ideas of what they were looking for, seeking instead to generate 'middle range' theories based on their data. Once this had been done, consideration could be given to how the middle-range theories fitted with broader social theories. The gap between grand theories about society and specific (often small-scale) research projects could be bridged through the grounded theory method.

Harding (2006: 131–132) describes the process of grounded theory, suggesting that it should begin with data collection but that analysis should start as soon as there is sufficient data to work on. This data is put into different categories and the categories are used to form abstract concepts; theory building involves arranging these concepts into a logical scheme. The categories, abstract concepts and theory should all be modified as more data is collected.

There is no doubt that Glaser and Strauss' ideas could be applied to Criminology, even though it hardly existed as an academic subject at the time that they were writing. There would clearly be little point in a student conducting a small number of interviews about experiencing temptation to commit crime in order to determine whether control theory (or an aspect of it) was right or wrong. Instead, they could begin by conducting their interviews, then analyse their data as described above and see if they could build some sort of explanation or theory for what they had found, before looking to see where in the existing literature there was material that could be compared to their explanation/theory.

The collection of data without reference to existing literature and theory has led to the slightly cynical – but almost certainly accurate – criticism voiced by Barbour (2008: 197) that a grounded theory approach is sometimes used because the researcher is too lazy to read the relevant literature. At a more conceptual level, it could be questioned how far a researcher ever approaches their subject without any pre-conceived ideas. Researchers quite naturally and correctly choose to examine subjects where they have an interest and where they are motivated to find out more; this interest is often linked to having strong views about the subject.

Research objectives

So it may be difficult to conduct research in a manner that reflects entirely the principles envisaged by the grounded theory approach. Identifying one or more research objectives represents a middle way between testing a specific theory (or answering a specific research question) and approaching a subject with a completely open mind. Research objectives are less specific than research questions and are defined by Davies et al. (2011: 353) as:

The purpose for which the research is being carried out. They can be basic (couched in terms of exploration, description, understanding, explanation or prediction) or they can be of an applied nature (e.g. to change, to evaluate or to assess social impacts).

For example, my colleague Mary Laing (then Mary Whowell) undertook a PhD study examining male sex work in Manchester (UK). Male sex work is an under-researched area compared to female sex work and the motivation and opportunity to undertake the research arose from Mary's voluntary work with a project providing front-line services to men who sold sex on the street. Three objectives were set for the research:

1   To document sex work practice by mapping the where and when of street-based male sex work in Manchester.
2   To describe how men perform sex work on the streets and specifically explore how they sell sex.
3   To critically explore how male sex work is regulated by formal and informal bodies.

The research design was inductive and evolved as Mary undertook participant observation and interviews with stakeholders and sex workers. She produced important findings in relation to each of these objectives, including the following:

1   The history of certain spaces within Manchester was key to understanding why they became de facto 'red light landscapes'.
2   Male sex workers developed means of walking, looking and dressing that enabled them to generate business, while at the same time being able to blend into the background of the street.
3   Outreach teams played a central role in the regulation of sex work. (Whowell, 2009)

Deduction, Induction and the Student

Most students opt to adopt a deductive approach to their research and there are several good reasons for this. The idea of conducting research to seek to answer a research question is relatively easy to grasp and can keep you focused throughout your study. Constantly asking 'is this helping to answer my research question?' is a good way to ensure that you don't get diverted into writing about literature, or collecting data, that is not relevant to your study.

Secondly, many university research processes assume that a deductive approach is being taken: you may be asked to specify a research question, or to produce a detailed plan for your research, as part of your dissertation preparation or ethical approval processes. It may not be acceptable to write on a form a statement such as *The research will collect data from forensic scientists who have worked extensively with West Midlands Police, with the themes and issues to be discussed in the dissertation being determined by the content of the interviews.*

However, it is important to be aware of the differences between deductive and inductive approaches and the choices that they present to the researcher. It is also important to remember that few projects are inductive or deductive in their entirety and most will include elements of both approaches. For example, a researcher may have a specific research question to answer but, after conducting the first few interviews, may adjust the interview guide (see Chapter 9) when it becomes clear that there is an important issue that was not covered by the original list of questions.

Textbox 2.1

What is the mistake? Grounded theory

Try to identify the mistake(s) that a student has made here and then have a look at Appendix 1 to see whether your view is the same as mine.

A student sets out to conduct research to establish whether the reasons for acquisitive crime that are suggested by traditional forms of strain theory can be applied to young shoplifters. She negotiates access to a number of anonymised pre-sentence reports written by members of a Youth Offending Service, which discuss the reasons for shoplifting offences being committed by young people. These reports are searched for references to frustration at being unable to achieve the material goals valued by society by legal methods. The student finds few examples of these feelings being discussed, with many more references to peer pressure. She concludes that, having conducted a grounded theory study, she has found that strain theory is unhelpful in explaining the actions of young shoplifters.

Quantitative Research, Qualitative Research and Other Methodological Approaches

The most discussed methodological divide in research is the one between quantitative and qualitative approaches. The most obvious difference between these two approaches is that quantitative research tends to collect limited amounts of data from large numbers of respondents, while qualitative research tends to collect more detailed data from smaller numbers. However, these two approaches also have a number of differences in terms of underlying assumptions and characteristics: the key philosophical difference is the one between positivism (which is associated with quantitative methods) and interpretivism (which is associated with a qualitative approach).

Positivism and Interpretivism

Bryman (1988: 13–21) notes that positivism is a concept that is often discussed without a clear definition, but identifies a number of characteristics that most discussions attribute to it. Positivism reflects a belief that the methodology of the natural sciences is applicable to the social sciences, despite the different subject matter (i.e. people, who have feelings, behave irrationally, etc.). Only phenomena that are observable should be recorded: feelings or subtle differences in perspective are not a matter for the researcher. It follows that positivists believe that there are objective and verifiable facts about the social world that the researcher should seek to identify.

In contrast, interpretivism focuses on seeking to understand people's experiences from their own, subjective perspective. It assumes that reality is socially constructed because different world views are created as people place experiences within their own social, cultural, historical and/or personal context: actions cannot be understood outside of this context. Instead of one, single objective reality, there are different forms of reality constructed by different people. So there can be no 'objectively' conducted research, as the values and world view of the researcher will inevitably influence the study (Hennink et al., 2011: 14–15).

The level of overlap between the positivist position and quantitative methodology, and between the interpretive position and qualitative methodology, will be demonstrated below. There will first be a discussion of crime statistics – an example that demonstrates particularly well the differences between positivist and interpretivist approaches.

Crime Statistics

Official crime statistics from 1857 were based on returns from police forces and the courts, and were originally thought to represent an objective view of the level of crime and of trends in crime (Maguire and McVie, 2017: 164–165). This reflected the prevailing positivist perspective of the time. However, there has been an increasing awareness of the limitations of these figures, culminating in the UK Statistics Authority announcing in 2014 that they did not reach the standard for national statistics (Hope, 2015).

The Crime Survey of England and Wales (formerly the British Crime Survey) was launched in the 1990s and was originally intended to be used alongside police statistics to provide a fuller, more objective picture by identifying the types of crime that were under-reported to the police. It is a household survey, asking a random sample of households about the extent to which they have been victims of crime (Maguire and McVie, 2017: 165). However, with time it has come to be regarded as an independent source that provides another, more accurate perspective on the level of crime (Hope, 2015).

There are substantial difficulties with the crime statistics provided by either method. Police statistics are believed to include fairly full representations of the most serious crimes and those crimes that need to be reported for insurance purposes. However, they do not cover crimes that are not reported to the police, so underestimate the levels of domestic violence, to take one example. In contrast, the Crime Survey of England and Wales focuses on 'personal' and 'household' crimes, but does not include crimes against organisations, drug-related offences or many forms of fraud (Maguire and McVie, 2017: 166–169).

Hope (2015) argues that the people who do not respond to the Crime Survey of England and Wales are among those who are most likely to be victims of crime, and that, by placing limits on the number of crimes that can be recorded against any one individual, the survey fails to acknowledge that some people experience crime almost continuously. The survey had not previously covered online crime but an experimental module included in the 2015–16 survey provided an estimate of 5.8 million 'fraud and computer misuse' crimes – only slightly smaller than the aggregate figure for all other forms of offence (Maguire and McVie, 2017: 172). This suggests that the failure to include this type of crime previously was a major difficulty with the survey.

The weaknesses of the different methods of compiling statistics demonstrate the problems in trying to establish an objective truth about the amount of crime taking place.

A positivist could argue that the imperfect tools that are available do not alter the truth that there is a 'real' figure for the amount of crime and that improvements to the method of measurement will bring us closer to it. However, the interpretivist could, in turn, point to different interpretations of what should be considered a crime. This issue has proved particularly controversial in the case of rape, with some police forces being heavily criticised for making decisions not to record some allegations of rape as a crime because of a lack of supporting evidence. For example, Northumbria police re-opened 54 rape cases in 2014 after Her Majesty's Inspectorate of Constabulary criticised the manner in which decisions to record 'no crime' for such alleged offences were taken (www.theguardian.com/uk-news/2014/oct/06/northumbria-police-reopen-54-rape-cases-deemed-no-crime).

Characteristics of Quantitative Research

The close links between a positivist view of the world and quantitative methodology are reflected in the characteristics that Bryman (1988: 21–40) attributes to a quantitative approach. Some of these are discussed below, with my examples:

- **Measurement:** Quantitative methodology seeks to measure social phenomena in a similar manner to natural phenomena such as heat. In addition to the amount of crime, measures are also sought for phenomena as diverse as satisfaction with the criminal justice system (Hope, 2015) and the amount of time that detectives spend investigating crimes (Fallik, 2018).
- **Causality:** Although we cannot produce the same sort of 'laws' as the natural sciences, for example that heating water to 100 degrees Celsius at sea level will always produce steam, quantitative researchers seek to identify some factors that make others more likely. For example, research has consistently shown that people who define their ethnic origin as 'mixed race' are more likely to be victims of crime than people who class their ethnic origin as 'White' (Phillips and Bowling, 2017: 194).
- **Generalisation:** The quantitative researcher does not just want to find what is true for the people who are subjects of the research, but also to generalise to others. So, if they cannot collect information from an entire population, they will tend to choose a random sample from which they can make statistical inferences about all the people in the population. When the Crime Survey of England and Wales adjusts its sampling strategy, there is often a debate as to the impact on the generalisations that can be made to the population (see, for example, Hope, 2015). Sampling is discussed further in Chapter 7.
- **Replication:** In the natural sciences, research is sometimes repeated to produce the same result continuously, for example every experiment to stretch a spring demonstrates the truth of Hooke's Law (https://phys.org/news/2015-02-law.html). In the social sciences, it is more usual to use the same measure repeatedly in order to track changes over time. The Crime Survey of England and Wales is often used to measure changes to levels of crime against individuals in England and Wales (although the difficulties associated with this are noted above) and the Commercial Victimisation Survey does the same for crimes against businesses. As the 2017 commercial survey used a similar methodology to the 2012 survey, it reported with confidence that there had been no significant increase in shoplifting in this period, but that the cost of shoplifting to retailers had increased, due to a higher number of incidents involving items worth over £50 (Osborne, 2018: x).

- **Individualism:** Although the quantitative researcher typically deals in statistics, it is the aggregate of individual views that is of interest, rather than the impact of interactions between individuals. So, for example, South Africa's Medical Research Council conducted an anonymous survey of men in which 28% said that they had raped a woman or girl and 3% that they had raped a man or boy. The survey simply counted up the number of respondents who gave each answer rather than addressing the cultural issues, or the nature of relationships between men and women, that may have contributed to making rape such a disturbingly common experience (Smith, 2009).

Textbox 2.2

Example of a study with classic quantitative characteristics

One study that demonstrated the key quantitative characteristics of causality and measurement concerned gang membership. Researchers used a measurement of the extent to which a young person was involved in a gang that had been used in English-speaking countries – based on answers to six questions such as 'Which of the following best describes the ages of people in your group?' – and sought to apply it to Latin America. They then considered whether membership of gangs increased the amount of deviant behaviour that young people were involved in (or whether the reverse relationship was true – young people who were involved in substantial delinquent behaviour were more likely to join gangs). They concluded that the questions used to measure gang membership needed to be adjusted if they were to be applied to more countries but, with these modifications, the measure could help to predict delinquency among individuals and groups (Rodriguez et al., 2017: 1165–1184).

Characteristics of Qualitative Research

Bryman (1988: 50–69) identifies the characteristics, and underlying principles, of qualitative research that are tied to its interpretivist roots. Again, some of these are presented below with my examples:

- **Naturalism:** Qualitative researchers argue that quantitative research methods – for example, structured interviews – create an artificial environment in which individuals are unlikely to provide information that truly reflects their behaviour. In contrast, qualitative data collection techniques – particularly observation – are thought to have the benefit of recording people in their 'natural' state. To illustrate this point, research into policing through quantitative methods such as surveys has often proved difficult for reasons such as many police officers tending to form a close-knit group who are distrustful when asked to provide information to outsiders (Nix et al., 2019: 531). Instead, many classic studies of policing have collected qualitative data through ethnographies. In some cases (e.g. Holdaway, 1983), the researcher could be confident that they were seeing 'natural' behaviour because they were themselves a police officer, and in others (e.g. Rowe, 2007) a researcher spent an extended period of time with police officers to build trust and enable officers to relax into their regular patterns of behaviour (ethnography is a research design that is discussed further in Chapter 5).

- **Ethogenics:** Individual actions can often only be understood by considering them as part of a wider 'episode' in an individual's life. If we see, or have an account of, the whole of an episode then we can begin to identify the belief system that has led a person to act in a particular way. So, confrontations between supporters of different football clubs can often be best understood by considering the history of rivalry between the clubs and sometimes also the areas in which they are based.
- **Seeing through the eyes of others:** Consistent with the interpretivist position that there will be multiple perspectives on any situation, qualitative researchers are committed to 'seeing through the eyes' of others. The researcher must seek to understand, although not necessarily to share, the point of view of those being studied. So, for example, Sleath and Brown (2019: 519) studied Integrative Offender Management, a government initiative designed to co-ordinate the work of different agencies with responsibility for offenders. They found, through qualitative interviews, that there were a range of perspectives on this approach, with some professionals and offenders viewing it as limiting the opportunities for re-offending, some professionals feeling that it increased offenders' perceptions that they were seen as criminals, one offender believing that it increased the risk of re-offending once the surveillance was finished, one professional feeling that offenders became frustrated which led to an unwillingness to co-operate with agencies, and one offender arguing that it limited the opportunities to look for work.
- **Description and contextualism:** Qualitative researchers believe it is important to view human behaviour in context, so describing the scene, or understanding the background to the problem, is essential if we are to understand what is going on. So, for example, Holdaway's (1983: 1) policing ethnography begins with a description of Hilton, the area covered by his police station:

Two years before my research began in the mid-1970s a social survey of the area identified its housing conditions as the worst in the borough; only about one-fifth of the 53,000 people who lived in Hilton had exclusive access to hot water, a bath and an inside lavatory. In the central area of the subdivision, it was estimated, one family in six was headed by a single parent, and 9 per cent of families had four or more children.

- **Flexibility and lack of structure:** Qualitative researchers tend to conduct studies that are towards the inductive end of the spectrum and to change their approach as unexpected issues are raised by research. For example, my colleague Thomas Raymen undertook a study of a parkour community in the North East of England – parkour being an activity that is seen as on the border between a leisure activity and deviance, because it involves moving around urban spaces in an unconventional manner (climbing up scaffolding, jumping over walls, etc.). Thomas introduced visual methods and photography part way through his data collection when it became clear that photography was a key element of the culture of the community. He initially took his own photographs but, when this provided little insight, he worked with his participants to take and select the images to include in the research output (Raymen, 2017).

Textbox 2.3

What is the mistake? Cybercrime

Try to identify the mistake(s) that a student has made here and then have a look at Appendix 1 to see whether your view is the same as mine.

A student conducts research into awareness of cybercrime among students by conducting interviews with six of his peers. He reported his key findings as:

- Students used the same password for an average of 3.8 purposes.
- 100% of students admitted that they sometimes did not take enough security precautions when online.
- One third of students had lost money at some point in their life due to cybercrime.

The student concluded that, as the university had 18,000 students, approximately 6,000 were likely to have suffered financially from cybercrime at some point in their lives and the university should undertake a major awareness-raising campaign on this issue.

Mixed Methods Research

Given that quantitative and qualitative methods are based on such different methodologies, it is sometimes suggested that they cannot be combined within one research project (Spicer, 2012: 480). However, writers such as Moses and Knutsen (2007: 293–294) argue that the distinction between the two approaches is an unhelpful one and that many studies will include elements of both quantitative and qualitative methods – a mixed methods approach. The methods are treated as being of equal status, in contrast to triangulation, where one is used to 'check' the other. Spicer (2012: 485) suggests that combining methods can facilitate asking a wider range of questions than would be the case if just one approach was used.

An example of a study that made good use of both quantitative and qualitative methodology is one that examined the use of various measures to tackle the perceived anti-social behaviour of young people. This research was conducted in four Community Safety Partnership areas: two London boroughs and two cities in the North of England. Quantitative data was collected by identifying all the young people in the area who – within a two-year period – had received an Anti-Social Behaviour (ASB) warning letter, signed an Anti-Social Behaviour Contract (ASBC) or been made the subject of an Anti-Social Behaviour Order (ASBO). Quantitative data was obtained by tracking these young people through databases held by local youth offending services. Qualitative data took the form of interviews with staff of youth offending services, together with young people and parents who they had worked with (Lewis et al., 2017: 1233–1234).

The quantitative data demonstrated that the system was not dealing with young people as policymakers had hoped. Although Anti-Social Behaviour Contracts had been intended as a measure to 'nip crime in the bud', in over 40% of cases they were signed after a young person had been charged with at least one criminal offence and, in some cases, quite large numbers of criminal offences. Young people were found to have been charged with more offences after they signed Anti-Social Behaviour Contracts than before, including more serious offences (Lewis et al., 2017: 1243–1244).

The qualitative data provided reinforcement to these quantitative findings, while also identifying other difficulties and some strengths of the system. The problems with processes were further illustrated by some professionals highlighting a lack of evidence for young people's alleged anti-social behaviour and some parents disputing claims about their children's activities. Professionals and parents were quoted at some length to illustrate this point (Crawford et al., 2017: 20–21). Linked to this issue, some young people and parents were reported to believe that they were offered little choice over signing agreements that were meant to be voluntary (Crawford et al., 2017: 18). The qualitative data demonstrated that some young people did not understand the processes that they were going through, with one quoted as saying 'I remember signing something, but I don't know what it was!'

One positive finding that emerged from the qualitative data, and that was not evident from the quantitative databases, was that families sometimes welcomed their children becoming involved in the system for dealing with anti-social behaviour because it could create access to other services (Crawford et al., 2017: 20). In addition, parents noted the positive support that could be found among family, friends and neighbours (Crawford et al., 2017: 21).

The overlapping but also distinctive contributions made by the quantitative and qualitative elements to this study demonstrate the value of using mixed methods in some circumstances.

Critical Research

Critical criminology is a long-established tradition, recognised as a major perspective on the causes of crime, and boasting its own international journal. It is linked to critical research, which rejects the principles underlying both quantitative and qualitative approaches and suggests that 'the aim of social research should be to change society for the better' (Henn et al., 2009: 27). Critical researchers believe that the dominant values of society are those of powerful groups and that research that does not address these values will inevitably reproduce existing power relations. They have sought to challenge structures of power exerted on the basis of gender, ethnicity, social class and disability (Henn et al., 2009: 29–38).

A classic study that took a critical approach was Hall et al.'s (1978) research into the perceived crisis of street robberies in the early 1970s. These crimes became known as 'muggings' (although there was no definition in law of such a crime) and, in the view of Hall et al., were used to present African-Caribbean people as presenting an inherent risk of violence, thus reinforcing the dominant position of those who were White.

The concern of critical approaches to change power relationships has resonance with the principles of action research. Reason and Bradbury (2006: 1) acknowledge that action research is an ambiguous concept but offer this definition: 'a participatory, democratic process concerned with developing practical knowing in the pursuit of worthwhile human purposes'. Participatory action research, sometimes referred to as participatory appraisal, is particularly concerned with changing the power relationships between researchers and respondents, reducing the distinction between the two roles (Lopes, 2006: 216–217). Examples of how this can be achieved in practical terms will be considered in Chapter 5.

Key points for your own research

- Be clear, and make explicit in your methodology section, whether your approach is primarily inductive or primarily deductive.
- Do not describe your research as grounded theory unless you are confident that its characteristics justify this description.
- In the case of deductive research, be clear as to what answer you have reached to the research question or what has been the outcome of the testing of your chosen theory or theories.
- In the case of inductive research, identify any objectives that were set for the research and, if so, whether these objectives have been met.
- While choices of qualitative methodologies in particular are often affected by practical factors – for example, a limited number of respondents or a student not feeling comfortable using statistics – it is important also to conduct and report the research in a manner that is consistent with the underlying assumptions and characteristics of your chosen methodology.
- Where mixed methods are used, be sure to identify the contribution of the quantitative and the qualitative elements.

Key points when reading other people's research

- If the research is deductive, consider whether the hypothesis to be tested or the research question(s) to be answered has been specified and whether a clear outcome to this process has been discussed.
- If the research claims to be inductive – and especially if it is described as grounded theory – consider whether it has followed the process of collecting and analysing data before making a substantial review of the literature.
- Identify whether a clear and convincing rationale had been provided for the selection of quantitative, qualitative, mixed methods or critical methodology.
- Consider whether the research has been conducted in a manner that is consistent with the underlying principles of the chosen methodology.

Further reading

A further example of a piece of research that tested the value of theory in explaining a particular type of crime – specifically the use of situational crime prevention theory to explain environmental crime – is:

Husman, W. M. and van Erp, J. (2013) 'Opportunities for environmental crime: a test of situational crime prevention theory', *British Journal of Criminology*, 53: 1178–1200.

Another study that clearly demonstrated some of the underpinning principles of quantitative research is one undertaken by Stansfield. This sought to measure attitudes to violence by creating a scale of 1–100 and showed a concern for causality by seeking to establish whether sport and other factors had an impact on 'risky' behaviour and violent attitudes:

Stansfield, R. (2017) 'Teen involvement in sports and risky behaviour: a cross-national and gendered analysis', *British Journal of Criminology*, 57: 172–193.

A further example of a mixed methods study – in this case looking at the impact of long-term imprisonment – is provided by Hulley, Crewe and Wright, who examined the difficulties experienced by long-term prisoners. The results are reported in separate articles, but the quantitative questionnaire data and the qualitative interview data both made important contributions to the findings:

Crewe, B., Hulley, S. and Wright, S. (2017) 'Swimming with the tide: adapting to long-term imprisonment', *Justice Quarterly*, 34(3): 517–541 (this reported primarily on qualitative interview findings).

Hulley, S., Crewe, B. and Wright, S. (2016) 'Re-examining the problems of long-term imprisonment', *British Journal of Criminology*, 56: 769–792 (this reported primarily on the quantitative survey findings).

Wright, S., Crewe, B. and Hulley, S. (2017) 'Suppression, denial, sublimation: defending against the initial pains of very long life sentences', *Theoretical Criminology*, 21(2): 225–246 (this also reported primarily on qualitative interview findings).

If you are interested in a new innovation to estimate the amount of crime in an area, based on Twitter posts, see:

Williams, M. L., Burnap, P. and Sloan, L. (2017) 'Crime sensing with big data: the affordance and limitations of using open-source communications to estimate crime patterns', *British Journal of Criminology*, 57(2): 320–340.

3

CONDUCTING A LITERATURE REVIEW

What you will learn in this chapter

By the end of this chapter, you will:

- Be able to select the most and least reliable sources in relation to your chosen topic
- Understand the importance of the perspective of the writer when reading any source
- Be able to find and select the literature that fits best with your chosen research topic
- Be able to identify the body of theory in which it is most appropriate to locate your own research

Introduction

This chapter is about looking for literature and choosing the sources that are most relevant and reliable to present alongside your own research. Detailed advice as to how to organise these sources into a literature review is provided in Chapter 13.

Literature, Induction and Deduction

It was noted in Chapter 2 that the point at which literature is searched for, read and evaluated depends on the methodological approach adopted. The deductive model of the research process involves the researcher searching the literature before beginning to collect data in order to ensure that testing out a theory, or answering a research question, will add to what is already known about the topic. In contrast, inductive approaches – and particularly grounded theory – involve the researcher collecting and analysing their data before deciding which literature is most relevant to place along-side their findings. While it was suggested in Chapter 2 that this distinction is often not as clear cut as some of the writing on methodology suggests, it is still worth think-ing a little further about the role of literature in these two types of approaches.

Charmaz (2006: 165), in the context of studies that have used grounded theory, describes how a literature review – conducted after data has been collected and analysed – forms a basis for comparison with the researcher's own findings:

> The literature review and theoretical framework can serve as valuable sources
> of comparison and analysis. Through comparing other scholars' evidence and
> ideas with your grounded theory, you may show where and how their ideas
> illuminate your theoretical categories and how your theory extends, transcends,
> or challenges dominant ideas in your field.

The key principle here is important, regardless of whether a grounded theory approach has been taken or whether your findings can be described as theory. For you to demon-strate that the findings that you have produced are useful, you must show how they contribute (albeit in a very small way) to the ideas that are discussed in the existing literature.

Silverman (2006: 340) identifies two similar purposes of the literature review that are typical of a deductive approach:

- To demonstrate that the research is building on the topics, methods and theories frequently used in the subject discipline;
- To demonstrate that the research is building on previous studies.

At whatever stage the literature is considered in the research process, it is important that you know how to search for it and how to evaluate which pieces of literature are most important to cite and quote in your work.

The Practicalities of Searching for Literature

When you are searching your university library or other catalogues for literature, you must think carefully about the search terms to use. You will often need to employ what is usually referred to as 'Boolean logic' (see Oliver, 2012: 42–43), which involves using some or all of the following terms: AND, OR, NOT. Almost all library catalogues and other types of search engine employ this logic. An example is provided in Textbox 3.1.

Textbox 3.1

Using boolean logic to search for literature on racial and religious hate crime

I searched my own university library catalogue for sources on racial and religious hate crime. Clearly it would not be sensible to use either *hate* or *crime* as keywords but the phrase *'hate crime'* (in quotation marks) would be more effective. Searching for this phrase produced a list of 126,925 references – the first 10 included some broad references which would be almost certain to have sections on racist and religious hate crime (e.g. Nathan Hall's (2013) book with the title *Hate Crime*). In addition, there were three that focused specifically on hate crimes based on the victim's sexuality. So clearly I needed to narrow down my search. I made it more specific by adding a further term:

   'hate crime' AND racial

Now my list was 29,148 items long and my first page included material about hate crime, racism, ethnicity and lynchings – topics which were more specific to my area of study. While some of this material covered religious hate crime as well as racial hate crime, there were texts specific to religious hate crime that would not be on the list. I tried to tackle this difficulty by typing in:

   'hate crime' AND racial OR religious

However, this extended my list to 2,646,223 items, suggesting that something had gone wrong. The difficulty was that my search had been read as asking for material about racial hate crime or any material connected to the word 'religious' (not just religious hate crime) – clearly a very large number of publications. So instead I typed in:

   'hate crime' AND (racial OR religious)

This time I had 52,983 references. When I looked down the list, there were (as would be expected) many of the same references as I had found when I had typed in *'hate crime' AND racial*. However, there was also one on Islamophobia, that had not been there before.

(Continued)

> Two footnotes to this example. The first is that I could have tried to achieve the same effect using the NOT command, i.e. 'hate crime' NOT sexual. However, the list would have been 100,805 references long and would have included one on the first page that was not relevant to my area of study – a book by Roulstone and Mason-Bish (2013) called *Disability, Hate Crime and Violence*.
>
> Secondly, you may be surprised to hear my satisfaction that my 'best' method had reduced the number of possible references to 52,983 – clearly there was much more sorting to do. My university library sorts references by relevance, giving me first those that seem most relevant to my search terms. However, it is also possible to order the search in a number of other ways: by date (with the most recent first), within a specific time period, selecting only those that are available in the university library or only those from academic journals, or combinations of these and other factors.

Sources of Literature

In selecting literature, there are two key issues to consider: the quality of the source that you are using and its relevance to your topic. To deal with the issue of quality first, research that appears in peer-reviewed academic journals (for example, *The British Journal of Criminology*) has been through a process of careful scrutiny by independent reviewers. One of the questions that is considered by the reviewers is whether the arguments that are presented in the article, and the conclusions that are reached, are justified by the material presented. However, it is important to reach your own judgement because there can be differing opinions on the same piece of work. Similarly, monographs and textbooks, usually written by academics, can usually be assumed to provide good-quality material, although you should again make your own evaluation of this. The simplest way to distinguish these sources from other books is that they will include a list of references.

One disadvantage of using these types of academic materials is that the information tends to be slightly dated by the time it is published. Other sources, particularly when published online, can provide more recent material. However, when considering online sources – which have not been through a process of peer review – it is even more important to be critical and, in particular, to consider the motivations of the writer. If you were writing about prisons, for example, these are some of the additional sources that you could use and some of the factors to consider when using them:

- The Howard League for Penal Reform is a very well respected charitable body, which has produced many reports on issues around crime and punishment. Its website explains that it is named after John Howard, who looked for 'a humane prison system for English gaols to follow' and that one of its aims is 'fewer people in prison' (https:// howardleague.org/about-us). While the quality of the Howard League's research and reports is high, it is important to bear in mind that it would be unlikely to produce work suggesting that harsher punishments for offenders are appropriate. The same could be said of another pressure group, the Prison Reform Trust.

- Her Majesty's Inspectorate of Prisons is also a very well respected body, noted for producing independent, and often uncomfortable, reports. Most of these reports are written about individual institutions (prisons, secure training centres, immigration removal centres, etc.) based on inspection visits, but there also thematic reports, discussing issues across several institutions. The inspection process is a thorough one, as described on the inspectorate's website:

Prison inspections normally span two weeks, with two days of preparation and research during the first week. The Inspectorate collects information from many sources, including the people who work there, those who are imprisoned or detained there, and visitors or others with an interest in the establishment. (www. justiceinspectorates.gov.uk/hmiprisons/about-our-inspections)

However, it is important to remember that independent inspections are not research projects and so will not necessarily follow the same approach that a researcher would with regard to methodological issues such as interviewing and sampling. The purpose of the inspection is to determine how well prisons are performing against the four features of healthy prisons, as defined by the inspectorate – safety, respect, purposeful activity and rehabilitation. So there will not be the same detailed consideration of issues such as inmate culture that have been discussed in other studies (e.g. Crewe, 2006).

- In contrast, individual prisoners' own accounts of prison life tend to discuss the inmate culture extremely effectively. Erwin James and John 'Ben' Gunn are two prisoners who have written insightful accounts of their own experiences in prison: Gunn's work appears mainly in the form of blogs, while James has written articles for *The Guardian* that have been compiled into books, for example *A Life Inside: A Prisoner's Notebook* (2003).

Again, the high quality of such accounts should not prevent you from considering their limitations: James and Gunn could only discuss direct experience of the prisons in which they had been held, which are a very small percentage of the prisons in the UK. In addition, both served very long prison sentences for murder and both men are intelligent and reflective: their experiences and views are likely to be very different to those of a short-sentence prisoner with little education or capacity to reflect on their own experience.

- The Prisons and Probation Ombudsman mainly reports on individual cases where prisoners or (less frequently) people under the supervision of probation services have brought a complaint to them, or where somebody has died in prison. However, they also produce 'learning lessons' reports identifying themes across a number of complaints (see www.ppo.gov.uk/document/learning-lessons-reports). These reports are extremely useful but it is important to remember when reading them that all the material relates to complaints, so will not deal with situations where prisoners and people supervised by the probation service are satisfied with the way that they are treated.

- Government reports can provide important information, but it is important to bear in mind that they tend to be written by civil servants who are representing the government's perspective rather than taking an objective view. So, for example, the HM Prison and Probation Service (2019) strategy for tackling drug use in prisons includes some helpful information:

Between 2012/13 and 2017/18, the rate of positive random tests for 'traditional' drugs in prisons increased by 50%, from 7% to 10.6%, and drug use in prisons is now widespread, particularly in male local and category C prisons. (HM Prison and Probation Service, 2019: 3)

However, the strategy document then discussed the money that was being provided to tackle the problem and made some bold claims as to what the strategy was expected to achieve:

We will also reduce the demand for drugs in prison by developing more meaningful regimes, providing more constructive ways for prisoners to spend their time and ensuring the balance of incentives encourages prisoners to make the right choices. (HM Prison and Probation Service, 2019: 4)

The report failed to mention, for example, the reduction in the number of prison staff between 2013 and 2018, which occurred alongside an increase in violence and a reduction in the amount of time that prisoners spent in purposeful activity, as noted by Her Majesty's Inspectorate of Prisons in its annual report of 2017–18 (HM Inspectorate of Prisons for England and Wales, 2018). This particular point demonstrates the value of comparing different sources to gain a rounded view of an issue.

- Government press releases and politicians' speeches should be treated with even more caution, as they often make use of research in a highly selective manner or not at all. For example, in 1993 then Home Secretary Michael Howard told the Conservative Party conference that 'prison works'. He repeated this assertion on a number of occasions, quoting a research study where interviewed prisoners said that the most important reason for wanting to avoid re-offending was that they did not want to go back to prison. However, the author of the research in question was quick to point out that Howard did not mention that 62% of those interviewed later reported that they had re-offended after their release so, whatever deterrent value prison held, it was not usually sufficient to prevent re-offending (Burnett and Maruna, 2004: 390–392).

- Broadsheet newspapers can be a vital source of up-to-date information, but it is important to consider the perspective that they adopt and the sources of information that they use. As you may gather from the number of references to *The Guardian* in this book, it is the newspaper that I read most and is quick to report findings that are critical of government policy, particularly when the government is Conservative. The criticisms are often based on the reports of HM Chief Inspectorate of Prisons or pressure groups such as the Howard League and the Prison Reform Trust. It is important when reading articles in *The Guardian* to remember that it is a left-leaning paper with liberal values such as wanting to see prisoners rehabilitated. I would expect more right-wing newspapers such as *The Daily Telegraph* to focus on the need to protect the public by keeping dangerous people in prison, while other broadsheets might be somewhere between these two perspectives. Similar considerations need to be applied with newspapers throughout the world: for example, *The New York Times*, a highly respected liberal newspaper in the USA, was unsurprisingly enthusiastic in its report on a 2019 agreement reached between many Democrat and Republican politicians. The agreement specified that criminal justice policies of mass incarceration should be changed and that policy should consider issues such as racial segregation in housing and the manner in which areas with high concentrations of minority ethnic groups were policed (www.nytimes.com/2019/05/16/us/politics/criminal-justice-system.html?searchResultPosition=2).

- Extreme caution should be exercised when reading reports in tabloid newspapers, which often seek to sell papers by playing on people's fear of crime and the perception that life is too easy for criminals. Here it is particularly important to check where they are taking their information from. For example, the Daily Mail online on Boxing Day 2018 published a story about an alleged Christmas party at a prison which it claimed was operating like a Butlins holiday camp (www.dailymail.co.uk/news/article-6530029/It-looks-like-Butlins-prison.html). The origin of this story was a film of prisoners apparently dancing on Christmas day, which had appeared on Facebook. The report said that the footage was 'believed' to be from HMP Lancaster Farms and quoted an unnamed former prison officer who said that the footage made him 'want to vomit'. There was no discussion of any attempts to verify whether the footage was genuine, when it had been filmed or whether it did in fact come from Lancaster Farm, but instead the article included a very detailed description of the dancing, together with numerous expressions of disgust from people who had watched it.

- Even more caution should be exercised when using websites that do not belong to an individual or organisation that you recognise as being linked to criminal justice. While everyone is entitled to express an opinion online, you should consider carefully whether there is any reason to quote or cite that opinion. For example, a website called Quora offers a quite reasonable argument for Australian prisons focusing more on rehabilitation, but without any supporting evidence or indication of expertise on the part of the writer, so there would be no reason to use this opinion as part of your literature review (www.quora.com/Should-prison-be-tougher).

Prisons have been selected here because there is a particularly wide range of materials available about them. In other areas, there are fewer sources available. For example, if your interest is in probation, you will be able to use one excellent specialist journal (*Probation Journal*) and the reports of HM Inspectorate of Probation, but other sources are likely to be limited. There are fewer books and book chapters on probation, few first-hand accounts of people's experience of being supervised by the probation service, and the large majority of complaints dealt with by the Prisons and Probation Ombudsman come from prisons. However, the key principles – considering the motivations of the writer, evaluating the methodology used, comparing the conclusions to the findings on which they are based and seeking to compare with other sources wherever possible – should apply regardless of the number of sources available to you in your chosen area.

As was discussed above, we should be particularly careful when listening to the claims that are made by the government or individual politicians about crime. Crime and criminal justice policy are often highly contentious issues in politics; politicians have a huge vested interest in distorting research findings in order to suit their own ends. Textbox 3.2 gives an example of a policy where bad use was made of research at several stages.

Textbox 3.2

Policy based on bad research – the Troubled Families Programme

The Troubled Families Programme was a major initiative of the coalition government of 2010–2015. It targeted 120,000 families who, according to Communities Secretary Eric Pickles, were acting in the following manner: 'These families are ruining their lives, they are ruining their children's lives and they are ruining their neighbours' lives' (Siddique, 2012). The 120,000 figure was based on research by the previous Labour government's Social Exclusion Unit in 2004, suggesting that there were 140,000 families in Britain who were experiencing five of the following seven disadvantages: no parent in the family was in work; living in overcrowded conditions; no parent with any qualifications; the mother suffering from mental health problems; at least one parent with a long-standing illness or disability; an income below the poverty line; and the family could not afford a number of food and clothing items. These indicators were all about poverty and exclusion, and none necessarily meant that the people involved were ruining the lives of themselves, their families or their neighbourhoods (Ramesh, 2012).

Louise Casey, who was placed in charge of the Troubled Families Programme, quickly produced a report in which she discussed her understanding of the families' troubles. Her conclusions reinforced many of Pickles' concerns, but the report was heavily criticised for the sampling method used in her research – this is discussed further in Chapter 7.

Prime Minister David Cameron claimed in 2015 that virtually all of the families who were involved in the scheme had been 'turned around' and that the taxpayer had been saved £1.2 billion in the process. However, this information was based on returns by local authorities, which only received money from the government if they reported that a family had been 'turned around' – so had a huge incentive to do this (Butler, 2015). An independent evaluation of the programme – which involved a much more robust methodology with extensive data collection (Day et al., 2016: 10) – reached a very different conclusion. It argued that the programme had made little progress towards the outcomes it sought to achieve (Day et al., 2016: 69).

Textbox 3.3

What is the mistake? Gun control

Try to identify the mistake(s) that a student has made here and then have a look at Appendix 1 to see whether your view is the same as mine.

A student writing a dissertation on gun control laws in the USA includes the following passage:

During the race for the Democratic nomination for the 2020 US presidential election, Senator Cory Brooker launched an anti-gun agenda which involved banning 'assault weapons' (although he failed to define these), requiring that different classes of weapon were licenced or surrendered and prosecuting those who failed to comply. Brooker could not answer the question as to whether people could ultimately be imprisoned for failing to give up weapons. Similar proposals had previously been ruled illegal by the courts or had been ineffective in their implementation – for example, attempts to register all semi-automatic weapons in New York resulted in only 44,485 registrations, despite estimates that over 1 million such weapons were owned within the state (National Rifle Association, 2019).

(The full reference is National Rifle Association (2019) 'Sen. Cory Booker (D-N.J.) pushes may issue federal firearm owner licensing and gun confiscation', www.nraila.org/articles/20190510/sen-cory-booker-d-nj-pushes-may-issue-federal-firearm-owner-licensing-and-gun-confiscation)

Finding an Appropriate Theoretical Background

In addition to being very thorough in discussing all the literature around your chosen topic, you should also link that topic to broader criminological questions by the use of a body of theory. Sometimes the body or bodies of theory to choose is obvious. For example, Shortland and Varese (2014) examined the factors that explained the differing levels of piracy among different parts of the coast of Somalia. The obvious body of theory in which to locate this discussion was protection theory, which considers the relationship between states and criminal groups.

However, the decision you make regarding the appropriate body of theory to use is not always this simple. You may find that there are too many possible bodies of theory to choose from and that trying to write about them all would mean that none of them could be considered in sufficient detail. Any piece of work about the causes of crime runs this risk. Rock (2017: 26–47), in common with other authors, identifies a long list of theories and concepts that may help to understand why crime is committed:

- Anomie
- Social disorganization
- Control theory
- Rational choice theory
- Routine activities theory
- Radical criminology
- Functionalist criminology
- Labelling theory
- Subcultural theory

It would be an impossible task for a researcher to suggest how their findings could contribute to all of these theories, so they would need to select those that seemed to have the clearest links to their specific topic. If, for example, they were examining robberies from people who had consumed large amounts of alcohol, they would probably select those theories that are most concerned with opportunistic crime, hence:

- Routine activities theory, which argues that an increase in crime is due to an increased number of targets for crime with fewer people to guard them (Rock, 2017: 35–36).
- Control theory, which examines why some people resist the urge to commit crimes while others do not (Rock, 2017: 31–33).

In other cases, a researcher may be faced with the opposite problem, i.e. there is no body of theory that obviously fits with their findings. So, for example, Brunton-Smith and

McCarthy (2017) sought to examine the impact of family relationships during a prison sentence on the likelihood of re-offending on release. There was no body of theory directly relating to this topic so they drew on the 'pains of imprisonment' theory, which argues that the experience of imprisonment places a major strain on family relationships (Brunton-Smith and McCarthy, 2017: 464). Their research supported a key assertion of this theory by showing that imprisonment tended to have a negative impact on family relationships, both those that were strong and those that were weak before incarceration. However, the authors also adapted this theory to apply it to their specific topic by noting that, in the minority of cases where family relationships improved, this had a positive impact on the likelihood of re-offending (2017: 476–477).

Other Issues in Literature Selection

Of course, the selection of the body (or bodies) of theory in which to locate your work is only one of the issues that must be addressed in deciding which literature to include in your review. As Oliver (2012: 59) notes, the choice of which material to include is a subjective one and it is important that you are clear about your reasons for discussing some issues in detail and excluding others, or only mentioning them briefly.

To illustrate the different directions that a literature review can take, let us use the example of a student who has read about the eventual dismissal of misconduct charges against police officers who were on duty at the time of the death of Sean Rigg (Gayle, 2019). The student is concerned about the length of time that it took to conduct the various investigations into Mr Rigg's death and, more broadly, the relationships between the police and minority ethnic groups. They decide to write a dissertation about deaths in police custody of people from minority ethnic groups and the manner in which these have been investigated.

The student conducts an initial search of the literature that is available and realises that their review could cover any of the following topics:

- The ethnic mix of the UK, both today and through history.
- Racial discrimination and racial disadvantage.
- Historical tensions between police and minority ethnic groups.
- The historical claims that there is institutional racism within police forces.
- The specific accusation of institutional racism made against the Metropolitan police by the MacPherson inquiry into the manner in which the murder of Stephen Lawrence was investigated.
- Issues around police accountability; who monitors the lawfulness of the behaviour of those who are there to enforce the law on others?

- The system for investigating complaints against the police and deaths in custody.
- Questions around what represents truly independent investigation.
- Questions concerning who has the competence and skills to undertake investigations.
- The invisibility of much police work.
- The experience of tensions between police officers and minority ethnic groups in other countries – most notably the USA.
- The manner in which complaints against police officers are dealt with in other countries.
- Cases where people from minority ethnic groups have died in police custody.

In seeking to limit the material that they include, the student might first decide that they are going to focus on the UK and so not include international comparisons. They might also decide that they are going to focus on the practical difficulties around investigating complaints rather than the more theoretical questions around police accountability and the invisibility of much police work, because institutional racism will be their theoretical background. Finally, they might decide that there will be only a brief discussion of the ethnic mix of the UK – it will be assumed that the reader is aware that Britain has become an increasingly multicultural society, so the starting point will be to discuss how some ethnic groups have been the subject of hatred and discrimination.

Using the remaining issues, the student might then decide that they best fit into three literature review chapters as follows:

Chapter 1 – Racism in Society and Police Forces (covering racial discrimination and racial disadvantage, the historically difficult relationship between police forces and minority ethnic groups, and the accusation of institutional racism made by MacPherson).

Chapter 2 – Deaths in Custody (acknowledging that there have been occasions when White people have died in police custody, but will discuss cases involving people from minority ethnic groups, particularly where there have been suspicions that the full truth about the death has not been told).

Chapter 3 – Investigating Deaths in Custody (considering the system for investigating deaths in custody, addressing questions over what an independent investigation is and asking who has the skills to complete one).

This would provide a suitable context for the student's research into the reported comments of relatives of people from minority ethnic groups who had died in police custody. These comments would be analysed to examine the extent to which they drew – either directly or indirectly – on ideas of institutional racism and/or a perceived lack of independence in the investigation process, and whether they sought to link these two factors together.

Using Literature from a Range of Perspectives

As Oliver (2012: 77) correctly notes, any discussion of literature should include the controversies around the subject. As discussed in Chapter 2, some research is conducted from a very specific (often critical) perspective. Some students choose to take this approach in their writing and that is completely acceptable, provided that they acknowledge that this is what they are doing.

However, for most students, one of the purposes of a literature review is to identify a number of different, and sometimes conflicting, perspectives on an issue. So, in the above example on deaths in custody, the student would need to examine both the case that was presented by the MacPherson report that the Metropolitan Police were institutionally racist, and the work of writers who argued that institutional racism does not exist or that it was wrongly defined by MacPherson.

To take a further example, a student might decide to write about Murray's (1990) argument that posited the existence of a growing underclass in Britain – a group of poor people who had separate values from the rest of society, characterised by high rates of illegitimacy, unemployment among healthy, working-age young men and violent crime. In critically evaluating Murray's work, the student would need to consider both the arguments of those who believed that an underclass did not exist (e.g. Deakin, 1990) and also those who accepted that there was an underclass but believed that it was created structurally rather than by the behaviour of the people concerned (e.g. Field, 1990).

Textbox 3.4

What is the mistake? The gangs matrix

Try to identify the mistake(s) that a student has made here and then have a look at Appendix 1 to see whether your view is the same as mine.

A student writes a dissertation examining the helpfulness of labelling theory for understanding initiatives to tackle youth crime in London and the outcome of these initiatives. As one example, she considers the Gangs Matrix and the criticism of groups such as Amnesty International that the matrix stigmatises and ruins the lives of young people (www.amnesty.org.uk/london-trident-gangs-matrix-metropolitan-police). To balance her work by presenting an argument in favour of the matrix, she uses the following document which she finds on the website of an organisation called *London for Victims*:

(Continued)

Gang Matrix Climbdown Puts Londoners at More Risk

It comes as no surprise that bleeding-heart liberals have forced the Metropolitan Police to take hundreds of young people off their Gangs Matrix. Once again, the 'human rights' of young thugs have been placed above the needs of Londoners who fear being stabbed every time they leave their home. We have seen youth crime, gun crime and murder rising by at least 10% every year and the deaths of Eraj Seifi, James Dowdell and Sundeep Ghuman are just some of the reasons why more needs to be done to keep guns, crime and violent young people off the streets. No one is arrested for being on the matrix and, if they commit no crime, they have nothing to fear. But there are plenty of young people there who are a danger to us all – and it is right that every police officer knows who they are and can be ready for their next attempt to create mayhem in the capital.

Keeping Track of Your References

Oliver (2012: 51–52) suggests that it is important to note the references of your material as you read it and I fully support this view. It is often tempting, when you feel that you are 'flowing' in your writing, to think that you can make a note of a reference later. However, it is very easy to forget to go back to do this. I write from bitter experience that it can be incredibly frustrating to read through your work, find a section that you think is really helpful, and then realise that you do not have the reference for the material. A huge amount of time can be lost searching for the missing reference.

Of course, you can keep your references stored as a Word document but there are also programs available that can assist you with this and enable you to re-use the references or present them in a different format. Many universities have access to a program called Endnote that does this, and there are also freely available web-based resources, such as Mendeley (www.mendeley.com/?interaction_required=true).

Key points for your own research

- Begin with the academic sources (books and academic journal articles) when looking for literature on your own topic.
- Also look for relevant reports, newspaper articles, etc., but consider carefully the quality of the material and the evidence that is offered for any assertions.
- Whatever source you are using, think carefully about the perspective of the writer and how it influences the material that you are reading.

- Select the most appropriate body or bodies of theory in which to locate the specific issue that you are studying.
- Be selective about the areas that you discuss in your literature review and have a clear justification for the areas that you include and those that you exclude.

Key points when reading other people's research

- Decide whether the research contributes to the body of theory that the writer discusses in the literature section.
- Consider the perspective of the writer and how this might have affected their choice of literature.
- Look briefly through the list of references and decide whether they form an appropriate background to a rigorous investigation of the topic.

Further reading

Two sources that provide good advice about searching for literature are:

Hart, C. (2018) *Doing a Literature Review*, 2nd edn. London: Sage (1st edn 1998).
Wakefield, A. (2018) 'Undertaking a criminological literature review', in Davies, P. and Francis, P. (eds), *Doing Criminological Research*, 3rd edn. London: Sage (1st edn 2000).

4

IDENTIFYING A RESEARCH QUESTION

────What you will learn in this chapter────────────────────

By the end of this chapter, you will:

- Understand the difference between a general question and a research question
- Be able to distinguish between independent and dependent variables
- Understand the differences between explanatory and descriptive research questions
- Be able to choose an appropriate research question for your own study

Introduction

As was noted in Chapter 2, research questions are associated with deductive research: the researcher begins with a specific question in mind and then seeks, through the research, to answer that question. Many research processes, especially for undergraduates, assume that students are taking a deductive approach and ask them to specify a research question.

Quantitative studies typically use a deductive approach, and the type of research questions that they address often reflect the characteristics of quantitative methodology. Their questions frequently centre on the issue of causality, e.g. which factors cause people to feel safe against crime? Although qualitative studies tend to be more inductive in nature, there are many examples of qualitative research which address a specific research question. Again, the types of questions asked frequently reflect the characteristics of qualitative methodology, for example they may be descriptive in nature.

There are pieces of research that seek to address a number of research questions and it may be that you find that you need to ask more than one research question to cover the full scope of your project. However, where possible, it is helpful to focus in on a single question, because this makes it easier to ensure that everything that you do contributes to answering this question.

Characteristics of Research Questions

It is hoped that all students will question the things that they see around them in the world. We should want to know what the world is like, how it came to be like that, why it is like that and whether it is right that it is like that. However, not all the questions that we have about the world are suitable for research. In some cases, this is because our questions are too difficult for research to answer. For example, the question of whether the threat of capital punishment reduces the level of murder is one that has been debated for decades, with no definitive answer having been reached and no obvious suggestion as to how research could be conducted to inform the debate.

In other cases, our questions are not research questions because they are not worth answering. I sometimes wonder to myself how long a person could live for if they took one of every item from a supermarket and then went to live on a desert island, but have to concede that I could not justify the resources needed to conduct research to answer this question!

Green (2008: 51–57) suggests that a researcher should begin with a broad (or general) question and then narrow it to one that fits the criteria for a research question. These criteria are that the question is:

- Interesting – if the researcher is not interested in what they are doing, it is virtually guaranteed that they will not pursue the task with any enthusiasm;
- Relevant – addressing the question should potentially contribute something useful to our understanding of social phenomena;
- Feasible – boundaries should be placed around the research to ensure that there is a realistic prospect that it can be successfully completed;
- Ethical – ethical issues are discussed in Chapter 6;
- Concise – the question should be as precisely worded as possible; and
- Answerable – this is the most important difference between a general question and a research question; it must be a question that is capable of being answered by a piece of social research.

Types of Research Question

There are two broad types of research question – explanatory and descriptive.

Explanatory research questions

A researcher might have a general question such as 'Has the requirement for new police officers to be educated to at least degree level changed the way forces deal with vulnerable groups?' However, substantial refining would be needed to convert this into a question that fitted the criteria listed above, for example: 'Are there differences in the way students on the second year of the Police Constable Degree Apprenticeship understand the needs of victims of crime, compared to officers who joined police forces in the last decade and do not have a degree?' This is an example of an explanatory research question because it seeks to explain the impact of the requirement for higher levels of education on a specific aspect of policing. The possible research designs that could be used to answer an explanatory research question such as this are discussed in Chapter 5.

Explanatory research questions draw on the idea of independent and dependent variables. The nature of the relationship is that an independent variable may have an influence on a dependent variable. To take some obvious examples:

- Age is an independent variable that has an impact on the dependent variable of whether a person is involved in committing crime (younger people are more likely than older people to commit crime).
- The area where a person lives is an independent variable that has an impact on the dependent variable of whether they are a victim of crime (people who live in poorer areas are more likely to be victims of crime than people who live in more affluent areas).
- The type of school that a person attended is an independent variable that has an impact on the dependent variable of whether they reach the most senior levels of the legal profession (people who went to independent, fee-paying schools are more likely to become judges than people who went to state schools).

In many cases, relationships are not so straightforward and there can be fierce debate as to whether an independent variable has an impact on a dependent variable. Even when]it is clear that there is a relationship between two variables, there can be substantial disagreement about the nature of that relationship. So, for example:

- Boris Johnson's election by the Conservative Party to be prime minister of the United Kingdom was based partly on the role that he claimed to have played in bringing down knife crime statistics when he was Mayor of London (Walker, 2019). However, critics pointed out that knife crime fell all across the country in this period of time, raising the question of whether Johnson's policies had any impact at all.

- There seems little doubt that people who are homeless are more likely to have addiction problems than people who are not homeless. However, it is also true that people with addiction problems are more likely to be homeless than people who do not have addiction problems. There has been a long-running debate as to whether homelessness or addiction should be seen as the independent variable in this relationship (see, e.g., Kemp et al., 2006: 320).

- Ethnicity is an independent variable which has consistently been shown to have an impact on the dependent variable of whether a person is stopped and searched by the police, with African-Caribbean people being particularly likely to be stopped and searched. There has been a very long-running debate as to the reasons for this relationship existing, with explanations including racial prejudice on the part of police officers, African-Caribbean people being particularly likely to live in areas with high crime rates and African-Caribbean people being particularly likely to be out of the house and so 'available' to be stopped and searched on the street (Waddington et al., 2004).

Controversies such as these are one of the reasons for explanatory research questions being asked, to try to establish the exact relationship (if any) between one or more independent variables and a dependent variable.

Explanatory research questions can be of two types:

1   Factorial – seeking to establish the influence of one independent variable on a dependent variable by holding the other independent variables constant. So, for example, Bond and Jeffries (2014) examined whether courts in New South Wales (Australia) made different sentencing decisions in cases where offenders were convicted of domestic violence offences, compared to violent offences outside of the domestic context. To be confident that any differences they observed were not the result of changes to other independent variables, they made comparisons based on offenders having similar social characteristics (age, gender and indigenous status) and similar numbers of previous convictions, as well as committing similar types of violent offence. When holding all these characteristics constant, offenders were less likely to be sentenced to imprisonment, and, if imprisoned, more likely to be given a shorter sentence, if the offence was committed in a domestic context. The factorial approach demonstrated the impact of one independent variable (whether the violent offence was committed in a domestic context) on the dependent variable (severity of sentence).

2   Multivariate – seeking to establish which of a number of independent variables has the most impact on a dependent variable. For example, Harding (2004) asked the research question: *Which factors have most impact on whether homeless 16–17-year-olds who are re-housed by Newcastle City Council are successful in living independently?* (The dependent variable of success was defined as: staying in the property for more than six months, not being evicted or abandoning the property, and not becoming homeless again within a year). The impact of 122 independent variables was examined, from a wide range of areas including young people's family background, their educational experiences, their financial position and their experience (if any) of having been in trouble with the police. It was found that the independent variables with the most impact were whether the young person had ever tried drugs, whether they had quite a few friends and whether they felt that they had control over visitors to their property.

Descriptive Research Questions

Descriptive research questions are commonly used in qualitative research studies. Some of the elements that De Vaus (2002: 23) suggests should be included in a descriptive research question are:

1   Time frame;
2   Geographical location;
3   Whether the researcher is interested in comparing and specifying patterns for sub-groups; and
4   How abstract the researcher's interest is.

So, an example of a descriptive research question might be: What are the feelings of safety or fear of crime among male and female students of Northumbria University, when walking home to city centre Halls of Residence after midnight on Friday and Saturday nights? Descriptive research questions may appear to lack the complexity of explanatory research questions because they do not involve dependent or independent variables, but providing answers to them can be just as challenging, as the later chapters on data collection and analysis will demonstrate.

Research Questions that Students Can Address

When students choose a question that they would like to address through their own research, probably the most common error is to choose one that cannot be answered within the time and resources that they have available to them. I have had many conversations with disappointed and frustrated students where I have had to point out that it is not feasible for them to address their preferred research question, because the only resource that they have available is the limited time that they can put into their dissertation project. Examples of common types of problem in this area are:

- Students seek definitive answers to questions about the causes of crime. There is sometimes enthusiasm to write a dissertation that seeks to answer a multivariate research question covering a large number of factors that may be linked to crime levels. Alternatively, a student may wish to ask a factorial question that seeks to examine the influence of one factor, such as childhood trauma or experience of school. However, the causes of crime have been examined by researchers for over a century without reaching any clear or definitive answer, so it is highly unlikely that a small research project will be able to answer such questions. In addition, such explanatory research questions tend to be addressed using large samples and specific research designs (see Chapter 5), which are far beyond the resources of an undergraduate. It would, however, be feasible for a student to undertake a study to answer a research question such as: *Which factors do students living in Simonside Terrace consider to be the most important causes of crime in their area?*

- Students seek to make over-ambitious international comparisons. People released from Norwegian prisons appear to have much lower levels of re-offending than those who leave prisons in the United Kingdom (see, e.g., Ugelvik, 2016: 395–396). However, to conduct research to examine the reasons for this difference would require a wide range of data from both countries, something that is far beyond the resources of most undergraduate students. An alternative would be to compare documents that governments of both countries produced about their prison system, but that would require the student to be fluent in two languages. However, a student who spoke only English and who wanted to make international comparisons could realistically compare the United Kingdom with another English-speaking country such as Australia (where there is also a high re-offending rate after release; see www.sentencingcouncil.vic.gov.au/statistics/sentencing-statistics/released-prisoners-returning-to-prison). An appropriate research question might be descriptive rather than explanatory, for example: *What are the similarities and differences between the aims of imprisonment in the United Kingdom and Australia?*

- Students ask questions about criminal justice that are too broad for them to answer. For example, they may ask whether neighbourhood policing is effective in reassuring communities. This is an example of a question that could be addressed through an undergraduate dissertation if it became more specific, particularly if the student limits it to a geographical area that they are familiar with. So, for example, a student with friends on the Norris Green estate in Liverpool might ask: *What (if any) benefits do young people on the Norris Green estate perceive from the deployment of police officers and Police Community Support Officers to work with their community?*

- Students ask questions that could be answered by online research, but only with a high level of access or a high level of skill in 'data scraping' (accessing online information without the agreement of the organisation that creates it – the ethics of such an approach are discussed in Chapter 6). Instead, they could concentrate on publicly available online material and ask a question such as: *Which were the types of crime that Greater Manchester Police most commonly asked for assistance with via Facebook in 2020?*

A related point is that undergraduate students in particular should not worry that their question is not sufficiently striking or different from what has gone before to be worthy of asking. At undergraduate level, there is not the same need to make an original contribution to knowledge that there is for a PhD student, for example. You can take a topic on which research has previously been completed and ask a slightly different question, adapting it to the resources that are available to you. So, for example:

- Hutton, Whitehead and Ullah (2017) found that specifically trained faith-based volunteers had reduced the risk of unsafe alcohol consumption practices – such as pre-loading and binge drinking – among young people in Adelaide, Australia. You might conduct a piece of research to address the research question: *To what extent are a group of people who I went to school with aware of the dangers of practices such as pre-loading and binge drinking, and who might they go to for advice or information about this?*
- Mitchell and Roberts (2012) found that the public underestimated the severity of sentencing for murder and that most people believed that the sentences imposed were too light. You could conduct a piece of research to address the question: *To what extent do a group of final year Criminology undergraduate students at my university reproduce the pattern seen among the public of underestimating the severity of murder sentences and believing that these sentences are too lenient?*
- Werth (2017) argued that the parole board in California, USA, made decisions on whether to release prisoners that were based on the impression created by the individual offender rather than the various tools that have been developed to measure risk. You might conduct a piece of research to address the question: *To what extent do the documents provided on the website of the parole board of England and Wales indicate that decisions about parole are made by objective measures rather than individual impressions?* (The website at which you can find these documents is at www.gov.uk/government/organisations/parole-board)

Textbox 4.1

What is the mistake? Coming out of prison

Try to identify the mistake(s) that a student has made here and then have a look at Appendix 1 to see whether your view is the same as mine.

A student gains permission from Bromsgrove Advice Centre, where she is a volunteer, to interview all the former prisoners who approach the centre asking for advice in February 2020. She decides to make her research question *Does staying in a hostel on release from prison increase the likelihood that an offender will rate themselves as being at a high risk of re-offending?* The student conducts six interviews with former prisoners approaching the centre for advice; the results are summarised below:

Offender	Age	Current addiction problem(s)	Sentence served	Housing situation	Self-assessed re-offending risk
Ajay	30	None	6 months	Living with parents	Low
Carl	22	Drugs	3 months	Hostel	High
Haider	24	None	2 years	Staying with friends	Low
Margaret	35	None	3 months	Living with partner	Low
Nick	21	Drugs/alcohol	4 years	Hostel	High
Tony	19	Alcohol	9 months	Hostel	High

The student concludes that staying in a hostel increases the likelihood that a recently released prisoner will assess their risk of re-offending as high.

Key points for your own research

- If you are seeking to answer a research question, be clear in your methodology section that you are using an approach that is predominantly deductive.
- You should also state clearly whether your research question is descriptive or explanatory (and, if explanatory, whether it is factorial or multivariate).
- However, you should be cautious about explanatory research questions – they are often beyond the resources of an undergraduate student to answer.
- You must choose a research question that it is realistic for you to address, given the time and other resources that are available to you.

Key points when reading other people's research

- Consider whether the research is primarily inductive or primarily deductive. If it is primarily deductive, has the research question to be addressed (or the hypothesis to be tested) been made clear? Even where the research question(s) are not specifically stated, it should be clear to the reader what they are.
- If the research question is an explanatory one, is it clear which are the independent, and which are the dependent, variables?

Further reading

For a further example of a study that asked a factorial research question, seeking to establish the impact of race on sentencing while eliminating the impact of other independent variables, see:

Hood, R. (1992) *Race and Sentencing*. Oxford: Clarendon Press.

For an example of a piece of research that asked a more complex multivariate research question than those discussed in this chapter, see:

Beauregard, E. and Mieczkowski, T. (2011) 'Outside the interrogation room: the context of confession in sexual crimes', *Policing: An International Journal of Police Strategies and Management*, 34(2): 246–264.

5

RESEARCH DESIGNS

─What you will learn in this chapter─

By the end of this chapter, you will:

- Understand the central role that research design plays in planning your research project
- Be aware of the distinction between different types of quantitative research design and the manner in which they seek to demonstrate the impact of one or more independent variables on one or more dependent variables
- Appreciate the contribution that is made by research designs that are typically qualitative or mixed methods in character, such as ethnography, case studies and participatory designs
- Be able to make an informed choice of the most appropriate research design for your own study
- Be able to design a piece of research with reference to principles of validity
- Understand the importance of a pilot study in any piece of research

Introduction

Davies (2006: 265) defines a research design as:

> A design or strategy that justifies the logic, structures and principles of the research methodology and methods and how these relate to the research questions, hypothesis or propositions.

A good research design will ensure that credible conclusions are based on the evidence generated by the research. It becomes a plan of action for the research. Decisions about practical issues that are discussed in later chapters – for example, sampling, data collection, data analysis – are all part of the research design (Davies, 2006: 265–266).

Before considering the range of designs that can be used by criminological researchers, it is necessary to consider the principle of validity and some related concepts. Validity must be a key concept when designing research; all the action that follows from the design will be worthless if the design is not valid.

Validity

Validity in research is defined by Jupp (2006: 311) as:

> The extent to which conclusions drawn from research provide an accurate description of what happened or a correct explanation of what happens and why.

There are specific methods of checking the validity of findings after analysing data, which will be considered in Chapter 12. However, validity is a concept that should permeate every stage of the research process: you should be constantly asking yourself whether the decisions that you make contribute to you describing and explaining the issue that you are examining as accurately as possible. Two ideas that are closely linked to validity are reflexivity and triangulation.

Reflexivity

The following definition of reflexivity is offered by Alexander (2016: 514):

> Reflexivity denotes a style of research whereby one addresses how the research process affects the results. It requires precision about the analytical methods and data collection procedures used, and emphasizes the researcher's own assumptions and beliefs through explicit statements of how the researcher's very presence affects what he or she is investigating.

As this definition indicates, it is important to be reflexive, i.e. to consider the influence that you may have had (intentionally or unintentionally) all the way through your research. For example, you should think about how you might have influenced the research findings – might the comments of any of your respondents be influenced by any of your personal characteristics? Take, as an example, the interviews that I conducted with police officers which are discussed in Chapters 12 and 13 of this book. The respondents were all people I had worked with, so I had to consider carefully whether what they knew about me through meetings and informal discussions might have influenced the answers that they gave to my questions.

Similarly, if you are collecting data from people you know, you should consider whether your position is that of an 'insider', and, if so, how that might affect the outcomes of the research (see, e.g., Myers, 2019). For example, if you collect data about environmental crime among your peers who know that you are an activist in this area, you must consider not only how your own assumption and beliefs may be affecting the research, but also whether your friends may be shaping their responses to fit with what they know about you.

Linked to reflexivity is the question of 'positionality', where the researcher is from a privileged and advantaged position compared to the people who they are collecting data from. This concern is most often expressed when conducting research in the area of international development (see, e.g., Gaywood et al., 2020), but could equally apply if data is collected from victims or offenders by staff or volunteers within the criminal justice system. In addition to the ethical difficulties that arise from this situation (see Chapter 6), it is important to consider whether respondents' expressed views may be influenced by the power relationship with the person conducting the research.

The importance of reflexivity is demonstrated by the move in recent decades towards social scientists discussing their own role in collecting and analysing data and producing findings, which represents an acknowledgement that their decisions are likely to have an impact on the outcome of the research (Fontana and Frey, 2008: 140–141). Steinke (2004: 186–187) suggests that a comprehensive and very detailed account of decisions made during the research process is required to ensure that the quality of the researcher's work can be assessed by others. While the word count for an undergraduate dissertation may not allow for this, it is important that your methodology section includes information about key decisions, to enable the marker to assess the validity of your research.

Triangulation

Triangulation is a method of ensuring validity that involves 'checking' one form of data collection by using another, and/or 'checking' one form of data analysis by using another. This is different to the mixed methods approach that was discussed in Chapter 2, where the two methods are treated as equals. So, for example, a researcher might conduct an online survey of 200 students to establish their views of crime prevention measures in the city centre. They might then follow this up with a small number of qualitative interviews with students who were not involved in the survey to establish whether the same pattern emerges from this alternative form of data collection. Although it adds to the time that your research will take, building triangulation into your research design is another way of increasing the likelihood that your eventual findings will be valid – and will be recognised by readers of your output as such.

Quantitative Research Designs

Robson (2002, cited in Semmens, 2011: 58–59) makes a distinction between fixed and flexible designs. Fixed designs tend to be used in quantitative research and involve working closely to a pre-determined format. A series of rules and procedures are followed to ensure that the research is as objective as possible.

The concepts of the dependent and the independent variable, which were introduced in Chapter 4, are very important to quantitative research designs. Many designs seek to measure the impact of one or more independent variables on one or more dependent variables. These designs can be either longitudinal – i.e. they involve collecting data at (or about) two or more distinct points in time – or cross-sectional, when all the data is collected at one point in time. The first five designs discussed below are all longitudinal.

The Classic Experimental Design

This is sometimes viewed as the 'purest' type of design and is the one that comes closest to the natural sciences. The steps that are taken are listed below:

1   Two groups of people are selected – an experimental group and a control group.
2   Both are measured according to some characteristic, attitude or opinion.
3   The experimental group are subjected to a stimulus while the control group are not.
4   Both groups are measured according to the same characteristic, attitude or opinion as in Step 2.
5   Comparisons are made as to whether the experimental group have changed more than the control group.

This approach is similar to the one used in clinical trials of new drug treatments, which are often referred to as randomised control trials. Patients with a medical condition will be divided into two groups, and one group (the experimental group) will take the new drug, while the other group (the control group) take a tablet that looks identical but in fact contains none of the drug (referred to as a placebo). If the experimental group see an improvement in their condition that is not matched by the control group, it is assumed that the drug has brought about a positive effect.

Before moving on to some criminological examples, you may be wondering why there is a need for the control group who take the placebo. There are two main reasons:

1   To ensure that any improvement in the condition of the experimental group has not come about because of an expectation of improvement, rather than because of the actual impact of the drug. If it was the expectation that had brought about the change, we would expect to see an equal change in the control group. In some cases, even the people administering the treatment will not know which is the genuine drug and which the placebo, to avoid any risk that their expectations could create bias.

2   To ensure that any improvement in the condition of the experimental group is not due to a factor that is nothing to do with the drug, for example a change in the weather. Again, if this were the case, we would expect to see an equal change in the control group.

The researchers will try to ensure that the experimental and control groups are carefully matched according to factors such as age, length of time with the condition, other health-related factors, etc. This is a further measure to ensure that greater improvement in the condition of the experimental group can only be attributed to the drug and not to other factors (for further, very helpful discussion of this process, see Yates, 2019: 163–168).

Classic experimental designs are used infrequently in the social sciences; one of the reasons is that it is difficult to create the conditions for them to be put into practice. This is illustrated by Yuille and Tollestrup's (1990) study of the impact of alcohol on eyewitness memory. Their study created three groups: one whose members were given an alcoholic drink; one group that was given a drink that smelled and tasted like alcohol (a placebo); and one group that received no liquid at all. The participants witnessed a dramatised crime scene where there was a complex series of actions: these actions, the appearance of the actors and the setting for the scene were all designed to be distinctive. The scene was video recorded so that the accuracy of recollections could be tested later.

Interviews in which the participants described the crime they had witnessed were compared for accuracy. The group who had consumed alcohol were judged to have produced accounts that were 91% accurate; the group who thought they had consumed alcohol or that had consumed no liquid gave accounts that were judged to be 93% accurate. The research suggested, therefore, that the consumption of alcohol reduces the accuracy of eyewitness accounts.

The reason that this example does not fit exactly with the classic experimental design is that there was no measurement of the accuracy of the respondents' recall before any alcohol was consumed. It is possible that the group who consumed alcohol had weaker recall even before they had their drink. So it could not be stated with certainty that it was the alcohol that had caused the accounts to be less accurate. This demonstrates the difficulty of designing research that fits perfectly with the classic experimental design, and explains why there are many criminological pieces of research that have some, but not all, of the characteristics of this design.

The Quasi-Experimental Design

This design also involves dividing research subjects into two groups, but this is done after the data has been collected rather than before. Typically, the researcher will be seeking to compare groups who have achieved two different 'outcomes', and looking for factors that may explain this difference. One study of this kind involved interviewing prisoners at three stages: prior to their release, 4–6 months after release and 7–20 months after release. Ten years after the prisoners' release date, data from the Home Office Offender Index and the Police National Computer was used to divide the sample into two groups: those who had returned to prison and those who had not. The interview data was examined to look for factors that could explain why one group had been imprisoned again and the other had not. The analysis suggested that a key factor that divided the two groups was the level of hope that they expressed in the interviews – those with higher levels of hope that they could avoid re-offending were more likely to achieve this, but only if they experienced relatively few social problems on their release (Burnett and Maruna, 2004).

The Panel Design

This type of design is a classic experimental design without the control group. Panel designs are much easier to conduct than classic experimental or quasi-experimental designs because there is no need to find ways to distinguish between two or more groups of respondents. However, they cannot be as specific when identifying the factors that have brought about change.

So, for example, Davis et al. (1996) collected data from people who had been victims of robbery, nonsexual assault or burglary in New York. The data was collected at two points in time – one month after the crime and three months after the crime – to measure the extent to which the respondent had psychologically adjusted at each point. The research produced a number of important findings. For example, the extent to which the crime disrupted victims' perceptions of the world was a key factor affecting their level of distress – those who no longer felt that the world was a safe and controllable place were likely to face most difficulties in adjustment. In addition, the study found that the level of distress experienced by victims was likely to decline with the passing of time (Davis et al., 1996: 29–31). However, there was no attempt to measure which factors affected changes to the levels of distress between the two time periods.

The Retrospective Panel Design

This design involves asking people about their behaviour, feelings, beliefs or attitudes, both at the present time and at some point in the past. Compared to the other longitudinal designs, this one is much easier to put into practice, because there is only one data collection point. However, one obvious weakness of this design is memory: people may simply not remember from a past period or may get the timeframe wrong and think that something that happened six months ago actually happened two months or two years ago.

So, in the example above, Davis et al. (1996) could have interviewed victims once, three months after the crime, asking them a series of questions about their feelings. The researchers could then have asked them how they had been feeling two months previously. This would have saved substantial amounts of time and also prevented people being 'lost' between interviews (249 people were interviewed one month after the crime but only 181 could be interviewed after three months) (Davis et al., 1996: 6). However, there would have been a substantial reduction in accuracy as it would have been very difficult for victims to recall exactly how they had felt two months previously.

The Quasi-Panel Design

This design involves collecting data from one group of respondents at one point in time, then from a different group of respondents at a second time point. Here the difficulties in establishing relationships between independent and dependent variables are even greater than with other panel designs. Take, for example, a piece of research that sought to measure changes in time about opinions of conditions in prisons. A first round of interviews might suggest that the majority view was that prisons should be made more comfortable, while a second round (conducted a year later) might show a majority to feel that prisons should be made harsher. However, if the people taking part in the interviews at the second stage were different to those who took part at the first stage, the researcher would not know whether there had been a genuine change in public opinion about prisons or whether the second group had always had more punitive attitudes.

Despite the difficulties, these designs are often used to measure change in society, with the Crime Survey of England and Wales being one obvious example. In addition to questions about personal experience of crime, the survey includes questions on opinions and attitudes, such as whether respondents think that the police are doing a good job in their area. The responses are used to measure changes to opinions with time, despite the difficulty noted above of not knowing whether the groups interviewed at different times had always held different opinions. However, the only way to avoid this difficulty would be to try to interview the same people ever year for the survey, which would be problematic in practical terms as respondents move to different locations, are admitted to residential care homes, etc.

Textbox 5.1

What is the mistake? Domestic violence questionnaire

Try to identify the mistake(s) that a researcher has made here and then have a look at Appendix 1 to see whether your view is the same as mine.

At the start of March 2020, a chief constable announces a new focus on domestic violence in her force's work. A researcher sends a questionnaire to all response officers in the force, asking them about the amount of time that they have spent on different types of incident during the first two months of the year. They then send out the same questionnaire again at the start of May, asking about the time that has been allocated to different incidents in March and April. The researcher concludes that the Chief Constable's announcement has led to response officers spending substantially more time dealing with domestic violence incidents.

Cross-Sectional Designs

All of the designs discussed above are longitudinal because, even if they do not involve collecting data from people at two or more points in time, there is an attempt to make some sort of measurement of the relationship between different time periods. However, much quantitative research is cross-sectional, with data collected through 'one-off' surveys.

To take one example of a piece of cross-sectional research, Menting et al. (2020) undertook an online survey of offenders which asked them about places they had lived/stayed, homes they had visited, places where they had been victims of crime, places where they had been perpetrators of crime, current and former school locations, work locations and leisure locations. Their analysis of the findings showed that the offenders were most likely to commit crimes in areas where they undertook regular non-criminal activities. This finding was consistent across all types of crime.

(In writing this section on quantitative research designs, I have used De Vaus, 2002: 31–37, adding criminological examples.)

Are Quantitative Research Designs Feasible for Students?

While all students of criminology are likely to read about research that is conducted according to some of the designs discussed above, you may feel that a cross-sectional design in the form of a survey is the only option that is available for your own research. You may, quite reasonably, believe that you do not have time to conduct a longitudinal study, the power to influence criminal justice interventions or the actors to stage a dramatised crime scene. However, this section includes examples and suggestions as to how you might be able to put into practice some other types of quantitative research design.

It is important to remember that longitudinal studies can take place over a short time period and can measure the effect of a stimulus that is watched or read. For example, I used a simple panel design with a group of my students to examine their opinions of the Hillsborough disaster (if you are unaware of the details of this tragedy, you might want to look at: www.theguardian.com/football/2017/jun/28/long-road-justice-hillsborough-inquest-timeline). At the start of a seminar, I gave each students a handout which asked them (if they were willing to take part) to give their name or a pseudonym and then to answer the questions shown in Textbox 5.2. (This exercise was undertaken as former Chief Superintendent David Duckenfield was about to begin his third trial for manslaughter and others were facing trial for conspiracy to pervert the course of justice.)

Textbox 5.2

Questions asked of students about the Hillsborough disaster

Please give a scale score from 0 to 10 to indicate how far you agree with each of these statements, with 0 representing 'totally disagree' and 10 representing 'totally agree':

Despite all the time that has passed, it is correct that the Crown Prosecution Service is prosecuting police officers where there is sufficient evidence of wrongdoing.

Score 0–10:

(Continued)

South Yorkshire Police cannot be criticised for the decision to open an exit gate to allow fans into the ground when there was a danger of crushing in the street outside.

Score 0–10:

Chief Superintendent David Duckenfield has already been tried twice (with the jury unable to reach a verdict on either occasion) but justice demands that he faces a third trial.

Score 0–10:

The families receiving inaccurate information about the death of their loved ones caused untold suffering.

Score 0–10:

There is not enough focus on the activities of the fans that contributed to the disaster.

Score 0–10:

No matter what mistakes were made on the day, no one intended that people should die so it is inappropriate that any criminal charges are brought.

Score 0–10:

There should be no return to having standing areas at big football matches.

Score 0–10:

After collecting in the answers to these questions, I then showed the students a BBC documentary about the disaster that was critical of the strategy adopted by South Yorkshire Police on the day. After watching the documentary, students were given the same set of questions again. The material in the documentary appeared to have an effect because there were now lower mean agreement scores for comments or statements that defended the police – for example: *There is not enough focus on the activities of the fans that contributed to the disaster* – and higher mean scores for statements that were critical of the police, e.g. *Chief Superintendent David Duckenfield has already been tried twice (with the jury unable to reach a verdict on either occasion) but justice demands that he faces a third trial.*

One student made an excellent suggestion as to how this research could be improved: students could be asked in the first questionnaire how much they already knew about the Hillsborough disaster. This would have enabled me to measure whether those who had little prior knowledge had their opinions changed more than those who were already well informed about the events of that day. Nonetheless, I was able to conclude that, among my group of students, being presented with a critical account of the role of South

Yorkshire Police at Hillsborough led them to have less sympathetic opinions of the role of the police on that day.

Vignettes – i.e. brief accounts or descriptions – can also play a crucial role for a student seeking to conduct a piece of research that uses one of the designs described above. It is often difficult to use an example that involves real crime, for both practical and ethical reasons, so the creation of mini-stories that involve plausible accounts of a crime can be an extremely helpful tool.

To take one example of a study that had many similarities to a classic experimental design, Munoz et al. (2016) examined the question of why voters in Spain often re-elected politicians who were known, or believed, to have been involved in corrupt practices. The study essentially represented three separate experiments, each involving a pair of vignettes. All of the vignettes began by stating that a judge had accused the town's mayor of corruption by awarding a substantial contract to a company that had paid bribes to public officials. At the end of the vignette, respondents were asked, on a scale of 0 to 10, how likely they would be to vote for the mayor, with 0 representing 'would never vote for him' and 10 representing 'would certainly vote for him'. The differences in each of the three experiments were:

- In vignette one, the mayor had been a good economic manager, but in vignette two he had been a bad one.
- In vignette three, the mayor's party backed him against the allegation, but in vignette four they promised 'appropriate action' against him.
- In vignette five, the mayor's two predecessors had been involved in corruption scandals but in vignette six the town had no history of corruption.

The results showed that respondents tended to give low scores to the likelihood of re-electing the mayor under all conditions. While bearing in mind this overall position, two of the factors examined had an impact:

- Respondents were more likely to say that they would vote for the mayor again if he had a good economic record than if he had a bad one.
- Respondents were more likely to say that they would vote for the mayor again if his party backed him than if the party promised 'appropriate action'.

However, whether there had been previous corruption scandals had no impact on the likelihood of respondents saying that they would vote for the mayor again. This research did not meet all the conditions for a classic experimental design because it is possible, for example, that the respondents reading vignette one were more tolerant of corruption under any circumstances than those reading vignette two. Nonetheless, the study provided some important indicators as to the factors that might explain why politicians who are accused of corruption are sometimes re-elected.

I used a similar approach in one of my lectures where I sought to establish whether a history of domestic violence affected my students' views on the rehabilitation of people convicted of the most serious crimes. Half the student group were given the scenario in Textbox 5.3.

Textbox 5.3

First rehabilitation scenario presented to students

Andy was convicted of murder 15 years ago for the killing of an acquaintance in a fight. He had claimed self-defence, that the victim had used violence first, but witnesses confirmed that Andy had struck the first blow and had continued to punch the victim after he had lost the ability to defend himself. The judge passed a life sentence but attached a minimum tariff of 15 years because witnesses confirmed that there had been provocation: the victim had repeatedly mocked Andy over his disabled son, using highly insulting and prejudicial language. Andy had never been in trouble with the law before.

In the course of his sentence, Andy has acknowledged that the killing was not self-defence and that he was rightly convicted of murder. He has been in trouble once during his sentence – he was involved in a fight with another inmate (in which both suffered minor injuries) approximately one year into his sentence, shortly after he had heard that his partner was ending their relationship, having met someone else. Since then he has been a model prisoner, taking courses on anger management and consequential thinking, being constantly on an enhanced level of privileges, and training for a new career in financial management. He has been in an open prison for the last year, undertaking voluntary work, helping a charity with their accounts. The charity has given him an excellent reference.

Andy's brother has offered him accommodation for as long as he needs it once he is released. He does not have a specific offer of employment but is ready to apply for jobs and is confident that his new skills will enable him to find work quickly. He has kept in touch with both his children by letter and hopes to meet with them again in due course.

Andy understands that, if he is released, this will be on life licence; he is prepared to comply with whatever conditions are applied. As a member of the parole board, is your decision that Andy should be released or that he should spend more time in prison? What is the key reason for your answer?

The other half of the student group were given the same scenario but with a change at the end of the first paragraph. Their version read:

Andy had never been convicted of a crime before but, a few months before the murder, his partner made a statement that he had assaulted her. However, she later withdrew the statement and refused to press charges.

I discovered that the addition of the domestic violence allegation had no impact, possibly because I appeared to have misjudged my students' confidence in the process of rehabilitation. In the case of the scenario where Andy had never been in trouble with the law before the murder, 12 students said that Andy should be released and two that he should remain in prison. However, in the case where there had been the report of domestic violence, all 14 students said that he should be released. The qualitative comments focused on Andy's attempts to rehabilitate himself and a belief that he should be given a second chance.

Despite the limitations of my method, I was able to conclude that my students would consider other factors more important than a possible history of domestic violence when deciding whether to release a long-term prisoner.

Qualitative Research Designs

In contrast to fixed designs, flexible designs tend to be associated with qualitative methods and involve adopting an approach that can develop as the research progresses. The researcher exercises less control over the research setting (Robson, 2002, cited in Semmens, 2011: 58–59).

The designs discussed in this section of the chapter are described as qualitative because they usually involve the collection of mostly qualitative data, although none of them preclude quantitative data collection. It should be noted that a qualitative researcher will often identify an issue, set research objectives and collect data to meet these objectives without their study fitting the pattern of any of the designs outlined below. However, these designs are presented as options to consider in your research and to look for in the research of others.

Ethnography

Ethnography is a type of research design that has been highly influential in the development of criminology. It has its roots in classic anthropological studies of pre-industrial societies, which a researcher would go to live in for several months, as was the case with Margaret Mead's (1943) famous study of Samoa. Such approaches have subsequently been criticised for reflecting colonial values (Bacon et al., 2020: 4). Studies of working-class communities in the United Kingdom also involved researchers going to live in the environment that they were studying: Young and Willmott (1957) spent three years living in East London to collect data for their study, while Dennis, Henriques and Slaughter (1969) went to live in an unnamed Yorkshire mining village for a year.

Ethnographies with criminological themes have historically taken a similar approach. Whyte's (1955) classic study involved living for 15 months with a family in an area of Boston notorious for overcrowding and crime. Patrick (1973) undertook a self-directed study based on his experience of working as a young member of staff at an approved school in Scotland. He became friendly with a pupil (to whom he gave the pseudonym of Tim) and joined him on his returns to Glasgow on weekend leave. This leave involved Tim meeting up with his gang, giving Patrick the opportunity to observe first-hand the gang violence that was a major problem in Glasgow at the time. For example, part of his description of one incident was as follows:

> The man fell forward into the path of a few boys from the Young Team who were making for the exit. Beano later described what happened next: 'We did a Mexican dance oan his face'. (Patrick, 1973: 54)

Ethnography has played a particularly important role in providing an understanding of policing; showing how the public face of the profession is often very different from the culture that prevails out of sight of the public. Bacon et al. (2020: 2) argue that ethnography 'offers an unreplicable insight into the processes, structures and meanings that sustain and motivate this social group'. Ethnographies of policing have involved the recollections of police officers after completing their police service (e.g. Young, 1991), research conducted while serving as a police officer (e.g. Holdaway, 1983) or academics spending substantial amounts of time with police officers (e.g. Ramshaw, 2012). The first two examples contain elements of auto-ethnography, where the researcher gives a personal narrative but links their story to the social and cultural context of the time (see, e.g., Wall, 2008).

However, some more recent studies of crime have been described as ethnographic, despite there being no data collection through observation and no direct experience of the field that is being studied. Instead, a detailed understanding has been gained through interviews with people who have that direct experience. Mercan (2018) used interviews with a group of men he had known as a child, and who had subsequently became involved in crime, to understand the world of the 'professional' burglar. Fontes' (2019) understanding of transnational gangs from Guatemala was developed through detailed interviews with just one former gang member, although Fontes had also spent time volunteering with gang rehabilitation organisations and visiting gang members in prison to familiarise himself, as far as he ethically could, with the field.

So ethnography can take many forms. As Hammersley (2018) notes, it is an approach to research that is difficult to define, but there are four characteristics that tend to be evident in ethnographic studies:

Subject matter – ethnography is the study of a group or culture. The ethnographer is concerned with the ordinary, the study of people's daily routines (Fetterman, 1989: 11). So an ethnographic study of a criminal court would choose a time period in which there was likely to be a typical range of cases, rather than one involving a celebrity that was certain to generate large amounts of media interest.

Qualitative principles – although ethnography can incorporate quantitative data, it has at its heart the qualitative principle of 'seeing through the eyes of others', i.e. understanding the range of perspectives of those involved in the group or culture. As Fetterman (1989: 15) argues: 'This paradigm embraces a multicultural perspective because it accepts multiple realities. People act on their individual perceptions …'.

Inductive principles – the ethnographer's approach should be a flexible one and they should be willing to keep an open mind (Fetterman, 1989: 11): qualities that are associated with inductive research. It is often practical, as much as conceptual, factors that drive a flexible approach to ethnography. This is illustrated by Blaustein's (2016: 251) comment on his ethnographic research into community policing in Sarajevo Canton, Bosnia-Herzegovina:

> The choice of methods was very much determined by the nature of the access and the need for flexibility due to the unpredictable schedules of the officers as well as that of the author whose time was split between the research and a placement with UNDP [United Nations Development Programme].

Data – as was noted above, ethnography no longer necessarily involves an extended period of participant observation. However, the collection of a substantial amount of data is an essential part of the process.

Netnography

Netnography is discussed as a sub-section of ethnography because it involves using traditional ethnographic principles but applying them to research that is conducted online. It is the study of culture or a way of life, but part or all of the data used consists of what Kozinets (2020: 16) describes as 'online traces'. He defines this term in the following manner:

> When people post images or video or text online, or when they comment, share or do anything else that is accessible online to anonymous or networked others, what they leave behind are online traces.

Netnographers sometimes supplement these online traces by collecting other forms of data such as interviews (Kozinets, 2020: 16).

One example of a study that used netnography was that of Banks (2012), who examined 'advantage play' subculture. 'Advantage play' involves a number of legal strategies by which individuals seek to make money from online gambling: for example, accepting a free bet on an outcome from one company, and then betting on an alternative outcome with another company, with the amount of the second bet chosen to ensure a profit whichever outcome occurs. The researcher took part in advantage play and also joined an online forum of advantage players for a period of 18 months.

The criminal element that the study incorporated was 'savage' gambling sites that are involved in identity theft, money laundering and theft of payments from gamblers by not paying out winnings. Advantage players reported on, and discussed, these sites online (Banks, 2012: 177–178).

Personal exchanges and group discussion online provided 1,791 'threads' for analysis (Banks, 2012: 176). As will be noted in Chapter 6, the ethics of online research are complex; Banks offered the following justification for undertaking the research covertly, without declaring his role as a researcher:

> The decision to engage in covert research was not taken lightly. However, advantage players by the nature of their activities are furtive individuals. In particular, they demonstrate a deep commitment not to promote themselves, their profits or their actions. (Banks, 2012: 177)

It was noted that, although informed consent was not requested either before or after the study, the risk to participants was minimised by ensuring anonymity in the manner in which the research was reported. The risk to the researcher only took the form of the danger of losing a small sum of money (Banks, 2012: 177).

Can ethnography be for me?

One obvious question raised by these studies is whether it is possible for an undergraduate student to undertake ethnographic research, given than they do not have 18 months to spend as part of an online forum (as Banks did) and that any study that proposed using methods such as those of Patrick in Glasgow would be received with horror by an ethics committee! Despite the difficulties, I believe it may still be possible for you to undertake some forms of ethnographic study. Some hypothetical examples where this would be feasible are:

- A student in a university which has a Howard League penal reform local group interviews members of the group about their experience of its campaigns and activities.

- A student who lives in an area where there is a high level of crime writes an auto-ethnography of their experience of living in the area.
- A student joins an online discussion group debating whether corporate crime should be more severely punished and asks for the agreement of the group to conduct a netnography.

Textbox 5.4

What is the mistake? Study of Rothbury

Try to identify the mistake(s) that a researcher has made here and then have a look at Appendix 1 to see whether your view is the same as mine.

A student with family who live in Rothbury, Northumberland, decides to undertake a historical ethnographic study of the time in July 2010 when police were hunting for Raoul Moat in the countryside around the village. Shortly after his release from Durham Prison, Moat shot his ex-girlfriend, her new partner and a police officer. The police manhunt lasted seven days and eventually led to Moat shooting himself dead (www.bbc.co.uk/news/10513994) by a river in the village. The student collects data by interviewing her family members and their friends from the village about the experiences and feelings that they had during those seven days, having first checked that they are unlikely to become upset by an interview on this topic.

Case Studies

For many researchers, and for you as a student, resource implications may mean that a case study is the research design that is most feasible to use. A case study can be described as a 'detailed examination of a single example' (Flyvbjerg, 2006: 220). A researcher can make one case, or several cases, the subject of their study. There is no consensus as to how many cases would mean that the research could no longer be considered a case study – I suggest that, if there are more than five, the study should not be described in this way. Case studies can be quantitative, qualitative or mixed methods, although they tend to be predominantly qualitative in nature. Some recent examples of case studies demonstrate the very wide variety of forms that 'cases' can take:

- In a study of international perceptions of – and responses to – wildlife crime, Sollund and Runhovde (2020) used Brazil, Columbia, Uganda and Norway as case studies.

- To illustrate the importance of understanding 'the situated life experiences and biographies' of individuals who engage with violent extremism, Walklate and Mythen (2016) used the case study of the January 2015 terror attacks in France.
- To demonstrate the problems and possibilities associated with translating the offence of coercive control into practice, Barlow et al. (2020) used the case study of one police force area in England.
- Urbanik et al. (2017) examined the question of how 'street codes', which governed behaviour and violence in disadvantaged neighbourhoods, were affected by major neighbourhood change. They used as a case study Regent Park, Canada's oldest and largest public housing neighbourhood, which was undergoing restructuring.

It is important to correct one common misunderstanding of the term 'case study'. Where research output includes a detailed description of the circumstances of an individual from whom data was collected, this can be a very effective part of the presentation of the findings (as will be discussed further in Chapter 13) but is not a case study, unless that individual was (or a very small number of individuals were) the only subject of the research from the start.

Case studies are sometimes criticised for producing findings that cannot be generalised. For example, although not an academic piece of research, one of the objections that was raised to the MacPherson report was that it sought to generalise its findings about institutional racism in the Metropolitan Police largely on the basis of one case, i.e. the investigation into the murder of Stephen Lawrence. Lea (2000: 221) suggests that, in order to effectively demonstrate that institutional racism existed, 'it would be necessary to survey a series of such inquiries and look for patterns of behaviour which could then be located in patterns of institutional operation'. In contrast, a subsequent investigation of the Metropolitan Police by Her Majesty's Inspectorate of Constabulary found that the technical failings of the investigation into the murder of Stephen Lawrence had been shared by several other major cases (Brain, 2010: 290).

A number of points can be made to counter the criticism that case studies cannot be generalised. Firstly, as was noted in Chapter 2, generalisation is predominantly the concern of the quantitative researcher, while qualitative researchers aim for a more detailed understanding of specific situations. In addition, Flyvbjerg (2006: 224–225) argues that there have been single cases that have had much wider relevance, particularly when the findings take the form of a 'black swan' (the belief that all swans are white is disproved simply by seeing one that is black). So, for example, the widespread assumption that, in the post-MacPherson era, better police selection and training had prevented racists from becoming police officers was devastatingly disproved by the documentary *The Secret Policeman*. In this 2003 documentary, an undercover journalist trained as a police officer and recorded eight of his fellow trainees making racist remarks and engaging in racist behaviour (Brain, 2010: 334). While it is unlikely that a student would produce research findings with similar impact, a further point to consider is Yin's (2003: 10) argument that the aim of case studies should not be to generalise but to contribute to theory. So a student who found among a small group of their Criminology colleagues that there was strong support for the chemical castration of sex offenders should not conclude that this is the view of all students (or even all social science students within their own university), but might instead use their findings to contribute to theory about the factors that influence people's views on crime and punishment.

It is important to remember that case studies do not necessarily involve empirical data (i.e. data collected from human subjects). So, for example, Strobl undertook a case study of policing in the Eastern Province of Saudi Arabia where the aim was to 'harness what information is available', largely through documents, to better understand the role of policing in the province (Strobl, 2016: 547).

Strobl (2016: 545) notes that, in case study police research, understanding the historical and political context is crucial to understanding the case. Similarly, Yin (2003: 13) argues that one of the unique features of case studies is that the context is crucial to the research. Taking two hypothetical examples of case study research projects illustrates this point:

1   An undergraduate wishes to conduct a case study of the experience of burglary in an area where large numbers of students live and where many have had their houses/flats broken into. She decides to collect data by interviewing some of the students she knows who have been burgled and two neighbourhood police officers who have been offering advice to students about securing their property. Important contextual factors to consider and discuss in this case study would include the number of students in the city where the university is located, the nature of the student housing market in the city, the socio-economic profile of the city and of the neighbourhood, crime trends nationally and locally, the experience of crime among students in the city and the approach taken to neighbourhood policing in the police force area and the neighbourhood.

2   A student wishes to undertake historical case study research, based on an analysis of documents, into the miscarriage of justice experienced by the Birmingham Six. The six were wrongly convicted of two fatal bombings in Birmingham in 1974 and served almost 17 years in prison before their convictions were quashed (Lissaman, 2011). The historical contextual factors the student would need to consider would include the troubles in Northern Ireland, the IRA bombing campaign and the fear that it created, the public pressure on police forces to obtain convictions, the lack of procedural safeguards to prevent confessions being forced from suspects, the corrupt practice within the West Midlands Serious Crime Squad, the quality of forensic science evidence available at the time, the unwillingness of judges to

question the verdicts of juries and the widespread belief before the 1990s that Britain had 'the best criminal justice system in the world' (for reasons that were rarely specified).

Participatory Research Designs

It was noted in Chapter 2 that participatory approaches seek to change the power relationship between the researcher and the people who are the subject of the research. Participation can happen at all stages of the research process, but a participatory approach is often particularly evident in the form of the output. For example, the output from Pain and Francis' (2004) research, which examined the experiences of crime and community safety of socially excluded young people, included a spider diagram on which young homeless people had written directly their view of police officers, ranging from 'never had bad encounter' to 'do as they please' and 'perverts'. There were also timelines on which young people wrote their experiences at different ages of being both victims and perpetrators of crime (Pain and Francis, 2004: 100–101).

Diagrams enable the views of respondents to be represented in more direct form than traditional methods of reporting findings such as identifying trends and selecting quotations from qualitative interviews. However, elsewhere Pain and Francis (2003: 51) note that even diagrams cannot be considered to be completely the work of the subjects of the research: 'inevitably participants' words and diagrams are reinterpreted and re-presented to become the findings'. Pain and Francis (2003) argue that, on its own, the use of diagrams does not represent a different philosophy of research – ideally participants should also be involved in analysing and interpreting findings and in action taken to address issues raised by the research.

Research projects that involve training, learning from and working alongside peer researchers can go further in reducing both the distinction between the researcher and the respondent, and the power differences between them. For example, research into the lives of sex workers in Tyne and Wear was led by my colleagues Adele Irving and Mary Laing, but a number of peer researchers (women with varied experiences of the sex industry) were involved in shaping the research design, interviewing their peers and disseminating the research findings. The research report noted that:

> It is important to state that the peer researchers were central to the development and execution of the project. They were consulted on and engaged with all aspects of the research ... (Irving and Laing, 2013: 16)

Participatory research designs are difficult to put into practice: for example, training peer researchers requires very large amounts of time and skill. So, the new researcher might well want to avoid such designs until they have gained more experience. However, you should be able to look at pieces of research that claim to have a participatory approach and consider how far they represent a genuine transfer of power to the research participants.

Piloting

Whatever design you decide on for your research, it is important to include a pilot study, which is essentially a practice before you begin the main study. Although research is often completed to a tight timescale, which can make a pilot difficult to fit in, all sorts of unexpected difficulties can be revealed by a pilot. Finding these difficulties and tackling them can save huge amounts of frustration when the main study is undertaken. This is particularly true of quantitative studies – I have known the disappointment of having to ignore the answers given to a survey question by almost 200 respondents because I suspected that many had misunderstood what was being asked.

The respondents for a pilot study should not be the same individuals who will be included in the main part of your research. However, they should be as similar as possible. So if, for example, my research consisted of interviews with magistrates who sat in Newcastle Magistrates' Court, I might seek to conduct two pilot interviews with magistrates from other courts in the North East of England. Alternatively, if I were analysing tabloid newspaper articles from 2020 to determine their view of the impact of illegal drug use, I might undertake a smaller analysis of tabloid newspaper articles from 2019 as a pilot study.

Key points for your own research

- Do not feel that your research has to conform perfectly to one of the research designs described in this chapter. These are provided as examples for you to consider; many published pieces of research match these designs only partially or not at all. What does matter is that you have a logical plan as to how you will answer your research question(s) or address your research objectives.
- However, if the plan for your research does fit (or partially fit) one of the designs discussed in this chapter, it is important to identify this.
- Clearly describing your research design, and the reason for choosing it, is an important means of ensuring the validity of your study. Validity is a factor that should be borne in mind throughout the design process.
- It is fine if part of the justification for your choice of research design is practical, so long as it is also made clear that the design is a suitable one to answer the research question or address the research objectives. One common reason for choosing a

(Continued)

case study approach is that a student may have access to a particular environment through personal contacts or voluntary work.

- Although a new researcher is not prohibited from using some of the more complex research designs such as ethnography and participatory designs, it is important to consider carefully whether these are realistic, given your experience and the time and resources that are available to you.
- Think about the options – such as the use of vignettes – that may enable you to put a research design into practice effectively, even with limited resources.

Key points when reading other people's research

- Consider whether the researcher has provided enough information to demonstrate that they are using the design that they claim to. For example, if they say that they have used a classic experimental design, have they compared the measures taken before and after some of the respondents were subjected to an intervention?
- Consider whether the researcher has chosen the most appropriate design for their study. For example, if they are seeking to establish very specifically the relationship between an independent variable and a dependent variable, they should not be conducting an ethnographic study.
- Identify whether the researcher has assessed the weaknesses of their chosen design. For example, if they have used a panel design, have they considered the full range of factors that might have brought about any change in respondents' attitudes or opinions?
- Consider whether the claims made by the researcher about their findings fit with the design that they have used. Look for obvious weaknesses such as making inappropriate generalisations from a case study.
- When reading the methodology section, look for indications that the researcher has considered issues of validity when choosing their research design.

Further reading

For a broad view of the process of research design, see:

Creswell, J. W. and Creswell, J. D. (2017) *Research Design*, 5th edn. London: Sage (1st edn 1996).

Another example of a study that used vignettes and had many features of a classic experimental design is:

Rebellon, C. J., Piquero, N. L., Piquero, A. R. and Thaxton, S. (2009) 'Do frustrated economic expectations and objective economic inequity promote crime?', *European Journal of Criminology*, 6(1): 47–71.

For a broader discussion of criminological ethnography, with accounts of many classic studies, see:

Treadwell, J. (2020) *Criminological Ethnography: An Introduction*. London: Sage.

To read more on some of the issues associated with case studies, I recommend:

Swanborn, P. (2010) *Case Study Research: What, Why and How?* London: Sage.

6

ETHICAL ISSUES

████████ What you will learn in this chapter ████████ ─────────────────

By the end of this chapter, you will:

- Be aware of studies that have raised major ethical concerns and be equipped to judge whether the approach taken was justified
- Understand the importance of gaining ethical approval for any research that you propose to undertake
- Be aware of the types of research for which you are likely and unlikely to gain ethical approval
- Be able to identify the ethical concerns that are most likely to affect your own research project and to put in place measures to deal with these concerns

Introduction

When considering ethical issues as an undergraduate student, there are two important questions to consider:

1   What is good ethical practice, minimising the risk of harm to the participants and the researcher, and maximising the benefit that is likely to be derived from the research?
2   Which approach is likely to be approved by the ethics committee?

Of course, it is hoped that the answers to these two questions will be very similar. However, it is important to remember that there is no clear consensus on many ethical issues.

As a result, while I have tried to provide specific advice on some occasions in this chapter, on others I have only been able to highlight the issues that it is important to consider. As a general guideline, whatever system of ethical approval your university has in place, those administering it are likely to err on the side of caution when considering research proposed by undergraduate students. So, it is sensible to consider ways of exploring your proposed topic that will raise the fewest possible difficult ethical questions.

Why Ethics are Important

Homan (1991: 1–3) suggests that the justification for undertaking social research ethically rarely begins at the point of ethics as many people understand it, i.e. a consideration of moral values and what is right or wrong. Instead, codes of practice are developed, and it is noted that failure to keep to them may make it more difficult to undertake social research in the future. This tendency to concentrate pragmatically on the interests of researchers is one reason why it is important to pause and consider when it was first established that an ethical approach to research was necessary.

In legal proceedings at Nuremberg from 1946 to 1947, the US authorities examined the evidence against 23 German doctors accused of murdering people with learning disabilities and torturing concentration camp victims under the pretence of conducting medical research. Sixteen of the doctors were found guilty and seven were sentenced to death (MacDonald, 2016: 181). Among the 'experiments' that had been conducted by the doctors were the infection of wounds, the infection of people with malaria and typhoid, and the use of poisons. One outcome of the trials was the issuing of 10 rules known as the Nuremberg code, which remain influential in modern-day medical research and in other areas such as Psychology (Homan, 1991: 9). The code can be found at https://media.tghn. org/medialibrary/2011/04/BMJ_No_7070_Volume_313_The_Nuremberg_Code.pdf

The legacy of Nuremberg, together with the very personal nature of some of the information gathered, goes some way to explaining why medical research has a particularly high ethical threshold – anyone wanting to conduct research that involves contacting respondents thought the National Health Service, or collecting data on National Health Service premises, can expect to go through an extremely lengthy and thorough ethical approval system. Other academic disciplines such as Criminology do not have such extensive processes, but all universities now have ethics committees to consider research proposed by staff and students. These committees carefully scrutinise proposals to ensure that all research reaches high ethical standards.

In addition to universities' own ethical system, researchers are increasingly required to go through further processes of research approval. For example, the website of the Prison and Probation Service states that:

All researchers wanting to conduct research with staff and/or offenders in prison establishments, National Probation Service (NPS)/Community Rehabilitation Companies (CRC) regions or within Her Majesty's Prison and Probation Service (HMPPS) Headquarters are required to formally apply for research approval to the HMPPS National Research Committee (NRC). (www.gov.uk/government/organisations/her-majestys-prison-and-probation-service/about/research#amendments-to-your-research)

So, gaining ethical approval for any piece of research is likely to be a time-consuming process. This is one reason why, throughout this book, I encourage you to consider using approaches that present fewer ethical challenges, such as analysing documents or collecting data from friends, family and acquaintances.

The Ethical Issues to Consider

Both the British Society of Criminology and the American Society of Criminology have their own codes of ethics to guide staff and students in this area. The British Society's code (www.britsoccrim.org/docs/CodeofEthics.pdf) contains some sections that are more likely to be relevant to staff and postgraduate students than to undergraduates, such as those on responsibilities to colleagues and to sponsors/funders. However, of fundamental importance is the section on researchers' responsibilities to research participants. Many of these points are covered in the discussion below, where I highlight key ethical questions that may affect the work of undergraduate researchers, while also considering some classic studies that raised difficult ethical questions.

Harm to Participants

Studies which involve causing harm, or possible harm, to participants have always been hugely controversial, and would almost certainly fail to gain ethical approval today. One such example was the Stanford prison experiment, in which researchers at Stanford University created a mock prison within the university and randomly chose stable young men to act the part of prisoners or guards. The experiment was meant to run for a fortnight but had to be abandoned after six days because of the violent and abusive behaviour of the guards towards the prisoners (Haney et al., 1981). Here, the psychological and physical harm to respondents had to be balanced against the greater understanding that the study provided of the impact of institutions, positions of power and powerlessness, etc.

This is, of course, an extreme example and one that is far removed from any research that you are likely to undertake. However, it is important to remember that research participants can suffer harm even when all that is required of them is to talk about themselves and their experiences: crime and related issues can be distressing to discuss. Both victims of crime and offenders are likely to be from vulnerable groups, so it is particularly important to be sensitive to their feelings if you are collecting data from them. When collecting data from criminal justice professionals about their work, or from members of the public about attitudes to crime, the risk of harm is lower, but it is still something that you need to consider.

What this means in practice is that, as part of the process of gaining informed consent, you should indicate clearly which topics the data collection will cover. Respondents should be assured that they can decline to answer questions and end the interview or leave the focus group if they feel that they cannot carry on. In addition, you should be alert to signs that a respondent is struggling to answer questions on a topic and offer to move on to the next one.

Harm to the Researcher

In addition to potentially causing harm to participants, researchers should also consider any risks to themselves that may arise from their research. In the past, some criminologists have placed themselves in extremely dangerous positions during their research: the study of Patrick (1973) with a Glasgow gang, which was discussed in Chapter 5, is one such example. One impact of the greater ethical regulation of research is that studying offenders in the course of their crimes is all but impossible now. Infiltration of criminal groups is the role of the undercover police officer and the investigative journalist, not the academic researcher. Quite recently, I was approached by a student who wanted to contact a dangerous group from an online forum; I had to be very clear that such a proposal had no chance of gaining ethical approval.

When collecting data from people who present even a slight risk of responding angrily to the research, the location becomes an extremely important issue to consider. Offices of organisations that have acted as gatekeepers are often suitable places for interviews because there are already measures in place to protect staff, for example a window that enables observation from the place where other staff are working. It is unlikely that ethical approval would ever be given to a student project that involved interviewing people in their own homes.

More likely than the threat of physical harm during your research is the possibility that someone will tell you something that you find distressing. This situation is dealt with below, under the heading of confidentiality.

Informed Consent

The question of when it is justified to conduct research in which respondents do not give fully informed consent for their participation is a difficult one and is at the heart of the controversy surrounding some very famous (or perhaps infamous) studies. One example is Humphreys' (1970) research in which he posed as a lookout for men who undertook homosexual acts in public toilets. By noting the car registrations of the men involved, Humphreys was able to obtain their addresses from friendly police officers (without revealing his purpose in asking). He subsequently called at their houses on the pretext of conducting a social health survey (and claimed, surprisingly, that none of the men recognised him). Humphreys (1970: 171) offered a spirited defence of his approach and undoubtedly gained information about the type of people who were involved in homosexual acts in public toilets that would not have been available using more conventional methods. However, the deception involved in the study would today be seen as breaching the principle of informed consent.

The British Society of Criminology's ethical code identifies research that has exposed racism and other social harms as the exception to the principle that participants should give fully informed consent to take part in research. However, as noted above, this type of research quite often involves risks to the researcher and is something that you would be highly unlikely to gain permission for as an undergraduate.

Studies that involve observation often present specific difficulties. Covert observation – where the respondents do not know that they are being observed – offers no opportunity for respondents to indicate in advance that they consent to take part. In the case of the research of Patrick and Humphreys, discussed above, such consent would almost certainly have been refused. Some studies – most frequently psychological experiments – have tried to get round difficulties such as these by asking participants to give their consent at the end of the observation, i.e. retrospective consent. However, any form of covert observation is likely to face major ethical questions.

Even when observation is overt, there are likely to be difficult questions to face. For example, Rowe (2007) is one of a long line of researchers who have gained informed consent from police officers to observe them in the course of their duties. However, this consent clearly cannot extend to members of the public who the police interact with. This is not a problem to which there is an easy solution, but a reasonable compromise is to seek prior consent from those you know are going to be observed and retrospective consent from anyone who you observe unexpectedly for a substantial period of time. Of course, what is substantial is subjective and a matter of judgement. For example, if a member of staff interrupted a meeting that you were observing to say that there was a telephone call for one of the participants, you would not be expected to seek permission from that staff member. However, if someone you had not expected to be part of the meeting arrived late and took a full part in the discussion, you would need to ask their permission at the end to include their contribution as part of your data. If the unexpected arrival said no to you recording your observations of them, this would probably mean that much of the meeting you observed could not be used as data: this would be hugely frustrating, but something that you would have to accept.

There are other forms of data collection where gaining informed consent is problematic or unrealistic: for example, when analysing a police drama, it is not possible to gain the informed consent of all the actors involved. However, for the more popular forms of social science data collection – questionnaire, interviews and focus groups – it is possible to seek informed consent from respondents, meaning that they understand as fully as possible what is required of them before agreeing to take part in the research. Even when respondents are keen to get on with the data collection, you must take the time to explain what the research involves and what will be required of them.

An idea of the types of information that should be given to respondents to ensure informed consent is provided in Textbox 6.1. This is taken from a piece of research which I was involved in where people were interviewed about their housing situation shortly after their release from prison. Data was also collected about respondents from an agency that worked with them. My university uses a system whereby respondents read (or have explained to them) a research information form which tells them what the research will involve, before they decide whether to sign a participant consent form to say that they agree to what is proposed. This is the research information form.

Textbox 6.1

Research information form for recently released prisoners

We would like to know whether you are willing to take part in a piece of research examining the housing situation of people who are released from custody. The reason that you have been asked to take part is that we are interested in your opinion of the value of the support that you have received, or are currently receiving, to successfully make the step of leaving custody and moving into independent housing. In order to make a full assessment of your situation, we would like to interview you soon and then possibly again in a few months' time.

We have a consent form where we ask if you can help us in two ways:

- Firstly, by agreeing that we can ask people who have worked with you about your circumstances before, during and after your time in custody. This will also involve collecting information from the records that they hold about you. We can provide a list of the types of information that we will ask about if you would like us to.

- Secondly, by agreeing that we can interview you soon and possibly again in a few months' time, to get some more detail about your past and present housing circumstances and your perspective on services that you have received.

If you agree to take part in the research, we can assure you that:

- You will be under no obligation to answer any interview questions that you do not wish to.
- You can end an interview at any time of your choosing.
- You can withdraw your permission for us to use information we hold about you, either from the interview(s) or from people who have worked with you, at any time until the completion of the research project.
- All information about you will be stored securely and destroyed within two years of the completion of the project.
- No information will be placed in any report that could enable you to be identified as someone who took part in the research. This means that your name or any other identifying information will not be included. The only information we would have to share with other people would be any about crimes not yet known to the police which you disclose to us or about issues that may affect the safety of children or young people.

If you would like any more information about the research, you can contact one of the research team: Jamie Harding 0191 227 3545 (jamie.harding@northumbria.ac.uk)

It is very important that information is provided about the project in a manner that is appropriate to potential respondents; especially careful thought should be given to this issue when respondents are vulnerable. Ethics committees are usually very cautious about providing consent for research with these groups and some universities may simply specify that permission will not be granted to undergraduates to collect data from them. You should consider carefully the most appropriate method of ensuring that consent is asked of people who may have limited language abilities and ability to understand. There may be potential respondents who would find it difficult to read information about your research project and/or would be reluctant to sign a consent form (for example, because they associate a signature with a legal requirement). For this reason, the option should always be offered to go through the information verbally with a respondent and gain verbal agreement. Ideally, this conversation should be recorded, but sometimes a researcher just has to report that all the necessary information has been given and consent has been provided verbally.

Research with children (i.e. those under the age of 16) always requires the consent of a parent or guardian and should usually involve some form of consultation with the children themselves about their participation. You should consider a wide range of communication methods: for example, would choosing an emoji be an easier way for a child to indicate whether they are willing to take part in the research than answering 'yes' or 'no'?

In many cases, data collection takes place at one point in time and so consent only needs to be provided once. However, where research takes place over a longer period, it is good practice to remind respondents of the consent that they have given and to check that it still applies. For example, a researcher who is undergoing an extended period of participant observation may need to remind all those involved in the setting of their role from time to time. If you are going to interview a respondent on two separate occasions, on the second occasion you should give a reminder of the consent that was given and the option to refuse to answer questions or to withdraw from the research at any point.

Gatekeepers

One of the reasons why it is so time-consuming to undertake research into a field where you don't already know someone is that there is likely to be at least one gatekeeper to negotiate with. This will certainly be the case if you are seeking to collect data from victims or offenders, and increasingly if you are seeking contact with criminal justice professionals.

The gatekeeper is the person who determines whether respondents can be asked to take part in the research. They are usually a staff member in a senior position in an organisation. So, for example, if I wished to interview bank staff about the extent to which they feared armed robbery, I would certainly not begin by queueing up at the bank's service counter and then asking if there was anyone available to take part in my research. My first step would be to contact the manager of the branch(es) where I wished to collect data and to ask for their permission to contact their staff. Alternatively, I could ask the manager if they were willing to give staff my contact details and encourage them to get in touch with me if they were willing to take part in the research. The manager might have to refer the request to a higher authority within the bank, i.e. a second gatekeeper. I would need to allow plenty of time in the plan for the research for this request to be considered.

> **Textbox 6.2**
>
> **What is the mistake? Interviews with vulnerable respondents**
>
> Try to identify the mistake(s) that a researcher has made here and then have a look at Appendix 1 to see whether your view is the same as mine.
>
> A researcher gains permission to undertake research at a drug rehabilitation centre. The staff of the centre say that, although all their service users are vulnerable, there are some who they feel could give an interview. They ask the researcher to wait in the common room; if suitable service users come in and are willing to be interviewed, the staff will suggest that they go into the common room and approach the researcher.
>
> A service user approaches the researcher and says that the staff have told him about the interview and he is willing to take part. The researcher asks if the service user is happy to read and sign the consent form, to which the answer is 'yes'. The form is signed and the researcher begins the interview. However, after the first few questions a second service user comes in and begins to contribute their own answers to the questions. The researcher uses the contributions of both service users as part of their data.

Anonymity

When collecting data from people, there are relatively few methods where the researcher does not know who has given which response to a question – postal and online questionnaires are the only examples (see Chapter 8). However, although the researcher who has conducted an interview or focus group knows who has given which answer, it is very important that their output does not enable an individual to be identified, unless this is with their prior agreement. This is most likely to be an issue when you are collecting data from people with specialist roles. For example, if you are conducting a case study of a Youth Offending Service's supervision of arsonists, and you interview the only officer who specialises in this area, it is unlikely that you will be able to write up your research in a manner that keeps them anonymous. Instead, you should show them everything that you intend to write about them and ensure that they are happy with this.

If you are conducting research among friends, it is important not to include quotations with phrases that are likely to be identified as being frequently used by one person. Equally, you should avoid quotations or examples that could obviously be linked to one person's experience. So, for example, if you interview a number of friends who have roles with the police as special constables, it might be obvious who you are talking about if you write:

One respondent reported feeling extreme fear when, on their first night shift, they accompanied a police officer to the scene of a stabbing and the officer disarmed the person with the knife.

The identity of the respondent who reported this could be better protected if you wrote:

One respondent reported feeling extreme fear when, soon after taking on the role, they accompanied a police officer to a scene where they both faced physical danger.

Confidentiality

Confidentiality is often confused with anonymity and there are clear links between the two, particularly when gaining agreement from respondents as to whether identifying information can be included in your output, as discussed above. Confidentiality is about ensuring that research participants are fully aware of who will have access to the information that they provide during your data collection. Academic staff or postgraduate students may need to share data with a research team or give audio recordings to a transcription company to type up. In these cases, all those involved should be aware of the need not to pass on information unnecessarily. However, as an undergraduate researcher it is unlikely that anyone else will need to know who said what in response to your questions. Even when discussing your data with your supervisor, you should be careful to do this without identifying respondents.

Focus groups create particular difficulties in relation to confidentiality. You can guarantee what you as the researcher will do with the comments that are made during a focus group discussion, but can only ask that respondents do not repeat the remarks of other respondents, with no way of enforcing this. This may be particularly important because most focus groups are made up of 'communities of interest', i.e. pre-existing groups who all know each other, as will be discussed in Chapter 9. It must be made clear before the focus group starts that you can only guarantee that you will not use information inappropriately, but that you are requesting that focus group members do the same.

Students sometimes ask me whether they should include completed consent forms as an appendix to their dissertation, as evidence that they have really collected their data and not just made it up. I always reply that this is a breach of confidentiality and it would be much better to include a blank copy of the consent form to show the information that has been provided to respondents.

The need for confidentiality must be balanced against the need to protect yourself from harm if you hear about something that is distressing in the course of your research.

It is essential that you discuss anything that you hear that has upset you with someone who can support you through this, such as your dissertation supervisor or a trusted friend – in severe cases, you may want to seek help from professionals such as those working in your university's counselling service. Ideally, you should discuss the distressing revelation without identifying the respondent but, if this is unavoidable, you should ensure that the person that you are speaking to is aware of the need not to repeat the information. The question as to whether to intervene when you hear about (or observe) a distressing situation is dealt with below.

Intervention

Linked to the issue of confidentiality is the question of when the researcher should intervene if, in the course of their research, they observe (or hear about) something going on that causes them major concern. The traditional view in the social sciences has been that the researcher should take the view of the detached reporter on the situation and that any attempt to intervene may 'contaminate' the research setting that they are examining. This is the type of approach that we are used to seeing in wildlife programmes, where television teams rarely intervene to change the situation that they are observing, no matter how distressing it may be for the animals involved and for viewers. A rare exception occurred when the film crew on the television programme *Dynasties* intervened to save a group of penguins who were trapped in a ravine; the crew subsequently had to defend their actions (Mohdin, 2018).

The question of when to intervene in the social sciences was vividly raised when Van Maanen (1983, cited in Miles and Huberman, 1994: 293–294) witnessed acts of police brutality during his research, which he wrote about in his field notes. Although he did not join in with the violence, he did not protest or report it to anyone because this would almost certainly have ended his access to the setting. Such controversial examples are rare and likely to fall well beyond the experience of the new researcher. However, there are several other situations that you may encounter where the question of whether to intervene is highly relevant.

A respondent may express a view that is offensive or factually wrong, in which case you will need to decide whether it is appropriate to challenge this view. This question is addressed in Pryke's (2004) excellent discussion of a research situation where he was faced with some respondents who justified or minimised acts of genocide. The first time this happened, he simply moved on to the next question – an approach that he later regretted: 'However, in retrospect I felt somewhat disgusted by my silence … my lack of response seemed to collude with the denial of the atrocity'.

He then changed his approach so that, while not directly disagreeing with respondents, he asked more challenging questions that sought to explore the justifications further, such as:

Are you saying that the rapes and murders didn't happen?

Was there ever a point when you felt you had to condemn it?

The point of ethical principle that is raised by Pryke could be applied to numerous other scenarios: what would you do, for example, if one of your participants used a racist term? Would your response differ between a respondent who was not aware that the term was offensive and one who used it deliberately to offend? There are no clear answers to these questions, but it is important to have considered them before beginning data collection. My advice to a new researcher is to end an interview if a participant is repeatedly expressing views that you find offensive.

Another scenario where the issue of intervention arises is one where, during your data collection, you become aware that a respondent could benefit from some sort of service – e.g. counselling or money advice. You clearly do not want to discuss this in the course of your interview or focus group discussion. However, you may decide afterwards that you want to do something to facilitate the person accessing the support that they need. While talking about their circumstances to a support agency would clearly be a breach of confidentiality, you could quite reasonably and ethically provide information to the respondent about how to contact the agency and the type of support that it provides.

The need to respect confidentiality may be over-ridden if you think there is a risk of serious harm to your respondent or someone else, for example if their responses suggest that they are part of a violent and/or abusive relationship. This is a situation that I strongly suggest you discuss with your supervisor or another member of academic staff at the earliest possible opportunity. Where there is a danger to children, the National Society for the Prevention of Cruelty to Children's excellent ethical guidance leaves no doubt as to what the appropriate course of action is: 'If a researcher suspects that a child might be at risk of harm then the research must be stopped until that child's safety is secured' (https://learning.nspcc.org.uk/research-resources/briefings/research-with-children-ethics-safety-avoiding-harm). This is a huge responsibility and another reason to think very carefully before undertaking data collection with children.

Finally, given that our discipline is Criminology, it is to be expected that crime will be discussed as part of our research. If you are able to negotiate ethical permission to collect data from people who have committed crime, or who may have done so, it is important that you consider what your response will be if they discuss committing an offence for which they have not yet been convicted. My strong advice is that you should make it clear when you first meet respondents that, if this situation should arise, you may need to report the crime to the police. If, despite this warning, a respondent still tells you about an offence that they have committed but not been convicted for, you face a difficult choice between respecting the confidentiality of the respondent and seeking the wider public good. The choice that you make may depend on the nature of the offence discussed – most researchers would take a different approach to the reporting of an act of criminal damage from several years ago to a situation where there was ongoing exploitation of a vulnerable person.

Online Research

Online research raises several specific ethical questions; discussion of these ethics has perhaps not kept pace with the extra research opportunities that have become available with new forms of social media. Franzke et al. (2020) provide ethical guidelines for online research, which point to specific risks, such as the amount of violent and upsetting material that is easily available via the internet. So your own welfare is a major ethical issue to consider, and to make provision for, if you are proposing to look for information or images that have the potential to cause distress.

Another important issue is the ease with which vulnerable groups (such as people with learning disabilities) can be contacted via social media, without any gatekeepers being involved. This means that particular care should be taken to ensure that participants give fully informed consent, with appropriate safeguards in place.

More generally, the issue of informed consent is an important and difficult one when research is conducted online. It is not problematic when supermarkets use data from loyalty cards for research purposes, for example, because this is specifically agreed to before anyone is provided with a card. Similarly, we are told when we go onto many websites that the site uses cookies, i.e. that our internet usage will be monitored for the benefit of the organisation that owns the webpage, and usually agree without giving much thought to the consequences of this. However, someone providing the information to enable the probation service to conduct a risk assessment of them (for example) is unlikely to be able to object if data pertaining to all the service's risk assessments is subsequently analysed by a university under a licence agreement (this is sometimes discussed under the heading of 'big data', which is discussed in Chapter 10). As Franzke et al. (2020) note, various mechanisms have been suggested to ensure that consent is provided (or at least reasonably inferred) in this type of research. When information that an organisation holds, but which is not publicly available on their webpages, is obtained online without their permission – a process sometimes referred to as 'data scraping' – this raises even more questions and is an issue where the legal and ethical framework is still emerging. The danger of the misuse of digital data was highlighted in 2018 when it emerged that a company called Cambridge Analytica had taken information from the Facebook profiles of over 50 million people to use in targeted political advertising (Cadwalladr and Graham-Harrison, 2018).

Of course, licence agreements and data scraping will probably seem a long way from any internet-based research that you are considering. There is little difficulty with analysing information that organisations make publicly available on their website. For example, most Criminology departments publish profiles of their lecturers, so these could be analysed to show how many lecturing staff have previously worked in the criminal justice system (and in which areas). However, questions of consent become difficult in the case of more personal information: you should avoid assuming that because someone has posted something on the internet, there are therefore no restrictions on its use for research purposes. The approach adopted by my university, which seems sensible, is that information can be used freely when there is no password protection. However, other types of online information – for example, in the area of Facebook to which friends need to be invited – should be used only with the express permission of the person who posted it.

If you are filling in an ethics form to propose some online research, particularly if it involves a recently developed social media application, bear in mind that the person reading the form may not be completely up to date with virtual communication – it would be sensible to spell out to them exactly what the app in question does!

Textbox 6.3

What is the mistake? Metropolitan police research

Try to identify the mistake(s) that a researcher has made here and then have a look at Appendix 1 to see whether your view is the same as mine.

A researcher conducts a piece of research into the personal and professional pressures faced by new police recruits who move from elsewhere in the United Kingdom to take up their first post with the Metropolitan Police. The most senior officer at West Hendon Police Station agrees that their station can be used as a case study, provided that she is given a copy of the final report. She circulates details of the research and reports back to the researcher with the names and contact details of six officers who fit the criteria and are willing to be interviewed. The researcher arranges times to interview each of the officers and gives them a consent form that explains the purpose of the research, why they have been selected to take part in it, the topics that the interviews will cover, their right to refuse to answer questions or to withdraw from the research at any point, the option to see a transcript of the interview in case there is anything that they wish to change on reflection, and a promise that nothing will be presented in the research report that will enable individual officers to be identified. All the officers sign the form before their interview commences.

As part of their report, the researcher includes the following paragraph:

For all respondents keeping in contact with their family was an important coping mechanism for the difficulties associated with being in a new location. On occasions this contact was prioritised over their professional role. For example, one respondent reported that: 'Sometimes when I'm on a shift I get the chance to sneak away and ring my sister and the bairn for a few minutes.'

Giving Yourself the Best Chance of Gaining Ethical Approval

As this chapter has demonstrated, it is easier to identify ethical issues for researchers to consider than to give specific advice as to what is best ethical practice. Such advice inevitably involves a good deal of subjective judgement, which is why there are differences in the types of proposed student research that are permitted by the ethics committees of different universities and even different departments within the same university.

Before seeking ethical approval for your proposed research, you should read your university/department's policy carefully and also consult your supervisor – they may know whether previous projects similar to yours have gained ethical approval. In addition, you should ensure that your ethics forms discuss all the ethical issues that are relevant to your proposed project – and all the measures that you intend to put in place to deal with these issues – in as much detail as possible. In my experience of being on an ethics committee, many students have been asked to re-submit their forms, or refused permission to undertake the research, because they have not provided enough information, but none because they have provided too much!

If you do get asked to adjust your approach by the ethics committee, this can be very disappointing, but it is important to read the feedback carefully and re-design your research to ensure that all the committee's concerns are addressed.

Key points for your own research

- Read carefully the guidance that your university provides on ethical issues before deciding on the nature of your research project. There is no point in proposing research with children, for example, if your university has a rule prohibiting this type of research.
- Consider carefully which of the issues discussed in this chapter are most applicable to your own research project.
- Once you have identified the most relevant issues, determine the steps that you will take to ensure that your research is conducted in an ethical manner.
- Ensure that you provide as much information as possible when seeking ethical approval for your research from your university.

Key points when reading other people's research

The ethics of published studies can be difficult to evaluate because journal articles and other academic publications often include little or no discussion of the way ethical issues were dealt with in the course of the research. However, if you are reading about a piece of research that involves a method where there are likely to be major ethical issues, for example a piece of covert observation, there should be some discussion of how those issues were dealt with. Similarly, in the case of online research, particularly where there is 'big data' involved, a discussion of consent should be included – as was the case with Banks' (2012) research into online gambling, which was considered in Chapter 5. If there is no such discussion, it is appropriate to identify this as a weakness when writing about the research.

Further reading

One of the most famous studies that raised difficult ethical questions was Milgram's study of obedience, where the principle of informed consent was breached and there was a serious risk of psychological harm to participants. However, the study also raised questions about obedience to authority that would have been difficult to examine by other means. There are huge numbers of sources debating the study and its findings; one good account is:

Gibson, S., Blenkinsopp, G., Johnstone, E. and Marshall, A. (2018) 'Just following orders? The rhetorical invocation of "obedience" in Stanley Milgram's post-experiment interviews', *European Journal of Social Psychology*, 48: 585–599.

There are also clips on YouTube and a full-length film called *Experimenter* that consider Milgram's work.

If you are interested in considering further the complex issues around informed consent, a good source is:

Wiles, R., Crow, G., Charles, V. and Heath, S. (2007) 'Informed consent and the research process: following rules or striking balances?', *Sociological Research Online*, 12(2).

For more discussion of the issues associated with online research, see:

Sugiura, L., Wiles, R. and Pope, C. (2017) 'Ethical challenges in online research: public/private perceptions', *Research Ethics*, 13(3–4): 184–199.

If you are interested in specific issues around using WhatsApp for research, you could read:

Barbosa, S. and Milan, S. (2019) 'Do not harm in private chat apps: ethical issues for research on and with WhatsApp', *Westminster Papers in Communication and Culture*, 14(1): 49–65.

7

POPULATIONS AND SAMPLES

What you will learn in this chapter

By the end of this chapter, you will:

- Be able to assess which populations are easiest to identify and which are more difficult
- Understand the reasons for using random sampling and the circumstances in which it is appropriate to use it
- Be able to put random sampling techniques into operation, should you need to
- Understand the different principles associated with sampling in qualitative studies
- Be able to select a sampling method that is appropriate for a qualitative study

Introduction

Choosing who or what to collect data from can have a crucial impact on the outcome of your research. This chapter considers the range of methods by which this can be done and the circumstances under which it is appropriate to use each method. The importance of accurate sampling is perhaps best understood with reference to occasions where it has been done badly. So this chapter includes not only the regular, hypothetical *What is the mistake?* feature but also two real-life examples where research has been discredited because of poor sampling.

Defining a Population

In most pieces of research, there is a population, which can be defined as everyone or everything from which data can be collected. The most well-known example of a piece of research that seeks to collect data from an entire population is the UK census, which is conducted every 10 years and seeks to collect data from every person normally resident in the UK.

There are clear advantages to collecting data from an entire population because it saves any debate about whether the right people or things have been selected. However, there are also several potential difficulties:

1   Most obviously, it can be very time-consuming. If you are proposing to collect data from your seminar group, it may be possible to collect data from every member. However, one reason why the UK census is only taken every 10 years is the very large cost of such an exercise: it is estimated that the 2021 census will cost £906 million (Shaw, 2020).

2   Even though the aim may be to collect data from the entire population, in practice there are still likely to be people who don't respond. This occurs even with the census where, despite stringent efforts to collect data from every member of the population, some people are still missed by enumerators (http://news.bbc.co.uk/1/hi/uk/2277835.stm). Difficulties associated with non-response are considered further below.

3   It can be difficult to establish exactly what the population is. In some cases, this is not a problem: for example, your university will have a list of the population of students studying Criminology courses which is likely to be completely accurate. However, in other cases, 'populations' only consist of those who are known to belong to a particular group: for example, the population of people who have reported being a victim of crime to the police, or approached an agency such as Victim Support, is not the same as the population of all victims of crime. Similarly, the population of known offenders will not include those who have avoided falling under suspicion for their crime. There may also be debate as to who should be considered to be part of a population: for example, there has been much criticism of the choice of young people to appear in the Metropolitan Police's gang matrix database (see, e.g., Mayor of London Office for Policing and Crime, 2018).

The question of exactly who should be included in a population is not just of academic interest. Waddington et al. (2004) demonstrated the importance of this question to an issue that has caused enormous debate in policing circles for decades. After the report of Lord Scarman into the Brixton disorders of 1981 (Scarman, 1982), a number of writers had examined the differences between the ethnic breakdown of a local population and the ethnic breakdown of those who were stopped and searched by the police in the area. Their analyses had consistently suggested that some minority ethnic groups (particularly young African-Caribbean men) were more likely to be stopped and searched than others (e.g. Newburn et al., 2004). However, Waddington et al. (2004) argued that the comparison with the population who were living in the area was inappropriate – instead, what should be considered was the population of people who were in public places and therefore 'available' to be stopped by the police. They suggested that the 'available' population was very different from that of the residential population of an area – for example, older people were less likely to be found in public places than younger people.

Waddington et al. (2004) used the concept of the 'available population' to guide their research in Reading and Slough. They drove around an area where there was a high level of stop and search, making judgements as to which of the people they saw were adults and whether their ethnicity should be classified as 'White', 'Asian', 'Black' or 'Other'. They then did the same with CCTV footage from a shopping centre. The ethnic classifications were chosen to be consistent with earlier Home Office research. It is highly undesirable to give an ethnic classification to a person that is not one of their own choice, but there was no alternative in this case. The percentage of people in each ethnic group who were observed from the car and through the CCTV footage was then compared to the percentage who police records showed had been stopped and searched. Waddington et al. (2004: 897) suggested that, while Black and Asian people appeared to be over-represented when stop-and-search figures were compared to the resident population, a very different position emerged when considering the available population:

> The result is that, in Reading, the pattern of stop and search reflects pretty closely the available population, whilst in Slough there is significant disproportionality, with white people being over-represented among those stopped and searched and Asians under-represented.

Sampling

All samples are chosen from a sampling frame, which consists of all the units that could be included in the sample. In most cases, the sampling frame is identical to the population. The sampling frame does not have to consist of people: it can be a collection of newspaper articles, job advertisements or crime locations. In the case of Coupe's (2016) study of burglary and the police response to it, the sampling frame was 5,768 case files on burglaries from two divisions of a large UK police force. From the 5,768 case files, Coupe chose a random sample of 695 and gave questionnaires to the police officers who had been involved in investigating each burglary, asking for some more information (Coupe, 2016: 567–568).

However, for the sake of simplicity, it will be assumed for most of this chapter that a sample is being chosen from a sampling frame of people.

Random sampling

Random samples, or probability samples, are associated with quantitative methodology. A key characteristic of random samples is that every element of the sampling frame has an equal chance of selection (De Vaus, 2002: 70–71); the researcher's judgement as to who would be a 'good' sample member plays no part in the decision making.

Another characteristic of random sampling is that it makes possible the use of inferential statistics. These statistics, which are discussed further in Chapter 11, examine the likelihood that a pattern seen in a random sample would also be evident in the population.

All random samples involve some element of choosing numbers at random, which is most easily done using an online random number generator (such as www.random.org/integers). The techniques associated with different methods of random sampling will be discussed briefly below, before considering as an example the highly sophisticated random sampling method adopted by the Crime Survey of England and Wales.

Simple random samples

This technique involves taking the sampling frame and giving each of the individuals in it a number. Numbers are then chosen at random (using a random number generator) and the individuals corresponding to those numbers form the sample. (If the random number generator provides the same number twice, it is just ignored the second time and a further number is chosen to replace it.) Simple random sampling is easy to understand but can be time-consuming when choosing a large sample. It has the advantage that no knowledge is needed of the individuals in the sampling frame (e.g. their age) before the sample is chosen. However, a corresponding difficulty is that there is no guarantee that the sample will be representative of the sampling frame in terms of gender (men or women may be over-represented) or any other characteristic.

Systematic random samples

If you were choosing a systematic random sample, you would begin by giving each member of the sampling frame a number, as you would for a simple random sample. The next step is to calculate what fraction of the sampling frame you want to go into your sample – for example, if you were choosing a random sample of 200 offenders from a probation caseload of 1,000, this would be one-fifth of the sampling frame. So, in this example, you would choose every fifth person on your list. The random element would be introduced because you would decide at random whether to start at the person numbered 1, 2, 3, 4 or 5. This could be decided by using a random number generator (asking for a random number between one and five) or by rolling a dice (of course, you would roll again if you rolled a six). Depending on the outcome of the random number generation or dice roll, the first few offenders to appear in your sample would be those numbered:

1, 6, 11, 16, 21 or

2, 7, 12, 17, 22 or

3, 8, 13, 18, 23 or

4, 9, 14, 19, 24 or

5, 10, 15, 20, 25

Systematic random sampling has the advantage over simple random sampling that it is quicker, particularly when choosing a large sample. Otherwise it shares the same advantages and disadvantages, i.e. no prior knowledge of the characteristics of the people in the sampling frame is required but it cannot be guaranteed that the sample will be representative of the population. One other factor that occasionally needs to be considered with systematic random sampling is that systematic bias can occur: for example, if choosing half the house numbers in a street for a survey of crime prevention measures taken, a systematic random sample may consist entirely of people living on one side of the street (i.e. of odd or even numbers). This could be a problem if the side of the street in question backed onto an unlit alleyway, which increased the risk of crime. However, it should be emphasised that systematic bias is quite a rare difficulty.

Stratified random samples

Stratified random samples are designed to overcome the difficulty associated with simple and systematic random samples – namely, that there is no guarantee that the sample will be representative of the population. Choosing a stratified random sample can ensure that the individuals selected are representative but only in terms of certain, carefully selected variables.

To illustrate this point, imagine that you have a sampling frame of 1,000 people, where half self-identify as male and half as female. You decide that you would like to choose a random sample of 100 which reflects the gender balance of the sampling frame. To achieve this, you would list the 1,000 people in the sampling frame with the 500 women first, followed by the 500 men. You would then choose every tenth name from the list, with a random number generator determining whether the starting point was 1, 2, 3, 4, 5, 6, 7, 8, 9 or 10. If the random number generator chose the number 4, then the people included in the sample would be those numbered 4, 14, 24, etc., through to number 994. However, whatever the starting point, this sample would include 50 women and 50 men.

It is possible to stratify by more than one variable. In the above example, the sample could have been stratified by gender and employment status if the population was listed in the following order:

- women in employment
- women not in employment
- men in employment
- men not in employment

It is important to note that a stratified sample is still a random sample because each member of the sampling frame has an equal chance of selection and the researcher has no control over who is chosen. This method provides control of some characteristic(s) of the sample, but not which individuals appear in it.

One difficulty with stratified random sampling is that it requires accurate information about the key variables prior to the sample being selected. In the above example, the researcher would need to have accurate information about the employment status and self-identified gender of each person in the sampling frame. Gender, or any other characteristic, should not simply be assumed from people's names.

A further difficulty is that stratified random sampling cannot guarantee that very small groups are represented: in the above example, if there were only four men who were not in employment, the likelihood is that none of them would be included in the sample. It is also important to stratify by the most appropriate variable(s) for the research study in question: for example, in a study of 'risky' practices in relation to alcohol consumption, it may be more appropriate to have a sample that is stratified by age than one that is stratified by employment status.

Textbox 7.1

When sampling goes wrong – first example

Although not a criminological example, the 1936 US Presidential Election first drew the public's attention to the need, in some circumstances, for samples that are representative of the population. The magazine *The Literary Digest* conducted an opinion poll suggesting that the Republican candidate, Alf Landon, would win the election. This poll was based on the magazine's usual sample taken from telephone subscribers, car owners and registered voters. The magazine distributed ten million questionnaires, of which two million were returned. However, George Gallup predicted a victory for the Democratic candidate, Franklin D. Roosevelt. He argued that the *Literary Digest* had over-emphasised the views of rich people – telephones and cars were both luxury items at that time (Osborne and Rose, 1999: 377–378). The Democrats won the election and the boost to Gallup's reputation continues to have effects today as his polling organisation is still flourishing.

Multi-stage cluster samples

This type of random sampling method is the most complex and is usually used when choosing samples from a very large sampling frame, particularly for national studies where there will be face-to-face interviews and there is a need to limit the travelling done by interviewers. It involves a series of random samples; a basic model is shown below:

- A series of larger areas are randomly chosen.
- Within each selected larger area, several smaller areas are randomly chosen.
- Within each selected smaller area, a series of streets are randomly chosen.
- Within each selected street, a series of property numbers are randomly chosen and interviews are conducted at these addresses.

In practice, the process is never quite this simple, as the example of the Crime Survey of England and Wales (discussed below) demonstrates.

The Crime Survey of England and Wales

The sampling strategy used in this survey has a section of its own in this chapter for several reasons:

- Most students are likely to discuss the survey in some form during their undergraduate degree, so it is helpful to have information as to how its data is produced.
- It demonstrates some of the difficulties that need to be considered when using a complex random sampling strategy, particularly a multi-stage cluster sample.

- Despite modifications, there remain criticisms of the sampling strategy, which demonstrates the difficulties in having confidence that the trends that we see in a random sample will be reproduced in a population.

Kantar Public (2017a: 6–13) provides a detailed description of the sampling strategy for the 2016–17 survey. The main sample was of 35,000 adults (those aged 16 or over) who were living in private households in England and Wales. Another sample that was selected, of 3,000 10–15-year-olds, is not discussed here. The steps involved in choosing the addresses where one of the adults was to be interviewed is outlined below in a slightly simplified form:

1   A target was set for the number of interviews in each of the 42 police force areas of England and Wales (although the City of London Police was combined with the Metropolitan Police); the minimum target for an area was 650. This was a departure from the principle of representative sampling because it meant that the smaller police force areas were over-represented – if the sample had been representative of the population geographically, some areas would have had targets of less than 650. It was agreed that each police force area could be up to 50 interviews above or below its target.

2   The number of households that needed to be approached in each area in order to achieve the target figure for interviews was decided, based on response rates to previous surveys. In most areas, the expected response rate was approximately two-thirds. So, in an area where the target was 1,000 interviews, the number of households to be approached would be approximately 1,500.

3   With each police force area, a series of geographical areas or strata was created, each with an approximately equal number of addresses. Across England and Wales 1,639 of these strata were chosen by a stratified random sampling method, with the stratifying variables being the expected victimisation rates (based on previous surveys) and spatial distribution (i.e. how 'spread out' certain features were in the area).

4   These chosen strata were then ranked according to the density of addresses within their borders: all of the strata with the highest density were selected, together with half of those with a moderate level of density and a third of those with the lowest density.

5   Within each of the selected strata, approximately 38 addresses (chosen from the postcode address file) were selected by random sampling.

You may wonder why all the highest density strata were selected at Step 4 but only one-third of the least dense strata. The reason is to keep (as far as possible) to the principle of every household having an equal chance of selection. To illustrate the reason for this, let us take two hypothetical strata with extreme population differences:

- A is a high-density stratum with 3,800 addresses in it so, if it is chosen, each household there has a 1 in 100 chance of being among the 38 selected to be in the sample.
- Area B is a low-density stratum with 76 addresses in it so, if it is chosen, each household has a 1 in 2 chance of being among the 38 selected to be in the sample.

Area A therefore needs to be given a bigger chance of being selected to compensate for the smaller likelihood of any individual household within the area being one of the 38 that is chosen.

So, the sampling method used in the Crime Survey of England and Wales largely conforms to the random sampling principles inherent in multi-stage cluster sampling, except for the target of 650 interviews for the smallest police force areas. However, Hope (2015) is highly critical of the approach used, arguing that the desire to ensure a high level of representation from every police force area has led to the over-representation of rural and suburban areas, and the under-representation of inner-city areas where crime is most common. In Hope's opinion – which I agree with – this means that the survey underestimates the level of crime.

Sample Size and Sample Error

A question that I am often asked is how large a sample needs to be. In the case of quantitative survey research, having 20–30 respondents can produce some illustrative findings, but there is little point in producing even simple statistics such as percentages or means until the number of respondents reaches about 50.

For larger-scale studies, the size of a random sample has an impact on the likely accuracy of any inferential statistics used, but not quite in the way that might be expected. A common misunderstanding is that random samples are less accurate when the population is larger. In fact, it is the size of the sample that is the determining factor, unless the sample makes up a very large proportion of the population. So, there is unlikely to be much difference in accuracy between a random sample of 2,000 of the 2 million + prisoners in the USA and a random sample of 2,000 of the 83,000 prisoners in the UK. This seems illogical, but it is a well-established mathematical principle.

The confidence that we have that the findings from a random sample would be reproduced in the population can be measured using something called the sampling error. To illustrate what this means, let us take a hypothetical example, where a random sample of respondents has been taken and 55% say that they support the restoration of capital punishment for certain crimes. If the sampling error were 4%, we would then be able to say that we were 95% confident that, in the population, the percentage of people who support the restoration of the death penalty is between 51% and 59%, i.e. 4% above or below the figure that we found in the sample (95% confidence is a commonly adopted standard in the social sciences).

Of course, the key question is how we find the sampling error; it is here that the sample size is crucial:

> *If the sample size is 100, the sampling error is 10%*
>
> *If the sample size is 400, the sampling error is 5%*
>
> *If the sample size is 1,100, the sampling error is 3%*
>
> *If the sample size is 1,600, the sampling error is 2.5%*
>
> *If the sample size is 2,500, the sampling error is 2%*
>
> *If the sample size is 10,000, the sampling error is 1%*

(De Vaus, 2002: 81–82)

This explains why many political opinion polling organisations select random samples of 1,000–1,500: beyond this number there needs to be a very large increase in cases for a small increase in accuracy. In fact, Gallup (and other polling organisations) often make inferences to a population of over 250,000,000 in the USA from a sample of approximately 1,000 people.

Quota Sampling

Quota sampling is discussed here because it seems quite different from the purposive, qualitative approaches to sampling that are discussed in the next section. It is not a random sampling strategy, although it seems similar to stratified random sampling; Rowlingson and McKay (2005) suggest that it produces similar samples to those chosen using a stratified approach. The word 'quota' is used because the researcher has quotas of people within certain categories that need to be filled.

To take an example, I might decide to do some research at a case study university into beliefs about the sexual harassment of students by staff. If my aim were to conduct 100 short interviews, I might decide that – to ensure that the views of men, women, staff and students were all well represented – I should seek to interview:

- 25 female students
- 25 male students
- 25 female staff
- 25 male staff

If the weather was good, and because the interview was short, I might decide to stand in the main university quadrangle, interviewing people as they came past. I would go on trying to interview people in each category until I had 25 completed interviews, when I would stop. So it might be that, towards the end of the process, I had interviewed 25 people in three of the categories but only 20 male staff. So, at this point, I would only go on interviewing male members of staff who came past.

One weakness of this approach is that it takes no account of people who classify their gender as non-binary. It is important also to note that it is not a random or probability sample because, although the sampling frame is every staff member and student of the university, they do not all have an equal chance of selection. There are two reasons for this:

1 Most universities have considerably more students than staff. As the same number of staff and students are chosen for the sample, this means that an individual staff member has a higher chance of being included in the sample than an individual student.
2 Choosing people who walk through the university quadrangle means that those staff or students who frequently attend the university have a higher chance of being selected than those who often work at home or have other reasons for staying away from the campus, for example students who work long hours in part-time jobs or staff who frequently attend international conferences.

Quota sampling can be an excellent method of ensuring that some groups are well represented. It may be more important that the views of these groups are thoroughly examined than that the sample is representative of the population.

Qualitative Sampling

Random or probability sampling is not used in qualitative studies for several reasons:

1 There is no desire to determine whether the findings can be generalised to the population using inferential statistics – this tends not to be a concern of the qualitative researcher.
2 Sometimes the size of the sample to be selected, or the sampling frame to be selected from, is so small that it would be very difficult to ensure that the sample is representative.
3 In contrast to the concern to avoid bias among quantitative researchers, qualitative researchers regard it as essential to select sample members subjectively and with a purpose, which is why their approach is often referred to as 'purposive sampling'. Fetterman (1989: 43) introduces a similar term when he suggests that

ethnographers – whose work was discussed in Chapter 5 – use a process that he calls judgemental sampling: which he describes in the following way: 'ethnographers rely on their judgement to select the most appropriate members of the subculture or unit, based on the research question'.

As is the case with many aspects of qualitative research, there are less clear 'rules' about how samples should be chosen than is the case with quantitative studies. For example, there is no qualitative equivalent to sampling error: a qualitative researcher must use their own judgement, based partly on the resources available to them, to determine the most appropriate sample size. This is a particularly difficult judgement because, as was seen in Chapter 5, case study research has been conducted on the life of just one individual and other pieces of qualitative research frequently involve small numbers of respondents. However, if one of the purposes of the research is to identify themes in the data (see Chapter 12), then I would suggest as a very crude rule of thumb that at least five respondents are required.

There are also no clearly prescribed methods for choosing who should be in a qualitative sample; the approach used often develops as a research study progresses. However, there are some commonly employed strategies, which are identified by Patton (1990, cited in Flick, 1998: 69–70) and with my examples added:

- *Criterion sampling* – this involves choosing all sample members according to some specific criterion. So, for example, Carpenter et al. (2016) undertook research into the way non-suspicious deaths were dealt with by Australian professionals. Their research took place in one jurisdiction, where they interviewed 34 coronial professionals – coroners, forensic pathologists, coronial nurses, etc. These staff were all selected on the basis of having long experience in their role (Carpenter et al., 2016: 700).
- *Selecting critical cases* – this approach is taken where there are cases that seem likely to contribute most to answering the research question(s) or meeting the research objectives. So, for example, Fitz-Gibbon and O'Brien (2017) sought the views of legal professionals on the naming of children who are convicted of homicide. They decided that the professionals who were critical of their research were those who had been involved in at least one reported criminal trial involving a child homicide offender. Accordingly, these were the people who were selected for their sample. This approach is similar to criterion sampling, but with more emphasis on selecting those cases that have the most essential knowledge and/or experience.
- *Selecting typical cases* – here the idea is to understand the field from the centre. So, let us say, for example, that a researcher in 2018 looked at the statistics for changes to levels of police-recorded crime from September 2017 to September 2018 (these are available from www.ons.gov.uk/peoplepopulationandcommunity/crimeandjustice/

datasets/policeforceareadatatables). These figures are broken down by police force area and ranged from a 32% increase in Lincolnshire to a 4% reduction in Staffordshire, with the overall figure for England and Wales being a 5% increase. The researcher might decide that, for a study of factors affecting change in the level of police-recorded crime, they would include in their sample the six police forces that were closest to the England and Wales average, i.e. those where the rate of crime increased by 4%, 5% or 6%. These forces were West Yorkshire, Northamptonshire, Nottinghamshire, West Mercia, Suffolk and Thames Valley.

- *Selecting extreme or deviant cases* – this is an approach that is used when it is thought that sampling the extremities may give the best understanding of the field as a whole. So, for example, a researcher wishing to examine the impact of social class on the approach to sentencing taken by magistrates might seek to create a sample consisting of magistrates from the most privileged backgrounds and those from the most disadvantaged backgrounds.

- *Seeking maximum variation in the sample* – this approach seeks to demonstrate the range of differences within the population. So, for example, the research of Kavanaugh and Anderson (2017) into the relationship between alcohol, drugs and crime in the nightlife of Philadelphia focused on an independent record store that was a hub for nightlife. From the people who used the record store, they chose a sample that gave maximum variation in terms of race/ethnicity and gender.

Textbox 7.2

Maximum variation sampling – an example with documents

Imagine that I want to do some research on the topic of people dying in prison. I decide to use as my data source the reports of the Prisons and Probation Ombudsman (www. ppo.gov.uk) into deaths in custody. My intention is to analyse a maximum variation sample of eight of these reports, as this is all that the time I have available will allow. I set a parameter that the deaths must have occurred since 1 May 2020 and, on the day that I begin the research (29 June 2021), find that there are 44 reports of deaths within this time period. So my sampling frame is 44 cases. In addition to the date of the death, four other pieces of information are given on the site where the reports are listed and I decide to seek maximum variation in each of them. The pieces of information are:

(Continued)

- Prison – there are a small number of prisons that had more than one death during the time period in question, but I ensure that every case selected for analysis is from a different institution.
- Age – I seek a range of ages, even though most prisoners who die are recorded as having an age in the range 61+.
- Cause of death – in the sampling frame, 41 deaths are recorded as being from natural causes, with two recorded as self-inflicted and one as 'Other non-natural'. I include the two self-inflicted deaths and the non-natural death in the sample to ensure that it covers the maximum range of causes.
- Action plan – the reports into 30 of the 44 deaths are accompanied by an action plan. This includes the reports into the non-natural death and both the self-inflicted deaths, so it is important to include in the sample some of the deaths by natural causes that did not have an accompanying action plan.

Table 7.1 provides details of the deaths that were chosen for analysis.

Table 7.1 Cases selected for maximum variation sample

Date of death	Prison	Age of prisoner	Cause of death	Action plan?
14.2.2021	Elmley	61+	Natural causes	Yes
21.1.2021	Altcourse	51–60	Natural causes	No
4.8.2020	Holme House	31–40	Natural causes	Yes
25.7.2020	St Leonards	22–30	Self-inflicted	Yes
20.7.2020	Dovegate	22–30	Other non-natural	Yes
5.6.2020	Littlehey	51–60	Natural causes	No
17.5.2020	Bure	41–50	Self-inflicted	Yes
5.5.2020	Norwich	61+	Natural causes	No

This example provides an important reminder that maximum variation sampling, like all forms of qualitative sampling, is not representative: this sample was chosen to deliberately over-represent some of the less common features, such as younger prisoners and those whose deaths were not classified as being from natural causes.

Theoretical Sampling

Although qualitative sampling strategies may develop as the research progresses, theoretical sampling is the name given to an approach where there is a clear decision to choose as few of the sample as possible at the start of the study. It is an approach associated with grounded theory – a form of inductive research that was considered in Chapter 2 – where sampling, data collection and data analysis tend to be undertaken together, rather than one by one in turn.

When using a theoretical sampling approach, a small number of respondents should be selected initially. Data from them should be collected and analysed, with further sample members chosen on the grounds that they can add to the analysis and the theory that is being built (Harding, 2006: 131–132). To take an example, a piece of grounded theory research exploring fear of crime in a neighbourhood might begin by interviewing a small number of residents of the neighbourhood, with the early data analysis indicating that residents had particular fears around waiting at bus stops. The researchers might then decide that the next people to include in the sample should be those who live near bus stops, to determine whether they are particularly fearful about leaving the house.

Sampling Methods Dictated by Circumstances

There are two sampling methods that should not be used if there are alternatives available but that are sometimes necessary because of the lack of any realistic alternatives. For many students, the only choice that is realistically available is a convenience sample. As its name suggests, this means collecting data from the people you have easiest access to, i.e. your family, friends and colleagues, with the sample often being recruited via social media such as Facebook. Collecting data from such a sample clearly reduces the difficulties with negotiating access (see below), although it in no way dilutes your ethical obligations to your respondents. One obvious difficulty with this approach is that respondents are being chosen for reasons of convenience rather than because they are most likely to contribute data that could help to answer the research question(s) or meet the research objectives.

A snowball sample is often the only option when seeking to recruit a sample from a population that is hidden and therefore hard to reach. The researcher depends on one sample member to recruit others and has no idea who, beyond those recruited, is in the sampling frame. For example, Sung et al. (2016) undertook a piece of research among undocumented immigrants from Latin America in Palisades Park, New Jersey. This group was, by definition, hidden – there was no list of members and being identified by the immigration authorities as an undocumented migrant would be likely to lead to deportation. The sample was recruited by the researchers making initial contact with migrants from different street corners along the two main thoroughfares (Broad Avenue and Columbia Avenue) in Palisades Park. They then asked these migrants to contact others who fitted the criteria for the sample, i.e. people they knew who: (1) were aged 18 or over; (2) were born in a Latin American country; (3) had entered the United States through land routes; and (4) remained undocumented at the time of recruitment.

Textbox 7.3

When sampling goes wrong – second example

Louise Casey (2012) was a government adviser who produced a report entitled *Listening to Troubled Families*. This was based on the Government's Troubled Families Programme (discussed in Chapter 3), which focused on 120,000 families who had substantial involvement with a range of agencies. In the report, Casey (2012: 1) wrote in a very clear and definitive manner when describing the findings of her research:

> What came from these families' stories were that they had entrenched, long-term cycles of suffering problems and causing problems. Their problems were cumulative and had gathered together over a long period of time – perhaps over generations. Listening to the families there was a strong sense of them having problems and causing problems for years. The longevity of their relationship with services was also striking. In many cases their problems began with their own parents and their parents' parents, in cycles of childhood abuse, violence and care which are then replayed in their own lives.

However, critics were quick to point out that Casey's sampling strategy did not justify her generalising to the population of troubled families. The sample she chose was of only 16 families and eight of these families (half) had four or more children, compared to only 4% of families in the general population (there was no indication that this percentage was higher in the Troubled Families Programme). It was correctly considered inappropriate for Casey to draw such sweeping conclusions from a very small sample that was unrepresentative of the population on a key variable (Levitas, 2012). Had the conclusions been presented as illustrative of the types of factors that can cause the difficulties of some families, particularly larger families, this would have been far more in keeping with the sampling strategy.

Negotiating Access

In deciding which people to seek to collect data from – regardless of whether you want a population or a sample – ease of access is an important factor to consider, particularly as an undergraduate student with a limited amount of time and authority. This is one of the reasons why a convenience sample of friends, colleagues, etc. may be the only option that is available to you. Your lecturers are another group where there is likely to be relatively easy access.

In contrast, prisons are one of the most difficult areas from which to access respondents and even collecting data from staff of criminal justice agencies, rather than offenders or victims, is likely to present difficulties in terms of access. For example, a piece of research that involved interviewing probation officers would require approval from the national Prisons and Probation Service (as discussed in Chapter 6), as well as a senior officer in the local probation service. If this approval were to be given, it would probably only be after a substantial delay and period of negotiation, after which there would be the difficult task of trying to find a gap in the probation officers' diaries when they would be available for data collection.

The people who determine whether you can have access to those from who you want to collect data are often referred to as gatekeepers, as discussed in Chapter 6. It is very important to determine who, if anyone, are the gatekeepers to the sample or population that you want to contact, and how long negotiation with them might take, when planning the likely timescale for your research. Of course, it goes without saying that politeness and diplomacy are skills that are needed when undertaking such a negotiation. Giving comprehensive information about the project, and being flexible about who you will collect data from and when, are other essential qualities when seeking to arrange access.

Non-Response

Difficulties with negotiating access are one reason why plans for sampling and data collection often need to be adjusted as the research progresses. Another is non-response. No matter how good the sampling strategy that is adopted, it can need re-thinking if the people who you would like to collect data from are either not available or are unwilling to take part in the research.

In the case of qualitative data collection, non-response can often be dealt with by substitution. If a piece of research sought to interview Chief Constables from all 42 police forces in England and Wales to ask their opinion of government policing policy, there would probably be few adverse effects if some Deputy Chief Constables had to be interviewed instead.

In contrast, non-response can be a major difficulty for quantitative studies, where replacement of non-respondents by others is often viewed as an inferior option, even when the use of a random number table makes it easy to select a replacement. The desire to generalise from a random sample makes a low response rate problematic, particularly if it can be shown that one group (e.g. older people) is less likely than others to have responded. Political opinion polls have sometimes incorrectly predicted general election results partly because of different response rates between groups. In particular, those who have responded to the polling companies' surveys have tended to be those who are most interested and engaged in politics, while those who are less interested (but still vote) have tended to be non-respondents (Wells, 2018).

So, with quantitative surveys it is particularly important to use every possible ethical method to maximise the response (these methods are discussed in Chapter 8). Some studies also seek to 'weight' responses: if, for example, the response rate among most age groups is approximately 60%, but among those aged 16–25 it is 30%, the responses of the 16–25-year-old respondents may be made to 'count double' to seek to overcome this difficulty. 'Weighting' may feel uncomfortable – and cause you to ask why one person's responses should be regarded as more important than another's – but it is widely used in quantitative studies (see, e.g., Huq et al., 2017). However, it is something that I would not recommend that you do until you are considerably more experienced in quantitative research.

Textbox 7.4

What is the mistake – prisoner research

Try to identify the mistake(s) that a researcher has made here and then have a look at Appendix 1 to see whether your view is the same as mine.

A student volunteers in a charity shop where there is a prisoner who also volunteers on day release from an open prison. The student explains that she wants to write a dissertation about the impact of prison conditions on the population who are incarcerated there. The prisoner agrees that he will distribute to his fellow prisoners a questionnaire asking them what they think about their current living conditions. The student is very happy to accept his offer. The student uses the questionnaire responses to argue that criticisms of the lack of purposeful activity for prisoners are unjustified.

Key points for your own research

- Decide whether there is a clearly defined population to collect data from. If there is and you have the resources to collect data from the entire population, this should be your first option.
- If you need to select a sample, choose a method that is consistent with your overall approach to the research: quantitative studies tend to use random samples and qualitative studies tend to use non-random samples. If your research utilises mixed methods,

you will need to think further about the research question(s) or research objectives to determine which is the most appropriate approach.

- Whatever sampling method you choose, remember the key underlying difference – random samples seek to exclude subjective judgement from the sampling process, while purposive samples require subjective judgement to be used.
- Consider carefully how you will need to negotiate access to your sample and factor this into your plan for the research. Although convenience samples are not ideal, they are sometimes the only option because access to other respondents will not be possible.
- Make every ethical effort to maximise the response rate from those originally chosen for your sample. Carefully consider the implications of adding new people to the sample because of non-response.

Key points when reading other people's research

- Determine whether the researcher has adequately described their approach to choosing respondents: sometimes writers do not give much more information than the number of respondents, which gives the reader no opportunity to assess whether the sampling method used is appropriate.
- Consider whether the method of choosing respondents is appropriate to the research question(s) or research objectives: it is a common mistake to place too much emphasis on generalisation when a purposive sample has been chosen.
- Determine whether appropriate steps have been taken to access the sample: although this issue will not necessarily be discussed in detail, as a minimum the gatekeepers who provided access should be identified.
- Consider whether the conclusions drawn are justified by the sampling strategy: for example, it should be acknowledged that research findings arising from a very small sample of respondents are likely to be illustrative.

Further reading

For a broad introduction to sampling, see:

Daniel, J. (2011) *Sampling Essentials*. London: Sage.

A further example of criterion sampling is provided by the following study of Norwegian prisoners, where prisons were selected to ensure a good representation of certain types of prisoner:

Laursen, J., Mjaland, K. and Crewe, B. (2019) '"It's like a sentence before the sentence": exploring the pains and possibilities of waiting for imprisonment', *British Journal of Criminology*, 60(2): 363–381.

For an example of a piece of research where even a snowball sample was difficult to collect, see:

Pryke, S. (2004) '"Some of our people can be the most difficult": reflections on difficult interviews', *Sociological Research Online*, 9(1).

PART II

DATA COLLECTION

Introduction to Part II

Social science research in general, and criminological research in particular, has traditionally been based on empirical data, i.e. data that is collected directly from humans. Chapter 8 examines the collection of quantitative empirical data and Chapter 9 does the same for qualitative empirical data. However, the options for students to collect this type of data are now more limited than they once were, as ethics committees have focused more on the possible risks to respondents of being involved in research and other factors have limited the availability of human subjects. So Chapter 10 focuses largely on analysing data that already exists, in the form of quantitative and qualitative datasets, documents, images, television programmes and films. It is included in this part of the book to encourage you to think widely about the range of data that could be included in a criminological research project.

Of course, availability is not the only factor that should determine the type of data that you decide to use in your research project. The data must be suitable to answer your research question(s) or meet your research objectives. There is a two-way process here: it is also appropriate to consider the types of data that you can collect or use, and the way in which it needs to be analysed, when setting your research question(s) or objectives.

I mention data analysis here because it should be a central part of your decision making around data. It would be unwise to use questionnaires with closed questions if you hate calculating statistics. On the other hand, if you love producing bar charts, there will be no opportunity to do this if your data is collected through focus groups. It is my hope that, after reading Part 2 of this book, you will feel a degree of confidence about analysing any type of data, particularly the statistics that frighten so many students. However, you will of course prefer some forms of analysis over others, and it is right that this factor influences your decisions regarding the type of data to collect and use.

Many researchers, including me, find the most satisfying and exciting part of any research project to be collecting and working with their data. There is much technical discussion in the following three chapters: for example, about suitable forms of questions for research interviews. This material is included because it is important for you to understand and to put into practice when working with data. However, I hope the chapters will also give you a feeling of excitement about the data for your research project, which will – albeit in a very small way – say something new about the world.

8

COLLECTING DATA THROUGH SURVEYS

┏━━━ What you will learn in this chapter ━━━┓

By the end of this chapter, you will:

- Understand the role that surveys have played in increasing our understanding of crime
- Be able to select a suitable topic for a survey that you could conduct
- Understand the possible reasons for choosing to collect survey data face to face, by telephone, by post or online
- Be able to design a survey logically, with well-written and appropriate questions
- Know the practical (and ethical) steps that can be taken to maximise the response to a survey

Introduction

Surveys are the most common form of quantitative research and have played a crucial role in the development of Criminology. They can be part of a longitudinal research design, such as classic experimental designs or panel designs, which were discussed in Chapter 5. However, surveys are most often cross-sectional pieces of research that collect data at one moment in time.

Surveys involve the collection of data through pre-set questions, which can be asked face to face, by telephone, by post or online. They collect data quickly and cheaply and are excellent at providing a broad overview of the experiences, opinions or attitudes of a substantial number of people. Their limitations include the lack of opportunities for respondents to introduce variations on the researcher's choice of answers or to take the data collection in the direction that is of most interest to them.

This chapter will consider the topics on which you might be able to conduct surveys, as well as the techniques that you will need to use to make a survey effective. However, I will first demonstrate the value and limitations of surveys by showing what they have (and have not) taught us about the experiences of victims and perpetrators of crime.

Surveys of Victims of Crime

Surveys play an important role in increasing our understanding of the extent and nature of victimisation. In addition to the Crime Survey of England and Wales (and the Scottish Crime and Justice Survey), the Commercial Victimisation Survey, previously undertaken on a sporadic basis, is now conducted every year (Home Office, 2019).

Racially motivated crime is a specific area where surveys have played a particularly important role in raising awareness. In the 1980s, surveys of such crimes led to a greater understanding of the experiences of victims and a realisation that police statistics only recorded a small percentage of racially motivated incidents. For example, Newham Council gave a 'racial harassment questionnaire' to residents from minority ethnic groups, which found that one in four Black residents had experienced some form of racial harassment in the previous year and that two-thirds of these respondents had been victims on more than one occasion. The pressure created by surveys such as this led to racially motivated crimes being included in the British Crime Survey (now the Crime Survey of England and Wales) for the first time in 1988 (Bowling, 1993: 236).

However, this example also demonstrates the limitations of surveys. Bowling (1993: 238–239) argues that they do not present a complete picture because they cannot show how one incident is related to another. For example, a perpetrator may take encouragement from going unpunished after racially harassing one victim and so return to harass them again. Bowling (1993: 244) argues for surveys to be combined with other methods such as ethnography, life history interviews and case studies in order to present a fuller picture.

Bowling's critique has relevance beyond racially motivated crime; victim surveys such as the Crime Survey of England and Wales have been criticised for failing to capture the full experience of people who are repeatedly victims of crime. The survey places a 'cap' on the number of times that any one respondent can report being a victim of crime in any year. The reason for this is that a very small number of respondents tend to report a very high level of crime against them. However, limiting the number of crimes that these respondents can report is thought to lead to substantial underestimates of the level of violent crime: statistical analysis of the survey suggests that 70% more domestic violence incidents would be recorded if the cap were to be removed (Hope, 2015).

Surveys of Perpetrators of Crime

In contrast to self-report surveys of victims of crime, self-report studies of perpetrators have been subject to relatively little academic debate and appeared to reach the peak of their popularity at the end of the last millennium (see, for example, Junger-Tas and Marshall, 1999). However, some more recent examples are noted here:

- The Offending, Crime and Justice Survey was conducted among 5,000 10–25-year-olds in England and Wales every year from 2003 to 2006. It was a panel survey, with the same young people asked about their experience of committing crime on repeated occasions. Key findings were that there was a small group of prolific offenders who were involved in very large amounts of crime, including the most serious offences, and that anti-social behaviour could be a precursor of criminal activity (Hales et al., 2006).
- The Netherlands Longitudinal Lifecourse Study (NELLS), conducted in 2010, was a large-scale survey of the living situation and attitudes of 15–45-year-olds. Respondents were asked if, in the previous 12 months, they had been involved in the following activities: 'stolen something from a person or a shop', 'damaged or demolished property of others', 'carried a weapon (knife, gun)', 'threatened someone', or 'kicked or punched someone or participated in a fight' (Leerkes et al., 2019: 172–173). The outcome of the survey echoed that of previous self-report studies by raising questions over crime, policing and ethnicity. Police data showed that people of Turkish or Moroccan origin (the two largest ethnic minority groups in the Netherlands) were over-represented among crime suspects, even when taking account of gender, age, urbanisation and social and economic status. However, in the NELLS, both groups reported similar or lower rates of offending as native Dutch respondents when controlling for socio-economic status (Leerkes et al., 2019: 182).

The accuracy of self-report studies of perpetrators is even more difficult to assess than is the case for victim studies. Respondents may not report all the offences that they have committed, even with the promise of anonymity. However, there is some evidence that respondents will admit to even the most serious crimes in research of this nature: for example, in a survey in South Africa, more than one in three men admitted that they had committed rape (Smith, 2010).

Surveys and Students

The discussion in the previous two sections was included because of the great importance of surveys to our understanding of crime and to enable you to take a critical view when examining the data provided by such surveys. However, even with the protection of anonymity (discussed further below), an ethics committee is likely to raise objections to you undertaking a survey that asks respondents about their experience as victims or perpetrators of serious crimes (e.g. assaults).

So if you wish to undertake a survey – and I personally think it is extremely important to encourage students to use this method – you will have to think carefully about the topic. There is a much lower risk of ethical objections to surveys about offences that the police would be unlikely to take action against unless they found an offender 'in the act'. For example, while urinating in a public place is an offence, a survey asking long-distance runners about the most discreet places to go if caught short in an area with no public toilets is unlikely to result in a major police operation! Dropping litter, disturbing neighbours with noise late at night, failing to clean up after dogs and fare evasion on public transport are other examples of survey topics which present relatively low ethical risk.

An alternative is to ask survey questions that are related to crime but not directly about experiences as a victim or perpetrator. One popular example of such a topic is fear or worry about crime (see, e.g., Roh et al., 2013). The Crime Survey of England and Wales regularly asks about the level of worry that respondents have about a series of types of crime, for example, 'how worried are you about having things stolen from your car?' The options that respondents have to choose from are 'very worried', 'fairly worried', 'not very worried', 'not at all worried' and 'not applicable' (for those who do not have a car) (Kantar Public, 2017b).

Related to fear or worry about crime are feelings about safety: another area where you could ask survey questions without raising major ethical difficulties. For example, when conducting a survey of students that addressed several crime-related issues, I asked the following questions:

- How safe do you feel around the place that you live during daylight hours?
- How safe do you feel around the place that you live during the hours of darkness?
- How safe do you feel on the campus during daylight hours?
- How safe do you feel on the campus during the hours of darkness?
- How safe do you feel in the city during daylight hours?
- How safe do you feel in the city during the hours of darkness?

For each question, the options offered were 'very safe', 'quite safe', 'not very safe', 'not at all safe' and 'not applicable' (this last option was offered because, for example, there were some students who did not come onto campus during the hours of darkness).

Attitudes and opinions about crime are another area where you could propose a survey and feel confident that it would not face major objections from the ethics committee. For example, I conducted a survey where students were asked to read a brief account of the major theories/explanations of crime and then to give each one a mark out of 10, according to its helpfulness. Rational choice/routine activities theory achieved the highest mean mark, with biological explanations having the lowest.

Of course, there are many other areas where you could undertake surveys and I offer a few more suggestions below:

- A survey of attitudes to crime that students experienced among their peers in their teenage years. If questions were also asked about the characteristics of people who were in the peer group (e.g. whether they were comfortably off or poor, whether they received free school meals, etc.), this data could be used in the context of subcultural or strain theories.
- A survey that asked whether students aspired to work in different parts of the criminal justice system, together with questions about their attitudes to crime and punishment. This data could be used to evaluate whether, for example, students who wanted to work in the probation service were more concerned with rehabilitation, while those who wanted to work in the prison service gave higher priority to deterrence and incapacitation.
- A survey of attitudes to a piece of legislation such as the 2006 Health Act which made it illegal to smoke in any pub, restaurant, nightclub (and most workplaces and work vehicles) in the UK (British Heart Foundation, 2021). The survey could ask whether respondents feel that the health benefits of the ban outweigh the inconvenience to smokers of having to go outside to smoke. There would be scope to compare the responses of smokers and non-smokers.

Forms of Quantitative Data Collection

Older textbooks about survey research discuss the advantages and disadvantages of three main forms of data collection: structured face-to-face interviews, structured telephone interviews and postal questionnaires. Of course, the advent of the internet has changed this picture, with huge numbers of surveys made available through a range of online platforms. However, relatively little has been written about the merits of online surveys, so the literature on postal surveys is discussed below because they share some of the advantages and disadvantages of their more modern, online counterparts. It should also be noted that this is still a form of data collection that is used on occasion, no matter how dated it may seem to post a blank questionnaire to potential respondents, with a self-addressed envelope to return the completed version in.

Each of the main forms of data collection for surveys will be discussed in more detail below. Firstly, Table 8.1 compares the forms in terms of some key characteristics.

Table 8.1 Comparisons between different methods of survey data collection

Characteristic	Face-to-face interviews	Telephone interviews	Postal questionnaires	Online questionnaires
Amount of researcher time required	Very high	High	Low	Low
Chance to establish rapport	High	Medium	Low	Low
Likely response rate	High	Medium	Low	Low
Risk of bias	High	Medium	Low	Low
Anonymity possible?	No	No	Yes	Yes
Opportunity to correct misunderstandings?	Yes	Yes	No	No
Opportunity to categorise responses?	Yes	Yes	No	No
Control over who is giving the response?	Yes	Yes	No	No
Control over the order that questions are answered in?	Yes	Yes	No	Some
Capacity to deal with embarrassing subjects?	Medium	Low	High	High
Researcher safety a consideration?	Yes	No	No	No
Ability to reach a range of populations?	Variable	Variable	High	Variable
Can identify reasons for non-response?	Sometimes	Sometimes	Rarely	Rarely

Structured Face-to-Face Interviews

Structured face-to-face interviews are a traditional method of collecting survey data that incorporate several advantages, most notably they facilitate the types of interpersonal non-verbal communication that is not possible when collecting data through other means. There is also the opportunity for the interviewer to repeat or re-phrase a question that has been misunderstood, although they must be extremely careful not to introduce bias in the way they do this.

Face-to-face interviews (like telephone interviews) also enable the interviewer to listen to a respondent's answer to a question and place the answer into one of a number of pre-set categories. For example, the Crime Survey for England and Wales for 2017–18 (Kantar Public, 2017b) asked respondents why they thought that an incident might have been racially motivated. The interviewer had to listen carefully to the response and identify which of the following categories the response fitted into:

- Racist language used (comments, abuse, etc.)
- Because of victim's race/country of origin
- Because of offender's race/country of origin
- Because offence only committed against minorities (e.g. doesn't happen to anyone else)
- Because some people pick on minorities
- Because it has happened before
- Some other reason
  (More than one option could be chosen)

Of course, this categorisation requires a high level of skill on the part of the interviewer.

Data collection that involves visiting people at home for face-to-face interviews has a reputation for achieving high response rates, although the picture is more complex than has often been assumed (De Vaus, 2002: 127). Calling at home addresses has the advantage that the interviewer may be able to distinguish between respondents who are not willing to participate and those who are not available (which has an impact on the response rate, as discussed in a later section). For example, the Crime Survey for England and Wales of 2017–18 (Kantar Public, 2017b) asked the interviewer to note whether they believed a property to be unoccupied and to list one or more reasons for this, with the following options offered:

- Property is boarded up
- No furniture or other sign of occupation
- Neighbour confirmed property is unoccupied
- Front garden overgrown
- Post piled up
- Other reason (specify):
- NONE OF THESE
- Don't know

It should be noted that the survey employs experienced interviewers who are confident to talk to neighbours or to look through letterboxes for signs of post piling up – you may feel that you are some way from this stage! Indeed, for the student researcher, face-to-face interviews are more likely to be conducted with people you know in settings that you are used to sharing with others, such as a Hall of Residence, coffee shop or Students' Union. Such interviews will normally be conducted by appointment. The alternative is the intercept interview, which I do not recommend.

The intercept interview involves the interviewer approaching people as they come into a public place. High streets/shopping centres are the most popular locations for such surveys – while not giving a perfect representation of the population, they tend to provide a wider cross-section than is the case at locations meeting more specialised interests such as gyms or theatres. Intercept surveys have the obvious advantage of time because a skilled interviewer can interview large numbers of people relatively quickly. However, they have difficulty securing reasonable response rates, with large numbers of refusals as people are eager to get on with other tasks (Blair et al., 2015: 72–73). I am sure that I am not the only person who has developed a technique of avoiding eye contact and very obviously swerving away from the interceptor, only having to use 'I'm sorry, I have to get to work' on the occasions when I do not spot them in time!

More generally, the disadvantages of face-to-face interviews include the large amount of interviewer time that is required, particularly if interviews are being conducted in homes or places of work across a wide geographical area. Face-to-face interviews can be longer, often taking twice as long as telephone interviews, which has advantages in terms of level of data collected but costs in terms of interviewer time. They are the form of quantitative data collection which requires the researcher to think most carefully about their personal safety. There is also the greatest risk of interviewer bias – no matter how professional the interviewer, the respondent may be influenced by their appearance. For example, in studies of racial attitudes, respondents have been shown to be particularly likely to give 'socially desirable' responses where the interviewer is from a different ethnic group to them (Blair et al., 2015: 71–72).

Structured Telephone Interviews

Structured telephone interviews share some of the advantages of those that are conducted face to face, for example there are opportunities for the interviewer to carefully re-phrase misunderstood questions and to decide which category to place a response into. The most obvious advantage over face-to-face interviews is that time is saved because there is no need to arrange a venue or to travel to it; interviews also tend to be conducted at a faster pace. Telephone surveys enable interviewers to call back far more often than would be possible if the researcher is physically calling at someone's house (Blair et al., 2015: 64). There is clearly no risk of bias arising from the appearance of the interviewer, although their accent, tone of voice or any hesitation before speaking can all affect the answers that are given.

One of the disadvantages of telephone interviews is that the interviewer cannot take note of the non-verbal reactions of respondents. There are also limitations to the type of question that can be asked. Obviously, it is not possible to ask a question that requires the use of a visual aid such as a photograph (Blair et al., 2015: 66), but it is also difficult to discuss very personal subjects over the telephone, particularly when the respondent must state their answer rather than tick a box or point to an answer on a response card. There are some impacts on quality; there is evidence to suggest that telephone surveys tend to produce short answers to open-ended questions and less accurate responses than internet surveys (Blair et al., 2015: 67).

An issue that is unlikely to affect your own research, but which you should bear in mind when reading the findings of large telephone surveys, is that it is very difficult to obtain a comprehensive sampling frame. This issue was very different when telephones were only available as landlines and researchers would choose samples from telephone directories, which listed the telephone numbers of most of the people living in the area. This did not eliminate all difficulties – for example, some people did not have a telephone at all – but it is now particularly difficult to draw up an accurate sampling frame for telephone inter-views, due to some people having both landlines and mobile telephones and others having one or the other. However, many studies do not require nationally representative samples: for instance, in studies conducted in workplaces, it is usually reasonable to assume that all potential respondents will have a landline that they can be contacted on.

In addition, some studies chose samples of mobile telephone numbers by randomly selecting the digits, although this, of course, means that the researcher cannot choose a stratified sample (see Chapter 7). For example, Huq et al. (2017: 1107) used this method in a survey, measuring the extent to which the public trusted the police, although it should be noted that this survey achieved a very low response rate of 6.3%.

Postal Questionnaires

For organisations, postal questionnaires offer the advantage of being cheaper than face-to-face or telephone interviews, as they require little researcher time – once the questionnaire is designed, the main cost comes in the form of printing and postage. However, as a student researcher, your time may be a resource that you can offer to your project, while it may be more difficult to find the money for the extensive printing and posting of questionnaires.

Postal questionnaires eliminate the risk of interviewer bias and can reach people at widely dispersed addresses throughout the world. They provide respondents with time to go and look up information that they are uncertain of. A postal questionnaire can be completely anonymous if there is no identifying marker (such as a reference number) on the questionnaire, although this makes it impossible to target follow-ups at people who have not responded. Information can be provided in a range of formats: for example, respondents could be provided with a map and asked to mark on it places of interest (Blair et al., 2015: 53).

There are several difficulties associated with postal questionnaires. Responses often take four weeks or longer to arrive (Blair et al., 2015: 53–55), which may be a problem if you are working towards a tight dissertation deadline. Postal questionnaires are unsuitable for people with poor literacy, a visual impairment or language difficulties. There is no opportunity to correct misunderstandings, to probe, to offer explanations or to help. Even when a telephone number is provided for respondents to call if they are uncertain about what is required, this tends to be used very infrequently – instead, a section of the questionnaire will be skipped or the questionnaire abandoned altogether (Blair et al., 2015: 52). There is no control over the order in which questions are answered or whether the questionnaire is passed on to another person to complete (De Vaus, 2002: 126–131). Use of the postal service is declining for anything other than mail order goods. Even when sending letters was a more common phenomenon, postal questionnaires tended to produce low response rates, largely because they are easy to ignore, which increases the risk that the people responding are not representative of the sample or the population. However, this problem is not evident in all studies – where respondents feel strongly about a subject then even postal questionnaires may achieve high response rates and enclosing a 'thank you' gift in the envelope can also encourage people to respond.

Online Questionnaires

Online surveys can collect data in various forms, such as the sending of a questionnaire as an attachment to an email. Many webpages have 'pop up' surveys: at its simplest level, these can be asking about the level of satisfaction with the service received while visiting the page. In addition, respondents can be contacted and asked questions via mobile telephone (Sue and Ritter, 2012: 14–20). However, the most popular method is to send out a link to a survey which has been put together on one of the large number of online platforms that are available.

The researcher may email the link to all the people that they would like to fill in the questionnaire with an instruction – or at least an implication – that they should not pass it on. This gives them some control over who is included in the sample. An alternative approach is one where the researcher actively encourages the sharing of the link, often via social media such as Facebook, which creates an electronic snowball sample (see Chapter 7).

This approach often results in the researcher having more respondents, although less control over the characteristics of the sample. A study that used such an approach is Miles-Johnson's (2016: 609–611) survey of the opinions that transgender people held of the police, where the link to the survey was shared via various online groups used by the transgender community.

Online questionnaires offer many advantages when compared to other forms of data collection. They can be distributed very quickly – around the world if necessary – and at low cost. Responses are usually received within 10 to 20 days. A variety of additional media can be provided to those with a sufficient level of IT skills, for example respondents can be asked to watch a film clip and then answer questions about it. There is evidence to suggest that respondents give more detailed answers to open questions than is the case with postal questionnaires (Blair et al., 2015: 57–58). Data collection through online questionnaires can be a helpful approach when working with hard-to-reach groups, if they are suitably skilled in IT.

Another key advantage that online questionnaires have over postal ones is that most software that hosts online surveys has the power to ensure that one question is not asked until another has been answered. However, this power must be used carefully, bearing in mind that a respondent may be genuinely unable (or unwilling) to answer a question.

The extra assurance of anonymity that online questionnaires provide means that questions about attitudes or opinions are more likely to be answered, sensitive issues can also be discussed, and they are particularly helpful for the type of self-report questionnaire discussed earlier in this chapter. For example, Menting et al. (2020) undertook an online survey where data was collected from a random sample of people from a sampling frame provided by The Hague Police Service in the Netherlands. The criteria that people needed to meet to be included in the sampling frame were that they were aged 18–26, had been suspected of an offence in 2014 and had a known home address. Respondents were asked about locations in which they undertook a range of activities, including being perpetrators and victims of crime. One of the conclusions of the researchers was that offences were usually committed in or near to an area where the respondent regularly undertook non-criminal activities (Menting et al., 2020: 317).

Of course, there are also disadvantages associated with collecting data through online questionnaires. They cannot cover the entire population – while almost everyone has a postal address, fewer people have access to the internet or feel comfortable clicking a link that is sent in an email. For this reason, internet surveys tend to be undertaken with defined groups of people with a reasonable degree of IT skills. In addition, while it is possible to know the email addresses of the entire population of a workplace, this is not the case for other sampling frames.

Internet surveys appear to produce slightly different patterns of response to other forms of data collection, with more 'don't know' responses and more extreme responses on agree/disagree scale questions (different types of questions are discussed below). In addition, 10–15 minutes is thought to be the maximum length of time that a respondent is prepared to spend completing them (Blair et al., 2009: 59–62).

Although the evidence is limited, it appears that online surveys may have even lower response rates than postal questionnaires. The self-report offending survey of Menting et al. (2020: 309–310), referred to above, highlighted this difficulty. The sample were written to through the post and asked to go to a website to click onto an online survey. Despite the offer of a 50-Euro gift card for participation, the response rate was only 12.4% (Menting et al., 2020: 309–310).

Other Modes of Survey Data Collection

Although the main forms of survey data collection are discussed above, it is important to note that these are not the only options. For example, the self-administered questionnaire is not usually presented to the respondent by the researcher but by someone who is acting on their behalf. So, for example, a researcher could undertake a survey of burglary victims across a wide geographical area by leaving questionnaires at several offices of the voluntary organisation Victim Support. They would instruct the staff/volunteers in the offices to ask any victim of burglary who came into the office whether they would be willing to fill in a questionnaire. This method could be adapted so that staff/volunteers asked permission to share an email address with the researcher and the researcher sent a link to an online survey to the victim by email.

The self-administered questionnaire has the obvious advantage that far more data can be collected than if the researcher were to sit in a single Victim Support office and wait for suitable people to come in. It also eliminates the risk of bias on the part of the researcher in the way that they collect the data, although this is replaced with the risk that the staff/volunteers of Victim Support will create bias by the way in which they ask potential respondents to participate. Indeed, the greatest difficulty with this approach is that it requires a substantial 'buy-in' on the part of people who are not researchers: the staff/volunteers must be willing to give up their time to assist with the data collection; they must be clear as to exactly who should and should not be asked to take part in the research; and they must have the information to enable them to answer questions about the survey.

A final approach to consider is the group-administered questionnaire, which is given out to respondents while they are in one place together. So a group of offenders who have been brought together for an offending behaviour programme might be asked to complete a questionnaire, or a group of students might be asked to fill in a questionnaire on a criminological topic at the end of a seminar. The questionnaire can be completed in paper form or online – either in a computer lab or (more commonly today) by asking people to go online through their telephone or another device. The role of the researcher may be to give help where needed (in a non-directive manner), check finished questionnaires for completeness, and so on. This method has the advantage of efficiency – questionnaires can be completed by several people at the same time. However, there is a substantial risk of contamination of the data through copying, discussing answers or members of the group asking questions of one another. In addition, the researcher may feel under considerable pressure if several people want to ask questions at the same time.

Textbox 8.1

What is the mistake? Historic crime survey

Try to identify the mistake(s) that a researcher has made here and then have a look at Appendix 1 to see whether your view is the same as mine.

A student is writing a dissertation about historical attitudes to crimes that have largely been committed by men against women, such as domestic violence, sexual assault and rape. Her mother is the mobile warden of a number of sheltered housing complexes and agrees to provide residents of these complexes with a link to an online survey. The survey asks respondents about any past experience that they have had as victims or perpetrators of relevant crimes, and about the reaction of anyone who they told about this experience.

Designing Surveys

The difficulties involved in designing surveys and writing appropriate questions are often underestimated by students and others. This section will offer advice on the process while also highlighting some of the most commonly made mistakes.

My first piece of advice to anyone designing a survey is to begin by reminding yourself of the purpose. What are you trying to achieve? Next, think about the topics that you will need to ask about to achieve this purpose. It is important not just to think directly about your topic – in which case you would have a very small number of questions and collect a very limited amount of information – but to think around it. To show what I mean, I will go back to an example mentioned earlier in the chapter of a survey of attitudes to crime that students experienced in their teenage years. The survey can consist of one direct question, which could be worded as follows:

Please could you give a score from 0 to 10 as to how far the peer group that you were with as a teenager held pro-criminal attitudes? 0 means that your peer group was totally opposed to criminal behaviour, while 10 means that your group saw no difficulty at all with criminal behaviour.

This would provide a certain amount of information. However, a fuller picture could be provided by adding some further questions about related topics, for instance:

As a teenager, did you have friends who committed criminal damage?

This could then be repeated for other types of crime. You could also ask:

Did anyone in your teenage peer group talk about plans to commit criminal damage?

IF YES TO THE PREVIOUS QUESTION: Did anyone else in the peer group challenge them over their plans?

Again, this question could be repeated for other types of crime. You could also ask whether members of the group ever encouraged each other to commit crime, whether there were any crimes that were condemned by group members and what opinions were expressed of the police. You could end by asking an open question:

Is there anything else about the attitudes to crime in your teenage peer group that you think it is important to note?

As you begin to type up possible questions, or topics for questions, it is unlikely that they will appear on the page in the order in which you will eventually ask them. You will need to spend some time thinking about the best order for questions to ensure that the survey flows as smoothly and logically as possible.

Finding Indicators for Concepts

It was noted in Chapter 2 that a belief that social phenomena can be measured is one of the key underlying principles of quantitative methodology. However, most quantitative researchers would accept that the social phenomena that they seek to measure are usually complex and that the measures used are often approximations.

I suggested above that, if the questionnaire about attitudes to teenage crime also considered poverty, a question could be included as to whether anyone in the peer group received free school meals. This can clearly only be an approximate indicator of whether someone has experienced poverty as a child or teenager for several reasons, for example: the test that is applied to determine whether a family is eligible for free school meals is an imperfect one; the question does not distinguish between those who received free meals for a short period and those for whom it happened throughout their childhood/teenage years; and some families may have obtained free school meals fraudulently. An accurate measure of childhood/teenage poverty would include a complex analysis of income and expenditure over several years; clearly no respondent would know this about members of their peer group. They would be far more likely to know whether any of the group had received free school meals, which is a much simpler (although less precise) measure of poverty.

Textbox 8.2

A study that used an indicator for desistance

Burnett and Maruna (2004), in their research into desistance among former prisoners (discussed in Chapter 5), used the measure of whether someone had returned to prison as an indicator of whether they had been successful or unsuccessful in their attempts to desist. This was not a perfect indicator of desistance, because it is likely that there were people in their sample who had committed imprisonable offences of which they had not been convicted, and possible that there were some who had been imprisoned when they had not committed the offence. However, it was the best indicator that was available to the researchers.

Some other indicators that are not perfect but may be the most useful way to measure a concept in a survey are as follows:

- Whether a respondent has been involved in youth crime might be measured by asking whether they have had contact with the Youth Offending Service.
- A respondent's attitude to motoring laws might be measured by the number of times they have had penalty points on their licence.
- The level of support that a family offers a prisoner might be measured by the number of visits that they make to them.

Open and Closed Questions

There are many types of questions that can be asked in a survey, but a key distinction is between open and closed questions. Typically, surveys consist mainly of closed questions, where the respondent chooses from a number of pre-set options. For example:

Have you ever attended a criminal trial, for any reason?

☐ *Yes*

☐ *No*

This is the ideal type of subject for a closed question because it is a simple factual matter where respondents are very unlikely to want to give an answer other than 'yes' or 'no'. It is possible that someone may not be able to remember whether they have attended a criminal trial or may have been in court (e.g. over a breach of tenancy conditions in a rented property) and not known whether this represented a criminal trial, but the large majority of people will have no difficulty in choosing 'yes' or 'no'. One key advantage of closed questions is that the responses are easy to quantify and report on – in this example: *'30 respondents (20%) said that they had attended a criminal trial; 120 (80%) that they had not'*.

One of the difficulties with closed questions is that they do not allow the respondent to modify any of the choices that are offered, so you need to think carefully whether options need to be added such as 'don't know', 'can't remember', 'not applicable' or 'other'. When the 'other' category is used, there is often a follow-up question where the respondent is asked to give more detail. For example:

What was your favourite British TV crime drama shown in 2019?

☐ *The Capture*

☐ *Criminal: UK*

☐ *A Confession*

☐ *Dublin Murders*

☐ *Giri/Haji*

☐ *Line of Duty*

☐ *Luther*

☐ *Manhunt*

☐ *Unforgotten*

☐ *The Widow*

☐ *Vienna Blood*

☐ *Other*

☐ *Don't know*

☐ *Not applicable: don't watch TV crime drama*

A supplementary question would then be needed: *If you have answered 'other', please could you say which was your favourite?* This would give respondents an opportunity to choose dramas that I did not include on the list because my personal (and biased!) opinion was that they were less likely options, such as *Grantchester, Shetland, Vera or Midsomer Murders*.

This question demonstrates another advantage of closed questions – they can act as an aid to memory. A respondent who had enjoyed *Manhunt* might not have thought of giving this answer until prompted through the list of options. However, it also demonstrates the potential of closed questions to create bias if every possible option is not listed – in the scenario where a respondent had most enjoyed watching *Midsomer Murders* but did not think of it when asked the question, they would not be prompted and so would choose another option.

So, if it is not possible to list all the possible answers, an open question may be more appropriate. An open question is one where there is no list of possible answers and a respondent is left to respond as they think most appropriate. So the question *What was your favourite TV crime drama shown in 2019?* could be asked without any options being given. This would avoid the difficulty of creating bias by providing some dramas as options but not others. However, there would be a danger that respondents would fail to remember the drama that they had enjoyed most, would not be certain which year a drama had been shown or would make an inappropriate choice (e.g., answering *24 Hours in Police Custody*, which is a documentary rather than a drama).

More generally, open questions give the respondent the freedom to make their own choice but can be difficult for the researcher to classify. For example, if you were to ask respondents*: What word would you use to describe the serial killer Harold Shipman?* you might receive a very wide range of responses that were difficult to place into clear categories, beyond them all being negative.

Asking mainly open questions tends to be a characteristic of qualitative, rather than quantitative, research. In surveys, open questions are likely to have more limited roles, such as acting as follow-ups to closed questions, for example:

- If you have answered 'other', please specify?
- Please give reasons for your answer?
- Is there anything that has not been asked about but which you think it is important to say?

When asking questions which require numerical answers (e.g. how often, how much, how many), a survey may offer the respondent ranges to choose from. This is particularly important when it may be difficult or embarrassing to give a precise answer. For example, when asking a respondent's age, a series of bands are often offered (such as 18–25, 25–40, 40–60, 60 or over), which may help some respondents who would be unwilling to give their exact age in years, particularly if the data collection is face to face or by telephone. The 2017–18 Crime Survey for England and Wales asked about the amount of time that a respondent's house was left unoccupied on an average weekday, but acknowledged that most respondents would be unable to give a precise answer, so offered the following options:

☐ *Rarely*

☐ *Less than 1 hour*

☐ *1 hour or more but less than 3*

☐ *3 hours or more but less than 5*

☐ *5 hours or more but less than 7*

☐ *7 hours or more*

(Kantar Public, 2017b)

One disadvantage of the banded approach to numerical questions is that they create an ordinal variable, meaning that it is not possible to calculate statistics such as the mean – this issue is discussed further in Chapter 11.

For any closed question, it is very important to make it clear to the respondent whether they are required to choose just one answer or whether several can be given. An example of a question to which only one answer could be given was one in the 2017–18 Crime Survey for England and Wales, where respondents who had been a victim of crime were asked to identify the time at which the crime occurred, choosing one of the following options:

☐ *During week*

☐ *At weekend – Friday evening*

☐ *At weekend – Saturday*

☐ *At weekend – Sunday*

☐ *At weekend – Early Monday morning*

☐ *At weekend – can't say when*

(Kantar Public, 2017b)

In contrast, if a respondent said that a crime where they were the victim might have been a hate crime, they were asked if the offender was motivated by any of the following factors and could choose as many as they thought appropriate:

☐ *Your religion or religious beliefs*

☐ *Your sexuality or sexual orientation*

☐ *Your age*

☐ *Your sex*

☐ *Any disability you have*

☐ *Your gender identity (e.g. transgender)*

☐ *Don't know*

☐ *None of these*

(Kantar Public, 2017b)

This question about motivation is an example of one which is dependent on the answer to a previous question: it was only asked to respondents if they had said that they had been a victim of crime and that they believed the crime might have been a hate crime. A question that determines whether a further question should be asked is sometimes referred to as a 'filter' or 'screener' question.

Questions where several options can be chosen make the type of quantitative data analysis that is discussed in Chapter 11 more difficult. So it may be worth avoiding these questions, even if this means that you do not get quite the level of detail that you want. For example, if you were asking a question about your respondents' opinions on the causes of youth crime, the data would be difficult to analyse if you asked a question in this format:

> Please read this list of factors that people have suggested are linked to youth crime. Please tick all of those that you think are major reasons for young people committing crimes.

So you might instead ask the question in the form:

> Please read this list of factors that people have suggested are linked to youth crime. Please tick the one that you think is most likely to cause young people to commit crime.

There would then be a list of factors for the respondent to choose from.

Questions with Scales

Some questions seek to measure where on a scale a respondent's attitude or opinion lies. One possible method of doing this is by asking for a score out of 10 – here is an example from the 2017–18 Crime Survey of England and Wales:

> How much is YOUR OWN quality of life affected by crime on a scale from 1 to 10, where 1 is no effect and 10 is a total effect on your quality of life?

(Kantar Public, 2017b)

Similarly, another possible format to the question about the causes of youth crime would be to list possible causes and then ask the respondent to say for each one, on a scale of 1–10, how far they agree that it causes young people to commit crime. This would again avoid some of the difficulties with analysis that are caused by a 'tick all that apply' question.

An alternative type of scale offers respondents a range of options as to how far they agree or disagree with a statement. For example, the New Zealand government surveyed the public in 2014 about their perceptions of crime and criminal justice. One set of questions presented respondents with a series of statements about punishment and asked them to choose from the options 'strongly agree', 'agree', 'neither agree nor disagree', 'disagree', 'strongly disagree' or 'don't know'. The statements included:

- Prisons keep the public safe by securely containing offenders.
- Prisons give offenders the help they need to stop offending.
- People on community sentences are well managed.
- Parole is effective in reducing re-offending.

(Ministry of Justice, New Zealand, 2014: 11)

Scenarios can also be used for creating scales of attitudes, for example in a police integrity measure that has been put into practice in several countries (Gottschalk, 2010). Police officers are given various scenarios, involving incidents that they might choose to report to senior officers, where their responses are scaled from 1 (not at all serious, I would never report it) to 5 (very serious, I would always report it). The scenarios are wide ranging, for example: a police officer who attended a burglary at a jeweller's shop and kept for himself a watch that he reported as stolen, two police officers who pursued and overpowered a car thief then punched him as a punishment for fleeing and resisting, and a popular police officer who accepted free gifts of food and drink from local restaurants and bars on days off (Gottschalk, 2010: 53–54). When a slightly adapted list of these scenarios was put to Norwegian police officers, the results showed that they regarded cases involving corruption to be the most serious, followed by those that involved physical abuse, with those that involved evidence manipulation considered least serious (Gottschalk, 2010: 61).

Demographic Questions

Finally, most surveys include questions asking about the demographic characteristics of respondents. These are typically placed at the start or end of the survey. Many of these questions have become more nuanced as awareness has risen of the complex forms that identity can take. For example, questions about ethnic origin used to typically offer the respondent the choice of classifying themselves as 'White', 'Black', 'Asian' or 'Other'. In contrast, a survey that I was involved in – about students and crime/safety – offered the following options for ethnicity:

- ☐ *White: English / Welsh / Scottish / Northern Irish / British*
- ☐ *White: Irish*
- ☐ *White: Gypsy or Irish Traveller*
- ☐ *Another White ethnic origin*
- ☐ *Mixed / multiple ethnic groups: White and Black Caribbean*
- ☐ *Mixed / multiple ethnic groups: White and Black African*
- ☐ *Mixed / multiple ethnic groups: White and Asian*
- ☐ *Another Mixed / multiple ethnic origin*
- ☐ *Asian (or Asian British): Indian*
- ☐ *Asian (or Asian British): Pakistani*
- ☐ *Asian (or Asian British): Bangladeshi*
- ☐ *Asian (or Asian British): Chinese*
- ☐ *Another Asian ethnic origin*
- ☐ *Black (or Black British): African*
- ☐ *Black (or Black British): Caribbean*
- ☐ *Another Black / African / Caribbean ethnic origin*
- ☐ *Arab*
- ☐ *Another ethnic origin*

This was followed by an open question:

> If you have answered 'Another White ethnic origin', 'Another Mixed/multiple ethnic origin', 'Another Asian ethnic origin', 'Another Black/African/Caribbean ethnic origin' or 'Another ethnic origin', please could you specify?

Similarly, questions about gender should no longer simply offer the options of 'male' or 'female', but should also include an 'other' category, with a request to specify in cases where this category is chosen. You might also consider including a further question such as: *Is your gender identity the same as the one assigned to you at birth?* with respondents being given the option of answering 'yes' or 'no'.

Mistakes with Questions

The examples provided so far in this chapter have indicated the type of wording that is appropriate for survey questions. However, it is important to be aware of the types of mistakes that are commonly made:

1   Using language that is too complex or technical, for example: *In your opinion, which factors are most closely linked to desistance among young offenders?* Most Criminology students would understand this question, but desistance is a concept that may be unfamiliar to others, so better wording for a wider group of respondents would be: *In your opinion, which factors are most closely linked to young offenders stopping committing crime?*

2   Using questions that are longer than they should be – you should always ask yourself whether the same question can be asked in fewer words. For example, the question *Do you believe that the motivation of most offenders to commit their crimes is a simple calculation of the benefits of offending against the possible costs of being convicted?* could be changed to *Do you believe that most offenders calculate the benefits and the possible costs before committing crimes?*

3   Using questions that ask two things at once – this is a surprisingly easy mistake to make, for example asking *Have you been a victim of crime in your Halls of Residence or on campus?* If a respondent answers 'yes', you will not know whether the crime was committed on campus or at the Halls of Residence. Two separate questions are required here.

4   Using questions that are leading – for example, questions that ask *Do you agree that…* tend to produce high levels of agreement. This difficulty can be aggravated when the remainder of the question uses emotive or biased language to suggest that a particular response is required, for example: *Do you agree that the death penalty is the only sure method to ensure that murderers cannot commit their terrible offences again?*

It is also possible to word questions in a manner that few people will disagree with by using terms that allow no exceptions such as 'always', 'never', 'everybody' or 'nobody'. So, still on the theme of capital punishment, the wording of the following question encourages a negative response: *Supporters of the death penalty argue that murderers can never be reformed, regardless of the circumstances of the killing. Do you agree?*

Bias can also be created by having unbalanced answer categories. If you were to ask respondents how far they agreed with a statement such as 'Poor parenting is an important factor when considering why young people commit crime', it would clearly create bias to provide respondents with more negative than positive response categories, for example: 'agree', 'neither agree nor disagree', 'disagree', 'strongly disagree', 'completely disagree'.

5   Using questions with no clear frame of reference – you are likely to get a range of responses that are difficult to compare if you ask a question such as *'How often do you watch reality television programmes about policing?'* One person may tell you how many hours that they spend watching such programmes in a week, one may tell you how many series in a year and another may name the programmes that they watch. A better wording of this question would be: *'In a typical month, how many hours do you spend watching reality television programmes about policing (please give an estimated number of hours if you are not certain)?'*

(De Vaus, 2002: 97–99, with my examples)

Textbox 8.3

What is the mistake? Legal status of cannabis survey

Try to identify the mistake(s) that a researcher has made here and then have a look at Appendix 1 to see whether your view is the same as mine.

A student gains ethical permission to distribute an online questionnaire among their friends. This questionnaire seeks to determine attitudes to the legal status of cannabis, and whether these attitudes are influenced by the respondent's age, gender or history of cannabis smoking. After a suitable introduction (see next section), the questions that the student includes in the questionnaire are:

1   What is your age?
2   What is your gender?

   ☐ *Male*
   ☐ *Female*

3   How many times have you smoked cannabis during your life?
4   Please indicate which of these statements is closest to your position on the legal status of cannabis?

   ☐ *The law should not be changed*
   ☐ *Cannabis should be re-classified*
   ☐ *The use of cannabis should be legalised*

5   Do you agree that everybody should be able to chill out with cannabis without fear of prosecution?

   ☐ *Yes*
   ☐ *No*

(Continued)

6   To what extent do you feel that the claims about mental health problems have been overstated?

☐ *Not at all*
☐ *A little*
☐ *Quite a lot*
☐ *A large amount*
☐ *A very large amount*

Thank you for your help in completing this questionnaire.

The Introduction to the Survey

There are several pieces of information that should be included in the introduction to your survey to make the potential respondent aware of what is involved in participation, to encourage them to take part and to satisfy the ethical principle of informed consent. The method of providing this information, and of asking for consent, varies between the different methods of administering surveys. In a traditional interview – conducted in a home or office or by telephone – the respondent might be sent a letter telling them about the survey and asking them to sign a consent form, which they could then return in a self-addressed envelope. More commonly now, an email could be sent with the information and the respondent asked to click on 'I agree' if they are willing to participate. These options have the ethical advantage that the respondent does not complete the survey immediately after giving consent, so has time to re-consider their decision.

For postal surveys, information is usually sent about the survey in the same envelope as the questionnaire. It seems reasonable to assume that the respondent who completes the questionnaire and returns it in a self-addressed envelope (or hands it to a researcher who calls at the door) has agreed to take part. With online surveys, there are two methods by which information about the survey can be provided and consent requested:

- The potential respondent can be sent the information in an email and asked only to click the link to the survey if they agree to take part.
- The first page of the survey can provide the information and the potential respondent can be asked whether they agree to take part in the survey under these circumstances. If they answer 'no', the online programme defaults to the end of the survey and they

are thanked for their interest. This approach is more appropriate if you are posting the link on social media platforms and/or creating a snowball sample by asking other people to forward the link.

Both these methods have the disadvantage that the respondent goes straight into the survey, without any chance to re-consider, as soon as they have agreed to take part. This disadvantage could be avoided by asking potential respondents to email the researcher to say that they are willing to take part, and then sending them the link. However, this approach would be likely to substantially reduce the response rate, so would only be appropriate for surveys on the most sensitive topics.

It is not possible to give a definitive list of the information that should be given to a potential respondent before the start of a survey because this will vary according to the nature of the research. However, the following should always be explained:

1   The purpose of the survey – care should be taken not to make unrealistic promises about major changes arising from the research, but it should be explained that the survey is important and may bring about some beneficial outcome (a practical change, increased understanding of an issue or both).

2   How the potential respondent was chosen – it is important to emphasise that the chosen people should be the ones to respond, and not substitutes, if the research is to achieve its objectives. This is more important when using some sampling strategies (particularly random sampling) than others (e.g. electronic snowball samples), but in all cases the value of participation should be made clear. To balance the previous point, guidelines for good ethical practice should be followed by informing respondents that they are not under any obligation to respond and that they do not have to complete the survey once they have started. It should also be made clear whether respondents can miss out questions and whether they can withdraw any of their responses at a late stage (this will not be the case with an anonymous survey because there will be no way of knowing which answers were given by a specific respondent).

3   Information about how the data will be used and stored, with guarantees of confidentiality or anonymity as appropriate. This is also a matter of ethics.

4   A realistic indication of how long it will take to complete the questionnaire or interview.

5   Contact details, should the person have any questions at a later date (even if these have been provided in earlier communications).

Much of this information should also be supplied when undertaking data collection through qualitative methods (as discussed in Chapter 9).

The Role of the Pilot

Both the questions, and the order that you ask them in, should be tested through a pilot study. It was noted in Chapter 6 that a pilot is particularly important when conducting survey research. Your survey is likely to provide higher quality data if you can try it out with people you trust and ask them to give you some feedback as to whether the questions are easily understandable, whether the order is logical, whether the survey maintains their interest, etc.

Securing a Response

The importance of response rates was discussed in Chapter 7. There are some methods of maximising response that should be employed whatever the mode of data collection, such as providing an effective introduction to the survey, as discussed above. Small incentives can boost the number of responses, although you may not have the resources to provide these and they are often impossible to administer in online surveys.

Interviews conducted face to face or by telephone require people to set a specific time aside to answer the questions. Wherever possible, you should contact potential respondents in advance to arrange a time that is convenient to them. You should be ready for people to postpose the interview if something unexpected comes up, but also attuned to when the real reason for someone being evasive is that they do not want to complete the survey. In the case of face-to-face interviews, you should choose a location that is convenient for the respondent while also minimising the risk to your personal safety.

For postal surveys and, to a lesser extent, online surveys, appearances can play an important part in boosting response rates: a well presented survey, with clear instructions as to what is required for each question, will encourage a respondent to participate to the end. If you need to send reminders to complete the survey, you should send another copy of the questionnaire with the letter or re-send the link in an email.

The key reason for taking these measures is that surveys with low response rates raise particular questions as to how far the respondents are representative of the population. This was illustrated by criticisms of surveys conducted by the Independent Police Complaints Commission (now the Independent Office of Police Conduct), which were made by Shamik Dukta, of the Police Action Lawyers Group (PALG), to the House of Commons Home Affairs Committee (2013, Ev5):

> It would be important, I think, to look at the reports that are produced by the IPCC, but to do so with a degree of healthy concern about some of the statistics that are produced. For example, I was looking at their submission on appeals and

they referred to over 50% of those who replied to their satisfaction survey being satisfied ... They say that 6,476 appeals have been lodged. Now of those, only 789 people responded to the questionnaire. Of those 789, 54% said they were satisfied. So, we are looking at, in total out of all the appeals received, 6.5% of people who wrote back to the IPCC to say 'We are satisfied with what you have done' – less than 7%.

However, you should not despair if, like many students and other survey researchers, your best efforts result in a lower response rate than you had hoped for. This is a very common experience and not one that you should blame yourself for. It is important to acknowledge the low response rate when writing your methodology section and to ensure that you do not make unrealistic claims about your findings (see Chapter 13), but not to suggest that your data has no value because of a modest number of responses.

Skills for Collecting Survey Data

Many of the skills needed to collect survey data are in the writing of the questions and, if an online program is used, knowing how to use the program. However, when collecting data face to face or by telephone, there are a series of additional skills that are required in preparing for, and conducting, the interview.

It is important to make yourself very familiar with the survey questions and the routing instructions (e.g. *if 'yes' go to question 15; if 'no' go to question 18*) because, during the interview, you need to be focusing on the respondent's answers, not trying to work out your way around the questionnaire. You should also consider in advance what to do if a respondent says that they do not understand a question or gives an answer that suggests that they have misunderstood: is there a way of re-wording the question that does not change its meaning? When preparing for a face-to-face interview, if there are questions that a respondent may be embarrassed to give a verbal answer to, you should write the options on a card to hand to them, so that they only have to give a response such as 'number three'.

When it comes to the interview itself, you should seek to establish a degree of rapport with your respondent, without saying anything about yourself that suggests that you are hoping for particular answers to questions. Of course, the situation is different if you are interviewing someone you know well, in which case you should ask them to try not to consider anything that they know about you when giving their responses.

Similarly, you should respond neutrally to answers, with phrases such as 'thank you for that' rather than saying anything that suggests that you are pleased, displeased or surprised by an answer. Questions should be asked slowly and clearly. When reading possible responses to the respondent (e.g. 'agree', 'disagree', 'neither agree nor disagree'), it is important that the options are evenly spaced and that each is expressed in the same tone of voice. If a respondent chooses an option before you have finished listing them all, you should continue to offer all the choices (politely, of course) before asking them to give their answer again. Where a respondent appears to give an answer to a later question, you should still ask that question at the appropriate point in the schedule, but preface it with a phrase such as 'I think we may already have covered this, but …'.

Finally, there are some skills that apply specifically to face-to-face interviews. Try to avoid the presence of third parties (e.g. a partner, friend or colleague), who may influence the respondent's answers. If a third party insists on giving their own answers, offer to conduct the survey with them afterwards (but, of course, do not use their data because they are not part of your sample). Try to sit opposite the respondent and use eye contact to establish rapport. Your appearance should be appropriate to the setting that you are going into; you would be expected to dress in a conventionally smart manner to conduct interviews in a police station, while a more relaxed style would be appropriate to a Students' Union. You should seek to create a neutral impression through your appearance: for example, in the days when political opinion poll interviews were conducted face to face, interviewers were told not to wear blue, red, orange, green or black in case respondents thought that they were representing a particular party!

Key points for your own research

- Choose an appropriate topic for your survey, bearing in mind the need to gather useful data on a topic that is of interest to you, but also to gain ethical approval.
- Devising surveys is a considerably more difficult task than most people imagine. Make sure that you allow plenty of time for it and try not to get frustrated at the amount of re-writing that is involved.
- Carefully consider the type of questions that are most suitable for each issue that you wish to ask about: open, closed, scales, etc.
- Check that your questions are in the most logical possible order and that they avoid common mistakes such as asking two questions at the same time.
- Consider all the options when deciding how to administer the survey. Once the questions have been devised, it can be temptingly quick to put them online and then distribute the link, but make sure that you only take this approach if you have weighed up the other options.
- Conduct a pilot. It is impossible to foresee all the ways in which questions can be misunderstood and very important to check whether they work before your main survey is distributed.

- Take all feasible and ethical steps to encourage people to respond to your survey.
- Make sure that the introduction to your survey clearly states the reasons for undertaking it, the protection that respondents will be offered in terms of confidentiality/anonymity and other relevant information.

Key points when reading other people's research

- Consider whether a survey is the most appropriate method of collecting data on the chosen subject: surveys work best when establishing broad overviews of characteristics, behaviour, attitudes and opinions. They do not work so well in other areas, for example where personal narratives are required.
- Consider how the method of data collection may have affected the nature of the sample and the response rate, and whether this is acknowledged by the author, for example has a researcher who has conducted a mobile phone survey considered that the groups who are less likely to own a mobile (and/or less comfortable using one) will be under-represented?
- The response rate should always be discussed in survey research. You should look for this figure and consider whether the researcher has made claims that are realistic, given that many surveys have quite a low level of response.
- Many accounts of survey research include specific questions that were asked to respondents and the number who gave each answer. Decide whether you are satisfied that the questions are consistent with the good practice described in this chapter, for example that the wording does not imply that a particular answer is expected.

Further reading

For further advice about designing questionnaires, see Chapter 5 of:

Andres, L. (2012) *Designing and Doing Survey Research*. London: Sage.

To see examples of well-structured questionnaires and well-worded questions, see the UK data service's website at:

http://discover.ukdataservice.ac.uk/variables

For a further example of a self-report survey, see:

Selwyn, N. (2008) '"High-jinks" and "minor mischief": a study of undergraduate students as perpetrators of crime', *Studies in Higher Education*, 33(1): 1–16.

For a discussion of the under-reporting of certain types of crime in the Crime Survey of England and Wales, see:

Maguire, M. and McVie, S. (2017) 'Crime data and criminal statistics: a critical reflection', in Liebling, A., Maruna, S. and McAra, L. (eds), *The Oxford Handbook of Criminology*, 6th edn. Oxford: Oxford University Press (1st edn 1994).

9

QUALITATIVE METHODS OF DATA COLLECTION

┌─ What you will learn in this chapter ─┐

By the end of this chapter, you will:

- Be aware of the range of methods that can be used to collect qualitative criminological data
- Understand the reasons for choosing one method of data collection rather than the others
- Understand the issues that limit the circumstances in which some data collection methods can be used
- Be able to demonstrate the skills that are needed when using different methods of qualitative data collection
- Be aware of the manner in which criminological studies have put different forms of qualitative data collection into practice

Introduction

This chapter will consider four key methods of collecting qualitative data: observation, interviews, focus groups and questionnaires (although questionnaires are mainly used for collecting quantitative data, as was discussed in Chapter 8). In choosing the best data collection method, or combination of methods, to use for your study, it is important to consider not only the strengths and weaknesses of each method but also the feasibility of using them. For example, while bringing together a focus group of serial killers to discuss their understanding of the value of human life would be a truly unique piece of research that could yield hugely valuable data, the chances of it ever happening are virtually nil! Similarly, observation is a particularly difficult data collection method to use so there are quite limited circumstances in which this is viable.

This chapter gives more space to the skills required by the researcher than was the case for the quantitative methods of data collection discussed in Chapter 8. While collecting quantitative data is undoubtedly a skilled task, the range of abilities needed is not quite as extensive as is the case for qualitative data collection: this chapter will help you to develop these abilities.

The majority of the chapter discusses interviews and focus groups, as these are the most frequently used methods of qualitative data collection. However, first there will be a consideration of observation – which is closely tied to the historical development of qualitative methods – and questionnaires, which are more often used for surveys but can also have a role in qualitative studies.

Observation

The use of observation has historically been closely tied to qualitative methodology and particularly ethnography (which was discussed in Chapter 5), because it is seen to embody the principle of naturalism: people are observed in everyday settings without the artificial structure of asking them to take part in an interview or to complete a question- naire (Coffee, 2006: 214–216). Bryman (2008: 257) makes two important distinctions. The first is between structured and unstructured observation:

Structured or systematic observation – the researcher employs explicit rules as to what to record and observes for a specific length of time, so what is looked for is pre-determined. One example is the study of shoplifting undertaken by Buckle and Farrington (1984) in a depart- ment store – the researchers followed a sample of shoppers and made very specific notes based on their observations:

For each person followed, the observers recorded the date and day, the time of entry into and exit from the store, the total cost of all purchases made, and the sex, race and estimated age of the person and of any companions. In addition, of course, they made a detailed record of the behaviour of anyone who shoplifted. (Buckle and Farrington, 1984: 67)

Structured observations are often associated with quantitative methods, but for simplicity are discussed in this chapter. They are used less frequently in the social sciences than the unstruc- tured alternative.

Unstructured observation – the researcher records as much as possible of what they see in order to develop a narrative account of the behaviour observed. So, for example, Brent and Kraska (2013: 364) provide the following extract from their fieldnotes when observing people who were involved in 'cage fighting' – the focus is on providing a holistic picture:

Shirts off, bare knuckled and ready to 'throw', the fighters start closing the gap between one another. Cautious of the other, each fighter takes a defensive stance – both wary of being too aggressive and 'gettin tagged'…

As the research progresses, the researcher will tend to decide which are the key areas to concentrate on, so the focus will become narrower. Unstructured observation can be a bewildering task for a new researcher but, as with all forms of data collection, your confidence will grow as you gain experience of using it.

The second important distinction is between participant and non-participant observation (Bryman, 2008: 257):

Participant observation – the researcher immerses themselves in the social setting that they are studying and takes part in relevant activities. This was the approach of ethnographers such as Patrick, who studied a Glasgow gang, and a number of studies of the police, as was discussed in Chapter 5. Participant observation is only likely to be possible when the researcher is already a member of the group in question or has someone who can introduce them to the group, i.e. an informal gatekeeper (Fetterman, 1989: 43–44).

Non-participant observation – the researcher observes a social situation but takes no part in it. Non-participant observation can either be simple, where the researcher has no control over the situation they are observing, or contrived, where the researcher alters or even creates the situation. Simple observation would, for example, involve sitting in close proximity to a police station and observing people going in and out. In contrast, one example of a contrived piece of non-participant observation was the creation of a simulated prison by Haney et al. (1981), who observed how participants reacted to being given the role of prisoner or guard. The disturbing results of this study were mentioned in Chapter 6.

Most observation will be classified as either structured or unstructured and as either participant or non-participant. Observation can quickly provide a large amount of data, although this often makes analysis a more complicated task. However, the obvious point to make about all of the studies listed as examples above is that they present substantial ethical difficulties: you, as a modern-day student, faced with a rigorous ethical approval system, would be highly unlikely to gain agreement to conduct a study that was similar to any of these. Observation tends to be problematic for social science research generally, but particularly when dealing with criminological topics.

So, if you do wish to use observation, you need to think carefully about settings in which it might be ethically acceptable to use it. You might, for example, gain ethical approval to conduct participant observation with your seminar group, which would limit you to topics around how people learn about criminology. An alternative is to observe films or television programmes about crime – these options will be discussed further in Chapter 10.

Questionnaires

As was discussed in Chapter 8, questionnaires usually consist mainly of closed questions, with any open questions asking for more detail or for any information not covered earlier. Such questionnaires provide largely quantitative data.

However, there are also some questionnaires where the majority of questions are open and much of the data collected is qualitative. I have used an online questionnaire to gain qualitative data from police officers, on the subject of the manner in which they used reflective practice in their work, as discussed in Textbox 9.1.

Textbox 9.1

Qualitative questionnaire with police officers on reflective practice

The questionnaire consisted of only two questions. The first was:

> Please give an example from your policing career when you were disappointed with the outcome of your actions and decided to take a different approach the next time a similar situation arose. Did this changed approach lead to a better outcome?

The second question was:

> Please give an example of an instance where you decided to take a new approach to a situation and were not sure what the outcome would be. Once you had put your plan into action, did you consider it to be a success and did you modify it for the future?

Although there was a limited response to the questionnaire, those who did answer provided some rich qualitative data. One example of an answer to the first question was:

(Continued)

I dealt with an incident where a puppy had been out of control and had bitten a child. I spoke to the victim who stated she just wanted the owner spoken to and did not want to make a complaint. I have then spoken to the dog's owner and the following day the victim has made a complaint to the inspector stating she was not happy the owner had been spoken to and wanted to make a complaint. I explained that she was happy with this the day before but as I had no evidence of this I could not prove it. I then had to go to get statements and begin a prosecution into the offence. Since then, when I have come across similar instances I now always get a pocket notebook entry from the victim and have them sign it. This shows that if they change their mind that I have only done as they have asked.

One response to the second question was:

I came across a male going door to door who transpired to be collecting for a fake charity which was made up by him. As I dug into the case I came across numerous fraud offences with over 100 victims. I had not come across a case this big before so I decided, rather than attend each one, to do a pro forma statement that had blank spaces for each individual to fill in specific information. I then posted these to all the victims. This was a new approach for me and I was not sure if it would work but it was the only practical way I could think to deal with it. I had responses from most of the victims and the offender ended up being charged. The case even ended up in crown court and the offender was convicted. I did consider it to be a success and would do the same in the future if I came across a similar situation.

If you are considering using questionnaires to collect qualitative data, there are obvious advantages in terms of the ease and speed with which they can be distributed, as was discussed in Chapter 8. However, these are particularly difficult questionnaires to write, as the researcher must use great skill to encourage respondents to express themselves fully when there is no one there to prompt them – open-ended questions are assumed to work best when they are asked verbally (De Vaus, 2002: 129). Questionnaires of this nature should not be used with groups who are likely to find difficulty in writing or in expressing their opinions.

Interviews

Interviews have historically been assumed to be the 'gold standard' for qualitative research (Barbour, 2008: 113) and there is sometimes an assumption that a decision to use this data collection method requires no justification. However, it is important to consider the reasons for choosing interviews, such as their flexibility and adaptability (Robson, 2011: 280). The qualitative interview provides an opportunity for you to listen to the views or experiences of one respondent for an extended period of time and to ask probing questions to explore ideas further. Hennink et al. (2011: 109–110) note a range of areas where interviews are particularly helpful:

- in determining how people make decisions;
- in examining people's beliefs and perceptions;
- in identifying motivations for behaviour;
- in determining the meanings that people attach to their experiences;
- in examining people's feelings and emotions;
- in extracting people's personal stories or biographies;
- when covering sensitive issues; and
- in examining the context surrounding people's lives.

So, to provide some criminological examples, you might use interviews to establish what people believe to be the key impacts of environmental crime, what motivates people to volunteer with a Youth Offending Service, or how some retired probation officers saw the nature of their job change during their working life.

Hennink et al. (2011: 110) suggest that interviews are 'primarily used when seeking to capture people's individual voices and stories'. Miller and Glassner (2011: 133) argue that they do not provide an objective view of the social world that the respondent inhabits but demonstrate the meanings that they attribute to this world and their experience of it. So, in the above examples, the interviews would not be used to measure the impact of environmental crime, to provide a definitive list of possible reasons for volunteering with a Youth Offending Service or to write a historically accurate account of developments within the probation service. Instead, they would build a picture of these issues from the perspectives of the respondents.

Interviews require a researcher to spend a substantial amount of time with each respondent, so are resource intensive. In addition, they lack some specific advantages of other techniques, being seen as less 'naturalistic' than observation and not providing the same opportunities to explore collective understandings that are offered by focus groups.

Interviews can take many different forms. The discussion here will be limited to three types that are frequently used in qualitative studies: semi-structured interviews, unstructured interviews and life history/biographical interviews.

Semi-Structured Interviews

Semi-structured interviews are likely to be appropriate in many research situations and are recommended if you are a new researcher because, as their name suggests, they provide some structure and guidance, without taking the standardised approach of the quantitative survey interview. You have a guide to follow when collecting the data, meaning that there are certain topics where questions are asked of every respondent, and analysis is likely to be easier because there is some data on these topics from everyone.

When conducting a semi-structured interview, you can work from either a list of topics or specific, open-ended questions. These are used only as a guide, because you will also need to ask unplanned probes where you respond to issues that are raised by the respondent. The topics may be raised in a different order to the way that they appear on your list and you need good listening skills in order to be able to establish whether all the required topics have been covered (Roulston, 2010: 14–15). The use of probes will be discussed further, and an example of a semi-structured interview guide provided, later in this chapter.

Unstructured Interviews

While many qualitative researchers prefer a semi-structured approach, Gillham (2005: 45) suggests that there are three situations in which an unstructured interview may be most appropriate:

- In the early stages of the research, when the researcher is looking to identify key themes which can then be asked about specifically in subsequent, more structured data collection;
- When a more structured approach might be inhibiting or constraining for the respondent;
- When discussing an aspect of the respondent's life where asking questions might interrupt the thread of the narrative.

The unstructured interview appears on the surface to operate in a similar manner to a conversation. The interviewer may have a single question that they begin with, then ask follow-up questions based on the response to the first one, or they may have notes of a number of points that they wish to raise in the course of the interview (Bryman, 2008: 438). However, this list of points is shorter than would be the case for a semi-structured interview.

Unstructured interviews tend to produce the 'richest' data. However, they are also very time-consuming to analyse, as it may be difficult to find commonalities between different interviews. In addition, the potential for interviewer bias is particularly high, because the interviewer may decide to ask follow-up questions about the topics that they are most interested in and ignore others. If your research topic particularly lends itself to unstructured interviews, and you feel confident to undertake them, that is great, but they may be an option that you want to leave until you have gained some more experience of research interviews.

Life History/Biographical Interviews

These interviews can focus on the entire life of a respondent or one part of their life. They can be combined with the collection of various kinds of personal document such as diaries, photographs and letters (Bryman, 2008: 440). The focus of these interviews is on process. Life experiences are examined in a more holistic way than with other types of interview: breadth of topics covered is likely to be sacrificed for depth of information. These interviews can be semi-structured or unstructured but they lend themselves particularly well to an unstructured approach, with the researcher allowing the respondent to tell their story as they see best (Fielding, 2006: 159–161; Hesse-Biber and Leavy, 2011: 133–134).

One difficulty with life history/biographical interviews for the social sciences is that they cannot be generalised, but their popularity has grown in recent years as a number of advantages of this form of data collection have been identified (Bryman, 2008: 440). An example of how they were used in a criminological study is provided in Textbox 9.2.

Textbox 9.2

How a study put biographical interviews into practice

Collison (1996) undertook biographical interviews with young male offenders in which he explored what it meant to them to grow up male in a situation where they were on the margins of society. He concluded that drug taking, drug dealing and 'normal' crime were important ways in which they established masculine identities on the street.

Designing the Interview Guide

As its name suggests, the interview guide simply guides the interview, rather than prescribing the format, and is essentially a memory aid (Hennink et al., 2011: 112). However, putting together an interview guide is a task that you may find difficult the first few times that you try it.

As was mentioned above, the guide may include full questions or, alternatively, words or phrases as reminders of topics to cover. The advantage of full questions is that you can think in advance about the wording and so avoid questions that are leading or confusing. However, there is a danger of using the guide inflexibly, almost like a structured interview schedule, in which all questions are asked in the same order without any unplanned follow-up questions (King and Horrocks, 2010: 38–39). Despite this risk, having full questions written may well prove reassuring in your first few interview projects.

King and Horrocks (2010: 36–37, citing Patton, 1990) describe different types of question that can be asked during a qualitative interview. Background/demographic questions ask for factual information that may influence the analysis, such as the respondent's age, ethnicity or occupation. These questions are usually asked near the start of the interview. A number of other types of questions will usually be asked as the interview progresses:

- Experience/behaviour questions that focus on actions that could have been observed by the researcher had they been present;
- Opinion/value questions that seek to establish what the respondent thinks about the topic and how their thoughts relate to their values;
- Feelings questions that focus on respondents' emotional experiences. They should be worded carefully to avoid confusion with opinions/values questions, so questions are better to begin with 'What feelings are provoked by ...?' rather than 'How did you feel about ...?';
- Knowledge questions that are concerned with what a respondent considers to be a 'fact' rather than anything that is necessarily true objectively.

In addition to these types of questions, qualitative interviews depend heavily on the use of probes. These can be divided between topical probes (which are planned in advance) and unplanned probes (which are not). Topical probes involve the interviewer listing specific issues to raise if they are not covered by a respondent in answer to a question (Hennink et al., 2011: 119–120). The interview guide in Textbox 9.3 includes examples of such probes: for example, if a respondent did not mention whether a job that they held was full or part time, the guide reminded the interviewer to ask for this information.

Textbox 9.3

Example of an interview guide

This is a guide that was put together for interviews with people in prison, as part of a research project that examined the relationship between offending and housing. The guide sought to explore several issues that have been shown to be linked to both homelessness and offending, such as childhood trauma, mental health problems and addiction. It was also designed to address a respondent's housing situation and, if they had had a previous prison sentence, any housing-related support that had been provided when they had been released.

Please could you tell us about the places that you have lived since you were in the family home or in care?

In the case of each place lived probe for who lived with (if anyone), why moved there, why moved on

Have you ever been homeless?

(IF YES) How did this come about and what did you do to tackle it?

Did you have a happy childhood?

Were you ever cared for by the local authority, rather than by your family, as a child?

Did you get any qualifications through education or training? (IF YES) Please could you tell me what they are?

Did you have any difficulties in reading and writing? (IF YES) Were you given any help with these difficulties?

Did you regularly attend school?

Please could you tell me about any jobs that you have had? *(Probe for full-time/ part-time and types of job)*

What job have you held for the longest time?

Did you enjoy working?

Have you experienced financial difficulties at any point in your adult life?

(IF YES) Please could you tell me what they were and when they occurred?

Are you currently in a relationship with a partner?

Do you have any children? (IF YES) Were you seeing them regularly before you were sentenced to custody?

(Continued)

Do you have any family who would be willing to help you in a time of difficulty? (IF YES) Could you tell me who they are and what type of help they could provide you with?

Do you have any friends who would be willing to help you in a time of difficulty? (IF YES) Could you tell me who they are and what type of help they could provide you with?

Have you ever had any periods of illness? (IF YES) Please could you tell me what the illness was? How long did it last? What was the impact (e.g. loss of work)?

(IF NOT ALREADY DISCUSSED) Do you consider that you suffer, or have suffered in the past, from any mental health difficulty such as depression? Please could you tell me what impact this difficulty has or had on you? Have you received any help for this difficulty? Was the help that you received useful to you?

Has drug use ever been a problem for you? (YES/NO)

IF YES: At what age did drug use become a problem for you?

What happened as a result of your drug problem? Did you receive any help for your drug problem? *(Probe for help inside and outside prison)* (IF YES) Was this help useful to you?

Do you consider yourself to have a drug problem now?

Has alcohol use ever been a problem for you? (YES/NO)

IF YES: At what age did alcohol use become a problem for you?

What happened as a result of your alcohol problem? Did you receive any help for your alcohol problem? *(Probe for help inside and outside prison)* (IF YES) Was this help useful to you?

Do you consider yourself to have an alcohol problem now?

Which event in your life do you think had the most impact on your current situation?

At what time in your life were you happiest? Why?

At what time in your life were you unhappiest? Why?

Was there a point in your life when you would particularly have welcomed some extra help? (IF YES) What was the point and what type of help would you have welcomed?

Please could you tell me a bit about your history of involvement with the police?

IF NOT COVERED ABOVE: Have you been in custody previously?

IF YES: Did you receive any help with your housing while you were in custody the previous time(s)? *(Probe for usefulness of help)*

What was your housing situation when you came out of custody the previous time(s)?

(Continued)

Please could you tell us a bit more about your housing situation before you went into custody (present time)?

Can you tell us about any help that you are currently receiving with your housing?

What has been the most useful element of this help?

Are there any elements of this help that have not been useful?

Is there any help that you have not received but which would have been useful?

Unplanned Probes

In addition to the topical probes discussed above, a qualitative researcher needs to use probes that cannot be planned in advance. A key judgement during an interview is to know when and how to use unplanned questions, comments or sounds in order to elicit further information. A number of types of unplanned probes are shown in Table 9.1.

Table 9.1   Types of unplanned probe

Type of probe	Purpose	Typical words used
Motivational probe	To show that the interviewer is listening and encourage a respondent to say more	'Ah-ha', 'Mmm' or 'Yeah'
Amplification probe	To encourage a respondent to provide more detail	'Can you tell me a little more?' or 'Can you give me an example?'
Exploratory probe	To explore a respondent's feelings about a situation they have discussed	'How did you feel when...?' or 'Why did you think it was important to...?'
Explanatory probes	To encourage the respondent to explain opinions, feelings or behaviour	'What exactly made you feel...?' or 'Could you tell me why you believe...?'
Clarification probe	To provide greater clarity in areas such as the order of the events that a respondent is discussing or the definition of a term that they are using	'Could you just confirm...?' or 'Would you mind just explaining to me...?'

Sources: Hennink et al. (2011: 129–130); Legard et al. (2003: 150–152)

Qualities of the Qualitative Interviewer

Knowing when and how to use unplanned probes is one of a number of important skills that you will need to develop as a qualitative interviewer. Oppenheim (1992: 67) notes that it is a highly skilled task to persuade people to talk freely about their thoughts and feelings for a period of up to an hour. The nature of the relationship between the researcher and the respondent is clearly crucial to the success of an interview. Steinke (2004: 185) suggests that a key check for the quality of an interview is to examine whether a working relationship has been developed between the researcher and the respondent: if it has not, the interview is likely to yield little useful data.

Chapter 8 discussed the risk of unintentionally creating bias in survey interviews. This risk is even greater with qualitative interviews, so it is crucial to think of the possible impact of your observable and/or hearable characteristics and to seek to neutralise this impact as far as possible. The impact of personal characteristics is demonstrated by Lewis' (2006: 184) finding that offenders from minority ethnic groups were more likely to say in an interview that they would like to be supervised by a probation officer from the same ethnic group if the person conducting the interview was themselves from a minority ethnic background.

Hennink et al. (2011: 124–128) note the importance of the early stages of the interview for establishing and maintaining rapport: they suggest that it is very important to take some time to engage in everyday conversation after meeting a respondent and to continue to encourage them to relax as the interview progresses. However, the need to establish rapport must be balanced against the danger of creating bias.

A good interview should feel like a conversation to the respondent, but does not represent a two-way dialogue as the role of the interviewer should be to elicit information and views (Hennink et al., 2011: 109). So, this is an important balance that you will need to strike: being friendly enough to encourage your respondent to feel that their answers are wanted and appreciated, but not allowing the interview simply to become a conversation. This may be particularly difficult when interviewing someone you know already, where you may need to explain that this will be a different interaction to the ones that you are used to. Offering to answer questions at the end of the interview (e.g. on your own opinions) may be the most effective method to maintain both rapport and an appropriate distance.

It may be particularly difficult to maintain a neutral approach when faced with a subject that you feel strongly about or when the respondent expresses views that you find offensive. Although your university ethics procedures may prevent you from asking questions around the most sensitive topics, or those where views are highly polarised, it is not possible to eliminate the possibility that you may unexpectedly find yourself feeling offended by a view that has been expressed. This issue was discussed in Chapter 6.

Further skills required by the qualitative interviewer are listed by Bryman (2008: 445, adapting Kvale, 1996):

- structuring and finishing the interview, making clear when the interview is complete and asking if the respondent has questions;
- balance – not talking too much and dominating the interview, but equally not saying so little that the respondent feels that their answers are 'wrong';
- clarity – asking simple and easy-to-answer questions;
- gentleness – letting the respondent finish and giving them time to think;
- being critical – while being gentle, also being prepared to point out apparent inconsistencies in the respondent's answers;
- remembering and referring back to what has previously been said;
- interpreting and clarifying what is said, but without imposing your own meaning on the responses.

A final, very important point to make is that you should not feel discouraged if some of your interviews are shorter than you hoped they would be. Sometimes, no matter how skilled your approach, there are respondents who cannot be persuaded to discuss issues in any great detail. Even short interviews can include valuable data for analysis: I was recently involved in a research project where, for a number of reasons, the longest interview was about 25 minutes, but the research team were still able to reach some important conclusions.

Modes of Data Collection for Interviews – Meet, Call, Video or Type?

Qualitative interview data can be collected face to face, by telephone, through mediums such as Zoom or Microsoft Teams that allow virtual face-to-face contact, or by typing into mobile phones, laptops, tablets, etc. Face-to-face contact is usually the preferred method because a full range of communication is possible, with both interviewer and respondent able to respond to the non-verbal signs given by the other. For example, you may note that a respondent looks uncomfortable when asked a question and offer to move on to the next topic. However, it is in face-to-face interviews that the risk of bias is greatest because of the range of ways in which it can be created: through the interviewer's appearance, facial expression, gestures, etc.

In addition to the more limited forms of communication that can take place, another reason for telephone interviews frequently being considered an inferior alternative is that respondents may slip into their habitual method of telephone conversation: either the brief and to the point answers typical of the workplace or a conversational style used in discussions with friends. These difficulties can be reduced by informing respondents about the likely duration of the interview, briefing them thoroughly about the purpose, pre-arranging a time of day for the call when a respondent is unlikely to be disturbed and encouraging them to find a private setting in which to take the call (King and Horrocks, 2010: 80–82). However, there remains a risk that the conversation may become too task focused and stronger probing may be necessary if responses become too 'factual'. Specialist devices are available for recording telephone conversations (King and Horrocks, 2010: 82–83), although putting the telephone on 'speaker' may well be sufficient for recording.

The Covid-19 pandemic that began in 2020 meant that people across the world became more accustomed to video-based methods of face-to-face communication. The advantages and disadvantages of using one of these forms of communication (Skype) for research interviews were noted by Lo Iacono et al. (2016). The benefits observed were fairly obvious in terms of cost and convenience: people from around the world can be interviewed in an environment that is safe for both the respondent and the researcher. However, this form of communication depends on people having access to the appropriate technology so will be inappropriate for some research topics. In addition, it may be more difficult to build rapport (prior email communication may play an important role here), any interruption due to technical difficulties may damage that rapport, sensitive topics may be more difficult to discuss, eye contact is almost impossible to achieve and body language can only be perceived in the head and shoulders (meaning that some gestures will be lost). In addition, a respondent may unwittingly give something away about themselves that they would prefer the researcher not to know, for example if another member of their household appears in the background in the course of the interview.

There are a variety of options available for undertaking online interviews where the communication is typed rather than spoken, including email, chat rooms and instant messaging services. A key distinction here is between synchronous interviews, which happen in real time (i.e. one person starts typing when the other one stops), and asynchronous interviews (where there are gaps between contributions because people are doing other things; the interviewer and the respondent do not need to be online at the same time). Synchronous typed interviews are usually conducted using some kind of 'chat' or 'instant messaging' service, while asynchronous interviews tend to be conducted by email (Jowett et al., 2011: 355). Synchronous interviews are sometimes thought to produce very conversational styles of interaction, reflecting the nature of communication that many chat services are typically used for (King and Horrocks, 2010: 94–97).

Typed interviews share some of the advantages and disadvantages of video-based methods, for example they can reach participants worldwide but cannot be used for some groups of respondents such as prisoners and people from the poorest parts of developing countries. Concerns over the degree of rapport that can be achieved through typed communication have reduced with time as the amount of communication that takes place in this format has increased (King and Horrocks, 2010: 86–93). The lack of communication through body language, voice and facial expression is usually seen as a disadvantage. However, Pearce et al. (2014: 680) argue that the increased level of anonymity and invisibility of the interviewer can also be an advantage, particularly when dealing with sensitive topics: inhibitions, inclinations to give socially desirable answers and power imbalances can all be reduced. Respondents are also able to reflect on the dialogue so far because they have a written record.

In choosing your own method of communication for qualitative interviews, I encourage you to consider all the above factors but also the methods of communication that you feel most comfortable with. It is crucial that you feel as relaxed and comfortable as possible if you are to collect good-quality data.

Focus Groups

Focus groups provide extra challenges in terms of practical organisation and researcher skills, but they have some unique qualities that make them invaluable for collecting data in the right context. Wilkinson (2011: 168) defines focus group research as:

> … a way of collecting qualitative data, which usually involves engaging a small number of people in an informal group discussion (or discussions), 'focused' around a particular topic or set of issues.

Focus groups typically have 6–8 members. Their distinguishing feature is the interaction between the group members, which contrasts with an interview, where the interaction is solely between the respondent and the interviewer. Interaction between respondents has disadvantages because you as the researcher have a limited amount of control: it may be difficult to prevent the discussion from drifting into areas that are not relevant. However, as Barbour (2007: 35–37) notes, focus groups take some of the burden of interpretation away from the researcher because participants themselves can provide insights and commentaries in the course of the discussion. Oates (2000: 187) argues that focus groups force individuals to explain to others why they hold particular views and this can give a greater insight into the reasoning behind the opinions that people hold. Disagreement may also demonstrate the strength with which individuals hold their opinions.

Bloor et al. (2001: 5–6) note that focus groups also have a role in relation to exploring shared understandings. This point is illustrated by Onifade's (2002) finding that police officers from minority ethnic groups were more likely to acknowledge racism when data was collected through focus groups than through individual interviews.

There are some situations in which focus groups are clearly not a suitable method of data collection. They are unlikely to be effective when collecting data on sensitive topics or for contexts where people may not be willing to express their views in front of each other, for example when one group member is in a position of power over another. They are also unlikely to produce useful data where personal narratives are required or where participants strongly disagree with each other (Liamputtong, 2011: 8).

Textbox 9.4

How a study put focus groups into practice

Tang et al. (2001) sought to explore how Chinese people understood violence against women, at a time when the All-China Women's Federation was expressing concern about the growing numbers of reports of women's victimisation. A focus group study was conducted in Hong Kong, in parallel with studies in Taiwan and China. The Hong Kong study involved conducting six focus groups:

- One with male college students
- One with female college students
- One with male blue-collar workers
- One with female blue-collar workers
- One with 'homemakers'
- One with professionals

All the focus groups demonstrated a shared uncertainty about the definition of the term 'violence against women'. In one revealing exchange, a female college student discussed a range of aggressive behaviour that she felt the term referred to, but another focus group member suggested that these behaviours could also be used by women against men. Across the groups, there was a high level of agreement that terms such as 'abuse' should apply to a wide range of behaviours. Using abuse and violence interchangeably encouraged male group members to think more broadly about the dimensions of violence. The researchers concluded that, in order to encourage Chinese people to move away from very narrow definitions of violence against women, the phrase should be used interchangeably with 'woman abuse' and 'violation'.

The collection of data through focus groups was particularly appropriate in this case because it revealed shared understandings (or uncertainties), differences between groups in relation to these understandings and examples of people learning through interactions with each other. The article published by the researchers included some lengthy quotations of interactions between focus group members, which highlighted how these discussions contributed to a greater understanding of the subject matter.

Focus groups lend themselves to the use of materials such as images and video clips. For example, Waddington et al. (2015) showed focus groups members five clips from BBC documentary programmes involving encounters between police officers and members of the public. Each focus group member was then invited to assess the behaviour of the officers on an 11-point scale from –5 to +5. This was followed by a 10–20-minute discussion of the evaluations that group members had made (Waddington et al., 2015: 217–218).

Textbox 9.5

What is the mistake? Training and police officers

Try to identify the mistake(s) that a researcher has made here and then have a look at Appendix 1 to see whether your view is the same as mine.

A student wishes to understand better what role initial training has played in the biographies of police officers. He gathers together a focus group of officers with a range of experience and asks them to discuss their first memories of training, how (if at all) their training affected their expectations of working as a police officer, how far their training influences the way that they conduct their day-to-day work and what advice they would give to a new recruit about to start their initial training.

The Focus Group Guide

As with interviews, your preparation for conducting a focus group should include writing a list of topics to cover, specific questions to ask or a combination of the two. Although focus groups typically last longer than interviews, the guide is likely to be shorter, because interaction between respondents should ensure that issues are discussed for a greater length of time. You should be prepared with probes, but these are often not needed if group members interact effectively and explore each other's views. Less has been written about the types of question that can be asked in focus groups than is the case for interviews. Krueger (1998: 24–28) provides a list of types of questions which, although helpful, simply marks different stages of the discussion:

- Opening question – one that can be answered very quickly by everyone, often just a simple introduction.
- Introductory questions – broad questions that encourage respondents to discuss the areas of interest and to interact with each other.

- Key questions – these are most important and are central to answering the research question(s) or achieving the research objectives. Most of the discussion should be devoted to these questions.
- Ending questions – questions that finish the meeting by allowing respondents to state their final position, to respond to a summary of the discussion provided by the researcher and/or to discuss any matter that they consider important and which has not previously been mentioned.

However, this typology does not indicate how questions should be asked or what should be asked about. Considering the list of possible types of questions that were identified above for interviews, feelings questions are unlikely to be appropriate because sensitive topics are very difficult to discuss in focus groups. In addition, knowledge questions are unlikely to produce the interactions that are necessary for focus groups, unless respondents have different views of what is factually true. Background/demographic questions might be appropriate at the introductory stage, but most of the questions asked are likely to be about experience/behaviour or opinions/values.

Moderating a Focus Group

The researcher who leads a focus group is usually referred to as the facilitator or moderator. Moderating focus groups is a highly skilled task and, as with interviews, the quality of the data collected is highly dependent on the researcher. This section considers specific abilities that you will need when moderating a focus group.

Preparation

Finding a convenient time for focus group members to meet, and choosing and booking a suitable location, require good organisational skills on the part of the researcher. Making thorough preparations also involves undertaking tasks such as visiting the venue in advance and finding the best position for the recording equipment in the middle of the table (Barbour, 2007: 75–76). If you decide to use materials such as newspaper articles or film clips, ensuring that all such materials are available at the required time is another important element of the preparation.

Recording

While recording is advantageous but not essential for interviews, and note taking is a feasible alternative, audio or visual recording is essential for focus groups. The speed of discussion, and the limits to the control that you can exercise as a moderator, mean that it would be all but impossible to keep comprehensive notes and difficult even for a second researcher to do so (Barbour, 2007: 76–77). If a potential focus group member refuses to be recorded, and cannot be persuaded otherwise, you have little choice other than to very politely suggest that they do not take part in the discussion.

Video recording of focus groups can overcome the difficulties of identifying who is speaking, and of recording non-verbal behaviour, but may present problems in positioning the recorder to ensure that everyone is covered. It may also increase the self-consciousness of respondents (Barbour, 2007: 76–77). When using audio recording for focus groups, having a note-taker in addition to a moderator is a major advantage. The note-taker can keep track of the order of speakers (which may be difficult to tell from an audio recording), record the key issues to emerge from the discussion and note group activities and movements that cannot be captured by the recording device. In addition, in the later stages of the discussion, they can inform the moderator if there are any topics that have not yet been covered (Liamputtong, 2011: 63).

Encouraging interaction

Once the focus group begins, a key task of the moderator is to encourage interaction between the group members. As Wilkinson (2011: 169) notes, focus groups are not the same as group interviews and it is neither necessary nor desirable for questions to be answered by each respondent in turn; instead it is hoped that group members will respond spontaneously to the comments of others. The introductory question is crucial; it should encourage as many people as possible to participate and give the maximum opportunity for discussion of the issues that emerge (Finch and Lewis, 2003: 178–179).

If a focus group is working well, you will need to do little probing, because respondents will explore and sometimes challenge the views of other group members. However, you will need to take a more active role when there is a limited amount of interaction. Krueger (1998: 46) notes that unplanned probes may be crucial; you must be able to judge when to ask follow-up questions based on the importance of the issue, the amount of time available and the level of detail that is hoped for in the data.

Ensuring that all contribute

One of the consequences of focus groups being different from group interviews is that the moderator does not have control over the order in which people speak or the number of times each member contributes. Finch and Lewis (2003: 180–184) note that one role of the moderator is to regulate the dynamics of the group by ensuring that contributions are received from each group member, limiting the contributions of dominant respondents, drawing out reticent respondents and preventing people from talking simultaneously. As a moderator, you must be aware of a group member who has not yet contributed and sensitively invite them to do so, possibly through a direct question or by picking up on body language such as smiling or nodding: for example, 'I see that you are nodding there, can you tell me your views?' (Barbour, 2007: 80–82). It is important that you indicate from the beginning that the views of all group members are wanted and that disagreements should be voiced (Bloor et al., 2001: 49). Conversely, you must be able to shift attention away from a dominant speaker without them or others feeling that their views are being dismissed (Liamputtong, 2011: 81). In the case of a focus group that I conducted among lecturers about their experience of conducting seminars, one group member sought to close down discussion in response to a question and I had to be quite forceful in seeking the views of others:

Moderator: So, going back to Kevin's question, how do we measure whether a seminar's worked?

Evan: You can't.

Moderator: Well, others might think that you can.

Here this very blunt approach was effective, encouraging participation in the discussion from others without stopping Evan from taking part (I know Evan well and was confident that he would not take offence). In other cases, you may need to be gentler in ensuring that all are encouraged to participate without one speaker feeling that their contributions are not welcomed.

Textbox 9.6

What is the mistake? Conducting a focus group

Try to identify the mistake(s) that a researcher has made here and then have a look at Appendix 1 to see whether your view is the same as mine.

A researcher gains ethical approval to undertake a focus group with probation officers and the offenders that they supervise about the role that shortage of money has played in the offenders committing acquisitive crime. The researcher conducts this focus group at the offices of the probation service. As recording of conversations is not allowed on these premises, the researcher decides to note key words as the discussion is conducted and to write as full an account as they can immediately after the focus group has been completed. Their first question is:

Please could you tell me about the nature of your crimes and the role that poverty played in them [*Ask each offender and then their probation officer*].

Modes of Focus Group Data Collection

Like interviews, focus groups can also be conducted face to face, via telephone, through video-based mediums or by typing online. One of the key advantages of conducting focus groups face to face is that the full range of communication is possible: people can use facial expressions, nodding, etc., to communicate even when they are not speaking. In addition, respondents can indicate when they want to speak (e.g. by leaning forward) or note that someone else wants to speak and so wait for another opportunity.

However, the range of communication in a face-to-face focus group means that power imbalances tend to have the greatest impact when using this mode; the moderator has to be particularly vigilant in order to ensure that all contribute and no individual dominates the discussion. In addition, bringing focus group members together at a specific place and time is often a major challenge.

Telephone conferencing has advantages in terms of reducing the cost of bringing people together: it can reach remote populations or respondents who are geographically dispersed. In addition, focus groups conducted by telephone have been found to be less easy for an individual to dominate, probably because they cannot use body language to demand preferential treatment or assert their superior status (Barbour, 2007: 150). Of course, the lack of body language can also be a major disadvantage, as individuals cannot take cues from each other, most notably that one person is about to speak. As interaction is one of the defining features of focus groups, limiting this to what can be heard is clearly a major restriction. Telephone conferencing also requires the appropriate equipment, which may not be available if you are an undergraduate student.

Surprisingly little has been written about video-based focus groups. Kite and Phongsavan (2017) undertook a study where they used both face-to-face and video-based focus groups – the video-based ones used the Blackboard Collaborate tool. The groups on Collaborate had the advantage of being more convenient for respondents, although these respondents had a greater tendency to withdraw from the study. The quality of the data was similar to that produced in face-to-face groups, despite respondents being more easily distracted, both by irrelevant lines of discussion and other things going on in their home. Communication was slower and time was lost to technical difficulties. However, overall the study suggested that video-based focus groups were an important tool for the qualitative researcher. It seems likely that the Covid-19 pandemic has increased the number of people who are competent and confident in meeting people virtually, so video-based focus groups may have a greater role to play in the future.

If you are proposing to conduct a focus group with your peers, the use of text-based mediums may seem the 'natural' choice as most students are very familiar and comfortable with this form of communication. However, it is important to consider carefully all the implications of this mode of data collection. Bloor et al. (2001: 83) note that researcher effect is reduced when conducting discussion in online, typed form (as people cannot make assumptions based on the researcher's appearance or voice), but of course this advantage is reduced if you already know the respondents. It may be possible to discuss more sensitive topics in this format and having the data available in written format is another advantage.

However, there are several disadvantages of conducting focus groups in typed form. Assuming that the group is being conducted synchronously (i.e. with all group members online at the same time), pressure to type may lead to an individual abbreviating their comments, meaning that a full picture of their views is not established (Barbour, 2007: 150–151). Those who are quicker typists may be able to present their views more fully. Bloor et al. (2001: 83) note that, in an online environment, it is more difficult to detect deceit or establish rapport, but again this is less likely to be the case if your respondents are people who you already know.

Barbour (2007: 151–152) suggests that online focus groups will not replace the face-to-face mode of data collection but provide a useful extra tool for the qualitative researcher. As with interviews, I encourage you to consider all the points above when deciding on the most appropriate mode in which to conduct a focus group (or focus groups), but also to think about the mode that will feel most comfortable to you.

Textbox 9.7

Conducting a typed focus group

In order to identify further strengths and weaknesses of typed focus groups, I moderated such a group, where the respondents were five of my colleagues. Discussion was conducted via Communicator – a Microsoft tool that facilitates online discussion among everyone who is part of a particular network (in this case, my university). My instructions at the start of the discussion indicated that nobody should feel that they could not make a contribution on a topic because other members of the group had moved on to consider further issues:

> … please feel free to contribute, and to respond to other people's comments, as necessary. You may find yourself writing a response to a point that was made a few turns ago but that is fine, because there can't be the same sort of turn-taking protocols that occur in face-to-face discussions.

(Continued)

Everybody followed this advice and contributed as they saw fit, which I was very pleased about, but it made the discussion very difficult to 'steer', because group members would be typing a response to a previous point as I sought to move the conversation in a slightly different direction. However, I found a partial solution to this problem by having my pre-prepared questions typed in a different font to the main discussion. Respondents commented that, when I pasted these questions in, it made it clear that a change was required to the direction of the discussion.

The difficulty of several different topics being discussed at once was evident from the start. I learned that, in contrast to a face-to-face group, it may be best to nominate one respondent to answer the opening question because, if everyone types at once, the discussion can immediately be taken in any number of different directions. As you will see from the extract below, three of the four people who answered my first question gave broadly similar responses. However, Trevor introduced a different topic and there were two separate discussions going on for some considerable time:

Me: Please could we begin by people giving an example of a social problem that they are particularly concerned about and the reasons that they believe that this problem exists?

Evelyn: Last night I logged on to the internet to see all of the front pages of today's newspapers. It's about refugees and how we manage their needs.

Naomi: The problem of refugees.

Trevor: I am very concerned at the moment about anti-social behaviour on the Metro [*the light railway system of Tyne and Wear*] – especially by young teenage girls.

Naomi: The problem exists as a result of social, economic and political imbalances in the hierarchy of nations.

Lester: Social problem – refugee crisis. I think the problem is that we (e.g. the West) have contributed to the instability in the region that is causing people to flee but now our government doesn't want to take any responsibility.

Me: We'll maybe come back to Trevor's problem but do you think that it is inevitable that there will be refugees in some parts of the world?

Evelyn: Trevor - you're right. Thank goodness they're all back at school … Jamie – yes, but my issue is my utter embarrassment at the inaction and intransigence of our government.

Lester: The massively ramped up rhetoric around asylum, refugees etc. has created such a toxic debate the government won't face up to the issue as one that's primarily humanitarian.

Naomi: As inevitable as it is that the West will look after their own economic interests.

Trevor: This seems to be due to multiple factors – lack of social cohesion; lack of respect for authority; failure of the company involved to properly police behaviour; fear amongst members of the public (including me) to challenge such anti-social behaviour.

Piloting Data Collection

The importance of piloting quantitative methods of data collection was discussed in Chapter 8. It is particularly important to conduct a pilot in any study involving questionnaires, as it is difficult to alter them once the weblink has been created or the questionnaires have been sent out. The need for a pilot is not quite so pressing when collecting data through interviews or focus groups, as minor changes (e.g. to the guide) may be made as the research progresses. However, it is clearly advantageous to ensure that as few changes as possible need to be made once the research has begun.

Conducting a pilot study is particularly challenging with focus groups, due to the difficulties of bringing enough people together. However, when this opportunity is available it should be taken; feedback should be sought from the participants on subjects such as the wording of the questions and the dynamics of the discussion.

Key points for your own research

- Always have clear reasons for choosing your data collection method. It is a common mistake to choose interviews as a default option, or online methods only because you are comfortable using them, but it is important to carefully evaluate all the options that are available.
- Where you decide that interviews are the most appropriate option, further consideration should be given to the type of interview that will help you to obtain the best quality data.
- If you are thinking about using observation as a data collection method, be aware that there will be major ethical questions to address. This occurs in any situation where you want to observe 'real' people – although not, of course, when observing films or television programmes (see Chapter 10).
- If you decide to collect qualitative data through questionnaires, you should give very careful thought to the questions: will they make sense to the reader and do they encourage a full and detailed response? A pilot study is particularly important when using this form of data collection.
- You should use focus groups when you are interested in gaining insights into shared understandings or where you think the interaction between respondents can tell you something about the subject matter.
- When collecting data through interviews or focus groups, you should consider carefully which is the most advantageous mode of collection: face to face, by telephone, using video-based methods or through typed forms of communication.
- Collecting data by any means requires research skills, but the skill level is particularly high for conducting qualitative interviews and even higher for moderating a focus group. It is important to learn and think about the skills required, but practice is the best method of developing them.

Key points when reading other people's research

- Look for the rationale for the researcher's data collection method. If there is none given, you should consider particularly carefully whether the chosen method is the most appropriate one. If a rationale is presented, you should assess how convincing it is.
- Consider whether the researcher explains their data collection method fully. You would not expect to see an entire interview guide, for example, but a good account of a piece of research will identify the areas that respondents were asked about. If this information is not provided, it is correct to be concerned as to how the findings were reached.

Further reading

For more about the different methods of qualitative data collection, I recommend my own book:

Harding, J. (2018) *Qualitative Data Analysis from Start to Finish*, 2nd edn. London: Sage (1st edn 2013).

A good discussion of a range of topics around qualitative interviews is provided by:

Roulston, K. (2010) *Reflective Interviewing: A Guide to Theory and Practice*. London: Sage.

For an example of a criminological study that used semi-structured interviews, I suggest reading:

Lumsden, K. (2017) 'Police officer and civilian staff receptivity to research and evidence-based policing in the UK: providing a contextual understanding through qualitative interviews', *Policing: A Journal of Policy and Practice*, 11(2): 157–167.

The use of focus groups and the data that they provide is discussed further in:

Barbour, R. (2007) *Doing Focus Groups*. London: Sage.

For a discussion of focus groups conducted via a popular mobile-phone-based application, see:

Chen, J. and Neo, P. (2019) 'Texting the waters: an assessment of focus groups conducted via the WhatsApp smartphone messaging application', *Methodological Innovations*, 12(3).

10

ALTERNATIVES TO EMPIRICAL DATA COLLECTION

―――What you will learn in this chapter―――――――――――――――――

By the end of this chapter, you will:

- Be able to evaluate the choice to collect empirical data in the light of the non-empirical alternatives that are available
- Understand the advantages and disadvantages of obtaining and analysing secondary data
- Understand the locations and types of observations that can make for an effective physical trace analysis
- Have the ability to distinguish between a literature review and a documentary analysis and to undertake the latter
- Be able to undertake a range of types of analysis of visual materials, film and television programmes

Introduction

Chapters 8 and 9 suggested various methods that can be used to collect data by the traditional, empirical means that most people associate with social sciences research. However, the chapters also noted many difficulties that can be associated with such approaches, from both an ethical and a practical perspective. Students often do not consider the alternatives to collecting empirical data. While these alternatives will not be suitable for every topic of study, they can be helpful across a range of research areas, if you are prepared to think a little more imaginatively about data.

The title of this chapter has been chosen carefully because the first area discussed, secondary data analysis, involves using empirical data. However, the crucial point is that you do not collect this data yourself.

After a discussion of secondary data analysis and data collected through physical (rather than digital) traces, this chapter moves on to consider the use of documents, images and film/television programmes as data. These methods have much in common in that they are relatively straightforward ethically – it would not be expected that you should gain ethical approval from everyone who acted in a film or appeared in a TV documentary to analyse their 'performance' – and that the data is easily available. However, all raise the difficulty that it is not usually possible to go back to the originators of the data (the writer of the report or newspaper article, the person who appeared in the documentary, etc.) to check whether you have understood correctly.

Secondary Analysis

Secondary analysis involves a researcher undertaking their own analysis of data that has already been created. It can be survey data, data collected by qualitative methods or 'big data', which is held digitally but was not originally collected for research purposes.

Secondary Analysis of Survey Data

Secondary data analysis is a particularly important option for the quantitative researcher because of the huge amounts of time that can be saved by analysing the data from an existing survey rather than the researcher having to conduct their own. However, despite this great attraction, there are two important factors that may present difficulties if you wish to use this option. The first is that you have no influence over the questions that were asked or the selection of the sample from which the survey data was collected. You will need to think carefully about the extent to which it is appropriate to use the dataset to answer your own research question, or to meet your own research objectives – it is almost inevitable that some compromise will be necessary between what you would like to achieve and what is achievable using the existing dataset.

The second difficulty is that access to secondary data can either be impossible to negotiate, or difficult and time-consuming. The best source of quantitative datasets is the UK Data Archive, at www.data-archive.ac.uk

However, many of the datasets related to crime – such as the Crime Survey of England and Wales and the Commercial Victimisation Survey – are safeguarded, because of the danger that individuals could be identified from them. This means that access will only be granted, if at all, after a lengthy period of registration and the provision of substantial amounts of information. I could find only a very limited number of datasets in the crime and law enforcement section of the data archive that were open access; one example was the 1997 Prison Reading Survey, which is available at https://beta.ukdataservice.ac.uk/datacatalogue/studies/study?id=4359

So, difficulties of access suggest that using secondary survey data may only be an option for students looking at very specific topics. However, it is still important to be aware of this approach because of the substantial use that criminologists make of it: for example, the study discussed in Textbox 10.1.

Textbox 10.1

A study that involved secondary analysis of quantitative data

MacQueen and Norris (2016) undertook secondary analysis of the 2008–2009 Scottish Crime and Justice Survey, which has much in common with the Crime Survey of England and Wales. The survey asked respondents whether they had experienced domestic abuse and, if so, whether the police knew about this abuse. However, no one had previously undertaken an analysis of the independent variables that had an influence on whether the abuse became known to the police. The secondary analysis of MacQueen and Norris demonstrated that the police were more likely to know about the abuse if the victim was female, if they did not have employment, if the abuse took place on multiple occasions and if children had witnessed it. In contrast, the police were less likely to find out about abuse if the victims were young, male and/or in employment.

It was noted in Chapter 2 that domestic violence/abuse is one of the crimes that is believed to be underestimated in crime survey results. However, MacQueen and Norris' secondary analysis made an important contribution to understanding the types of abuse that most commonly become known to the police.

Secondary Analysis of Qualitative Data

The use of secondary data in qualitative studies is considerably less advanced than in quantitative research. There are a number of reasons for this, particularly that closeness to the research subject is seen as necessary to achieve the key goal of qualitative research of 'seeing through the eyes of others'. Some qualitative researchers have suggested that somebody looking only at transcripts (for example) will lose the understanding that comes from meeting the respondent and being aware of the context in which the data is being collected. However, others have suggested that such a 'distance' can ensure that the subjectivity associated with qualitative studies is less likely to turn into bias (Dufour et al., 2019).

Secondary analysis of qualitative data also raises ethical issues. The information given to respondents when they decide to take part in surveys often includes a statement that data may be used for secondary analysis and it seems quite impersonal for a line of data on an IBM SPSS Statistics software ('SPSS®') dataset (see Chapter 11) to be re-used by another researcher. This contrasts with the more personal nature of a qualitative research interview, which often depends heavily on the trusting relationship developed between the researcher and the respondent (Dufour et al., 2019). In addition, qualitative interviews tend to include large amounts of information that could enable respondents to be identified – names of people they know, places where they have lived or worked, job titles they have held, etc. Thompson (2003) suggests that these difficulties can be overcome by either returning to original respondents and asking them if the data can be re-used or by removing all identifying information from the transcript – but both represent substantial tasks.

I will illustrate this difficulty using an interview that I conducted with a police officer, which will be considered in the qualitative data analysis material in Chapter 12. If I were sharing the original transcript of the interview – rather than my analysis of the data – then large amounts of information would have to be removed to eliminate the risk that the officer could be identified, for example:

> So I've spent all of that time in uniform. I spent the first xxxx years on a Response shift, 24/7, at xxxx, which I loved. Then I joined the xxx Team at xxxx, so I was the xxxx. I intended just to go and join for a year and get a bit of experience and then do my crime skills, which would have been going into CID, but there were so many changes in the force that those opportunities just weren't there anymore, and I ended up staying as a xxxx in xxxx for several years …

Despite these difficulties, qualitative data is sometimes stored and made available for secondary analysis, and this is a requirement of some research funding councils. The UK Data Archive includes qualitative datasets, although, again, there are only a small number that are easily available.

Analysis of Public Records and 'Big Data'

The analysis of pre-existing data is not restricted to data created through surveys. One of the earliest pieces of criminological research, Durkheim's (1952, published in the UK) study of suicide involved secondary analysis of coroners' records to seek to establish which countries had the highest suicide rate.

Similarly, the first study of racial violence in the UK, which was commissioned by the Home Office in 1981, included the collection of some qualitative data but also some analysis of police crime records. These records were searched for incidents where the offender and victim were from different ethnic groups and police officers believed the primary motivation for the crime to be racial. The results were startling, suggesting that, compared to White people, Asian people were 50 times more likely to be the victims of racial violence and Black people 36 times more likely. The publication of the report into this study led to a large increase in the activities of police forces, and central and local government, to tackle violence of this nature. In addition, new methods of recording crime were introduced to make it easier to identify racial motivation (Bowling, 1993: 233–235).

Technological advances have led to large amounts of information being stored digitally and to the phrase 'big data' coming into common use. Researchers can sometimes access information that was not originally collected for research purposes, but which can be a very rich source of data. The researcher may analyse a single digital dataset or seek to combine several.

So, for example, Sosa et al. (2019) analysed the factors that could contribute to crime and deviance at or near casinos in Southern California by using three types of publicly available information:

1 Information from crime maps about the levels of crime in and around each casino;
2 The types of facilities that were available, as listed on the casinos' websites (e.g. an onsite hotel, slot machines, etc.);
3 Information available from the public website Yelp.com which enables consumers to share their reviews of businesses. This incorporated a score on a five-star rating system and comments. The researchers noted whether certain features appeared in these comments, for example positive or negative comments about the main gambling floor and instances of good and bad customer service.

A key finding of the research was that casinos with slot machines tended to attract lower levels of crime, as did those with higher star ratings. In contrast, casinos where there were comments about staff friendliness were associated with higher crime (Sosa et al., 2019: 160).

Digital datasets are also increasingly being used for practical purposes by criminal justice agencies such as police forces (see, e.g., Ferguson, 2017; Sanders and Sheptycki, 2017). There are ethical difficulties associated with big data, as was discussed in Chapter 6, and it is highly unlikely that you, as a student, will be given access to this data. However, as with other forms of secondary analysis, it is important to be aware of developments in this area, as you are likely to read (and should be ready to evaluate) increasing numbers of accounts of research that have used this approach.

Physical Trace Analysis

Garwood et al. (2000) discuss the use of 'sneaky' or 'unobtrusive' measures that can contribute to the study of crime and disorder, although it should be noted that some of these measures – such as the costs of maintenance associated with vandalism – would now usually be stored digitally as 'big data', as discussed above. However, some of the non-direct measures of crime they discuss could be used without reference to digital datasets, such as:

- Counting signs of vandalism and graffiti in an area, particularly in places that are often targets for such behaviour, such as bus stops and telephone boxes;
- Measuring the type and amount of alcohol consumption in public places by examining the number of empty containers left behind as litter;
- Estimating the amount of drug use by counting the number of indications such as burned foil (Garwood et al., 2000: 162–163).

Using such physical traces has obvious advantages over empirical data in terms of ease of access and gaining ethical approval, although ethical issues would still need to be considered. For example, a student who wanted to look for evidence of drug use in public toilets and lifts would have to clearly specify the safeguards that they intended to put in place (e.g. making their observations earlier rather than later in the day) to satisfy the ethics committee. However, a student who wished to study the location and content of graffiti would be likely to face less difficulty in gaining ethical approval.

Methods of Analysis of Documents, Images and Film/Television

So far, this chapter has discussed forms of data that are important for you to know about, but which you may feel you have little chance of accessing. However, when it comes to documents, images, films and television programmes, there are vast amounts of easily available information which you could use for your own analysis. Before considering each of these types of material in turn, it is important to discuss analysis in broad terms, because many of the forms of analysis overlap between different types of material. Although much of the published material based on these sources is unclear about the methods used, I have summarised in Table 10.1 which forms of analysis I believe can be used with which forms of data (although other researchers might have alternative views).

Table 10.1 Types of analysis that can be used for different sources of data

	Type of analysis that can be used			
Source of data	Structural analysis	Content analysis	Narrative analysis	Discourse analysis
Documents	x	x	x	x
Images		x		
Film/television	x	x	x	x

A definition of each of the forms of analysis that appears in Table 10.1 is presented below:

Structural analysis considers the aims that a document, film or television programme is seeking to achieve and then examines how material is put together to achieve these aims. It focuses on the overall picture rather than specific details.

Content analysis is defined by Neuendorf (2017: 16–17) as a research technique for analysing the content of communication, based on objectively measuring and quantifying specified characteristics. It is, by definition, quantitative in nature, involving substantial amounts of counting.

Narrative analysis is described by Moore (2014: 177) in the following manner:

Those using narrative analysis believe that the individual details of an event are assembled by a story-teller in such a way as to produce a narrative … A central premise of narrative analysis is that there are various ways of telling a story, that the details and 'facts' can be marshalled differently and with distinctive effects.

This form of analysis focuses, therefore, on the way a story is told.

Discourse analysis focuses on the way that language is used, and words are chosen, in order to convey meaning. It assumes that different choices of words can have different connotations, for example the phrase 'young criminal' is likely to create a slightly different mental image to 'young person who has been in trouble with the police'.

Narrative analysis and discourse analysis can also be used in relation to qualitative interview and focus group data, so they are also discussed in Chapter 12. Space has not allowed me to discuss every form of analysis with every form of data in this chapter, so I have used examples as follows:

- Documents – structural analysis is demonstrated using a report of an inspection of Her Majesty's Prison (HMP) Leicester; discourse analysis is considered through a study of the language used in newspaper reporting of sexual violence; and content analysis is discussed using a study of newspaper portrayals of asylum seekers.
- Images – content analysis is discussed using the same research into newspaper portrayals of asylum seekers and a study of images used in police recruitment material.
- Film/television – content analysis and narrative analysis are demonstrated in relation to the television documentary *Who Killed PC Blakelock?*

The examples used demonstrate that it can be difficult to distinguish clearly between one form of analysis and another. For example, my narrative analysis of *Who Killed PC Blakelock?* also has a structural element, because the different stories told of various incidents are part of the structure of the documentary. Similarly, the discourse analysis of reporting of sexual violence in newspapers may seem similar – except for some more elaborately defined categories – to the content analysis used to examine the way newspapers depicted refugees and asylum seekers. It is important to remember that methods of analysis overlap, and you should not feel that your own analysis must take exclusively one approach.

Some forms of analysis, i.e. structural and content analysis, are more concerned with what is done and said, while others, i.e. narrative analysis and discourse analysis, are more concerned with how it is said. However, all focus partly on the issue itself and partly on how it is discussed/portrayed. So analysing documents, images or TV and film material may tell you more about the way opinion on crime is shaped than about what causes crime and how it can be most effectively tackled. Analysis of this nature is less likely to lead to practical recommendations than, for example, interviewing young people who have previously been involved in crime and have now desisted. However, this does not make the analysis any less valuable.

Studying Documents

The extent of information that is available through documents was illustrated by the release by WikiLeaks in November 2010 of over 250,000 diplomatic cables, providing a huge resource for quantitative and qualitative researchers. The information revealed included examples of state-sanctioned crimes (Rothe and Steinmetz, 2013).

As with all other forms of data, it is important to consider the quality of documents and the appropriate use to put them to before beginning any analysis. Macdonald (2008) suggests that, although there may be a tendency to think of documents as being 'objective', they are socially produced, so it is important to question their authenticity, credibility and representativeness. Careful consideration should be given to the position and meaning of the writer. What are they trying to achieve by producing the document and how might this affect what is written?

The wide range of documents that can be studied in crime and criminal justice was discussed in Chapter 3, when we considered the literature review. This raises an obvious question: what is the difference between using a document as part of a literature review and treating it as a piece of data? The answer to this question may not always be obvious but my own view is that any document on which some original analysis is undertaken should be considered as data.

The difference can be illustrated by considering the example of a dissertation on the topic of suicide in prisons. One source of information on this topic is a report by Her Majesty's Chief Inspectorate of Prisons (HMCIP) into Her Majesty's Prison (HMP) Leicester, which was based on an unannounced inspection in 2018 (www.justiceinspectorates.gov.uk/hmiprisons/wp-content/uploads/sites/4/2018/05/HMP-Leicester-Web-2018.pdf). A student using this report as part of their literature review might write:

> The risk of suicide has been shown to be high in both male (Mandracchia and Smith, 2015) and female (Sharkey, 2010) prisoners. The factors that contribute to prisoners committing suicide have been acknowledged to be complex (see, e.g., Rivlin et al., 2013). HM Chief Inspector of Prisons (HMCIP) always includes an assessment of measures to prevent suicide or self-harm in its inspection of prisons, as part of its evaluation of the quality of a prison's safeguarding. For example, its inspection of HMP Leicester in 2018, noted (p. 5) that there had been three suicides since its previous inspection, although staff were making efforts to reduce the risks to prisoners.

However, a student undertaking a documentary analysis of the same report would consider it in much more detail. If they were undertaking a structural analysis, they might begin by considering the aims of the document in relation to safeguarding. A clear indication of these aims could be established by quoting (from p. 24 of the report) HMCIP's ideal picture of a prison with effective safeguarding procedures:

> The prison provides a safe environment which reduces the risk of self-harm and suicide. Prisoners at risk of self-harm or suicide are identified and given appropriate care and support. All vulnerable adults are identified, protected from harm and neglect and receive effective care and support.

Having established that the inspection and report were aiming to show how close the prison was to this ideal picture, the student could then look at the measures that were used in relation to safeguarding, and the outcomes that were recorded against these measures by the inspectors, as shown in Table 10.2.

Table 10.2 Measures of the effectiveness of safeguarding at HMP leicester

Criterion	Outcome
Number of suicides	Three since last inspection
Number of self-harm incidents	Higher than in similar prisons
	Reducing
Investigation of causes of self-harm incidents	Substantial
	Resulted in changes to procedures (on admission to prison)
Sharing of information between staff	Safer Custody meetings well attended
	Substantial information shared
Quality assurance checks by managers	Had been introduced
	Some open Assessment, Care in Custody and Teamwork (ACCT) plans missed out of checks
Safer custody team links to other departments	Improving
Quality of ACCT documents	Too varied – from excellent to very poor
Prisoner views	Felt well supported by staff
	Felt they could talk to listeners (listeners are prisoners trained by The Samaritans to provide confidential support to their peers who are struggling to cope or feeling suicidal; see www.samaritans.org/how-we-can-help/prisons/listener-scheme)
Listeners	Provided a good service
	Felt well supported by The Samaritans
Constant supervision processes	Good
Protection of prisoners at risk	No safeguarding policy
	No understanding of safeguarding issues among staff
	No manager responsible for this area
	No training for staff
	No formal processes for receiving intelligence reports

This analysis could then be developed in several ways: for example, there could be consideration of how far the measures used by HMCIP were consistent with its own ideal picture of a prison with effective safeguarding procedures, or how far the measures reflected the role envisaged for prisons in suicide prevention by the World Health Organization (2007).

Alternatively, the report into HMP Leicester could be compared with reports about other prisons to see whether there were trends in the strengths and weaknesses in relation to the prevention of suicide and self-harm.

There are very different steps involved in discourse analysis of a document. Although it is easy to see that discourse analysis is about choice of language, it is not always clear how you can go about analysing the words and phrases that are used. One piece of practical advice that I can offer you is to think about alternatives that could have been chosen. Take, as an example, a document that describes someone as 'spontaneous'. You could consider whether the person could alternatively have been described as 'impulsive', which would be seen less positively, or as 'reckless', which is undoubtedly a negative term. If these alternative words could plausibly have been used to describe the person, then you have grounds to argue that the author is seeking to present them in a positive light.

My second piece of advice is to concentrate on a very specific aspect of the material that you are analysing. This is well illustrated by Risdaneva's (2018) discourse analysis, which compared the language used to report sexual violence cases in two quality newspapers, *The Jakarta Post* (published in Indonesia) and *The Guardian* (published in the UK). There were any number of aspects of language that Risdaneva could have examined but she chose one very specific factor – the language used to describe the female victims (or alleged victims) and the male perpetrators (or alleged perpetrators).

A key finding of Risdaneva's study was that the language used by *The Jakarta Post* to describe the people involved, could often be described as 'functionalist', whereby people are named in terms of social roles which are immediately identifiable as positive or negative. (So, in other contexts, 'the teacher' is a social role that has positive connotations, while 'the prostitute' is one that has negative connotations). In 69% of cases, *The Jakarta Post* referred to the men in functional terms that reflected their legal status, and which were undoubtedly negative, using terms such as 'suspect', 'rapist', 'suspected rapist' and 'perpetrator', with 'suspect' being used particularly frequently. Women tended to be referred to as 'victim', 'detainee' or 'client'.

In contrast, *The Guardian* was more likely to use an approach described as classification, whereby people are described by certain key characteristics such as their age, gender, ethnicity, sexual orientation, etc. It referred to victims in terms such as 'women', 'girls', 'female student' and '19-year-old woman'. Perpetrators were typically referred to by their surnames (Risdaneva, 2018: 130–132).

Risdaneva's (2018: 135) conclusion was that *The Jakarta Post* described both victims and perpetrators in a manner that focused on their status in criminal cases. In contrast:

The Guardian's tendency to represent both perpetrators and victims as people instead of as parts of the legal processes indicated that the broadsheet attempted to focus the reports more on the crimes themselves rather than the participants involved in the cases.

Turning next to content analysis of documents, Moore (2014: 163) suggests that this approach is particularly well suited to studying the print media. An example of a piece of research that undertook content analysis of both the text and images used in newspapers was ICAR's (2004) study of stories about refugees and asylum seekers. This was a deductive piece of research which sought to test the following hypothesis:

> Newspapers often present images of asylum seekers and refugees that contain language, photographs and graphics likely to give rise to feelings of fear of and hostility towards asylum seekers and refugees among their readers. This effect is compounded by inaccurate and unbalanced reporting. (ICAR, 2004: 3)

This hypothesis was tested through a content analysis of newspaper stories about refugees and asylum seekers over a three-week period in 2003. A wide range of national newspapers were selected for study, together with eight local newspapers from different parts of London. The content analysis examined both the headlines and the text of stories. Some of the key findings were:

- The phrase 'asylum seeker' appeared in headlines 58 times.
- 14 of these headlines also included words associated with crime, i.e. 'arrested', 'jailed' and/or 'guilty'.
- Words indicating that the claim to be an asylum seeker was unfounded – 'bogus', 'false', 'illegal', 'failed' or 'rejected' – appeared five times in headlines and 103 times in the text of the articles.
- Words indicating that the asylum seeker was fleeing persecution in their country of origin – 'genuine', 'real', 'successful' or 'accepted' – did not appear in headlines at all and only eight times in the text (ICAR, 2004: 35).

This analysis, together with a similar one of images (which is discussed in the next section), led the authors of the report to conclude that their hypothesis was supported (ICAR, 2004: 98).

Textbox 10.2

What is the mistake? Manifesto analysis

Try to identify the mistake(s) that a researcher has made here and then have a look at Appendix 1 to see whether your view is the same as mine.

(Continued)

A student writing a dissertation on the effectiveness of criminal justice policies undertakes a structural documentary analysis of the 2015 Conservative Manifesto. Her findings from this analysis are that key developments in criminal justice policy in the period between 2010 and 2015 were building greater trust in criminal justice professionals, a focus on action rather than record keeping, greater numbers of offenders being supervised and rehabilitated on their release from prison, and the creation of new initiatives to tackle offences such as domestic violence and female genital mutilation.

Studying Visual Images

You probably do not need me to tell you that images play an increasingly important part in our communication as they can be very easily shared through applications such as WhatsApp and Instagram. The ease of taking and sharing images has been reflected in an increasing interest in the role that they can play in research.

Auto-photography, in which respondents are asked to take photographs that illustrate what is important to them in a particular subject area, is a methodology that has been used to examine topics such as homelessness (Johnsen et al., 2008). Advocates of this approach (e.g. Robinson, 2011) argue that photography can bring a deeper understanding of the everyday lived realities of people's lives than can be accessed through more traditional data collection methods. It is entirely feasible that you could undertake an auto-photography project: for example, by asking your fellow students if they would be willing, during daylight hours, to take photographs of places that they would be anxious about entering at night. However, this section will focus on a more common approach, i.e. the analysis of images that are already in the public domain.

The study by ICAR (2004), which was referred to in the previous section, included a content analysis of the images used to portray asylum seekers. The newspaper articles included 37 images of refugees or asylum seekers; the researchers divided the images into three groups:

- Nine were positive, showing an asylum seeker or refugee smiling and/or in a work or domestic context.
- 13 were neutral.
- 15 presented asylum seekers or refugees as criminals, by showing them being arrested or leaving court, by presenting police-style 'mugshots' of a head and shoulders against a blank background, or by showing a picture of Yarl's Wood detention centre, which was set alight by residents in the time period covered by the articles. (ICAR, 2004: 28–29)

So, the analysis of the images triangulated the analysis of the written text of the articles, supporting the hypothesis that newspaper reporting could provoke fear and hostility towards asylum seekers (ICAR, 2004: 98).

An analysis such as this depends crucially on decisions as to how each image should be categorised. For example, if the researchers had decided that the 'mugshot' style did not imply that an asylum seeker or refugee was a criminal, they would not have found their hypothesis to be so clearly supported. So, if you are undertaking an analysis of images, it is very important to decide before you start what your categories are and how you will decide whether an image fits a particular category (even if you must modify your approach as you progress with the analysis). This is crucial if you are to effectively justify the conclusions that your research reaches.

This process of creating categories, and deciding the criteria for placing images into them, is well illustrated by Jolicoeur and Grant's (2018) content analysis of images used in nine police recruitment brochures in a mid-western US state. The background to their research was that many police forces in the USA were facing difficulties in recruiting and retaining officers with the skills needed for the job. These skills were diversifying as officers were required to undertake a more community-focused method of policing and to make better use of new technology. However, recruitment materials that only portrayed the more traditional police role of enforcement seemed unlikely to attract recruits with these skills.

The researchers undertook very thorough preparatory work to establish the categorisation process that they were going to use. They decided to place each image from the recruitment brochures into one of three categories, according to clearly defined criteria:

- A legalistic policing role based on enforcement – an image would be placed in this category if it showed police officers wearing tactical uniform, arresting people, serving legal notices or stopping vehicles.
- A service policing role with the community at the core – an image would be placed in this category if it showed officers in standard uniform, interacting with citizens and/ or engaging with them in a social manner.
- A watchman role, where the focus is on preventing crime through informal methods – an image would be placed in this category if it showed police buildings and/or cars, interactions between police officers or anything else that held neutral connotations.

The effectiveness of this system was tested when the research team independently classified the images according to these criteria and found that there was a very high level of agreement between them as to which category each image should be placed in.

When the analysis was undertaken, it placed most of the images into the watchman category: they were neutral images of police officers, police buildings or police equipment. One third of the photographs showed legalistic images such as SWAT (special weapons and tactics) team members, officers using police dogs in enforcement, or arrests being made. In contrast, only 6% showed a service style of policing: informal interactions with the public, the provision of service or assistance to citizens, or social engagement with non-police officers. While there was some doubt as to whether neutral images should be placed in the watchman category, it was clear that legalistic images were used more than service images, which highlighted the inconsistency between the way the job was presented visually in brochures and the skills that were required of new recruits.

Studying Television Programmes and Films

There is a huge amount of crime-related material available through films, TV dramas, news reports, documentaries and 'reality' TV shows. This material can all be treated as data. However, there are few books or articles that discuss in any detail how this data can be analysed; books and journal articles often say little about the methodology that had been employed.

For example, Saunders and Vanstone (2010) undertook an analysis of the way four British films – *I Believe You*, *The Loneliness of the Long Distance Runner*, *A Sense of Freedom* and *McVicar* – portrayed the process of rehabilitation from violent crime. Their conclusion was that three of the four films demonstrated that:

> … individual change is a slow, incremental and often imperceptible process of self-awareness, motivation, and self-challenge which, while it can be helped on by professional intervention, is much more dependent on the accruing of social capital and movement through stages of life familiar to us all. In this sense, it might be argued that the limited attention given by British film to the subject of rehabilitation has, nevertheless, produced a surprisingly accurate reflection of how desistance works. (Saunders and Vanstone, 2010: 388)

However, the article discussing their work provides little indication of the methodology that was used to reach this conclusion, i.e. the way the films were analysed.

To provide you with an example of how television or film analysis might be carried out, I have undertaken a content analysis, and then a narrative analysis, of the excellent 2005 BBC documentary *Who Killed PC Blakelock?* This examines the riot at Broadwater

Fam in Tottenham, North London in 1985, the horrific murder of PC Keith Blakelock during the riot and the failure to convict anybody of his murder. This documentary is available on YouTube and is well worth watching.

After watching the documentary, I decided that the content analysis could take several forms: for example, I could look at the way the visual content was divided between images of the estate, reconstructions of events and the faces of people who were being interviewed. However, I decided instead to concentrate on the verbal content that came from the interviews.

The first stage of my analysis took a considerable amount of time. It involved going through all the interview material to record who was speaking, what they were speaking about and for how long. During this process, it became clear to me that there were several areas that could be covered by the second stage of the analysis:

- The factors contributing to the death of PC Keith Blakelock;
- The reasons for the identity of the murderers still being unknown;
- The reasons for the conviction of Winston Silcott;
- The impact of the riot and the murder on those involved.

(There would, of course, be some overlap between these areas.)

I decided to choose the first of these options, which meant that the analysis was concentrated in the first half of the documentary. The initial stage of analysis had suggested that there were four main factors that contributed to the death of PC Keith Blakelock:

- The architecture of the estate (which I coded as *architecture*);
- Tensions between the police and the local community (which I coded as *tensions*);
- Factors that led these tensions to escalate into a riot, including reports of riots elsewhere (which I coded as *triggers*);
- Policing decisions both before and during the riot (which I coded as *decisions*).

Table 10.3 shows the position that I had reached after the first two stages of my analysis:

1   Recording all the interview material according to who was speaking, on what topic and for how long;
2   Placing interview material that discussed causes of the murder into the categories of architecture, tensions, triggers and decisions.

Table 10.3 Analysis of the interview material from the *who killed pc blakelock?* Documentary

Interviewee	Time	Topic
Clasford Stirling, founder member, Broadwater Farm Youth Association	3.54–4.09 (15 seconds)	Princess Diana's visit to Broadwater Farm, nine months before the riot, to celebrate the improvements made to the estate
PC Paul McGee, retired police officer	4.09–4.23 (14 seconds)	Princess Diana's visit
Ibid.	4.29–4.47 (18 seconds)	Description of Winston Silcott making clear his displeasure at Princess Diana's visit
Stafford Scott, youth and community worker, Haringey Council, 1982–1987	4.57–5.19 (22 seconds)	Explanation of the reason for Winston Silcott's displeasure at the visit
Inspector Wally Poulter, retired police officer	5.36–5.51 (15 seconds)	The physical threat posed by Winston Silcott
Winston Silcott	6.10–6.21 (11 seconds)	The way he (Silcott) was presented in newspapers after his conviction
Ibid. (interspersed with reconstruction)	6.40–8.00 (80 seconds)	Account of an event from his schooldays when a teacher made a racist assumption that he had stolen an item
Stafford Scott	8.30–8.54 (24 seconds)	Discussion of the resentment felt by young Black men about the discrimination and stereotyping faced by them and their parents, and their determination to fight it
Sergeant Bob Hughes	9.47–10.13 (26 seconds)	The design of the Broadwater Farm Estate and the problems this caused for policing (*architecture*)
Wally Pouter	10.41–11.31 (50 seconds)	Account of an event in which a metal beer barrel was dropped from an overhead walkway onto the front of his car (*architecture*)
Clasford Stirling	12.52–13.07 (15 seconds)	Discussion of degrading treatment of young Black people by police officers (*tensions*)
Stafford Scott	13.10–13.32 (22 seconds)	Discussion of young Black people going 'off the rails' in response to the way that they were treated (*tensions*)
Winston Silcott	13.44–13.54 (10 seconds)	Account of being stopped by the police five times in four hours (*tensions*)
Ibid.	13.56–14.08 (12 seconds)	Explanation that he began burgling houses because he might as well do what everyone was assuming that he did (*tensions*)
Stafford Scott	14.50–14.59 (9 seconds)	Discussion of his conviction for burglary and explanation that young Black men wanted wider society to feel the same fear that they did (*tensions*)

(Continued)

Table 10.3 (Continued)

Interviewee	Time	Topic
Chief Inspector Alan Stainsby, retired	16.00–16.19 (19 seconds)	Criticism of the police's failure to address community relations in Tottenham (*tensions*)
Commander Jim Dickinson, retired	16.25–16.40 (15 seconds)	Justification for the young people on Broadwater Farm being the focus of police enforcement action (*tensions*)
Ibid.	17.05–17.12 (7 seconds)	Discussion of the need for high-profile policing to deter robbers (*tensions*)
PC Jeff Betts, retired	18.11–19.11 (60 seconds)	Account of incident when he was stabbed on Broadwater Farm (*tensions*)
Ibid.	19.18–19.37 (19 seconds)	Confirmation that Winston Silcott was suspected of his stabbing (*tensions*)
Stafford Scott	19.38–19.55 (17 seconds)	Complaint that Winston Silcott was always suspected, regardless of the circumstances (*tensions*)
Winston Silcott	19.56–20.17 (21 seconds)	Account of how the police asked to see him in respect of the stabbing of Jeff Betts (*tensions*)
Jeff Betts	20.44–20.51 (7 seconds)	Confirmation that it was not Winston Silcott who stabbed him (*tensions*)
Jim Dickinson	22.35–22.49 (14 seconds)	Criticism of a restructuring that led him to retire and not be replaced (*decisions*)
Sergeant Mark Parsons	23.44–24.15 (31 seconds)	Account of an incident that suggested that the police were unwilling to go onto Broadwater Farm for enforcement purposes (*decisions*)
Douglas Hurd, former Home Secretary	25.13–25.40 (27 seconds)	Account of the Handsworth riot 9–11 September 1985 (*triggers*)
Stafford Scott	26.38–27.09 (31 seconds)	Discussion of the shooting of Cherry Groce, which sparked the Brixton riot of 30 September 1985 (*triggers*)
Wally Pouter	27.21–27.35 (14 seconds)	Account of the police apprehension that a riot would follow in Broadwater Farm
Mark Parsons	28.05–28.20 (15 seconds)	Account of the stopping of a car owned by Floyd Jarrett (*triggers*)
Floyd Jarrett	28.21–28.27 (6 seconds)	Competing account of the stop (*triggers*)
Mark Parsons	28.28–28.39 (11 seconds)	Account of 'booking in' of Floyd Jarrett at the police station
Mark Parsons	29.02–29.19 (17 seconds)	Account of entering the property of Floyd Jarrett's parents, using key taken from him (*triggers*)
Floyd Jarrett	29.29–29.43 (14 seconds)	Account of being charged with assault and told that his mother had died of a heart attack (*triggers*)

Interviewee	Time	Topic
Mark Parsons	30.18–30.34 (16 seconds)	Account of Cynthia Jarrett's heart attack while he and a colleague were at the property (*triggers*)
Floyd Jarrett	30.39–30.55 (16 seconds)	Criticism of the police for the shooting of Cherry Groce (which triggered the Brixton riots a few days earlier) and the death of his mother (*triggers*)
Alan Stainsby	31.21–31.38 (17 seconds)	Account of his visit to the Jarrett family to express his regrets (*triggers*)
Wally Poulter	32.10–32.28 (18 seconds)	Recollection of his certainty that a riot was about to start
PC Richard Coombes, retired	33.04–33.23 (19 seconds)	Account of how he heard about the death of Cynthia Jarrett (*triggers*)
PC Steve Martin	33.48–34.01 (13 seconds)	Discussion of his inexperience when he was called to Broadwater Farm
Wally Poulter	34.18–34.38 (20 seconds)	Account of delivering the Broadwater Farm contingency plan to Wood Green Police Station, identifying what would be needed to take back the estate in a riot
Paul McGee	35.47–36.04 (17 seconds)	Account of attending a meeting where he was threatened
Ibid.	36.15–36.26 (11 seconds)	Account of taking the message of the threat against the police back to the police station
Stafford Scott	36.50–37.00 (10 seconds)	Account of taking a crowd away from Tottenham Police Station
Wally Poulter	37.01–37.21 (20 seconds)	Account of non-response to 999 calls from Broadwater Farm because of concerns over police safety (*decisions*)
Alan Stainsbury	38.29–38.46 (17 seconds)	Expression of concerns that police officers had been sent home before the hours of darkness (*decisions*)
Stafford Scott	39.04–41.16 (132 seconds)	Account of the confrontation between police officers and marchers who were heading towards Tottenham Police Station which started the riot
Steve Martin	42.03–42.35 (32 seconds)	Account of putting on riot clothing and picking up riot equipment
Richard Coombes	42.36–42.51 (15 seconds)	Account of getting into van to go to deal with the riot
Sergeant Chris Sevier	43.16–43.58 (42 seconds)	Account of arriving on Broadwater Farm during the riot

(Continued)

Table 10.3 (Continued)

Interviewee	Time	Topic
Bob Hughes	44.19–44.59 (40 seconds)	Account of arriving at the riot
Alan Stainsbury	45.40–46.10 (30 seconds)	Account of the inability of Wood Green control room to cope with the volume of calls it was receiving
Richard Coombes	46.31–46.45 (14 seconds)	Account of arriving at a quiet part of the estate
Steve Martin	46.46–47.01 (15 seconds)	Account of waiting in the quiet part of the estate
Bob Hughes	47.08–47.54 (46 seconds)	Account of being attacked with missiles
Chris Sevier	48.11–48.38 (27 seconds)	Account of his shield being hit by a bullet from a shotgun
Stafford Scott	48.51–50.04 (13 seconds)	Account of police throwing missiles back at the crowd
Bob Hughes	50.05–50.31 (26 seconds)	Account of throwing some masonry back into the crowd and causing injury
Chris Sevier	50.35–51.02 (27 seconds)	Account that suggested that someone was organising attacks on the police
Stafford Scott	51.03–51.19 (16 seconds)	Ridiculing of the suggestion that the attacks on the police were organised
Alan Stainsbury	51.38–51.52 (14 seconds)	Account of coming out of the control room onto the estate
Steve Martin	53.48–54.00 (12 seconds)	Account of going into Tangmere House to protect the fire brigade as they put out a fire in a shop
Richard Coombes	54.01–54.18 (17 seconds)	Recollection of saying that they needed to get in and out of Tangmere House very quickly
PC John Macaskill, retired	54.32–55.04 (32 seconds)	Account of frustration at being held on reserve rather than sent to the estate (*decisions*)
Richard Coombes	55.20–55.44 (24 seconds)	Discussion of the false sense of security experienced by the officers before they were sent into Tangmere House
Steve Martin	55.45–56.16 (31 seconds)	Ibid.
Steve Martin	56.19–57.07 (48 seconds)	Account of being confronted in Tangmere House
Richard Coombes	57.14–57.48 (34 seconds)	Ibid.
Alan Stainsbury	58.04–58.21 (17 seconds)	Account of hearing that a group of officers were in serious trouble

Interviewee	Time	Topic
Richard Coombes	58.40–58.50 (10 seconds)	Account of being forced backwards by the rioters and realising that their lives were in danger
Steve Martin	58.52–59.01 (9 seconds)	Ibid.
Richard Coombes	59.06–59.19 (13 seconds)	Ibid.
Steve Martin	59.20–59.37 (17 seconds)	Ibid.
Steve Martin	59.47–60.00 (13 seconds)	Account of trying to fight their way out of the building
Richard Coombes	60.16–60.51 (35 seconds)	Account of the fatal attack on PC Keith Blakelock
Steve Martin	60.52–61.28 (36 seconds)	Ibid.
Steve Martin	61.38–62.04 (26 seconds)	Account of attempt to clear the crowd around PC Keith Blakelock
Richard Coombes	62.05–62.23 (18 seconds)	Account of being knocked to the ground as he ran towards PC Keith Blakelock
Steve Martin	62.25–62.39 (14 seconds)	Recollection of the fear that he could be killed if knocked to the ground
Steve Martin	62.45–63.25 (40 seconds)	Recollection of drifting towards unconsciousness
Steve Martin	63.37–63.44 (7 seconds)	Account of being protected by firefighters
Alan Stainsbury	64.27–64.51 (24 seconds)	Account of arriving at the scene and seeing the reaction of Keith Blakelock's colleagues to his murder
John Macaskill	65.39–66.26 (47 seconds)	Account of the Metropolitan Police Commissioner, Kenneth Newman, arriving at the police station and having doors slammed on him
Steve Martin	66.35–67.04 (29 seconds)	Asking why Keith Blakelock had been killed
Inspector Dick Shepherd, retired	67.41–68.11 (30 seconds)	Account of visiting Keith Blakelock's family the day after his death
Detective Chief Superintendent Graham Melvin, retired	68.44–69.03 (19 seconds)	Account of how evidence was lost in the hours after Keith Blakelock's death
Winston Silcott	69.15–70.12 (57 seconds)	Account (with reconstruction) of being woken in police cell to be photographed, including a claim that police officers deliberately provoked an aggressive pose

(Continued)

Table 10.3 (Continued)

Interviewee	Time	Topic
Stafford Scott	70.34–70.53 (19 seconds)	Account of being threatened with arrest by a police officer in the weeks after the riot
Beverly Scott (Stafford Scott's mother)	71.00–71.21 (21 seconds)	Account of armed police arriving at her home
Stafford Scott	71.21–71.33 (12 seconds)	Account of being held at gunpoint and handcuffed
Beverly Scott	71.34–71.39 (5 seconds)	Account of her son's arrest
Stafford Scott	71.40–71.51 (11 seconds)	Account of being charged with Keith Blakelock's murder
Beverly Scott	71.52–72.00 (8 seconds)	Discussion of her change of attitude to the police after her son's arrest
Stafford Scott	72.20–72.47 (27 seconds)	Account of the 'climate of fear' that followed Keith Blakelock's murder and prevented people from testifying (for which he blamed the police)
Graham Melvin	72.48–73.03 (15 seconds)	Alternative account of the climate of fear based on the fear of detection on the part of those who had committed crimes
Graham Melvin	75.18–75.42 (24 seconds)	Account of how photographic evidence failed to demonstrate that Winston Silcott was at the scene of the murder
Winston Silcott	79.07–79.42 (35 seconds)	Explanation of his reasons for not giving evidence in his own defence at his trial
Winston Silcott	80.19–80.47 (28 seconds)	First part of account of his actions on the night of the riot
Winston Silcott	80.57–81.17 (20 seconds)	Second part of account of his actions on the night of the riot
Winston Silcott	81.32–81.55 (23 seconds)	Third part of account of his actions on the night of the riot
Winston Silcott	82.02–83.07 (65 seconds)	Fourth part of account of his actions on the night of the riot
Graham Melvin	84.55–85.15 (20 seconds)	Account of being suspended after Winston Silcott's conviction was overturned
Winston Silcott	85.44–85.58 (14 seconds)	Call for a public inquiry into every aspect of Keith Blakelock's murder
Mark Parsons	86.49–87.33 (44 seconds)	Stating his wish to express his condolences to the Jarrett family and the Blakelock family

The final stage of my content analysis was to produce a total figure for the amount of time devoted to interviewees talking about each of the causal factors:

- Architecture: 76 seconds
- Tensions: 233 seconds
- Triggers: 178 seconds
- Decisions: 114 seconds

This analysis suggested that the documentary presented the murder of PC Keith Blakelock as being largely the result of tensions between the police and the local community, with the factors that triggered the riot playing a significant part, and police decision making and the architecture of the estate being secondary factors.

A narrative analysis of the documentary would take a different approach, examining the way the story was told of events before, during and after the night of 6 October 1985. Like discourse analysis, it is often easier to say what narrative analysis is than to put it into practice. When using TV/film material, my advice is to look for a distinctive element of the manner of presentation and then to consider how this contributes to the understanding of the story that the material seeks to provide.

In the case of *Who Killed PC Blakelock?* I again focused on the interview material and noted a number of distinctive features:

- The use of exclusively police voices between 50.04 and 69.03, when discussing the key events of the riot;
- A prolonged period towards the end of the documentary when Winston Silcott was the only interviewee to appear;
- The use of pairs of interviewees to describe the same events, with alternating clips of their descriptions/analysis.

I chose the last of these features to examine further and, on re-reading Table 10.3 and watching the documentary again, noted that alternating the voices of interviewees was a technique used in two very different ways:

1   In some cases, it demonstrated that there was broad consistency between the accounts. One example was the descriptions of PC Steve Martin and retired PC Richard Coombes of the events immediately before and after the murder of Keith Blakelock (55.20–63.44). Another was the accounts of Beverley Scott and Stafford Scott of his arrest at gunpoint (71.00-71.51).

2   In other cases, it emphasised disagreement. So, for example, Sergeant Mark Parsons' (28.05–28.20) description of a range of reasons for being suspicious of the vehicle

being driven by Floyd Jarrett was immediately followed by Floyd Jarrett's assertion that the grounds for suspicion were spurious. Similarly, Stafford Scott's (72.20–72.47) account of a climate of fear after the riot, which prevented the community from co-operating with the murder inquiry, was followed by retired Detective Chief Superintendent Graham Melvin's alternative view that the only people who were fearful were those whose crimes might be detected.

So my narrative analysis concluded that the impact of alternating between two people who were giving their account of the same events often highlighted the difference in perspectives between the police and the community. The 'agreement' examples largely involved two police officers or two community members providing consistent accounts, while the 'disagreement' examples usually contrasted the views of a police officer and a community member. However, this conclusion was qualified by noting that there were occasions where 'police' and 'community' voices were largely in agreement: for example, Stafford Scott's (48.51–50.04) account of the police throwing missiles back at the crowd was followed by Sergeant Bob Hughes confirming that he did indeed do this.

Whatever form of analysis is used, it is important to remember that documentaries, like documents, are socially produced and inevitably reflect, to some extent, the perspective of the filmmaker. In the case of *Who Killed PC Blakelock?* the filmmaker, Professor Kurt Barling, makes clear in his introduction that his aim is to present the views of both the police and the community. He does this by including clips from the interviews with PC Steve Martin, retired PC Richard Coombes and Winston Silcott, and by ending the introduction with the following statement: 'Above all, it's a story of why eighteen years on, there's still a sense of injustice on both sides and how this stands in the way of resolving the unanswered question ...' (The words "Who Killed PC Blakelock?" then appear on the screen).

A contrasting example is provided by another very good but very different documentary called *The Boys Who Killed Stephen Lawrence*, which is also available on YouTube. The filmmaker, Mark Daly, makes clear from his introductory commentary that he is going to present his material from a perspective that is supportive of the Lawrence family, while being highly critical of the police and the five men suspected of Stephen Lawrence's murder (two of whom have subsequently been convicted): 'We watched as five White racists, suspected of the killing, treated the legal system with contempt. The police failed the Lawrences ...'.

In analysing this documentary, you would need to be constantly aware that Mark Daly's focus was on the injustice experienced by the Lawrence family, with little sympathy for any justification/mitigation for their actions offered by the Metropolitan Police and hostility towards the protestations of innocence of the five suspects.

So – when conducting research involving documents, television or film material – you must carefully consider the perspective of its creator and take this into account in your analysis. However, to reinforce a point made earlier, one of the difficulties with this form of research is that the author is rarely available for you to check your analysis (in contrast with a qualitative interview, for example, where you can ask a respondent a question that begins with a phrase such as 'Can I just check that I have understood …', as discussed in Chapter 9). To illustrate this point, I had the unusual (and very fortunate) experience of being able to put my analysis to the maker of the *Who Killed PC Blakelock?* documentary, Professor Kurt Barling. Part of his response demonstrated that I had not fully understood the importance of the different factors that the documentary portrayed as causes of the riot:

> The content analysis more or less reflects our objectives in seeking to explore the most salient issues giving rise to the events … I would say that the police decision-making was however not secondary but rather integral to the rising levels of tension in the run up to the riot/uprising/disturbances. In other words different decisions would have lessened the tensions and this was acknowledged by a number of the local officers on the ground in the film.

So there is always a danger that, no matter how thorough our analysis, our own understanding of the meaning of documentary, television or film material will not match that of the author, who is not usually available to answer questions.

Textbox 10.3

What is the mistake? Analysis of a television programme

Try to identify the mistake(s) that a researcher has made here and then have a look at Appendix 1 to see whether your view is the same as mine.

A student watches all the episodes from 1997 to 2002 of the BBC's *Rough Justice* programme, which focused on criminal cases where there was reason to believe that there had been a miscarriage of justice, and which led to several convictions being overturned. He concludes that, despite all the attempts that were made to improve it, the criminal justice system was just as often in error at the end of the millennium as it was in earlier decades of the twentieth century.

Key points for your own research

- Decide whether there are existing datasets available that might save you from having to collect your own data, or that could supplement the data that you collect. The ease of access to this data, and its capacity to answer your research question(s) or to meet your research objective(s), are key issues to consider when making this decision.
- Consider whether your research could incorporate physical trace analysis but be aware of the limited circumstances under which this is a helpful (and ethical) approach.
- Be clear as to whether you are using documents as part of a literature review or as part of a documentary analysis.
- Be aware that the content of documents, photographs, film and television material will be influenced by the perspective of the creator(s) of the material. Think about the impact that this perspective may have had.
- When using documents, images or films/television programmes as data, carefully consider the methods of analysis that are available and the method(s) that is/are most appropriate to use. Make your decision based on the nature of the material and on your research question(s)/research objectives.
- When undertaking a structural analysis, try to put yourself into the shoes of the person who was writing the document, or making the film or television programme. Think about the decisions that they made as to how to put the material together.
- Before undertaking a content analysis of any type of material, be clear as to what your categories are and the criteria that you will use to decide which material goes into which category.
- When undertaking a narrative analysis, examine the distinctive features of the storytelling and the effect that the storyteller is trying to create with them.
- When undertaking a discourse analysis, consider the words/phrases that could have been used instead of those that were chosen. Think about the impact of the choices that were made.
- Where appropriate, acknowledge that your own analysis may include elements of more than one approach – recognising that this is a strength and not a weakness.

Key points when reading other people's research

- Where a researcher is using secondary data analysis, try to find something out about the original study from which the data is drawn. In the case of data taken from well-known studies – such as the Crime Survey of England and Wales – this may be obvious, but it may be less so in other cases. Knowing about the original study will help you to judge whether the dataset chosen is suitable for the research question(s) addressed, or the research objectives pursued, through the secondary analysis.

- When reading analysis of films/television programmes, be particularly careful to evaluate whether there is adequate information about the methodology that is used. Of course, this is always important, but discussion of methodology is particularly likely to be inadequate in research of this nature.
- The distinction between structural analysis, content analysis, narrative analysis and discourse analysis is often blurred and much analysis of documents, film and television includes elements of a number of these approaches. However, it is important to identify which method(s) of analysis the researcher is using and whether they have followed the very broad underlying principles of this method/these methods.

Further reading

For an example of research that involved secondary analysis of the British Crime Survey (as it was then), see:

Feilzer, M. Y. (2009) 'Not fit for purpose! The (ab-)use of the British Crime Survey as a performance measure for individual police forces', *Policing: A Journal of Policy and Practice*, 3(2): 200–211.

For an example of a criminological study that uses documentary analysis, you could read:

Lister, S. (2014) 'Scrutinising the role of the Police and Crime Panel in the new era of police governance in England and Wales', *Safer Communities*, 31(1): 23–31.

Referred to briefly above, but worthy of more thorough reading, is one of the few books that seeks to provide some guidance on the different types of analysis that can be undertaken with media materials:

Moore, S. E. H. (2014) *Crime and the Media*. Basingstoke: Palgrave Macmillan.

To demonstrate the importance of perspective in telling a story, you might contrast the documentary *Who Killed Keith Blakelock?* with the account of the same events provided by a senior police officer (although not one who was personally involved in the riot at Broadwater Farm) in:

Brain, T. (2010) *A History of Policing in England and Wales from 1974*. Oxford: Oxford University Press.

PART III

DATA ANALYSIS AND PRODUCING YOUR OUTPUT

Introduction to Part III

After the excitement of collecting the data, the task of analysing it and writing about it may feel like a struggle. This is particularly the case when the findings are not quite as striking as you had hoped for, but point to a messier and more complicated truth – an experience that is familiar to almost everyone who has conducted research. However, analysing and writing about your data are crucial if you are to say something useful about your chosen topic of study, to justify the time that you and others have given to the study, and to pass your dissertation or fulfil your responsibility to the research funder.

Data analysis is a highly skilled task and takes quite different forms according to whether you have quantitative, qualitative or mixed methods data. Chapter 11 considers the preparation and analysis of quantitative data, dealing both with the situation where you type data into the IBM SPSS Statistics software (SPSS) and the one where you download data from an online survey program. Using an online program may seem like a timesaving option, but in reality data is likely to need a considerable level of 'cleaning' before it is ready to analyse. Once the data is ready, some of the methods of analysis that are available in SPSS are outlined in Chapter 11, before Chapter 13 considers the clearest ways to present quantitative findings, using both SPSS output and other methods such as writing a simple narrative.

One of the greatest challenges with qualitative data analysis is knowing where to start, so part of Chapter 12 is about the first steps that you can take to begin to make sense of such data. The chapter then takes you through various choices that you must make in analysis and some of the key approaches that are available: thematic, narrative and discourse analysis. Again, Chapter 13 moves from the analysis to the presentation of the findings, considering the principles that should guide you when seeking the right balance between writing about broad trends, discussing individual cases and providing direct quotations.

In addition to the presentation of data, Chapter 13 considers the other elements that should go into a good dissertation or research report (it also discusses research proposals). When you have finished reading Part III, you should be confident to analyse your data and to include it in your output, where it will sit alongside a discussion of the literature on your chosen topic, your methodology and a conclusion that brings your work together, providing a very clear message to your reader.

11

QUANTITATIVE DATA ANALYSIS

╭─ What you will learn in this chapter ─╮

By the end of this chapter, you will:

- Be aware of the programs that are available to analyse statistical data
- Be able to enter data into SPSS from hard copies of surveys
- Be able to download and 'tidy up' data from online survey programs
- Understand the circumstances under which it is appropriate to use descriptive and inferential statistics
- Be able to perform data analysis, and produce descriptive statistics, in SPSS
- Be able to interpret what descriptive statistics tell you about your data

Introduction

Many students (and lecturers!) avoid collecting and analysing survey data because of a fear of statistics. Reading academic journal articles which discuss statistical tests with obscure names and include expressions in the format ($p = 0.01$), sometimes with limited explanation for readers who are not familiar with the processes being used, can be an intimidating experience. However, this chapter will demonstrate that the discussion of data involving numbers does not have to be complex. Consider, for example, the section from my PhD thesis shown in Textbox 11.1, which discusses the financial circumstances of young homeless people who completed questionnaires. I hope that you will agree that there is nothing too complicated here!

Textbox 11.1

Section from PhD thesis dealing with debt

Thirty-one (33%) of respondents were in debt at the time of the first interview. The people or organisations owed the debt are shown in the table below:

Table 11.1 Who respondents owed debt to

Who debt owed to	Frequency
Parent(s)	13
Council	9
Other relatives	6
Friends	7
Catalogue	7
Benefit agency	2
Fuel company	2
Court order debts	2
Bank	1

Various items of expenditure had caused the debts, most commonly general living (in 10 cases – some respondents placed food in this category), rent (in six cases) and clothes (in four cases) (Harding, 2001: 172–173).

Simple statistics can provide us with important information about survey data. Even in a study which goes on to perform complex calculations, the first step is usually to have a look at the data to see which were the most frequently given answers to each question. So please be confident that you can undertake some useful analysis of a quantitative dataset, even if statistics is not an area where you feel comfortable.

Programs that Analyse Quantitative Data

There are large numbers of programs that can be used for analysing quantitative data but three that are of particular importance are:

- Microsoft Excel, which has the advantage of being familiar to many people and has the facility to perform a few statistical processes. Within the spreadsheet package, there is the capacity to calculate basic statistics such as totals and averages, but other forms of processing are more difficult and time-consuming than is the case in SPSS. So Microsoft Excel may be all you need when you have specific types of data and require specific forms of analysis; for example, if most of your questions ask respondents to give a score on a scale of 1–10 and you want to compare the average scores.

- The Statistics Package for the Social Sciences (SPSS), which can provide many functions more simply, and use a wider range of statistics, than Microsoft Excel. This program is widely used in universities, although the need to pay for a licence may prove a deterrent for organisations that do not undertake social sciences research so frequently. However, on the assumption that most readers of this book are in a university that has an SPSS licence, the majority of this chapter will demonstrate processes that are used in SPSS.
- R, which is a relatively new program and has the advantage of being freely available to download. It requires the typing of commands rather than the clicking of icons, so is probably easiest to use for people who are familiar with computer programming. However, the amount of advice that is available is growing, both through online users' forums and textbooks, one of which is recommended in the further reading section.

Preparing Data for SPSS

There is work that needs to be undertaken with data before even simple statistics can be produced, so this chapter starts at the point when you first receive your completed questionnaires in paper or electronic form. Of course, if you download a large national dataset – such as the Crime Survey of England and Wales (as discussed in Chapter 8) – the preparatory work will be done for you, so you can skip forward to the sections of this chapter that deal with data analysis. However, if you have conducted your own survey, the early sections on the preparation of data are essential. Data preparation is often a complicated and time-consuming process, but it is worth taking the care to do it well, because you will reap your reward when you come to do your analysis.

We will firstly consider the situation where you give out hard copies of a questionnaire and either collect them up or have them sent back to you. In this case, you will need to type the data into SPSS. I recommend reading this section even if you plan to conduct your survey using an online program (from which data can be downloaded), because some of the processes overlap for the two forms of data collection.

In order to demonstrate the process of preparing and typing in data, I am going to use three fictitious and very short questionnaires about labelling theory. Of course, this is just for the purposes of demonstration: if this was really the extent of your data, you would certainly not need to use SPSS to analyse it!

Textboxes 11.2, 11.3 and 11.4 include the data collected through these three fictitious questionnaires.

Textbox 11.2

Questionnaire 1 on labelling theory

1   Have you ever heard of labelling theory?

     ☐ *Yes*
     ☒ *No*

2   How far do you agree with the statement 'Everybody commits crime but only some people are labelled as criminals?'

     ☐ *Strongly agree*
     ☐ *Agree*
     ☐ *Neither agree nor disagree*
     ☒ *Disagree*
     ☐ *Strongly disagree*
     ☐ *Don't know*

3   Which types of crime do you think people are least likely to be convicted for?

     ☐ *Criminal damage*
     ☐ *Robbery, theft or burglary*
     ☒ *Sexual offences*
     ☐ *Violent offences*
     ☐ *Fraud*
     ☐ *Other offences*

3a   *IF YOU HAVE ANSWERED OTHER to Question 3: please could you specify?*

4   When considering every type of crime, how many times have you been a victim in the last year?

     2

Questionnaire 2 on labelling theory

1   Have you ever heard of labelling theory?

☐ *Yes*
☒ *No*

2   How far do you agree with the statement 'Everybody commits crime but only some people are labelled as criminals?'

☐ *Strongly agree*
☐ *Agree*
☐ *Neither agree nor disagree*
☐ *Disagree*
☐ *Strongly disagree*
☒ *Don't know*

3   Which types of crime do you think people are least likely to be convicted for?

☐ *Criminal damage*
☐ *Robbery, theft or burglary*
☐ *Sexual offences*
☐ *Violent offences*
☐ *Fraud*
☒ *Other offences*

3a   *IF YOU HAVE ANSWERED OTHER to Question 3: please could you specify?*

Shoplifting

4   When considering every type of crime, how many times have you been a victim in the last year?

Approximately 5 – my car has been vandalised a few times

Textbox 11.4

Questionnaire 3 on labelling theory

1   Have you ever heard of labelling theory?

   ☒ *Yes*
   ☐ *No*

2   How far do you agree with the statement 'Everybody commits crime but only some people are labelled as criminals?'

   ☐ *Strongly agree*
   ☐ *Agree*
   ☒ *Neither agree nor disagree*
   ☐ *Disagree*
   ☐ *Strongly disagree*
   ☐ *Don't know*

3   Which types of crime do you think people are least likely to be convicted for?

   ☐ *Criminal damage*
   ☐ *Robbery, theft or burglary*
   ☐ *Sexual offences*
   ☐ *Violent offences*
   ☐ *Fraud*
   ☒ *Other offences*

3a *IF YOU HAVE ANSWERED OTHER to Question 3: please could you specify?*

   Drunk and disorderly

4   When considering every type of crime, how many times have you been a victim in the last year?

   It depends what you call a crime

In order to prepare the data from these three questionnaires for SPSS, we need to convert them into a line of numbers. The method of achieving this may seem a little longwinded but I promise it is necessary! You should create a table that has the following columns:

- Question number – taken from the questionnaire
- Variable label – this column should state the piece of information which is being collected (the information may vary from respondent to respondent, hence the term 'variable')
- Variable name – SPSS has a column that requires a shortened version of the variable, without any spaces between letters, so this should appear here
- Value – here you give a number to all the possible forms that the variable could take
- Value label – here you show what each of the numbers means

This may seem a little strange in the abstract, but Table 11.2 shows how this would work in the case of the three questionnaires shown above.

Table 11.2 Table to convert labelling questionnaires into lines of numbers

Question number	Variable label	Variable name	Value	Value label
1	Heard of labelling theory?	HEARDLABEL	1	Yes
			2	No
2	Agree with principle of labelling theory?	AGREELABEL	1	Strongly agree
			2	Agree
			3	Neither agree nor disagree
			4	Disagree
			5	Strongly disagree
			9	Don't know
3	Type of crime people are least likely to be convicted for	TYPECRIME	1	Criminal damage
			2	Robbery, theft or burglary
			3	Sexual offences
			4	Violent offences
			5	Fraud
			6	Drunk and disorderly
4	Number of crimes actual or estimated	ACTEST	0	Not applicable
			1	Actual
			2	Estimated
4	Number of times victim	NUMVICT	999	Don't know

When drawing up a table like this, you will need to be flexible and ready to insert new lines as you go through, because this process almost always raises unexpected issues. This is illustrated by some of the key features of Table 11.2:

- Question 1 is the most straightforward – when it comes to typing the data into SPSS, if a respondent has answered 'yes' then 1 is typed in and if they have answered 'no' then 2 is typed in.

- Question 2 also presents few problems in terms of what to record. You might wonder why 'don't know' is 9 rather than 6 – this is an SPSS convention and, by following it, it makes it easier to spot the 'don't know' answers in your dataset.

- Question 3 demonstrates the most common method of dealing with a question that has an 'other' option: the answers given by those who have chosen this option can simply be added to the list. So there were five types of offences listed on the questionnaire – criminal damage; robbery, theft or burglary; sexual offences; violent offences; and fraud – and to these has been added the specific answer given by the third respondent who ticked the 'other' box, and then wrote 'drunk and disorderly'. However, although the second respondent ticked the 'other' box and then wrote 'shoplifting', this has not been added because I judged that it fitted with one of the pre-set options, i.e. 'robbery, theft or burglary'. (This is the type of tricky decision that you often have to make during the data preparation process.) The approach of adding the 'other' options to the list may become problematic if a very wide range of 'other' answers are given by respondents, but it is usually sufficient for a small survey.

- Question 4 demonstrates why there is a need to have a separate column for the question number and the variable label: the answer to the question includes two separate variables (i.e. two separate pieces of information) that need to be recorded. There is the number of crimes that a respondent reports but also whether the number they give is actual or estimated.

- However, there is a further complication with question 4 – the third respondent has provided no number at all, so it is not appropriate to classify their response as either 'actual' or 'estimated'. A 'not applicable' option is necessary and the SPSS tradition is that this is represented by 0. However, just to make matters even more complex, you must be careful not to use 0 as 'not applicable' for any numerical variable, i.e. one where the answer might actually be 0, such as 'How many friends of yours have been convicted of a crime?'

- You will see that 999 has been chosen as the 'don't know' value for the NUMVICT variable: this will be used for the third questionnaire, where the respondent provided neither an actual nor estimated number of crimes. The reasons for choosing 999 – rather than the usual value of 9 – is that it is possible that someone could have been a victim of crime nine times in a year, but not that they could have been a victim of 999 crimes, so there is no danger of misinterpreting the answer.

- Finally, you may wonder why only 999 has been given a label for question 4 and not the other answers, i.e. 5 and 2. This is because there is no need to give a numbered code to answers that are already numbers.

By referring to Table 11.2, I hope you can see that the data from the fictitious questionnaires in Textboxes 11.2–11.4 can be converted into rows of numbers that look like this:

Questionnaire One 2 4 3 1 2

Questionnaire Two 2 9 2 2 5

Questionnaire Three 1 3 6 0 999

To check that you have understood this process, I invite you to look through the fictitious questionnaire shown in Textbox 11.5 and then, referring back to Table 11.2, decide what the row of numbers should be to represent this questionnaire in SPSS.

Textbox 11.5

Questionnaire 4 on labelling theory

1 Have you ever heard of labelling theory?

☐ *Yes*
☒ *No*

2 How far do you agree with the statement 'Everybody commits crime but only some people are labelled as criminals?'

☐ *Strongly agree*
☐ *Agree*
☐ *Neither agree nor disagree*
☐ *Disagree*
☒ *Strongly disagree*
☐ *Don't know*

3 Which types of crime do you think people are least likely to be convicted for?

☐ *Criminal damage*
☐ *Robbery, theft or burglary*
☐ *Sexual offences*
☒ *Violent offences*
☐ *Fraud*
☐ *Other offences*

3a *IF YOU HAVE ANSWERED OTHER to Question 3: please could you specify?*

(Continued)

> 4   When considering every type of crime, how many times have you been a victim in the last year?
>
>   *1*

The line of numbers that you should have is:

2 5 4 1 1

The information that these numbers represent is:

2 (no) 5 (strongly disagree) 4 (violent offences) 1 (actual number) 1 (victim of one crime)

So now we have four lines of data and are ready to begin data entry. I encourage you to carry out this next stage with me. I will be using SPSS version 26 here, but much of what I do should be compatible with earlier versions.

Entering Data into SPSS

To enter the lines of data that were created above into SPSS, go into the SPSS program and choose the option to create a new dataset. This should take you to a screen where typing in these four lines of data is straightforward, giving you something that looks like this:

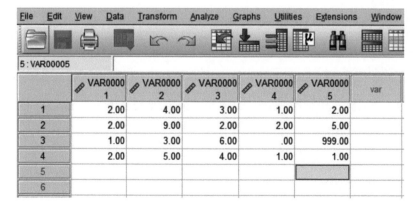

	VAR0000 1	VAR0000 2	VAR0000 3	VAR0000 4	VAR0000 5	var
1	2.00	4.00	3.00	1.00	2.00	
2	2.00	9.00	2.00	2.00	5.00	
3	1.00	3.00	6.00	.00	999.00	
4	2.00	5.00	4.00	1.00	1.00	
5						
6						

(Reprint courtesy of International Business Machines Corporation, © International Business Machines Corporation)

As with Word documents and anything else that you create, I encourage you to save your dataset regularly and now might be a good point to do so for the first time. To do this click on:

File

Save As

Give your file a name, keep the file type as SPSS Statistics (*.sav), choose a directory to save into and click **Save**. SPSS will produce a screen telling you what you have just done; close this down by clicking the X in the top right-hand corner. SPSS will ask you if you wish to save your output; choose **No** and you will find yourself back at the data file that you have just created.

If you look at the bottom left-hand corner of the screen, you will see that you are working in Data View. If you click the button next to this one, marked Variable View, you will come to a screen where you can take the next step, which is to give SPSS the information about what each of the numbers mean.

In the column on the left of the screen, headed with the word Name, type in the list of Variable Names from Table 11.2. The fifth column from the left, headed with the word Label, is where you type the Variable Labels; the outcome of this process should look like this:

	Name	Type	Width	Decimals	Label	Values	Missing	Columns
1	HEARDLAB...	Numeric	8	2	Heard of labelli...	None	None	8
2	AGREELAB...	Numeric	8	2	Agree with prin...	None	None	8
3	TYPECRIME	Numeric	8	2	Type of crime p...	None	None	8
4	ACTEST	Numeric	8	2	Number of crim...	None	None	8
5	NUMVICT	Numeric	8	2	Number of time...	None	None	8
6								
7								

(Reprint courtesy of International Business Machines Corporation, © International Business Machines Corporation)

If you now click in the first cell of the column headed Values (the one that is highlighted on the diagram above), you can tell SPSS what the Value Labels are for *Heard of Labelling Theory?* When you click this cell, a blue square should appear with three dots to the right of it. Click this square and you should come to the Value Labels screen. Now you enter the Value Labels:

Type '1' in the Value box

Type 'yes' in the Value Label box

*Click **Add***

Type '2' in the Value box

Type 'no' in the Value Label box. The box should now look like this:

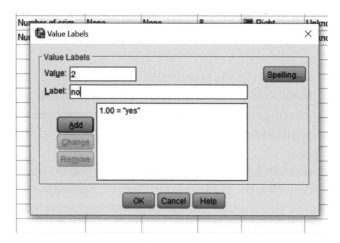

(Reprint courtesy of International Business Machines Corporation, © International Business Machines Corporation)

Now click **Add** and **OK**, at which point you have finished entering the Value Labels for this variable and can move the cursor down to add the Value Labels for the next one – *Agree with principle of labelling theory?* When you have put in the labels for all the variables, you can check whether you have done this correctly by going back to the Data View screen and clicking the icon at the top of the screen, near the right-hand side, that looks like this:

(Reprint courtesy of International Business Machines Corporation, © International Business Machines Corporation)

This will show the values that have been recorded for all the variables.

A very handy thing to know about Variable Labels is that they can be copied and pasted. So, for example, if you had several other variables like *Agree with principle of labelling theory?* – where the possible responses ranged from 'strongly agree' to 'strongly disagree' with a 'don't know' option – you could right-click on the Values cell for this variable and choose **Copy**. You could then go to other cells where you wanted these value labels to appear, right-click and choose **Paste**. This trick has saved me much time when working with survey data!

There are two more things that should be done at the Variable View screen. One is to tell SPSS which values are 'missing' and so should not be included in any calculation. We have three values that should be excluded in this way:

9 (don't know) for Agree with principle of labelling theory?

0 (not applicable) for Number of crimes actual or estimated

999 (don't know) for Number of times victim

Of these three, the reasons for listing 999 as missing are most obvious: it would clearly cause major distortions to calculations such as the average number of crimes if SPSS read this as someone having been a victim 999 times. The reasons for listing the others as Missing Values will become clearer later in this chapter. To begin entering these Missing Values, start by clicking in the cell which is in the *Agree with principle of labelling theory?* row and the Missing column. Once again, you should click on the blue square that appears. Choose **Discrete missing values** and type 9 in the first box, as shown below:

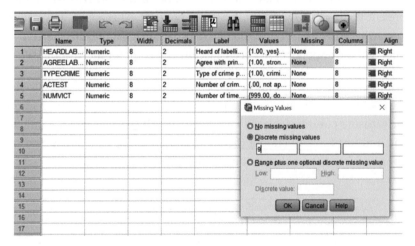

(Reprint courtesy of International Business Machines Corporation, © International Business Machines Corporation)

Then click **OK**. Do the same to add 0 as the Missing Value for *Number of crimes actual or estimated* and the 999 as the Missing Value for *Number of times victim*.

Finally, it is important to look at the column marked Measure, second from the right of the Variable View screen. If you click in this column, you will see that, for each variable, you are offered three choices:

1   Nominal – this applies to variables where the Values that are chosen to represent each Value Label are simply labels and any number could be chosen (which applies to *Heard of Labelling Theory?, Type of Crime People are Least Likely to be Convicted of* and *Number of Crimes Actual or Estimated*). So, for example, for *Heard of Labelling Theory?*, I have followed SPSS conventions with the Values, but it would have

made no difference to the calculations that I can do with this data if I had chosen completely different numbers, e.g.:

4 to represent 'not applicable'

27 to represent 'yes'

43 to represent 'no'

2   Ordinal – this applies to variables where the numbers chosen are in a sequence, such as *Agree with Principle of Labelling Theory?* The lower the number, the greater the level of agreement with labelling theory (except for 9 or 'don't know', which we have put into the Missing Values). Any questions asking, 'How far do you agree …' (or similar) will be represented by ordinal variables.

3   Scale – this is not an accurate statistical term but is used in SPSS where the numbers represent the 'real' answer given by the respondent. This applies to *Number of Times Victim*, where the number that you have typed into SPSS represents the 'real' number of crimes that the respondent has been a victim of (except for the Missing Value of 999).

For each variable, you should choose the appropriate measure, which should help to ensure that you only perform calculations that are appropriate (see later section). If you click in the Measure column for each variable, you will see that you are offered a drop-down menu and just have to choose the appropriate type of variable. At the end of this process, your Variable View column should look like this:

	Name	Type	Width	Decimals	Label	Values	Missing	Columns	Align	Measure	Role
1	HEARDLAB...	Numeric	8	2	Heard of labelli...	{1.00, yes}...	None	8	Right	Scale	Input
2	AGREELAB...	Numeric	8	2	Agree with prin...	{1.00, stron...	9.00	8	Right	Ordinal	Input
3	TYPECRIME	Numeric	8	2	Type of crime p...	{1.00, crimi...	None	8	Right	Scale	Input
4	ACTEST	Numeric	8	2	Number of crim...	{.00, not ap...	.00	8	Right	Scale	Input
5	NUMVICT	Numeric	8	2	Number of time...	{999.00, do...	999.00	8	Right	Nominal	Input
6											

(Reprint courtesy of International Business Machines Corporation, © International Business Machines Corporation)

Now (finally!) you are ready to start some calculations with your data. However, before you do this, we need to consider the alternative method of getting data into SPSS, i.e. downloading from an online survey program.

Downloading Data from Online Surveys

One of the obvious advantages of using online surveys is that the data can be downloaded straight into a program capable of analysis, without the need to type any of this data in. However, this is not always as beneficial as it first appears, because the data is likely to arrive in quite a 'messy' format and you will need to spend a considerable amount of time clean-ing it up. Many online programs download into Microsoft Excel and SPSS can read Microsoft Excel files, as we shall see later. So you have a choice of whether to do some of the 'cleaning' in Microsoft Excel or whether to move straight on to SPSS.

Of course, this is only a choice if you want to analyse your data in SPSS. As noted above, if the data analysis that you want to perform consists of numerical calculations – such as the average for single variables – then Microsoft Excel has everything that you need and there is no advantage to moving on to SPSS.

I am going to demonstrate the downloading of a dataset, and some of the issues that it raises, using data collected via an online program which asked the views of Northumbria University students about safety and other topics. When I downloaded this dataset into Microsoft Excel, a section of it looked like this:

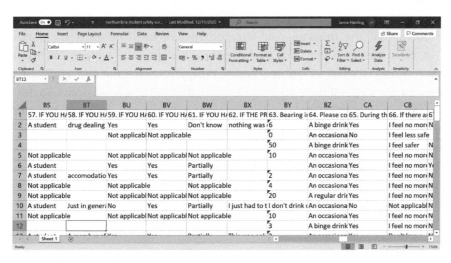

(Used with permission from Microsoft)

Of the variables shown on this screenshot, there was one which was suited to the type of analysis that Microsoft Excel is good at, because it was in the form of a number. This was from question 63 of the questionnaire:

63. Bearing in mind that 2 units of alcohol equates to a pint of lower strength (4%) beer, larger or cider; a standard glass of wine or a double measure of spirits, please could you estimate the number of units of alcohol that you consume in a typical week during the semester? It would be very helpful if you could just type a number here – we appreciate that this is likely to be an estimate and that the figure may vary from week to week.

To calculate the average or any other statistic for this question, Microsoft Excel must recognise that the answer given is a number rather than a word (or words). However, you will see that – in the column of the spreadsheet which records the answer to this question – there is an arrowhead in the top left-hand corner of each cell which indicates that the data is not recognised as a number. Thankfully, I was able to employ a simple solution to this problem, as follows:

1   I highlighted all the cells in the column relating to question 63.
2   When I did this, I saw a shape like a yellow diamond with a black exclamation mark in it next to these cells (unfortunately I am not able to copy this).
3   I highlighted this symbol and an arrow appeared to the right of it.
4   On clicking the arrow, I was offered several choices and selected **Convert to Number**.

This ensured that the program read the contents of most of the cells as numbers. However, there was still some work to do before calculating the average: Microsoft Excel will ignore those cells that are empty (because the question was not answered) but cannot create accurate statistics if there are some answers that still appear as words. So, for example, you can see from line 10 of the data that one person had answered 'I don't drink'. I needed to delete this answer and replace it with '0' for Microsoft Excel to be able to calculate the average accurately.

Once I had cleaned up the data in this manner, performing the calculation was quite straightforward. I moved the cursor to the cell below the column with the numbers for the weekly alcohol consumption, as per below.

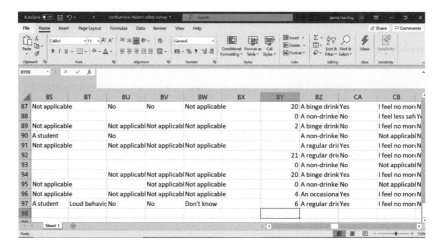

(Used with permission from Microsoft)

You will see, at the top of the screen towards the right, that there is a symbol that looks like this: Σ . I clicked the arrow to the right of this symbol and, from the options offered, chose **Average**. I then highlighted all the numbers in the column above the cursor and clicked the tick at the top of my screen on the left, between X and fx. The average number of units consumed per week now appeared in the cell at the bottom of the column.

So, Microsoft Excel was able to tell me something about my data. However, given the large number of nominal and ordinal variables in my dataset, it was hugely advantageous to move the data to SPSS to perform a wider range of analytical functions. So I opened SPSS and clicked **File**, then **Open**, then **Data**. Clicking the arrow by the 'Files of type' box meant that I could specify that I wanted to open a Microsoft Excel document. I found the file with the student survey data in it and then was ready to bring it into SPSS:

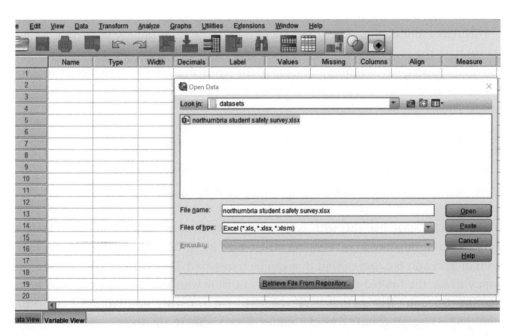

(Reprint courtesy of International Business Machines Corporation, © International Business Machines Corporation)

I then clicked **Open** and came to another screen, offering various options as to how the dataset could be presented, where I clicked **OK**. The outcome was a messy-looking dataset, which I will show you a section of here:

219

	@30.a.IFYOUHAVEANSWEREDYESPleasecouldyougivethereasons			@33.Howsafedo youfeelaroundthep acethatyouliveduri	@34.Howsafedoyou eelaroundtheplaceth atyouliveduringtheho	@35.Hows: oufeeloncar uringdaylighl
No		No	No	Very safe	Very safe	Very safe
No		No	No	Quite safe	Not very safe	Quite safe
No		Yes	Yes	Very safe	Quite safe	Very safe
Yes	ranking	Yes	Yes	Very safe	Quite safe	Very safe
No		No	No	Very safe	Very safe	Very safe
No		Yes	No	Very safe	Quite safe	Very safe
No		No	Yes	Very safe	Quite safe	Not very safe
No		Yes	Yes	Very safe	Very safe	Very safe
Yes	Like the course,having a placement, the facilities of the university and the cit...	Yes	No	Quite safe	Quite safe	Very safe
No		No	No	Quite safe	Quite safe	Quite safe
No		No	No	Quite safe	Quite safe	Very safe
No		No	No	Quite safe	Not very safe	Quite safe
Yes	Disability Support	No	No	Very safe	Very safe	Very safe
No		Yes	No	Very safe	Very safe	Very safe
No		Yes	Yes	Very safe	Quite safe	Very safe
No		No	No	Very safe	Quite safe	Very safe
		No	No	Very safe	Quite safe	Very safe
No		Yes	Yes	Very safe	Quite safe	Very safe

This screenshot demonstrates that downloading data from online programs does not always have the very large time savings – compared to typing the data in yourself – that you might expect. For example, at the top of the screenshot, you will see that there is the full question that each column records the answers to, but without any spaces between words. These questions included:

33. How safe do you feel around the place that you live during daylight hours?

34. How safe do you feel around the place that you live during the hours of darkness?

35. How safe do you feel on the campus during daylight hours?

If you get to a stage like this with your dataset, you must make a big decision. Do you want to put in the time to get it into a state where it can take advantage of all the functions of SPSS and produce output that can be transferred directly into Word? Or are you happy to use the limited functions that are available with the data in its present form, which will require that output is re-typed when transferring into Word (or any other word-processing program)? I would almost always choose the former option, but it is right to consider this question, bearing in mind the nature of your dataset and what you hope to do with the data.

If you do decide that you want the dataset to have the same level of functionality as one that you have typed in yourself, the first step is to go to the Variable View screen and to re-type the Variable Names and Labels. This is a time-consuming but simple task. However, it is more complicated to deal with the Values and Value Labels.

This is because, as noted above, SPSS can do the most with data if all Values are typed in as numbers and Value Labels are used to explain what each of the numbers means. This may seem like a slightly odd process to go through (to replace words with numbers and then put labels on the numbers to indicate which words they mean) but it is necessary if you want to have the full range of options as to what to do with your data.

Exactly how you convert the written answers in each column of your Data View screen into numbers depends on the nature of the dataset. You may decide that it is simplest just to re-type the data if:

- The dataset is small;
- You have questions where the answers need to be split into two variables, as was the case with the fictitious questionnaires above, where question 4 needed to be divided between *Number of crimes actual or estimated* and *Number of times victim*; and/or
- You have questions of a 'tick all that apply' nature, which are often in a particularly messy format when they are downloaded (it was suggested in Chapter 8 that it is good to avoid these questions if possible and there is not the space here to discuss all the possible ways in which they could be typed in).

However, if your dataset is sufficiently large, and you have closed questions where respondents chose one answer without any complications, it may be worthwhile to convert the data to numbers using the Find and Replace function in a similar manner to the way that you would use it in Word. So, for example, in my dataset, in response to Question 33 – *How safe do you feel around the place that you live during daylight hours?* – each respondent had selected from one of the options that was offered to them:

1 Very safe

2 Quite safe

3 Neither safe nor unsafe

4 Not very safe

5 Not at all safe

9 Don't know

To change the written answers to the numbers 1, 2, 3, 4, 5 or 9, I took the following steps:

Highlighted the column containing the answer to question 33

*Clicked **Edit***

Clicked **Replace**

Indicated that all answers of 'Not very safe' should be replaced with the number 4, as shown below:

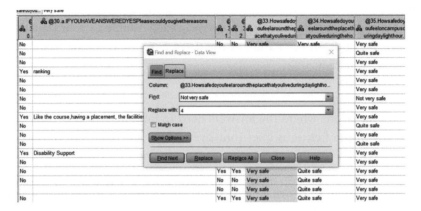

(Reprint courtesy of International Business Machines Corporation, © International Business Machines Corporation)

Clicked **Replace All** *and went through the same process to replace the rest of the written answers with numbers.*

You might ask why I started by changing 'Not very safe' to 4 rather than by changing 'Very safe' to 1. The answer is that, if I had specified first that 'Very safe' should be changed to 1, then the 'Not very safe' answers would have appeared as 'Not 1'. This would not be a particularly difficult issue to work around, but it does demonstrate that it is worth thinking about the order in which you make changes.

A difficulty with using the Find and Replace function in SPSS is that it can only work on one variable at a time. This is a frustration when dealing with a section of a question-naire like questions 33–35, where the same changes must be made for each variable. If you felt confident to make these changes in Microsoft Excel, before transferring the data to SPSS, that would be a substantial advantage, because in Microsoft Excel it is possible to use Find and Replace for several columns at once. In Microsoft Excel, the 'Find and select' function appears towards the right hand side of the main toolbar on the Home screen.

When the data is all converted to numbers, you can then begin to add Value Labels in the same way that you would when typing in data from paper questionnaires, as described above.

Producing Output and Statistics

Once you have either typed in and labelled your data or downloaded it from an online program and made the necessary adjustments, you are ready to start producing output and statistics from it. There are two broad categories of statistics:

1   Descriptive statistics, which help you to understand the patterns and trends within your own dataset. So, to take a hypothetical example, you might produce statistics to indicate, among the sample of people who completed your questionnaire, the percentage who said they felt 'very confident' that the criminal justice system is fair and impartial. A further level of analysis would be to determine whether men were more likely to give this response than women.

2   Inferential statistics, which seek to make inferences to a broader population. So if, in your dataset, men were more likely than women to say that they felt that the criminal justice system was fair and impartial, inferential statistics could indicate how likely it would be that this pattern would have been reproduced if the questionnaire had been completed by the entire population. (This is a simplified explanation of the principles behind inferential statistics; some of the books that I recommend in the further reading section offer a fuller account.)

You may well have seen accounts of quantitative research studies that use expressions of the nature ($p = 0.01$). These 'p values' are central to inferential statistics, representing the risk of error in assuming that a pattern seen in a sample would be reproduced in a population (again, this is a simplified explanation). P values have been the subject of much debate, with some arguing that they – and inferential statistics in general – are used too often and inappropriately (Gorard, 2016; Nicholson and McCusker, 2016; Spreckelsen and Van der Horst, 2016).

However, I have chosen not to discuss inferential statistics any further in this chapter for a different reason. The logic of inferential statistics is that they make generalisations from a random sample to a population. (Random samples were discussed in Chapter 7.) However, unless you have been able to access data from one of the publicly available datasets that were discussed in Chapter 8, it is unlikely that you will be working with a random sample. Most datasets that students collect through their own surveys tend to be via other sampling methods, often convenience sampling of people they know or snowball samples of people who can be contacted through social media. This is not a failing on the part of students – it is often the only option available – but it does mean that descriptive statistics are usually much more appropriate to use than inferential statistics.

To demonstrate some of the descriptive statistics that can be used in SPSS, I would like you to go to this book's companion website and look for the dataset called *Labelling Theory for Website*. This is an extended version of the dataset that you created earlier. Some more cases have been added (there are now a total of 80), together with some more variables, which have been coded as shown in Table 11.3.

Table 11.3 Additional Variables on *Labelling Theory for Website*

Question number	Variable label	Variable name	Value	Value label
5	Age in years	AGE	999	Don't know/not stated
6	Self-defined social class	CLASS	1	Working class
			2	Middle class
			9	Don't know
7	Whether support policy of avoiding custodial sentences for non-violent offenders under the age of 18	SUPPORTPOL	1	Yes
			2	No
			9	Don't know

For all three variables, the 'don't know' answer has been made into a missing value. Age is a scale variable and the other two are nominal.

We will now go through a few of the processes that you could use to analyse this data. Every time that I ask you to complete one of these processes, you will see that SPSS creates a separate output screen showing the outcome of your work. When we have finished discussing this output, you should close the output screen and click **No** when you are asked if you wish to save the output. You will then return to your data.

Examining Individual Variables

This is the first and easiest step to take and provides a good introduction to your data. For nominal or ordinal variables, the Frequencies command is the usual starting point. So, for example, you could examine the pattern of responses for the variable *Agree with principle of labelling theory?* To do this, click:

Analyse from the toolbar at the top of the SPSS screen

Descriptive Statistics from the menu that drops down

Frequencies from the menu that now appears to the right

You should now be at a screen that looks like this:

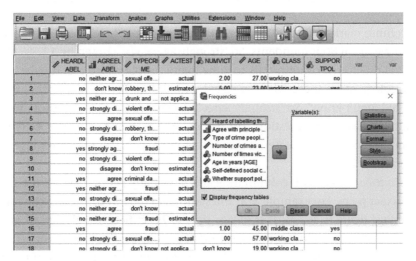

(Reprint courtesy of International Business Machines Corporation, © International Business Machines Corporation)

Highlight *Agree with principle of labelling theory?* (the second variable from the top) and use the arrow to move it across to the right-hand box. Then click **OK**. You should see an output screen where the key section looks like this:

Agree with principle of labelling theory?					
		Frequency	Percent	Valid Percent	Cumulative Percent
Valid	strongly agree	10	12.5	12.7	12.7
	agree	19	23.8	24.1	36.7
	neither agree nor disagree	19	23.8	24.1	60.8
	disagree	12	15.0	15.2	75.9
	strongly disagree	19	23.8	24.1	100.0
	Total	79	98.8	100.0	
Missing	don't know	1	1.3		
Total		80	100.0		

(Reprint courtesy of International Business Machines Corporation, © International Business Machines Corporation)

This is a frequency table, and it shows that the three most frequently given answers (each chosen by 19 respondents) were 'agree', 'neither agree nor disagree' and 'strongly disagree'.

You may be wondering why there are three columns where the headings include the word 'Percent'. These all tell us something slightly different about the data:

- The column marked 'Percent' tells us how many people gave a particular answer as a percentage of all 80 respondents. So 'strongly agree' was chosen by 12.5% of the 80.
- The 'Valid Percent' column tells us how many people chose a particular answer as a percentage of all those who expressed an opinion, i.e. excluding the one person who said 'don't know'. So 'strongly agree' was chosen by 12.7% of those who gave a definite answer to the question. This is one of the reasons why we specify what the Missing Values are in a dataset: it may be helpful to consider the percentages of those who gave firm answers.
- The 'Cumulative Percent' column indicates how many people gave all the answers to a particular point. For example, you will see that, in the row for 'agree', the cumulative percentage figure is 36.7%. This means that 36.7% either strongly agreed or agreed – a point that you might make when reporting your findings. You will also see that the cumulative figure has risen to 60.8% by the time you get to 'neither agree nor disagree'. By taking this figure away from 100, you could report that 39.2% either disagreed or strongly disagreed.

The frequency table that you have produced in SPSS, like all forms of SPSS output, can be copied and pasted into Word. Alternatively, you may decide to re-type the output in Word – presenting your output is a topic that will be covered in Chapter 13.

An additional option for presenting nominal or ordinal data is to use a Chart. You will see at the top of the Data View screen that there is an option to click on **Graphs**, which provides a range of options for producing visually appealing outputs: you may want to try these out. However, to provide a simple visual representation, you can use the **Charts** function within the **Frequencies** command. So, if you would now like to produce a frequency table and a pie chart to illustrate how respondents defined themselves in terms of social class, you should again click:

Analyse

Descriptive Statistics

Frequencies

You don't want to produce Frequencies for *Agree with principle of labelling theory?* again, so highlight this variable and use the arrow key to move it back to the left-hand box. Then highlight *Self-defined social class* and move it to the right-hand box. Click the **Charts** tab at the right-hand side of the screen, then choose **Pie Charts** and click

Continue and then **OK**. After the Frequency table, you should have a pie chart that looks like this:

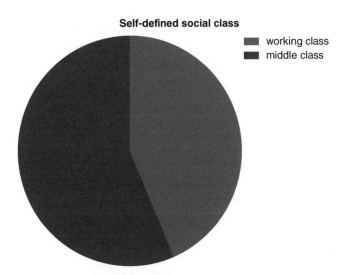

Self-defined social class

■ working class
■ middle class

(Reprint courtesy of International Business Machines Corporation, © International Business Machines Corporation)

Note that the two respondents who answered 'don't know' are excluded from the chart because their responses were classed as Missing Values.

You will have seen that you could also produce Bar Charts or Histograms. The question of which type of chart is most helpful to use in which circumstances is one that will be considered in Chapter 13.

Moving on to scale variables such as *Age in years* or *Number of times victim*, frequency tables and charts are not usually helpful. Instead, it is more appropriate to use simple statistics that summarise what is going on in the variable, most obviously the Mean and/ or the Median. I have used the word Average so far in this chapter, which many people regard as being the same as the Mean, but it is important to be aware of the Median as an alternative method of finding the 'middle' (or what is typical) for any variable. You may already be aware of the difference between the Mean and the Median, but in case you are not:

- The Mean is found by adding together all the values and then dividing by the number of values.
- The Median is found by listing the values from the highest to the lowest, then taking the one that is in the middle.

The Mean is the more commonly used figure. However, it can sometimes present a distorted picture. For example, if we were to take a mean for the annual income of 30 students in a classroom (grants + loans + wages + any other type of income), it would typically come to quite a low figure. However, if one of the Kardashian family, or some other very rich person, had enrolled to be a student and had joined the group, the Mean would rise hugely, giving a very unrealistic picture of the typical income of the people in the classroom. The difficulties caused by extreme values is a key reason why the Median can often give a better indication of what is typical for a variable than the Mean.

So we will look at the Mean and the Median for our two scale variables, *Age in years* and *Number of times victim*. To do this, again click on: **Analyse**, **Descriptive Statistics** and **Frequencies**. Now remove *Self-defined social class* from the Variable(s) box and replace it with *Number of times victim* and *Age in years*. Click **Statistics** and then check the boxes for the **Mean** and the **Median**:

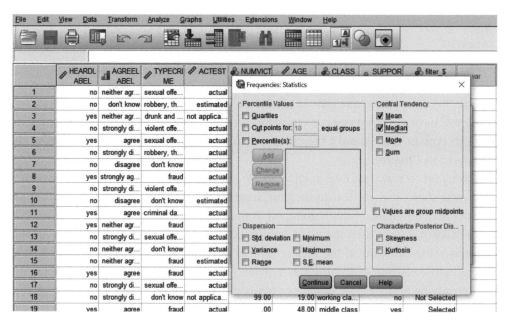

(Reprint courtesy of International Business Machines Corporation, © International Business Machines Corporation)

Click **Continue** and then **OK**. Your output should look like this:

Statistics		Number of times victim	Age in years
N	Valid	77	79
	Missing	3	1
Mean		1.3896	41.9494
Median		1.0000	38.0000

(Reprint courtesy of International Business Machines Corporation, © International Business Machines Corporation)

In the case of both variables, the Mean and Median are quite close together, which gives some confidence that both figures provide a good indication of what is going on at the centre of the dataset.

If you look below the output with the Mean and the Median, you will see that Frequency tables and Pie charts have also been produced for the two variables. (This happens because, unless you 'untick' a box, SPSS will continue to do the things that you asked it to last time, as well as any extra things that you have asked of it this time.) A quick look at the table and the chart for *Age in years* in particular should demonstrate why these are not helpful forms of output for scale variables!

The Median can also be used when considering an ordinal variable, although such a variable would typically be examined first by producing a frequency table, as discussed above.

Textbox 11.6

What is the mistake? Analysing a single variable

Try to identify the mistake(s) that a researcher has made here and then have a look at Appendix 1 to see whether your view is the same as mine.

A student undertakes a survey of students' feelings of safety in different locations at different times. His SPSS output in relation to one of the questions is shown below:

38. How safe do you feel in the city during the hours of darkness?					
		Frequency	Percent	Valid Percent	Cumulative Percent
Valid	Not at all safe	3	3.1	3.1	3.1
	Not very safe	22	22.9	22.9	26.0
	Quite safe	61	63.5	63.5	89.6

(Continued)

38. How safe do you feel in the city during the hours of darkness?				
	Frequency	Percent	Valid Percent	Cumulative Percent
Very safe	10	10.4	10.4	100.0
Total	96	100.0	100.0	

(Reprint courtesy of International Business Machines Corporation, © International Business Machines Corporation)

The student writes in his dissertation that 26.0% of the students surveyed felt not very safe in the city during the hours of darkness.

Examining Relationships Between Variables

Once individual variables have been examined, analysis can be extended further by looking at relationships between variables in a dataset. Here it is often important to remember the distinction between the independent variable and the dependent variable, which was discussed in Chapter 5. While it is not true in the case of every pair of variables, often it is clear that one variable is independent because it has an impact on the other (which is dependent). For example, because more crime is committed by men than women, gender is an independent variable which has an impact on the dependent variable of whether someone commits crime. Personal characteristics such as age, gender and ethnicity are always independent variables.

Crosstables between two variables

The best process to use when examining relationships depends crucially on the type of variables that you are dealing with. When both variables are nominal, crosstables are a very helpful tool. We will look now at how crosstables can be used to examine relationships between three pairs of variables:

- *Self-defined social class* and *Heard of labelling theory?* (where *Self-defined social class* is the independent variable because it is a personal characteristic).
- *Self-defined social class* and *Whether support policy of avoiding custodial sentences for non-violent offenders under the age of 18* (again, *Self-defined social class* is the independent variable).

- *Heard of labelling theory?* and *Whether support policy of avoiding custodial sentences for non-violent offenders under the age of 18* (here *Heard of labelling theory?* is the independent variable because it may have an influence on whether a respondent supports the policy).

It is important to note that there will be fewer than 80 cases appearing in each crosstable. This is because SPSS excludes from the table any missing values, i.e. any respondent who answered 'don't know' to either of the questions asked.

To explore the relationship between *Self-defined social class* and *Heard of labelling theory?* using a crosstable, click:

Analyse

Descriptive Statistics

Crosstabs

The independent variable should always be in the columns, so use the arrow key to move *Self-defined social class* into the Column(s) box and *Heard of labelling theory?* into the Row(s) box. Click the **Cells** button on the right of the screen and, at the next box, from the Percentages section on the left-hand side, click the box by the word **Column**:

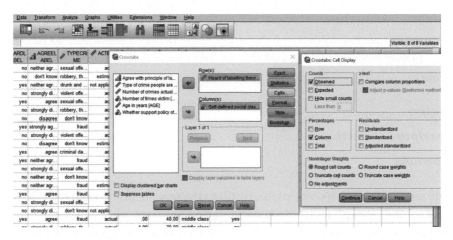

(Reprint courtesy of International Business Machines Corporation, © International Business Machines Corporation)

Now click **Continue** and **OK**. The output should look like this:

Heard of labelling theory? * Self-defined social class Crosstabulation					
			Self-defined social class		Total
			working class	middle class	
Heard of labelling theory?	Yes	Count	7	22	29
		% within Self-defined social class	20.6%	50.0%	37.2%
	No	Count	27	22	49
		% within Self-defined social class	79.4%	50.0%	62.8%
Total		Count	34	44	78
		% within Self-defined social class	100.0%	100.0%	100.0%

(Reprint courtesy of International Business Machines Corporation, © International Business Machines Corporation)

This output demonstrates the reason for asking for column percentages. It shows that the middle-class respondents were evenly split, with half (50.0%) having heard of labelling theory and half not having heard of it. In contrast, among the respondents who considered themselves to be working class, a minority (20.6%) had heard of labelling theory, while 79.4% said that they had not. So we can conclude that, in our sample, the middle-class respondents were more likely to have heard of labelling theory than the working-class respondents.

To create a crosstable to examine the relationship between *Self-defined social class* and *Whether support policy of avoiding custodial sentences for non-violent offenders under the age of 18*, click:

Analyse

Descriptive Statistics

Crosstabs

You will see that the previous crosstable is still in the box, so all you need to do is to move *Heard of labelling theory?* out of the Row(s) box and replace it with *Whether support policy of avoiding custodial sentences for non-violent offenders under the age of 18*, before clicking **OK**. You will see that a higher percentage of middle-class people (44.2%) than working-class people (26.5%) supported the proposal.

Finally, create a crosstable between *Heard of labelling theory?* (which should go in the Column(s) box) and *Whether support policy of avoiding custodial sentences for non-violent offenders under the age of 18* (which should go in the Row(s) box). You will see that a majority of those who have heard of labelling theory supported the policy (71.0%), compared to a small minority of those who have not heard of labelling theory (16.7%).

So, in our sample, we have found some degree of relationship between each of our pairs of variables:

- Middle-class people are more likely to have heard of labelling theory than working-class people.
- Middle-class people are more likely to support the policy than working-class people.
- People who have heard of labelling theory are more likely to support the policy than people who have not heard of labelling theory.

You might wonder, looking at these findings together, which variable has the greatest impact on whether a respondent supports the policy: social class or whether they have heard of labelling theory. To address this question, we can gain a better – although not perfect, as we will see – indication of the strength of relationship between two variables in a crosstable by using a statistic called Lamda. Lamda varies between 0 and 1; 0 means that there is no relationship at all between the variables, while 1 means that there is a perfect association (this would happen, for example, if all the middle-class respondents gave one answer while all the working-class respondents gave another). There are different opinions as to what all the possible values between 0 and 1 mean, but I am going to use the one provided by Argyrous (2011: 125):

0 No relationship

0–0.2 Very weak relationship

0.2–0.4 Weak relationship

0.4–0.7 Moderate relationship

0.7–0.9 Strong relationship

0.9–1.0 Very strong relationship

1.0 Perfect association

In order to use Lamda, go back to the crosstable that you have just created between *Heard of labelling theory?* and *Whether support policy of avoiding custodial sentences for non-violent offenders under the age of 18* (i.e. click **Analyse**, **Descriptive Statistics** and **Crosstabs**). At the crosstabs box:

- Click **Statistics**
- Select **Lamda** on the left-hand side
- Click **Continue**
- Click **OK**

In your output, after the crosstable you should see the following information:

Directional Measures

		Value	Asymptotic Standard Error[a]	Approximate T[b]	Approximate Significance
Nominal by Nominal Lambda	Symmetric	**.443**	.130	2.759	.006
	Whether support policy of avoiding custodial sentences for non-violent offenders under the age of 18 Dependent	**.433**	.140	2.420	.016
	Heard of labelling theory? Dependent	**.452**	.131	2.669	.008
Goodman and Kruskal tau	Whether support policy of avoiding custodial sentences for non-violent offenders under the age of 18 Dependent	.298	.106		.000[c]
	Heard of labelling theory? Dependent	.298	.105		.000[c]

a. Not assuming the null hypothesis.

b. Using the asymptotic standard error assuming the null hypothesis.

c. Based on chi-square approximation

(Reprint courtesy of International Business Machines Corporation, © International Business Machines Corporation)

Please don't be put off by the complicated nature of this table! We only need to be concerned with the top three numbers in the first column (the ones that I have put in bold). These are three possible values for Lamda:

- The first – Symmetric – we would use this if we were not sure which was the independent variable and which was dependent.
- The second treats *Whether support policy of avoiding custodial sentences for non-violent offenders under the age of 18* as the dependent variable.
- The third treats *Heard of labelling theory?* as the dependent variable.

Of these, it is clear that the second is the appropriate one to use. The value of .433 suggests that there is a moderate association between the two variables.

Now repeat the process with *Self-defined social class* as the independent variable – i.e. the one that goes into the Column(s) box – rather than *Heard of labelling theory?* You should see that, this time, the relevant value of Lamda is 0.000. This illustrates a difficulty with using Lamda, because clearly there was some relationship between the variables (middle-class people were more likely to support the policy than working-class people). Lamda can, therefore, mistake a weak relationship for no relationship at all. However, it has still shown us clearly that whether a respondent has heard of labelling theory has more impact on whether they support the policy than their self-defined social class.

Using crosstables to examine the relationship between three variables

We might want to explore further the moderate relationship between whether a respondent has heard of labelling theory and whether they support the policy by asking whether this relationship is equally strong among both working-class and middle-class respondents. This is the type of question that is important to ask to get a really detailed understanding of your data.

There are two ways that the question could be addressed – by splitting your data or by creating a three-way crosstable. Even though the three-way crosstable is quicker, I will show you the way to split your data because it is a technique that may prove useful when undertaking other types of analysis.

To split the data so that you only consider those respondents who classified themselves as working class, you should click:

Data

Select cases

The circle by 'If condition is satisfied'

If ...

At the next screen, use the arrow key to move *Self-defined social class* into the box at the top on the right-hand side. (It appears as the Variable Name CLASS.) Now use the calculator to click on = and **1**. Your screen should look like this:

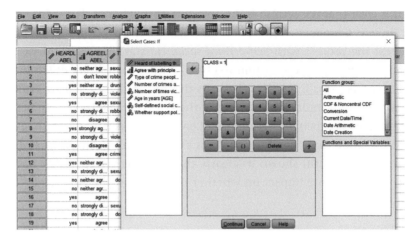

(Reprint courtesy of International Business Machines Corporation, © International Business Machines Corporation)

Click on **Continue** and **OK**. You will get some output telling you what you have done, but there are two ways that you can check that it has worked:

- On the Variable View screen, another variable will have been added with the name *filter_$*.
- On the Data View screen, the numbers on the left-hand side have a cross through them for every respondent who did not define themselves as working class.

Now run the crosstable for *Heard of labelling theory?* by *Whether support policy of avoiding custodial sentences for non-violent offenders under the age of 18*. This shows that 57.1% of working-class people who had heard of labelling theory supported the policy, compared to 18.5% of working-class people who had not heard of labelling theory.

Now repeat the process of splitting the data but this time specify:

CLASS = 2 (i.e. selecting the respondents who classified themselves as middle class)

Run the crosstable again and it shows that 72.7% of middle-class people who had heard of labelling theory supported the policy, compared to 14.3% of middle-class people who had not heard of labelling theory. So we can conclude that the pattern that we saw across the whole dataset – that people who had heard of labelling theory were more likely to support the policy – is reproduced when we consider each of the classes separately.

Very importantly, now that you have finished working with sections of your data and want to use the whole dataset again, you should click:

Data

Select Cases

The circle by All cases

OK

If you forget to do this, it can be extremely frustrating to discover that you are working with part of the dataset, when you thought you had been working with all of it – as I know from bitter experience!

A quicker way to show that the relationship between having heard of labelling theory and supporting the policy exists in both social classes is to create a three-way crosstable. To do this, go back into your crosstable which has *Heard of labelling theory?* in the Column(s) box and *Whether support policy of avoiding custodial sentences for non-violent offenders under the age of 18* in the Row(s) box. Now click on *Self-defined social class* and move it into the Layer 1 of 1 box at the bottom of the screen:

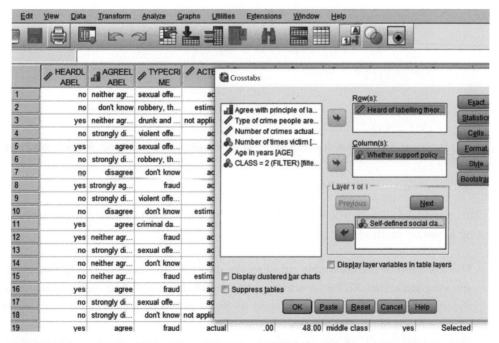

(Reprint courtesy of International Business Machines Corporation, © International Business Machines Corporation)

Click **OK** and the output should look like this:

Whether support policy of avoiding custodial sentences for non-violent offenders under the age of 18 * Heard of labelling theory? * Self-defined social class Crosstabulation

Self-defined social class				Heard of labelling theory?		
				yes	no	Total
working class	Whether support policy of avoiding custodial sentences for non-violent offenders under the age of 18	yes	Count	4	5	9
			% within Heard of labelling theory?	57.1%	18.5%	26.5%
		no	Count	3	22	25
			% within Heard of labelling theory?	42.9%	81.5%	73.5%
	Total		Count	7	27	34
			% within Heard of labelling theory?	100.0%	100.0%	100.0%
middle class	Whether support policy of avoiding custodial sentences for non-violent offenders under the age of 18	yes	Count	16	3	19
			% within Heard of labelling theory?	72.7%	14.3%	44.2%
		no	Count	6	18	24
			% within Heard of labelling theory?	27.3%	85.7%	55.8%
	Total		Count	22	21	43
			% within Heard of labelling theory?	100.0%	100.0%	100.0%
Total	Whether support policy of avoiding custodial sentences for non-violent offenders under the age of 18	yes	Count	20	8	28
			% within Heard of labelling theory?	69.0%	16.7%	36.4%
		no	Count	9	40	49
			% within Heard of labelling theory?	31.0%	83.3%	63.6%
	Total		Count	29	48	77
			% within Heard of labelling theory?	100.0%	100.0%	100.0%

(Reprint courtesy of International Business Machines Corporation, © International Business Machines Corporation)

This provides you with the same information that you found by splitting your data, but by a quicker method:

- The top third of the crosstable contains the data for the working-class respondents, showing again that 57.1% of working-class respondents who had heard of labelling theory supported the policy, compared to 18.5% of working-class respondents who had not heard of labelling theory.
- The central third of the crosstable contains the data for the middle-class respondents, showing that 72.7% of middle-class respondents who had heard of labelling theory supported the policy, compared to 14.3% who had not heard of labelling theory.

- The bottom third of the crosstable contains the data for all respondents, showing that 69.0% of all respondents who have heard of labelling theory supported the policy, compared to 16.7% who had not heard of labelling theory.

Working with scale variables

The two scale variables in our dataset are *Number of times victim* and *Age in years*. When working with scale variables, it is necessary to go through different processes to examine relationships between variables: if you want to demonstrate this, try asking for a crosstable between *Self-defined social class* and *Number of times victim*. You will see that this table is quite difficult to read.

In order to examine more effectively the question of whether one social class was likely to be the victim of more crime than the other, we could use the method of splitting the data demonstrated above. This would involve selecting the working-class respondents and asking for the mean and median number of crimes they had been a victim of, then selecting the middle-class respondents and doing the same. However, there is a quicker way to demonstrate this if you click on:

Analyse

Compare Means

Means

Use the arrows to put *Self-defined social class* into the Independent List box and *Number of times victim of crime* into the Dependent List box. Now click the **Options** button and you should come to a screen where you can see that the Cell Statistics that are already chosen – in the box on the right-hand side of the screen – are Mean, Number of Cases and Standard Deviation. Transfer across to this box also the **Median**. The **Standard Deviation** is not something that we need to be concerned about here, so transfer this across to the box on the left-hand side of the screen. Now click **Continue** and **OK** and your output should look like this:

Report			
Number of times victim			
Self-defined social class	Mean	N	Median
working class	2.0606	33	2.0000
middle class	.8810	42	.0000
Total	1.4000	75	1.0000

(Reprint courtesy of International Business Machines Corporation, © International Business Machines Corporation)

This output shows that there were 33 working-class people, and 42 middle-class people, who gave a figure for the number of crimes that they had been a victim of. Although the numbers are low, the mean figure for working-class people is more than double the one for middle-class people. In addition, the median suggests that the 'typical' working-class person was a victim of two crimes, while the 'typical' middle-class person was a victim of none. The data demonstrates that, among the sample, those who considered themselves working class were likely to have been victims of more crime than those who defined themselves as middle class.

The process of comparing means and medians is very useful when examining the relationship between a nominal variable (e.g. *Self-defined social class*) and a scale variable (e.g. *Number of times victim of crime*). However, when neither of the variables is nominal, correlation is the most useful type of statistic for exploring the relationship between them. There are two commonly used forms of correlation. Pearson's Product Moment Correlation Coefficient, usually described as r, is one measure, but this can only be used with two scale variables that meet quite stringent criteria (Pallant, 2001: 113–114). In contrast, Spearman's rho, although not so powerful, can be used to examine the relationship between any two scale variables, between a scale variable and an ordinal variable or between two ordinal variables. The value of a correlation can be:

- Positive (between 0 and 1) – this means that the value of one variable tends to increase when the other also increases. So, since I reached the age of 40, my marathon times have been positively correlated with my age – the greater my age, the more hours and minutes it has tended to take me to run a marathon.
- 0, which means no correlation at all between the variables. I have never tried to work it out, but I imagine that the correlation between my marathon times and the number of points that Newcastle United achieved in the last football season is close to 0 because these variables are completely unrelated.
- Negative (between 0 and –1) – this means that the value of one variable tends to decrease as the other one increases. So, since the age of 40, the number of press-ups I can do has been negatively correlated with my age – as my age has increased, the number of press-ups I can do has decreased.

As with Lamda, different opinions are expressed as to what should be regarded as a strong correlation, but a helpful set of guidelines is provided by Cohen (1988, cited in Pallant, 2001: 120):

.10 to .29 or – .10 to – .29 represents a small correlation

.30 to .49 or – .30 to – .49 represents a medium correlation

.50 to 1.0 or – .50 to – 1.0 represents a large correlation

We will calculate a correlation (Spearman's rho) between *Age in years* and *Number of times victim of crime*. To do this, click:

Analyse

Correlate

Bivariate

Transfer *Number of times victim of crime* and *Age in years* into the Variables box. In the Correlations Coefficient section, untick the box by **Pearson** and tick the box by **Spearman**. Click **OK** and the output you get should look like this:

Correlations			Number of times victim	Age in years
Spearman's rho	Number of times victim	Correlation Coefficient	1.000	–.623**
		Sig. (2-tailed)	.	.000
		N	77	76
	Age in years	Correlation Coefficient	–.623**	1.000
		Sig. (2-tailed)	.000	.
		N	76	79
**. Correlation is significant at the 0.01 level (2-tailed)				

(Reprint courtesy of International Business Machines Corporation, © International Business Machines Corporation)

The key figure is the Correlation Coefficient. Ignore the one that is 1.000 – this just means that the variable is perfectly correlated with itself, which is hardly surprising. It is the value of –.623 that is the important one. The negative value means that the variables are negatively correlated, i.e. that one tends to be higher when the other is lower. In other words, people of younger ages tend to be victims of higher numbers of crimes. The figure of –.623 represents a large correlation, suggesting a strong relationship between the two variables.

We could use another correlation to examine the relationship between *Number of times victim* and *Agree with principle of labelling theory?* To do this, once again click **Analyse**, **Correlate** and **Bivariate**. Move *Age in years* out of the Variables box and move *Agree with principle of labelling theory?* into the box. Click **OK** and you should get a correlation value of –0.119.

The next step is to stop to have a think! When using ordinal variables, such as *Agree with principle of labelling theory?* you often need to consider particularly carefully what a positive or a negative result means. Remember that the level of agreement ranges from 1 for strongly agree to 5 for strongly disagree, i.e. the lower the value of this variable, the more that someone agrees with labelling theory. So the negative correlation suggests that people who have been victims of higher numbers of crime tend to be more in agreement with the central principle of labelling theory, although the correlation is a small one.

This may seem a slightly surprising finding: you might intuitively expect people who have been victims of more crime to be less supportive of labelling theory, which is essentially sympathetic to those whom it regards as having been labelled as criminals. However, this demonstrates an important truth – that correlation is not causation. If two variables are correlated, one simple (and sometimes true) explanation is that the independent variable has affected (or caused a change in) the dependent variable. However, another explanation is that the relationship is more complicated than this.

To illustrate the type of factor that can complicate the relationship between two variables, you should run another correlation between *Age in years* and *Agree with principle of labelling theory?* You should find that there is a small, positive correlation of .191. This indicates that lower age is associated with lower numbers on the *Agree with principle of labelling theory?* variable (and lower numbers represent more agreement because 1 is 'strongly agree'). So younger people are more likely to agree with labelling theory, as well as being victims of more crime. This appears to at least partly explain why people who are victims of higher numbers of crimes are likely to be more in agreement with labelling theory. Age is an intervening variable in the relationship between number of crimes and level of agreement.

However, we cannot be more precise about what impact age and number of victimisations have on level of agreement without undertaking some more advanced forms of analysis – such as regression – which are beyond the scope of this book (but which are covered in the further reading at the end of this chapter). The most important point to consider here (and, where possible, explore) is the impact of any intervening variables. The possible impact of these intervening variables should be considered when writing up your findings.

Working with ordinal variables

There has been no separate discussion of ordinal variables here because the methods by which they can be compared to other variables are a combination of those that can be used with nominal and scale variables. Ordinal variables can be included in crosstables, although these are harder to read when you have questions with larger numbers of answers. You can also compare the medians of ordinal variables between different groups (it is not appropriate to use means), and you can use Spearman's rho to examine the relationship with scale variables or other ordinal variables.

Textbox 11.7

What is the mistake? Analysing relationships between variables

Try to identify the mistake(s) that a researcher has made here and then have a look at Appendix 1 to see whether your view is the same as mine.

A student conducts some research where three of the questions are:

7   *Have you ever been arrested?*

☐ *Yes*
☐ *No*
☐ *Prefer not to say*

7a *If you have ever been arrested, please could you tell me how many times this happened?*

8   *On a scale of 0–10, how well do you think the police do their job in the UK, with 0 representing extremely badly and 10 representing extremely well?*

The student uses Spearman's rho to examine whether students who have been arrested give higher or lower marks out of 10 to the police than students who have never been arrested. She also uses a crosstable to determine whether those students who have higher numbers of arrests are likely to give higher or lower marks to the police.

Key points for your own research

- Consider carefully the advantages and disadvantages of typing in your own data from a paper survey compared to downloading it from an online program: this factor should be part of your decision making about the mode of data collection (see Chapter 8).
- Another important decision to consider at the stage of data collection is which program would be most appropriate to analyse the data in.
- If you are using SPSS, decide how far you need to prepare your data in order to achieve the desired output. Time spent ensuring that your data is correctly labelled can reap rich rewards when it comes to the analysis.
- When analysing quantitative data, start by examining individual variables before moving on to look at relationships between pairs of variables.
- Be certain about whether each variable is nominal, ordinal or scale, and use processes that are appropriate to this type of variable.

- When examining the relationship between variables, think carefully about whether one of them should be considered independent and the other dependent – this could affect the manner in which you create and evaluate output. Consider also the possible impact of any intervening variable.
- Only use inferential statistics if you have a random sample and feel confident to use them.

Key points when reading other people's research

- When considering how much weight to give to statistical findings, try to find out as much as you can about how they have been created, particularly if they come from a source that may have an interest in mispresenting them (see Chapter 14 for more on this).
- If inferential statistics are used (usually indicated by expressions in the form $p =$ or by discussions of 'significant' findings), check that a random sample has been chosen – otherwise these statistics are of little value.
- A good source will explain what the statistics used are and what they demonstrate. So, even if you are not familiar with the types of statistics that are discussed (e.g. t tests), and the material includes tables and terms that are hard to understand, look for the part of the output that summarises what the findings are and what they mean.

Further reading

The book that I find most helpful in this area, because it devotes a good amount of space to descriptive statistics before moving on to inferential statistics, is:

Argyrous, G. (2011) *Statistics for Research*, 3rd edn. London: Sage (1st edn 2000).

If you do want to use inferential statistics, another book that I recommend – because its material is particularly clearly written – is:

Pallant, J. (2020) *SPSS Survival Manual*, 7th edn. New York: McGraw Hill Publishing (1st edn 2001).

If you are interested enough, and brave enough, to try to teach yourself R, I recommend:

Davis, C. (2019) *Statistical Testing with R*. Norwich: Vor Press.

Visit **https://study.sagepub.com/crimresearch** to access the dataset *Labelling Theory for Website* which you will need to interact with this chapter.

12

QUALITATIVE DATA ANALYSIS

What you will learn in this chapter

By the end of this chapter, you will:

- Feel confident looking at a qualitative dataset and taking some simple steps to analyse the data
- Be able to make an informed choice between thematic, narrative and discourse analysis, or an approach that combines two of these approaches
- Be able to identify and analyse key themes in a dataset
- Know how to explore the methods by which speakers seek to make their narratives persuasive
- Be aware of the choices respondents make about language and be able to identify the implications of these choices
- Have a range of options that you can use to check the validity of the findings of qualitative data analysis

Introduction

This chapter will focus on methods of analysing qualitative data which is obtained from interviews, with a section at the end about the extra opportunities that are provided by focus group data. The methods of analysing other possible sources of qualitative data – such as documents, visual images and television programmes/films – were discussed in Chapter 10.

It is very important to note that there are times when, despite your best efforts, the data that your research produces will offer limited scope for qualitative data analysis, because a respondent has given you only brief answers to questions. Of course, this is not to criticise the respondent, because they may only have a limited amount to say on a topic, may not feel comfortable to elaborate their views or may be speaking in a language that they are not completely familiar with (using a translator is not always feasible or desirable). However, it is important to consider from the outset the extent to which the data that you have collected provides opportunities for qualitative analysis and the types of analysis that could realistically be applied to it. You should never be marked down because your respondents did not discuss topics as freely or for as long as you had hoped that they would: the person marking your work should be asking whether you have made the best use of whatever data you have managed to collect.

This chapter will demonstrate some of the options that may be available to you for qualitative data analysis. The demonstrations will use data that I collected through interviews with eight police officers. This small research project had the following objectives:

- To establish the reasons for police officers joining the job;
- To explore experiences of training and starting work as a police officer;
- To consider the skills that were developed by being a police officer;
- To identify how the nature of the job had changed with time;
- To identify the most satisfying and more difficult elements of the job.

Before demonstrating how this data could be analysed, I will briefly discuss the subjective nature of qualitative data analysis and some key decisions that need to be made before beginning.

The Subjective Nature of Qualitative Data Analysis

The availability of statistical programs such as SPSS means that there are standard processes for analysing quantitative data, as was demonstrated in Chapter 11. In contrast, Auerbach and Silverstein (2003: 32) argue that there is no single 'right way' to analyse a qualitative dataset and that the decisions taken are inevitably subjective. However, it is crucial that there are clear and logical reasons for taking your chosen approach.

To briefly illustrate that qualitative data analysis can take different paths, but that these can all be valid if there is an appropriate justification for the decisions taken, a simple exercise is presented in Textbox 12.1:

Textbox 12.1

Exercise to identify commonalities in a dataset

Divide the following eight words below into two sets of four according to a key characteristic:

Gold Blue <u>Gnome</u> **Book Green Brown** <u>Goat</u> <u>Badge</u>

Please complete the exercise before looking at the different ways that it could have been tackled below.

As Table 12.1 shows, there are many ways in which this exercise could be completed (and these are just the ones that I can think of!), according to which characteristic you think is key, with none representing the 'right' or the 'wrong' way to complete the task.

Table 12.1   Possible methods of dividing groups

Method of dividing groups	Group 1	Group 2
First letter of word	Blue, Book, Brown, Badge	Gold, Gnome, Green, Goat
Number of letters in word	Gold, Blue, Book, Goat	Gnome, Green, Brown, Badge
Adjective or noun (all the adjectives are colours, of course)	Gold, Blue, Green, Brown	Gnome, Book, Goat, Badge
Whether word is in Bold type	Gold, Book, Green, Brown	Blue, Gnome, Goat, Badge
Whether word is underlined	Gold, Gnome, Goat, Badge	Blue, Book, Green, Brown

So the qualitative researcher is faced with constant difficult decisions and, in contrast to the quantitative researcher, has few guidelines as to the right way to make these decisions. Patton (2002: 457) argues that data should be allowed to 'tell their own story', but the exercise above shows that several different stories can be told, according to the decisions that you make about your data.

However, while there is no 'right' way, there are some methods of analysing qualitative data that are clearly wrong. You should never make decisions without a clear reason or try to get the findings to be what you want them to be (in which case subjectivity becomes bias). One way to reduce the risk of bias is to keep an account of key decisions (and the reasons for taking them) throughout the research process, but particularly when conducting data analysis, in order to later consider the implications of your approach (Jupp, 2006: 258). Gibson and Brown (2009: 195) suggest that keeping a research diary of thoughts and decisions may be a helpful way of showing how analysis has developed before key decisions are forgotten or the reasons for them become less clear with time. Notes or memos to yourself, which can be saved on your mobile phone or any other device, are other means by which decisions can be recorded.

There are also steps that can be taken to check the validity of the findings once your analysis is complete; these are discussed at the end of this chapter.

Key Choices that Are Made in Qualitative Data Analysis

Choosing Whether to Fully Transcribe

It is a major advantage to be able to audio record (or even video record) qualitative interviews, and essential to record focus groups, as was noted in Chapter 9. Once the recording is complete, you are left with the task of transcribing the material, which many researchers find to be the least enjoyable task of the whole research process, unless they are fortunate enough to have the funds to pay someone to do the transcription for them. However, transcription does have the advantage of ensuring that you are very familiar with your data before you begin your analysis.

Experienced researchers are sometimes able to selectively transcribe recordings, identifying in advance those parts of the discussion that are most likely to be key to the analysis. However, my advice to a new researcher is not to do this, unless there is a very obvious digression. For your first experiences of research, it is advantageous to have the full transcripts to work with – despite the large amount of time involved in producing them.

Choosing Whether to Use Computer Assisted Qualitative Data Analysis (CAQDAS)

One major decision that you must make is whether to use Computer Assisted Qualitative Data Analysis (CAQDAS). Many people assume that the use of a specialist computer package must inevitably improve the analysis, as is the case with most quantitative datasets, where programs such as SPSS provide benefits for analysing a dataset of any reasonable size (see Chapter 11). However, the value of computer packages for qualitative study is less easy to determine because so much depends on the interpretation of the researcher, rather than on the widely accepted techniques and formulae used to calculate statistics.

Computers undoubtedly have advantages in terms of efficiency, eliminating many physical tasks such as cutting and pasting chunks of text (Bryman, 2008: 565).

Programs such as NVivo can enable you to view all parts of a dataset very simply rather than hunting through manually or electronically stored documents, where there is always the danger that you will 'miss' something that you are looking for (Blismas and Dainty, 2003: 458; Gibson and Brown, 2009: 178).

However, computer programs take time to learn to use and there is a danger that the researcher will shape their analysis to fit with the program that is being used rather than considering what is most appropriate for the data (Blismas and Dainty, 2003: 458). The decision as to whether it would be beneficial to use CAQDAS should rest partly on the nature of your dataset – it is more likely to be helpful the greater the number of transcripts and the longer that they are – and partly on your preference. I urge caution in the use of such software when analysing your first dataset, unless you feel particularly comfortable with new programs or have collected a particularly large amount of data. Grasping basic principles of analysis is a demanding task in itself and learning to use a software package at the same time may put you under too much pressure. As you grow more experienced, you may feel more confident to use programs such as NVivo and find it easier to judge when it is most beneficial to do so.

Choosing Whether to Use Codes

Much writing on qualitative data analysis suggests that data will always be coded. However, it is important to remember that – like the use of CAQDAS – this is a choice and that coding is not helpful to everyone. Yin (2011: 188) argues that 'coding routines can produce their own distractions – for example having to attend to the mechanics of the coding process rather than struggling to think about the data'.

Coding involves attaching labels to data in a manner that captures the meaning while reducing the amount of content. Using codes becomes more important with larger amounts of data, where the use of full transcripts becomes increasingly awkward. However, if you have a relatively small amount of data, you must decide whether codes are helpful (because they reduce the space needed to represent an idea) or a hindrance (because, however carefully they are chosen, they reduce the level of information and may cause confusion over their meaning).

There is no one correct format for codes, with words or abbreviations both commonly used. I have shown in Table 12.2 an example of a section of transcript that I coded using abbreviations, with an indication of what the abbreviations mean at the end. It is a section taken from an interview with a police officer to whom I have given the pseudonym of Jack; he was responding to a question about the skills that he had developed as a police officer.

Table 12.2 Example of coding from interview with Jack

	Code
Communication would be the biggest one. Being able to talk to people is... it's a skill that you don't appreciate it until you work with a cop who hasn't got it and who makes the situation ten times worse, and obviously communication is about listening, not just talking. It's about knowing when to speak and knowing how to speak.	CSC LCSSF LTI
Not just external, not just with the public, but with your colleagues, your peers, your supervisors. I found that I very quickly became likeable, because I was able to explain things .... Yes, I suppose communication, to answer your question, was the skill I developed the most by far, and I suppose competence, as well.	CSPI CSCI IDC
It's funny how after you've been to ten people's houses in your first couple of weeks, you do start to feel like a cop and that does... and the people you're dealing with, the public, treat you like you're a cop because you are, so you start to think like you are and you start to feel more comfortable in the uniform and that confidence grows. And then because you're more confident, you become better at your job, and you come across more assured at jobs	FMCWE CLC

Explanation of codes:

CLC: confidence leads to competence

CSC: communication skills crucial

CSCI: communication skills with colleagues important

CSPI: communication skills with public important

FMCWE: feel more confident with experience

IDC: important to develop competence

LCSSF: lack of communication skills a serious failing

LTI: listening and talking important

Maintaining a set of codes becomes more complicated as more cases are added and it may become difficult to keep track of all the codes, which is one of the reasons some researchers prefer to use computer programs such as NVivo. There will also be difficult judgements to be made such as when to combine codes, when to replace them and when to sub-divide them. To take a hypothetical example, let us imagine that Jack was the first respondent whose answer to this question was coded, but that a second respondent said:

'If you have a police officer who cannot communicate effectively with the public, it can make your job more difficult.'

Here I would need to choose between three options:

- I could code this comment with the code that had already been used for Jack's transcript, i.e. LCSSF (which might not fit with the extent of the problem that the second respondent was reporting).
- I could create a different code to use for the second respondent's comment, e.g. LCSCCD: lack of communication skills can create difficulties.
- I could replace the existing code with a new code which covered the seriousness of the problem as perceived by both Jack and the second respondent, e.g. LCSP: lack of communication skills problematic.

My personal preference would be for the third option, but you could just as easily argue for one of the others.

So, there are difficult decisions to be made when coding and it is important to consider whether the time taken to create a clear set of codes will be repaid by being able to find your way around transcripts quicker. I recommend creating a set of codes for one part of your transcripts, and deciding if they are helpful for making sense of your data, before deciding whether to code entire interviews.

Two Suggested First Steps

Whatever decisions you make about using CAQDAS and using codes (see above), and about the form of analysis that you will use (see below), knowing where to start is often a huge problem when faced with your first set of transcripts from qualitative interviews. The task of making sense of the complex data that qualitative researchers collect can seem an overwhelming one (Patton, 2002: 440). This section will suggest two possible first steps – making summaries and using the constant comparative method. I must emphasise again that these are suggestions and that it is for you to decide whether one, both or neither are helpful to get you started with your analysis.

Making Summaries

Making summaries is an initial step that reduces an interview to the key points, helping you to see through the mass of detail and repetition to the points that are most relevant to the research question(s) or research objective(s). Miles and Huberman (1994: 51–52) suggest that the process of summarising an interview should involve the full transcript being reduced to a summary that fits onto one sheet of paper (or one page on a word processor), which makes it easier for the researcher to compare summaries.

It is often helpful to summarise one section of a transcript at a time. The process of summarising could involve the following steps:

1   Identify the research objective(s) that the section of the transcript is most relevant to.
2   Decide which pieces of information or opinion are most relevant to this objective/ these objectives and which are detail that do not need to be included in the summary.
3   Decide where (if at all) there is repetition that needs to be eliminated.
4   On the basis of these decisions, write brief notes.

This process assumes that an inductive approach is being taken and that the study is seeking to meet research objectives. If a deductive approach were being used instead, the researcher would need to consider how the section of the transcript could contribute to answering the research question(s) (see Chapter 2).

To take an example, let us consider how making summaries might work in relation to my research, where one of the objectives was to 'establish the reasons for police officers joining the job'. This objective was achieved with some questions about the process of applying and the motivation for applying. In the case of an officer whom I will refer to as Kevin, the relevant section of the transcript is shown inTextbox 12.2:

Textbox 12.2

Section from interview with Kevin

Me: And at what point did you first decide that you wanted to be a police officer?

Kevin: I was definitely not one of these people who, it's always been their dream, you know? I was never one of these people who grew up dressing up as a police officer and all that kind of stuff. My previous job was office-based and although it was fine, it was okay, I could tell at that point that it wasn't something I really wanted to do for the rest of my life, if you like. At that time, one of the ways the police were advertising the position of a police officer, was through the jobs paper. I looked at it and I thought, 'I quite fancy that,' and that was it, you know?

Me: Yeah. And what was it about the job or what you knew about the job that made you want to apply?

Kevin: Again, probably the traditional sort of, you know, I think I've already touched on not being in an office, you know, not being office-bound and having that sort of

(Continued)

> not knowing what to expect every day, all that … like I say, I know a lot of people who join the police have that kind of mentality. I can't say it was because I had a want to help people and stuff; I think I'm naturally that way inclined anyway. That kind of came … I think when you look at the qualities that a police officer needs, I thought, 'Yeah, I could do that,' as opposed to me thinking, 'What qualities have I got? What job could I do with my qualities?' Does that make sense? I looked at the job first and foremost and thought, 'Yes, I could do that,' as opposed to me thinking, 'Right, okay, what job fits me?' So it was more a case of, yeah, just thinking … it was probably more a case of not being entirely happy with where I was that made me look at being a police officer as opposed to seeking it out, if that makes sense. It was just a case of wanting that buzz of being out there and having more of an exciting job, I suppose.

When looking at Kevin's first answer, one of his key points is that he did not always want to be a police officer. There is extra detail, for example that he did not dress up as a police officer as a child, that does not need to be included in the summary. So the point that can be made in the summary is:

• Did not have long-term ambition to join the police.

Kevin makes the point that he did not begin by assessing his own qualities but rather looked at the qualities required of a police officer and then decided that he had them. He immediately repeats this point in order to reinforce it, but the repetition does not need to be included, so the point that can appear in the summary is:

• Saw recruitment advertisement and realised that he had the qualities.

The decisions made to arrive at the above two bullet points were fairly straightforward ones. A more difficult question was whether to include a point that Kevin made in both his answers – namely that he did not see the job that he had done previously as something that he had wanted to pursue in the long term, because it was office based and not exciting. I decided to include this point in the summary because, as the decision to apply to the police was a pragmatic one, Kevin's reasons for thinking that it would be a better option than his previous job seemed central to his thinking.

Another difficult decision was whether to include the comment Kevin made that he did not become a police officer specifically to help people. I decided that this point should not be included because the summaries would concentrate on those factors that officers identified positively as being part of their motivation.

So the summary read:

- Did not have long-term ambitions to join the police.
- Saw recruitment advertisement and realised that he had the qualities.
- Did not see his previous job as a long-term option.
- Wanted something more exciting than an office-based job.

Textbox 12.3 shows you the response to the same section of the interview with a police officer who is referred to as Jane. I invite you to read through this section and then go through a similar process to the one that I took you through with Kevin, identifying the points that should be included in a summary. Once you have done this, have a look below the textbox at the way that I did this task.

Textbox 12.3

Section from interview with Jane

Me: Right, great, thank you. And when did you first decide that you wanted to become a police officer?

Jane: I think I was pretty sure I wanted to be one when I was probably still in primary school, probably about eight or nine years old, my mam spent a lot of time and effort trying to persuade me not to. So, I don't think I fully committed myself to it until I was probably about 14–16.

Me: Right. A long-term ambition then? And what was it about the job that appealed to you?

Jane: So I think one of my main desires was to have no two days be the same. I wanted a mixture of being indoors and outdoors, I know this sounds ridiculous for somebody so young for this to actually be a consideration, but I wanted security. I wanted to know that there was always going to be a job there for us. And I wanted to work for a good employer, and that did mean something to me when I was that age.

I will now describe how I went through the four-stage process of summarising but do not be concerned if I made slightly different decisions to you – I must emphasise once again that there are no 'correct' answers when it comes to qualitative data analysis.

1   The relevant objective was still, of course, 'establish the reasons for police officers joining the job'.

2   When looking for detail that could be eliminated, I decided that the opposition that Jane faced from her mother did not need to appear in the summary – the key point here was that Jane had the ambition from an early age. Another key decision was that I should record that Jane wanted job security but that the specifics of this (a job that would always be there and a good employer) were extra detail that did not need to appear in the summary.

3   I did not think that there was any repetition to eliminate.

4   So the brief notes that I wrote were:

- Childhood ambition to be a police officer.
- Liked the variety and job security that the job offered.

It might be helpful at this point to consider how these points fitted into the summary of the full interview, which is shown in Textbox 12.4.

Textbox 12.4

Summary of interview with Jane

- *Held various roles as a police officer. 24/7 response policing is the 'bread and butter' but also enjoyed working in specialist teams.*
- *Childhood ambition to be a police officer.*
- *Liked the variety and job security that the job offered.*
- *Did jobs with customer contact before joining police.*
- *Feelings on starting training – excitement, anxiety, apprehension, the unknown, but determination.*
- *Memories of training – the law, exams, graduation.*
- *Feelings on starting work – apprehension, anxiety, knowledge of being the only new person, wanting to work out where she was in pecking order.*
- *Wanted to serve country, have order and routine, see the real world, earn a decent wage, help people, have excitement, grow up.*
- *Memories of first year – feeling proud of being the youngest person and the only woman.*
- *Job has nurtured nosiness, stubbornness and perseverance, not shocked by anything.*
- *Most satisfying elements – some convictions, people who she respects congratulating her.*
- *Difficulties – not having enough staff, not having staff with specialist skills, other agencies relying too much on the police because they are there 24/7.*

(Continued)

- *Not appropriate to come into the police with a fixed plan but wants to get promoted.*
- *Changes since started as a police officer – greater focus on vulnerability, less target driven so don't lock people up for being drunk and disorderly.*
- *Very negative media portrayal of the police.*
- *Has not seen a major change in police culture. Banter not so crude, but people still adopt similar roles on a shift.*
- *Best changes that could happen in policing: would like to work more closely with CPS and social services; would like time to look at people's problems more holistically; more police officers to realise that they are as much social services as armed services; better mental health support for traumatic experiences that police officers face; new recruits should appreciate the importance of physical fitness to surviving in the job and coping with the pressures.*
- *Very pleased to be a police officer.*

The original interview transcript with Jane covered over 12 pages. By reducing this to a single page, it became very easy to compare what Jane said about a range of topics – e.g. the best changes that could happen to policing – with the views of other respondents. It is important to remember that summaries are very useful for giving the big picture, but also that they are only a guide: you must keep returning to the transcripts for more detail.

The Constant Comparative Method

The constant comparative method can be a helpful early approach to identifying similarities and differences between cases in a dataset. It can be used alongside summaries or independently; as noted above, one of the values of summaries is that they make the task of comparing cases considerably easier. Much of the literature relating to the constant comparative method assumes that codes are used but this is not necessarily the case – the examples discussed below do not involve coding.

The constant comparative method is often associated with thematic analysis (which is discussed later in this chapter) but Barbour (2008: 217) argues that any form of qualitative data analysis involves constantly comparing and contrasting. Charmaz (2006: 54) describes the constant comparative method in the following manner:

> At first you compare data with data to find similarities and differences. For example, compare interview statements and incidents within the same interview and compare statements and incidents in different interviews.

A helpful approach to using the constant comparative method is to divide the process into three steps:

1   Make a list of similarities and differences between the first two cases to be considered.
2   Amend this list as further cases are added to the analysis.
3   Identify research findings once all the cases have been included in the analysis.

To show how the constant comparative method can work in practice, I will use as an example the question that we looked at in the last section – reasons for becoming a police officer – and begin by making comparisons between Kevin and Jane. I will then show how the picture develops when we add Jack's comments on this subject to the comparisons.

You will recall that I summarised Kevin's reasons for going into the job by listing the following points:

- Did not have long-term ambitions to join the police.
- Saw recruitment advertisement and realised that he had the qualities.
- Did not see his previous job as a long-term option.
- Wanted something more exciting than an office-based job.

Jane's reasons were then summarised as follows:

- Childhood ambition to be a police officer.
- Liked the variety and job security that the job offered.

So, the summaries point us immediately to a difference between the two respondents – Jane had a long-term ambition to join the police but for Kevin it was a pragmatic decision in response to a job advert. However, I was only able to find key similarities between Kevin and Jane in this area by carefully re-reading the transcripts of the relevant part of the interviews. Kevin discussed 'not being in an office, you know, not being office-bound and having that sort of not knowing what to expect every day', while Jane said: 'So I think one of my main desires was to have no two days be the same. I wanted a mixture of being indoors and outdoors'. My re-reading showed me that wanting a variety of tasks and the chance to work outdoors were two similarities in the motivations of Kevin and Jane.

When comparing cases like this, it can be difficult to know how to manage issues that are mentioned by one respondent but not another. Jane discussed job security and other advantages of working for a big employer. My interpretation of Kevin not mentioning this issue was that it was not so important to him, so this could be listed as a difference between the two officers. An alternative interpretation was possible – i.e. that it had been an important motivating factor for Kevin but one that he forgot to mention in the interview – but I thought that my interpretation was more plausible.

However, I decided to take a different approach, based again on my subjective interpretation, when faced with another point that was made by one respondent but not the other. Kevin said that he felt that he had the qualities needed for the job (when he saw the advertisement in the newspaper), but Jane did not mention this issue. So, did Jane doubt whether she had the qualities needed to be a police officer or did she not think to mention this point? I decided that the latter interpretation was more likely because it would be strange for Jane to harbour an ambition for so long while doubting whether she would be able to fulfil it.

For this reason, I was not prepared to list 'Kevin thought he had the qualities for the job, Jane did not' as a difference. However, it would certainly not be appropriate to list 'Kevin and Jane both thought that they had the qualities for the job' as a similarity, because this was based on an assumption in the case of Jane.

So, after comparing the comments of Kevin and Jane on the reasons for being a police officer, my lists of similarities and differences – based on a certain amount of subjective interpretation – looked like this:

Similarities:

Kevin and Jane attracted by working in different locations.

Kevin and Jane attracted by variety of tasks.

Differences:

Jane had a long-term ambition to do the job; Kevin's choice was pragmatic.

Jane was attracted by the job security; Kevin did not mention this.

While the constant comparative method is a good way to get started with a thematic analysis, it becomes more complicated as further cases are added. This can be demonstrated by considering the response of a third officer, Jack, to the questions about reasons for going into the job. The relevant section of the interview is shown in Textbox 12.5.

Textbox 12.5

Section from interview with Jack

Me: When did you first decide that you wanted to become a police officer?

Jack: I would say I was probably 20 at the time. One of my cousins joined at 18 and sang its praises. He was quite keen to go to work. He didn't mind going to work.

(Continued)

> | | We had a holiday, a stag do, and he was the only one lad of 20 of us who was looking forward to going back to work. |
> |---|---|
> | **Me:** | Right. And were you doing another job at that time? |
> | **Jack:** | I was, yes, I was manager of a centre that made payments to people, which was very helpful in terms of customer service. It got us through my police interview, because of my examples with angry customers. |
> | **Me:** | Yes, I can see that would be useful. You mentioned that your cousin was the only person looking forward to going back to work? |
> | **Jack:** | Yes. |
> | **Me:** | Were there particular things that you heard about the job or that you knew about the job that really appealed to you? |
> | **Jack:** | I liked the idea of a shift pattern: back in those days, you would work seven nights in a row and then have six days off. Every five weeks on a Thursday night, Friday morning, we'd be in the pub and he'd have six days off for free. Whereas, obviously, I was Monday to Friday. The shift pattern was nice. It was decent money. And the fact that he kept saying every day is different. Whereas, every day in my old job, was the same: it was Groundhog Day. |

Considering first the list of similarities between the interviews of Kevin and Jane, I noted that one reason that they both had for wanting to do the job – the variety of tasks involved – was shared by Jack so, of course, remained on the list. However, although both Kevin and Jane discussed the attractions of working between different locations, this was not mentioned by Jack and so ceased to be a similarity, instead becoming a difference between respondents.

Adding in Jack's data gave greater detail and complexity to the list of differences. Jack joined Kevin in discussing his choice of career as being made for pragmatic reasons, rather than joining Jane in having a long-term ambition. There was a difficult decision as to how to categorise Jack's discussion of the shift pattern and the pay: I decided to place these comments in the same category as Jane's discussion of job security under the broad heading of 'employment conditions'. This was a subjective decision; I could also have treated the two sets of comments as being about separate issues.

Adding new cases to the analysis can sometimes highlight that a similarity or difference has been missed previously. For example, Jack made clear that the description of the job by a serving police officer (his cousin) had been very influential in his decision to apply. This prompted me to re-examine the full transcripts of the interviews with Jane and Kevin to see whether there was any mention of a police officer who had influenced them. I found that Jane had a relative who had been a police officer and who she identified as an influence on her, although there was no such discussion in Kevin's interview. So this became a new factor to list among the differences between respondents.

Therefore, after adding the data of Jack, the list of similarities and differences became:

Similarities:

Kevin, Jane and Jack attracted by variety of tasks.

Differences:

Kevin and Jane attracted by working in different locations; Jack did not mention this.

Jane had a long-term ambition to do the job; Kevin and Jack's choice was pragmatic.

Jane and Jack attracted by aspects of the employment conditions; Kevin did not mention this.

Jane and Jack influenced by someone who was a police officer; Kevin was not.

This process demonstrates that, as the constant comparative method progresses and more cases are added, the list of similarities is likely to become shorter and the list of differences longer and more complex. However, even with larger numbers of cases, it remains a helpful way of making basic comparisons.

Choosing the Main Method(s) of Analysis

Boeije (2010: 76–77) helpfully notes that qualitative analysis consists of cutting data up to put it together again in a manner that seems relevant and meaningful. Bryman and Burgess (1994: 6) point out that many discussions of qualitative methods fail to address the choices that are available to the researcher in terms of how exactly such cutting up and putting back together can be done. Indeed, some books on qualitative methods often launch into the process of analysis without considering the options that can be taken. In contrast, other books identify a large number of methods of analysing qualitative data (e.g. Dawson, 2009: 119–125; Wertz et al., 2011). For the sake of space and simplicity, this chapter will concentrate on three methods: thematic analysis, narrative analysis and discourse analysis. These are sometimes presented as entirely separate approaches, but the discussion that follows will demonstrate that there is often a degree of overlap between them.

Thematic Analysis

Gibson and Brown (2009: 128–129) suggest that there are three sets of aims of thematic analysis:

1   Examining commonality – pooling together all the material across a dataset that has something in common. Commonalities which are discovered can then be analysed further, which may mean that subdivisions are found within them.

2   Examining differences – the researcher should also identify differences across the dataset and examine the relevance of them to the issues and themes that are being considered.

3   Examining relationships – the researcher should examine how different parts of their analysis fit together and contribute to an understanding of different issues and themes.

The third of these is the most complex; I have written about this elsewhere (Harding, 2017) but space does not allow it to be considered here. However, to provide you with an example of an outcome that can arise from this approach, Irving (2018: 238) looked at relationships between the current needs experienced by homeless people and their past experiences and concluded that: 'Those with the most complex needs engaged with had typically experienced some form of trauma at an early age and generally within the family home'.

Of course, examining commonalities and differences has much in common with the constant comparative method and can be seen as an extension of this approach. A commonality can be any feature that two or more cases have in common, including:

- a common characteristic such as being female;
- a common experience such as having been a victim of online fraud; or
- a common opinion such as believing that short prison sentences are counter-productive.

A difference, of course, can also cover any of those areas and, as we saw above, the pattern of differences can be a complex one.

Tables can be a helpful tool in providing a broad overview of similarities and differences. Tables come in many forms (Miles and Huberman, 1994), but a simple checklist may be the easiest to use for a new researcher. My recommendation for using a checklist table to look for themes in a particular section of the data is as follows:

1   Select the section from each transcript where a particular topic is discussed (e.g. the answer to a specific question).

2   Draw up a list of every issue that is discussed by respondents as you read through this section of the transcript.

3   Draw up your checklist table.

4   Re-read each transcript to see which boxes should be ticked for which respondent. This re-reading should be of the entire transcript, because the topic may be discussed in unexpected places. If you find a new issue that was not in your original list, you should add it and check for it in all of the transcripts.

5　Count up the number of times each issue is mentioned to see which might be considered themes. A theme, by definition, must appear more than once. However, when working with a large dataset you may decide, for example, that an issue must be discussed by at least four respondents to be considered a theme.

6　Consider also whether any of the themes have sub-themes, for example a pattern of difference within a broader area of commonality.

I put this process into action in my interviews with the police officers in the following manner:

1　I chose the responses to my question 'What is the most satisfying element of your job?' as the topic for which I would seek to identify themes.

2　I read all the transcripts and listed 10 issues that were discussed in response to this question.

3　I drew up the checklist table.

4　I re-read all the transcripts and ticked the relevant box each time I found that a respondent discussed one of the issues. The result is shown in Table 12.3.

Table 12.3　Issues associated with most satisfying elements of being a police officer

Satisfying element	Anna	Claire	Colin	Gavin	Jack	Jane	Kevin	Tom
Nature of the work	x	x	x		x	x	x	x
Gaining a conviction	x	x	x				x	x
Referring victims to support services	x							
Serving the public		x	x	x		x	x	
Protecting vulnerable people		x						x
Seeing a job through to the end		x			x			
Supporting people through sudden death			x					
Relationships with colleagues				x	x			x
Building relationships with people in neighbourhoods				x				
Solving longer-term problems							x	

5　With such a small sample, I decided that I should consider an issue to be a theme if two or more of my respondents mentioned it. This meant that four issues which were only mentioned by one respondent – referring victims to support services, supporting people through sudden death, building relationships with people in neighbourhoods and solving longer- term problems – were not considered to be themes. The six themes, listed from the most frequently discussed to the least frequently discussed, were: the nature of the work; serving the public; gaining a conviction; relationships with colleagues; protecting the vulnerable; and seeing a job through to the end.

6   I explored each of the six themes to consider whether any of them could be broken down into sub-themes. To take the example of gaining a conviction, some of the respondents (Anna, Colin and Kevin) concentrated on the positive impact this had for victims, while others (Claire and Tom) focused on preventing the offender from committing further crimes. To illustrate this different emphasis, Kevin said:

If you've been involved in something which has really affected your life, personally, you know, you want the police to be able to find that offender, bring them to justice and all that kind of stuff. And it is nice to be able to pass that message on …

While Tom's slightly different focus was illustrated when he said:

If you put heroin dealers away for example, those people destroy lives and they're indiscriminate, they'll sell heroin to children. So putting people like that away and making communities safer is brilliant.

Finally, it is important to note that thematic analysis, like every aspect of qualitative data analysis, involves subjective decisions. Using an example from the above analysis, although vulnerable people are part of the public, I made a subjective decision that what Claire and Tom said about them was sufficiently distinctive to make 'protecting vulnerable people' a separate theme from 'serving the public'. Once again, you should not be afraid to make such subjective decisions, so long as you have a clear rationale.

Narrative Analysis

Narrative analysis has traditionally been limited to subject areas such as the study of literature, but it has increasingly been used in the social sciences in recent years. The stories that people tell represent the way they make sense of events; narrative analysis does not seek to establish objective truth but to capture people's own understanding of their lived experience (Josselson, 2011: 225–226). Bryman (2008: 553) notes that narrative analysis is not restricted to biographical/life history interviews (which were discussed in Chapter 9) but can include accounts of much more specific events.

Josselson (2011: 226) makes an important distinction. Narratives can be considered on their own – sections of the text of one narrative are compared to other parts of the same narrative. An alternative approach, if there are multiple narratives, is to make comparisons between different respondents. It is this second approach that is demonstrated here.

Several writers (e.g. Elliott, 2005: 39–46; Grbich, 2007: 127–134) draw a further distinction between those approaches that focus on the content of the narrative (which is similar to thematic analysis, only applied to stories) and those where the principal concern is the structure and the language. Both thematic narrative analysis and structural narrative analysis will be illustrated here, using the accounts that the police officers gave of their feelings on their first day of training.

To conduct a thematic narrative analysis of these accounts, I used the process described earlier in this chapter and arrived at Table 12.4.

Table 12.4 Feelings described in narratives of first day of training

Feeling	Anna	Claire	Colin	Gavin	Jack	Jane	Kevin	Tom
Excitement	x		x			x	x	x
Anxiety/ nervousness		x	x		x	x	x	x
Apprehension						x		
The unknown						x		
Determination						x		x
Conscious of age		x			x		x	
Overwhelmed			x					
Doubting self			x					
Terror				x	x			
Like an imposter				x				
Like a fraud				x				
Odd				x				
Daunted								X
Intimidated								X
Proud								x

A quick look at this table confirms that anxiety/nervousness was the most common feeling that respondents discussed in their narratives, having been reported by six of the eight respondents (and Gavin, although he did not say that he felt anxious/nervous, reported that he was terrified!) Excitement was the next most common emotion to be described. These themes could next have been examined for sub-themes, as demonstrated previously.

An alternative, or complementary, approach would be to look at the way the officers structured their accounts to convey the feelings that they experienced at the start of their training. It is difficult to give a step-by-step guide as to how you might conduct such an analysis. However, my advice is to use a theme as the starting point and then to analyse the structure of what is said by considering factors such as the order in which ideas are presented, the choice of words and phrases, any use of metaphors, etc. This requires particularly detailed reading of the relevant sections of the transcripts.

My structural analysis of officers' accounts of their first day of training concentrated on the theme of nervousness/anxiety and looked for the ways in which these emotions were conveyed. I found that there were two broad approaches. The first was to demonstrate how emotional the experience was by listing a large number of feelings. So, for example, Jane said that she was feeling: 'a mixture of excitement, anxiety, apprehension, the unknown, but determination …'.

Jack's list was even longer and made use of some vivid images:

Terrified. Like an imposter syndrome. Felt like a fraud. Didn't feel as though I suited the uniform. Didn't want to wear uniform. Felt like a male stripper. Like a child in a man's uniform. A total imposter. Very nervous. Odd.

The second method by which respondents sought to convey their feelings of nervousness/anxiety was to point out the amount that was resting on them completing their training successfully. Claire and Colin emphasised that getting to the start of their training was the culmination of a long process:

I think I probably felt a lot of pressure to do well because it had been such a long journey to get into the police, you felt quite a responsibility to achieve. (Claire)

So there was a sort of air excitement because I'd ultimately achieved what I wanted to achieve in getting there, but then same time, there was a nervousness and a doubt within myself … (Colin)

Kevin also discussed the importance of this moment, but he looked forward rather than back, to the impact that it would have on the rest of his life: 'You were signing up for something for the rest of your life and you knew that, so it was a big step'.

Tom similarly looked forward, but focused on the consequences of the failure to pass the training: '… I can't fail, I can't leave, so I was really quite anxious about it … I've got to have super high standards …'.

So, after noting that nervousness/anxiety was the most frequently occurring feeling described in relation to starting training, my structural narrative analysis suggested that there were two main techniques for conveying this:

1 Emphasising the highly emotional nature of the moment by giving a substantial list of the feelings that were experienced.

2 Giving reasons for the nervousness/anxiety based on the importance of the moment – either because of the length of time that a respondent had been looking forward to starting training or because of the impact that succeeding or failing would have on the remainder of their life.

Discourse Analysis

Discourse analysis differs from conversation analysis, which is a study of the methods by which individuals achieve social practices such as greetings and giving directions (Greco, 2006: 42). While conversation analysis is concerned only with 'naturally' occurring every-day conversations, discourse analysis can be applied to a wider range of forms of the written and spoken word, including research interviews and official documents (Bryman, 2008: 499). Discourse analysis focuses particularly on the words and phrases that people choose to use and the role that these choices make in creating an image or view of the matter that is being discussed. So, it has something in common with structural narrative analysis.

There is little written about the practicalities of conducting discourse analysis (Muncie, 2006: 75). My suggested process is similar to the one that I demonstrated for structural narrative analysis and involves the following steps:

1 Read the transcripts.
2 Identify themes in the data.
3 Identify the language that is used to construct each theme.
4 Identify commonalities in the use of language in relation to each theme.

I used this process in relation to the responses to a question that I asked the police officers about the most difficult aspect of their job. A theme that I identified as occurring in seven of the eight interviews was that the police were over-burdened by tasks that should not be their responsibility, either because the tasks were unnecessary or because they would have been more appropriately performed by another agency. When considering the language that was used to discuss this theme, one common feature that I noted was the use of the word 'frustration' (or 'frustrating') by several respondents. Three examples are shown below:

> I think it's more frustrating when you're at court and the CPS [Crown Prosecution Service] prosecutor will come to you and tell you 'So, we've decided not to prosecute the case', then they'll tell you to go and tell the victim. Wait a minute,

you're telling me this here so why don't you come with me, and you tell the victim because when she says 'Why?' I can just say 'Because the CPS said'. You can tell them the reasons why legally. (Colin)

I know mental health is a massive part of our job now, but it's just so frustrating that we've spent hours and hours of our time, for example, sitting with mental health patients at A&E who are saying they're going to kill themselves, you know? For me, that's just so frustrating. Yes, absolutely, we should be involved, we should be involved in finding them and getting them to a place of safety and supporting them as much as we can alongside partners, but the most frustrating thing for me is that there's just an expectation that the police will be there for everything. (Claire)

Mental health is a real shame, because it's never going to go away, and we still carry the can for – and it's nobody's fault – for the lack of funding in mental health services. We'll always be involved. We have to be involved, and it's a shame, because we could make more of a difference if we could focus on vulnerability and reducing crime. We can turn up if they have a knife at their throat and disarm them, but then we need to hand it over to a professional. But we don't because there's no one to hand it over to … I'm not saying we walk away, this person needs help, but we could be out there doing what we're supposed to do, which would be to patrol the streets to prevent crime. But that doesn't happen, unfortunately; we end up sitting with a person who needs help, and we can't give them the help, so everyone gets frustrated. (Jack)

One level of analysis could simply identify the types of task that respondents were 'frustrated' about having to spend their time or energies on: explaining the reason for non-prosecution to a victim of crime (Colin), waiting with someone in the accident and emergency department (Claire) and giving longer-term help beyond the immediate crisis (Jack). However, I undertook a more thorough discourse analysis by considering why the word 'frustrating' (or 'frustration') was used rather than 'disappointing' or 'annoying'. My subjective interpretation was that 'frustration' implied not just a negative feeling about being given a task inappropriately, but a desire to be using time, energy, skills and knowledge in a more productive manner. There were several other elements from the quotations above that supported this interpretation:

- Colin's use of the word 'legally' at the end of his quotation emphasised that a member of CPS staff would have more appropriate skills and knowledge than him for the task.
- Claire and Jack both emphasised that the police should have a role in relation to mental health.

- Claire and Jack also discussed the tasks that would be appropriate for police officers to undertake in relation to someone with mental health problems: in Claire's case, finding such a person and taking them to a place of safety; in Jack's case, disarming somebody who presented a threat to themselves and others.
- Jack's use of a very graphic description – 'if they have a knife at their throat' – illustrated particularly vividly the situations for which the police were uniquely equipped.

So, the conclusion to my discourse analysis was that police officers chose the word 'frustration' (or frustrating) to avoid sounding as though they were not interested in victims of crime or people with mental health problems. Instead, the word was chosen to create a picture of officers being unable to spend their time and energy on the tasks that they were best equipped for.

The above discussion illustrates that discourse analysis, even more than other forms of qualitative data analysis, involves subjective interpretation on the part of the researcher. While I made every effort to check that my interpretation of the use of 'frustration' (or 'frustrating') was consistent with other aspects of the respondents' comments, it is still possible that another interpretation was the correct one. When using discourse analysis, it is particularly important to include checks on the validity of your analysis (see section on 'Checking the Accuracy of Findings' below).

Textbox 12.6

What is the mistake? First attempt at qualitative analysis

Try to identify the mistake(s) that a researcher has made here and then have a look at Appendix 1 to see whether your view is the same as mine.

A student is delighted to have conducted eight semi-structured interviews with members of her local Neighbourhood Watch group and has transcribed them from the audio files. She looks at all the advice she has been provided with about qualitative data analysis and decides to follow it carefully. So, she applies codes to all the transcripts and puts these codes into NVivo. Next, she writes a summary of all the transcripts and begins to make comparisons between them using the constant comparative method.

These processes leave her a little confused as to what is going on with her data, but she moves on to the next stages of the analysis. She looks for the main themes that occur in the data, examines narratives of incidents where respondents had called out the police and considers the language that respondents used to discuss their role within the Neighbourhood Watch group.

Analysing Focus Group Data

So far, this chapter has focused on the analysis of qualitative interview transcripts. There are extra challenges, but also extra opportunities, involved in analysing focus group data. Where research involves data collection from more than one focus group, there is the opportunity to undertake an extended thematic analysis, looking for similarities and differences between the groups. However, it is also possible to undertake a thematic, narrative or discourse analysis of the data collected from a single group.

Some of the methods suggested for the analysis of focus group data are very similar to those suggested for interviews: Barbour (2007: 117–119) discusses the use of codes and Onwuegbuzie et al. (2009: 6–7) suggest the use of the constant comparative method where there is more than one group. However, Krueger (1998: 20) advocates an approach that acknowledges, and takes advantage of, the distinctive features of focus group data: 'participants influence each other, opinions change, and new insights emerge'.

At a practical level, the first, distinctive step to take when analysing focus group data is often to create a table demonstrating who said what and to create codes for each contribution. To illustrate how this might work, Table 12.5 takes a section of the transcript from an online focus group, which I referred to in Chapter 9. Here the respondents were discussing anti-social behaviour (ASB) on the Metro – the light railway system of Tyne and Wear.

Table 12.5 Initial analysis of focus group data

Contributor	Comment	Codes
Leon	As a Metro user myself, I have noticed ASB particularly where there are groups of young people. I would however say that this is possibly the kind of behaviour I would have noticed when I was younger but in bus stops etc.	ASBGYP SEG
Naomi	Is it not kids being kids?	KBK
Trevor	Yes, good point Leon. It is always when they are in groups. Never alone (unless they are under the influence of something).	ASBGYP IODA
Evelyn	Although, saying that I did get verbals off a young man who was off his face and being stupidly loud. I asked him to quieten down and got the most awful mouthful.	ASBYPA IODA CYP
Leon	True Trevor, but it's kind of a rite of passage, an age thing – as Naomi says 'kids being kids' however when I was younger ASB wasn't the title we'd have given it. You're probably rare in that case Evelyn as most people wouldn't have confronted it.	KBK SEG CYP

Explanation of codes:

ASBGYP: anti-social behaviour in groups of young people

ASBYPA: anti-social behaviour by a young person who was alone

CYP: confronting young people

IODA: influence of drugs/alcohol

KBK: kids being kids

SEG: similar to earlier generations

It should be noted that giving the full statement made by each respondent in the middle column was only possible because this was a typed focus group, meaning that contributions were short. When using a table such as this for a face-to-face focus group – where contributions tend to be longer – it is likely that the middle column will need to summarise contributions to keep the size manageable. Another point to note is that this section of the transcript highlights one of the features of typed, online focus groups – participants are not always responding to the last comment that was made.

A table such as this can facilitate a simple thematic analysis, identifying the most frequently occurring issues and demonstrating similarities and differences between respondents. So, with the help of the table and the codes, the findings that I reached from this section were:

- Two respondents (Leon and Trevor) noted that the anti-social behaviour usually occurred when young people were in groups. Evelyn did not disagree but recalled one incident when a young person had behaved anti-socially on their own.
- Two respondents (Trevor and Evelyn) suggested that the anti-social behaviour usually occurred when the young people were intoxicated.
- Two respondents appeared willing to offer mitigation for the young people because of their age: Naomi suggested that it was 'kids being kids'; Leon agreed and also reported that there had been similar behaviour in his youth.
- Evelyn discussed confronting a young person who was behaving anti-socially, but Leon suggested it was rare for anyone to do this.

As an aside, it is important to note here that one difficulty with focus group analysis is that a consensus can sometimes be assumed when this is not the case. In the above exchanges, the two people who spoke about the youthfulness of those involved in the anti-social behaviour suggested that this offered some sort of mitigation. It might be assumed that there was a consensus in the group that this was the case. However, later in the discussion, Trevor indicated that he held a different opinion when he said: 'it's much more severe than "kids being kids". It's social deviance, creating fear of victimisation amongst commuters'. So, before assuming a consensus among a focus group, it is important that you establish just how many people have spoken in favour of a particular viewpoint.

If the whole transcript was used, it would be possible to extend this thematic analysis – or to use narrative or discourse analysis. However, as suggested by Krueger above, we will next consider how the analysis could take advantage of one of the distinctive characteristics of focus group data, namely that different group members sometimes express opposing points of view, in a way that would be inappropriate for an interviewer. By examining how a group member responds to their view being challenged, it is possible to learn more about the strength with which they hold their conviction. In one exchange, Trevor was challenged by a question from Leon about his view that anti-social behaviour was more than 'kids being kids':

> @Trevor – to what extent? What percentage is boisterous kids and what kind of percentage is actual ASB?

In response, Trevor made clear that his view was held very strongly by recounting a particularly distressing example of young people's behaviour:

> For example, the other night, a group of four girls (about 15 yrs old) were shouting racist abuse at an innocent man and playing music on their phone really loud. The guy got his phone out and filmed them. Their reply was 'F***ing delete that video, we are kids. If you don't we'll report you to the police'.

In addition to showing the strength of people's opinions, disagreements can also be extremely useful for telling us something about the nature of relationships between focus group members. We may look beyond the question of 'what', i.e. the subject matter of the discussion, and focus instead on the 'how', i.e. the way group members interact with each other (Morgan, 2010: 719). We saw above that Leon challenged Trevor's view about the seriousness of the anti-social behaviour by asking a question, which is a less direct method of disagreeing than simply putting an alternative point of view. If Leon was taking a more confrontational approach, he might have said:

> I disagree Trevor, because I think that few of the examples of kids being boisterous could be regarded as anti-social behaviour.

The contribution of another group member also suggested something about the nature of the relationship between the respondents. Lester said:

> I wonder if the problem is that the types of strategy that might once have
> stopped this behaviour aren't there, e.g. no/very few guards/ticket collectors.

Lester here presented an alternative view to Trevor's, i.e. that the difficulties were not due (or not entirely due) to the young people's tendency to criminality, but could be blamed in part on structural factors, i.e. a lack of staff on the Metro. My interpretation of his use of the phrase 'I wonder' was that Lester was seeking to avoid confrontation by presenting this as a possible point of view rather than stating clearly that this was what he believed. So the analysis of the interactions between group members suggested that there was a wish to avoid confrontation and to explore alternative points of view in a constructive manner.

You may feel that there is limited usefulness to exploring the nature of relationships between group members and that opinions on the reasons for anti-social behaviour among young people is a more important topic to study. You may also feel (quite reasonably) that, although the unique features of focus groups provide opportunities for distinctive forms of analysis, a new researcher should limit themselves to simpler approaches such as thematic analysis. However, it is useful to be aware of the extra opportunities that focus group data presents, particularly when examining areas of disagreement between respondents.

Checking the Accuracy of Findings

As was discussed in Chapter 5, validity must be ensured at every stage of your research project. However, it is particularly important to check the validity of the findings produced by qualitative data analysis, given the subjective nature of this part of the research process. There is no standard approach to take but, as Steinke (2004: 185) notes, to decide that the quality of qualitative research cannot be assessed would mean that such research was conducted in a random and arbitrary fashion.

Suggestions for measures that you could take to ensure the validity of your analysis include:

1   Reading the findings and then reading back through the transcripts. This is a good and simple method of checking that the story you are telling through your findings accurately reflects what was said by the respondents. Can the patterns that you believe you have found be seen when you look back at the original data? If not, you will need to re-consider your analysis or parts of it.
2   A further step is to check whether the respondents are satisfied with the findings, as recommended by Miles and Huberman (1994: 275–277) and Steinke (2004: 185).

There are difficulties associated with this step – for example, respondents may disagree with each other about the accuracy of the analysis – but it can provide an indication of whether you have unintentionally misrepresented the views that were expressed.

3   Silverman (2006: 47) argues that the validity of conclusions drawn by qualitative researchers are sometimes doubted when they have made no attempt to deal with findings that do not fit the patterns that they believe they have identified. Similarly, Miles and Huberman (1994: 271–275) suggest that the researcher should actively look for findings that do not fit with their chosen explanation and consider whether rival explanations may in fact be more accurate. It is useful to consider a hypothetical situation: if someone was seeking to discredit your findings and suggest alternative interpretations of the data, how much evidence would there be that their interpretations were correct and yours were wrong?

4   As was noted in Chapter 2, triangulation means checking the findings against the results produced by another method (Bryman, 2008: 379). So, at the simplest level, if your main data collection was through semi-structured interviews, you could then conduct a focus group or distribute some questionnaires to a similar group of respondents. If this alternative method of data collection yielded similar results, you would be much more confident that your findings were accurate. The time and resources available for a research study often make triangulation difficult or impossible, but this should be acknowledged in the methodology section of your output as a factor that could influence the validity of the findings.

5   You could ask a friend or colleague who is familiar with the subject matter of the research to read your transcripts and your findings, then to comment on whether the findings are justified. This may raise issues about confidentiality and certainly requires a very supportive friend or colleague. However, it can also be an extremely valuable measure: justifying findings to someone else can act as a very effective safeguard against any bias that you may have unintentionally introduced.

6   Alternatively (or additionally), you could find someone who does not know much about the subject, then tell them about the data and the findings, to get a detached view as to how well the two fit together. Again, another person's view – even that of someone who is not familiar with the subject area – can provide protection against bias.

Should any of these measures suggest that your findings are not entirely accurate, it will be necessary to re-examine your analysis, which may well be painful and frustrating. However, this is infinitely better than producing findings that do not accurately represent your data.

Key points for your own research

- Be aware that there is no 'correct' way to conduct qualitative data analysis; rather, choose an approach (or approaches) that helps you to best make sense of your data.
- Ensure that there is a logical reason for every decision you take, which could be used to defend your approach if you were questioned on it.
- Try out different tools such as coding and using CAQDAS to see whether they help with your analysis – but have no fears about abandoning them if they do not.
- Consider carefully what you are trying to achieve in deciding the form of analysis that you should undertake. If you are interested in establishing commonly held views or beliefs, thematic analysis is likely to be most appropriate. Where your interest is in your respondents' accounts of events, narrative analysis will probably be the best option to choose. A focus on choices of language, and how they seek to persuade the listener to accept a particular view, points you towards discourse analysis.
- However, be aware that the different approaches to analysis overlap and that it may be valid to use more than one when analysing the same dataset.
- When using focus group data, decide whether you are going to treat this data in a similar manner to interviews or to take advantage of some of the extra opportunities that are provided by the interactions between the respondents.
- Check the validity of your findings carefully, using as many techniques as you realistically can.

Key points when reading other people's research

- Any good piece of qualitative research should include at least an outline of how the data was analysed. If this is not provided, you should give less weight to the findings.
- Give particularly high value to any piece of research that discusses not only the method of data analysis, but also the checks on validity that have been made.
- The method of analysis should be appropriate when bearing in mind the aims of the research and the data collected: for example, if there are a very small number of cases (four or less), it is difficult to establish themes.
- The discussion of the data should be consistent with the method of analysis that the author claims to be using: for example, if they say they are using discourse analysis, the discussion of the data should focus on the use of language.
- When reading about focus group data that is published in books or academic journals, it is reasonable to expect that there will be some discussion of the interactions between respondents.

─Further reading─

For a more detailed discussion of the process of qualitative data analysis, I would (of course!) recommend my own book. Like this chapter, it focuses on practical steps that can be taken by the new qualitative researcher who is not certain how to go about analysing their data:

Harding, J. (2019) *Qualitative Data Analysis from Start to Finish*, 2nd edn. London: Sage (1st edn 2013).

There are numerous examples of research that involves thematic analysis and that demonstrates how this type of analysis can contribute to our understanding of criminological issues. For example, the following article includes a thematic analysis of interviews with trial prosecutors in Australia, examining their views as to how interviews with child witnesses in child sex abuse cases could be improved:

Burrows, K. S. and Powell, M. (2014) 'Prosecutors' recommendations for improving child witness statements about sexual abuse', *Policing and Society*, 24(2): 189–207.

For an example of a narrative analysis that makes use of focus group data, see:

Jägervi, L. (2017) 'Narratives of being a helper: the presentation of supporters and victims in Victim Support Sweden', *Victims and Offenders*, 12(5): 800–819.

For a piece of research that used discourse analysis to understand better how police officers perceive their job, I recommend:

Hirtenfelder, C. (2016) 'Masking over ambiguity: suburban Johannesburg police reservists and the uniform fetish', *Policing and Society*, 26(6): 659–679.

13

WRITING ABOUT RESEARCH

What you will learn in this chapter

By the end of this chapter, you will:

- Be able to write a strong research proposal under appropriate headings
- Be able to write an excellent final output for your research, in the form of a dissertation or report
- Know how to write a literature review that covers the most relevant areas of the most relevant sources, so setting the scene for your own research
- Be able to produce a methodology section that identifies the reasons for taking key decisions and the limitations of the approach taken
- Be confident about producing a quantitative findings section in which results are presented in whatever way is most helpful to the reader – whether through narrative, table or chart
- Be able to write a qualitative findings section where there is an appropriate mix of discussion of broad trends and individual cases, supported by quotations
- Understand the critical importance of the conclusion for demonstrating how your work fits together as a cohesive whole

Introduction

This chapter will consider two formats for writing about your research. The first is a research proposal, which is written before the study begins and is usually required for some form of approval – typically approval to conduct the research that you plan for your dissertation. The second is the final output: this could be your dissertation, but the advice is also relevant for other forms of output such as research reports. There are several differences between the proposal and the final output:

1   The proposal is likely to be considerably shorter, so will discuss the literature in less detail.
2   The proposal will not include research findings or a conclusion – clearly there is no way of knowing what these will be until the research is conducted.
3   The proposal will discuss the research in the future sense (this is what will be done) while the final output will discuss it in the past tense (this is what has been done).
4   The final output is likely to show that the expectations of the research proposal have not been fulfilled in every area: this is an almost inevitable feature of any piece of research, as has been discussed in earlier chapters.

Despite these differences, there are similar principles involved in writing a good research proposal and writing a good piece of final output, as will be shown below.

Writing a Research Proposal

Requirements for a research proposal vary from situation to situation and university to university, so it is crucial to read these requirements carefully before beginning to write. The nature of the proposal will be determined partly by the type of research that you intend to undertake: it is easier to be specific about a deductive research study than an inductive one. However, there are some key questions, listed below, against which a research proposal is likely to be evaluated in any institution and for any type of research:

- Is there a justification provided from the research literature for choosing either a deductive or an inductive approach? If the approach is deductive, have one or more clear and specific research questions been developed for the enquiry? Is it realistic to expect that this question could be answered by a piece of research within the constraints of time, access and other factors that are faced by the researcher? Alternatively, if a more inductive approach is to be taken, have the reasons for such an approach been clearly identified?
- Literature summary: Does the researcher have a grasp of the main sources of literature on the topic and the key issues that these sources raise? Does the research question clearly emerge from a study of the literature? If a more inductive approach is to be taken, is there an awareness of the types of theoretical question which may later be intertwined with the data analysis?

- Choice of methodology: Have the merits of quantitative, qualitative, mixed methods and critical methodologies been considered? Has the choice between these approaches been based not only on practical considerations but also underlying principles?

- Research design: Is the design appropriate to the research question that has been posed or the issue that has been identified for exploration? Has the researcher given thought to a range of potential designs, for example made an appropriate decision as to whether to use a cross-sectional or longitudinal approach?

- Data collection and analysis: Is there a clear statement of the data that will be used and, where appropriate, how it will be collected? Are reasons given for these choices? Has the researcher linked their approach to broader principles underlying inductive and deductive – and quantitative and qualitative – methodologies?

- Sampling: Has consideration been given to collecting data from the entire population? If this is not possible, is there a clear justification for the manner in which the sample will be chosen?

- Ethical issues: Is the researcher aware of these issues, not just in general terms but also as they apply to their own particular project? For example, have they considered the possible implications of taking part in the research for the potential respondents?

- Practical considerations: Has the researcher considered difficulties that may arise during the research and made contingency plans for these difficulties arising? For example, and perhaps most obviously, is there a plan to deal with a low response rate or a slow response rate?

My example of a fictitious research proposal is shown in Textbox 13.1. The author is an undergraduate student in a city where some students are employed part time as security guards in a local shopping centre. The word count for this proposal is a small one, so some of the above points can only be covered briefly.

Textbox 13.1

Good practice example of a research proposal

The dissertation will address the question: 'Do students employed as security guards in the CityHub shopping centre perceive themselves to be effective in reducing crime?'
    Rowe (2014: 219) notes that increasing concern over crime and disorder has led to the private sector becoming more involved in traditional policing tasks – part of a

(Continued)

process of pluralisation of policing. There has been limited research undertaken on the role of the private sector in providing security guards. Rowland and Coupe (2014) found that security guards in shopping centres were less easily identifiable to the public, and provided less reassurance, than police officers or PCSOs. However, one study from Finland (Kajalo and Lindblom, 2010) showed that shopping centre managers felt that security patrols were the most effective formal surveillance method in their centres.

As the research seeks to address a specific research question, it will be deductive in nature. The research will take a qualitative approach. This is partly because of the limited number of potential respondents that are available but also because the research is concerned to understand the perceptions of security officers – understanding the perspective of others is a central characteristic of qualitative methodology (Bryman, 2016: 375). Time constraints determine that the research will be cross-sectional, with data collected at one point in time, although some respondents will be able to reflect on being security guards for a substantial period of time.

Data will be collected from a convenience sample of students known to me who have worked as security guards in the CityHub shopping centre. Taking a convenience sample naturally limits the extent to which the results can be generalised but avoids the need to go through gatekeepers. Data will be collected through interviews, as the aim is to understand individual perceptions rather than collective understandings. The interviews will be semi-structured to enable respondents to talk about the issues that are of importance to them, while also having a common core of questions. This will facilitate thematic data analysis, where similarities and differences will be explored in areas such as the nature of the security guards' interactions with the public, any specific comments from the public about their role, any incidents where they have encountered crime or anti-social behaviour, etc.

The research will adhere to the British Society of Criminology's statement of ethics; an ethics form has been submitted to the university. One particular ethical concern is that, as the respondents are people known to me, they may feel under pressure to take part in the research. I will tackle this concern by emphasising the voluntary nature of the research and insisting that potential respondents take some time to think before confirming whether they wish to take part. I will ask all respondents to disregard any previous conversations that we may have had about their work and to speak to me as though I were a stranger.

Linked to this ethical question, the most likely practical difficulty is that few of the security guards that I know will be willing to take part in the research. If it looks as though my original approach will not provide enough respondents, I will switch to a snowball sampling technique, asking those who take part to approach any of their student friends who have also been security guards in the shopping centre. This possibility is covered on my ethics form.

References

Bryman, A. (2016) *Social Research, Methods*, 5th edn. Oxford: Oxford University Press (1st edn 2001).

Kajalo, S. and Lindblom, A. (2010) 'The perceived effectiveness of surveillance in reducing crime at shopping centers in Finland', *Property Management*, 28(1): 47–59.

Rowe, M. (2014) *Introduction to Policing*, 2nd edn. London: Sage (1st edn 2008).

Rowland, R. and Coupe, T. (2014) 'Patrol officers and public reassurance: a comparative evaluation of police officers, PCSOs, ACSOs and private security guards', *Policing and Society*, 24(3): 265–284.

Types of Research Output

Whatever the form of output at the end of your research (dissertation, research report, etc.), it is likely to include the following:

1   Discussion of the existing literature on similar subjects to your research;
2   A section which is usually called 'Methodology', although it covers both methodology and methods – see Chapter 2 for a discussion of this distinction;
3   Discussion of the research findings (sometimes referred to as the results);
4   A conclusion showing how the existing literature contributes to understanding the findings and vice versa.

The space devoted to each of these sections will vary considerably between different forms of output. Some of the most frequently used forms are:

• *Research reports for the workplace, professional bodies, pressure groups or other organisations.* The emphasis is usually on the research findings so the existing literature tends to be referred to only briefly, with a similarly short methodology section and the majority of the space devoted to discussion of the data. The conclusion concentrates on the implications of the findings for policy and/or practice, so is likely to include recommendations.

• *Undergraduate dissertations.* The literature is likely to form the majority of the content of the dissertation and will usually be divided into two or three chapters. The methodology and findings sections can either be a chapter each or combined into one chapter. The conclusion demonstrates the implications of the findings for the issues discussed in the literature chapters.

- *Master's dissertations*. These are likely to include more substantial discussions of both the existing literature and the research findings. The methodology usually forms a separate chapter and the findings may be divided into two chapters.
- *Doctoral theses*. The research findings are likely to be the major part of the output and will probably be divided into several chapters. The literature search will also be much more substantial than in undergraduate or Master's dissertations and should cover a very wide range of sources. The methodology section is particularly important to a thesis, as methodology and methods are likely to be key areas of assessment of the work. The conclusion must not only tie together the literature and research findings, but also include a substantial reflection on the impact of the chosen methodology and demonstrate how the thesis makes an original contribution to knowledge.

Your Final Output: The Literature Review

One method of reviewing literature is a narrowly focused systematic review or meta-analysis. This approach is widely used in fields such as health, but in recent years has become more common in social sciences research, particularly research that seeks to influence policy. This type of review involves bringing together all the previous studies in an area of interest, including those that have contradictory results. The researcher reaches a judgement about the state of knowledge in relation to the chosen topic (Wakefield, 2018: 75).

However, it is more common in the social sciences to conduct a 'traditional' or 'narrative' review. This involves the researcher bringing together a wide range of literature – which is relevant to their own study for a range of reasons – and arranging it thematically, although more rarely there may be a chronological approach (Wakefield, 2018: 73). A narrative review will typically include the following elements:

1 A discussion of the key theories that are relevant to the chosen topic;
2 Some historical context to the chosen topic;
3 Where appropriate, key policy concerns;
4 Previous research into the chosen topic and related topics.

Let us take the hypothetical example of a student who decided to conduct research into murder convictions that have been overturned in the UK in the last 10 years. For them, the four elements would be likely to include the following material:

1 The theory section would contrast two types of perspectives – those that see the law as treating everyone equally and those that are critical, arguing that the law and legal processes exist to protect the interests of people with power.

2   The historical context would involve discussion of some of the most noteworthy murder convictions that have been overturned prior to the past 10 years. It would examine the tendency for victims of miscarriages of justice to be from disadvantaged groups, for example minority ethnic groups, Irish Republicans or female victims of domestic violence.

3   The policy section would discuss the introduction of the Criminal Cases Review Commission and debates that have arisen over its role and funding.

4   The previous research section would look at books and journal articles that have been written about miscarriages of justice (e.g. Poysner et al., 2018). It would also consider policy-focused documents such as the Criminal Cases Review Commission's annual reports and reports of the All Party Parliamentary Group on Miscarriages of Justice.

Writing a good literature review is clearly dependent on finding the most appropriate sources, but it also requires skills in the selection, putting together and presentation of the material that is found. Your aim should be to demonstrate how your findings contribute to what is already known about the topic. Some practical advice on writing about literature follows.

The Beginning of the Literature Search Should Demonstrate the Importance of Your Own Findings

You should quickly establish why your own research is important and how it will add to what is already known about your chosen topic. Research in Criminology can be important because it provides greater understanding of a wide range of topics: the nature of crime, the causes of crime, public attitudes to crime or the criminal justice system, the characteristics of offenders, the experiences of victims, etc. Alternatively, or additionally, research may seek to establish how the world might become a better place: how some types of crime could be reduced, the public made more aware of the true nature of crime, police/community relations improved, offenders more effectively rehabilitated, etc.

It is important to note that undergraduate students do not need to demonstrate that their research will make a large contribution to knowledge. It may be that your study is similar to one or more that have been conducted previously, so it can either add support to, or question, the findings from the previous research. Alternatively, you may take a subject that has been examined at a national or an international level and provide a local perspective. For example, opinion polls in the UK have consistently suggested that a majority of the public support the restoration of the death penalty for certain crimes, but is this view reproduced among a group of social science undergraduates at your university?

You Should Be Selective

When you are writing about an area where there is substantial previous literature, you will have to be selective about which material to include in your literature review. The selection should be driven by the need to demonstrate the importance of your own findings.

Of course, selecting the most relevant previous work for discussion will, by definition, mean deciding not to discuss other published material or to make only a passing reference to it. Berg (2009: 388–389) notes the danger of failing to refer to classic works or recent studies that are of relevance to your subject. However, Rudestam and Newton (2007: 65) argue that, no matter how important an author or their research, it must only be discussed in proportion to its relevance to the topic under study. It is crucial that your literature search section concentrates on the most relevant existing work and does not become involved in a detailed discussion of areas that are not central to your own topic.

Where you want to indicate that you are aware of literature without discussing it in any detail, there is an academic skill to referring to sources only briefly. So, for example, Cox et al. (2018: 189) demonstrate that they are aware of studies that have argued that those who are victims of crime are also likely to be offenders, without going into detail about these studies:

> The idea that 'victims are conceptualized as individuals who have no experience of crime as offenders' (as first critiqued by Newburn and Stanko, 1994: 153) has been overturned by recent research on modern victimisation (see, e.g., Fagan et al., 1987; Lauritsen et al., 1991; Singer, 1981).

You Should Discuss Literature Thematically Rather Than Source by Source

An essential characteristic of a good literature search is that it is organised in the form of an argument rather than simply describing published work on your topic (Silverman, 2006: 341). It is relatively easy to write about literature source by source and there are a limited number of situations where this is appropriate. However, more commonly, the need to write thematically means that a source may be referred to on several occasions in order to illustrate different parts of an argument. Writing in this manner is challenging – even experienced researchers are likely to have to produce several drafts of a literature search to ensure that they are presenting a clear argument and citing sources in the most appropriate places.

Ray et al. (2004) provide an example of a thematic literature search in which some previous work is cited several times in order to develop an argument. Before presenting the findings of their own study of the role that shame plays in motivating racist violence, their literature search cites a previous study (Retzinger, 1991) on several occasions as the argument develops:

- They first refer to Retzinger (1991) to introduce shame as the theoretical framework they will use to analyse some of their data (Ray et al., 2004: 350).
- They later use Retzinger's work to develop this theoretical framework by citing her argument that shame can make people feel helpless and passive (Ray et al., 2004: 354).
- Later still, they use the work of Retzinger and that of another academic to show how shame can influence the moral justification that some racist offenders offer for their crimes (Ray et al., 2004: 354).

Your Final Output: The Methodology Section

As was noted in the introduction to this chapter, the methodology section will inevitably involve some degree of overlap with the research proposal and should cover all the areas/issues that were listed above as required for the proposal (except for the literature review). However, there are important differences from the proposal in that the methodology section of the final output will be more detailed, will be written in the past tense and will discuss the reality of what happened in the research process (and how the plans that were made at the start had to be modified). On this last point, it is important to note that research hardly ever sticks to the original plan and almost always needs to be modified in the light of difficulties along the way. This is not something that you should be ashamed of or seek to gloss over. In fact, a good methodology section will be the opposite of most Instagram accounts: instead of trying to present the best possible view, it will not be afraid to discuss all the imperfections, how they came about and how you sought to deal with them. The person marking your work will be expecting to read about difficulties that you encountered along the way and what you did to try to overcome them.

For each stage of the research process, the methodology should include a description of the actions taken, identification of the most important decisions and the reasons for taking them, and an acknowledgement of the limitations of the methodology/methods used. This should all be written with reference to the literature on research methods, using textbooks such as this one (for example, to support your reasons for choosing a particular approach). It should be emphasised again that acknowledging the limitations of your own methodology is not a weakness, but a strength, because it demonstrates your awareness of methodological issues. I would be pleased to read in any dissertation comments such as:

- As the data was collected by a questionnaire consisting of mainly closed questions, it provided a broad overview of respondents' opinions, but limited detail as to why they held them.
- The sample consisted of a small group of students so the data is helpful for illustrating how this group understood the experience of victimisation but may have limited applicability to a wider population.
- The data was collected through focus groups so provided some excellent insights into collective and shared understandings. However, in both groups there were some participants who made very limited contributions – despite the best efforts of the facilitator to encourage them – so it is not certain that these individuals agreed with the views on which the more vocal members of the groups expressed a broad consensus.

The above examples are all concerned with data collection, but it is also important to give a full and honest account of the factors that have influenced data analysis. You should acknowledge the subjective decisions that will (inevitably and rightly) have affected this stage of the research, particularly when you are working with qualitative data.

Textbox 13.2

What is the mistake? Writing a methodology section

Try to identify the mistake(s) that a researcher has made here and then have a look at Appendix 1 to see whether your view is the same as mine.

An undergraduate student submits a dissertation that includes this methodology section:

Data was collected via an online questionnaire. This method was chosen because the anonymity that it provides may encourage respondents to give opinions that they feel embarrassed to give with an interviewer present, especially with regard to a controversial issue such as assisted dying. The opening page described the subject and nature of the questionnaire and asked potential respondents not to click to go further unless they were happy with this. Respondents were told they could stop completing the questionnaire at any point and could leave out any questions they preferred not to answer. Although questions were worded to minimise the chances of a respondent becoming distressed, some sources of help were identified at the end of the questionnaire for anyone who felt upset. A snowball sample was selected, with the researcher's friends being contacted initially but then being asked to pass the link to the questionnaire on to their friends and other contacts. The response rate to the questionnaire was 100%.

Your Final Output: The Findings Section

The manner in which you write about your findings will be substantially different according to whether your data is quantitative or qualitative (of course, a mixed methods study will include elements of both). However, there are some principles that are common, whatever the nature of your data:

1 Most obviously, the manner in which you report your findings should present your data in a fair and unbiased manner. It is clearly unacceptable to discuss only those findings that support a particular point of view and not those that contradict it.

2 You should write in a manner that reflects the strengths and limitations of your data, including only material that contributes to an understanding of the subject. I suggest below that qualitative findings should discuss a mix of broad trends, individual cases and quotations. However, despite your best efforts, it may be that there have been few comments made that could helpfully be quoted to illustrate a point, which will mean that the number of quotations is reduced. Similarly, if very few respondents have answered a question on a questionnaire, then there is little point in presenting a crosstable involving the answer to this question and another variable.

3 The findings section should be consistent with your methodology/methods. If you have (quite correctly) noted in the methodology section that you have collected a limited amount of data from a very specific group of people, it is important that you write about the findings in a manner that reflects these limitations. To take the example used earlier in this chapter, if you have interviewed six students known to you about their experience of working as security guards in a shopping centre, you should not write:

> The data demonstrated that shopping centre security guards are viewed by the public as ineffective and ill equipped for their job.

4 Much more appropriate would be:

> All the respondents expressed the opinion that the public regarded them as ineffective and ill equipped for their job. It is not clear how far, if at all, this perception was accurate and whether it reflected the respondents' obvious student status: all were aged under 25 and none spoke with a local accent.

Other types of statements that acknowledge the limitations of your methodology/findings and which will bring you credit for your awareness of these limitations include:

- There were only two respondents who classified their ethnic origin as anything other than 'White: UK'. As a result, this part of the analysis of the survey findings concentrates on gender differences rather than those based on ethnicity.

- As only one of the respondents had been a victim of online fraud, this section concentrates on the perception rather than the experience of this form of victimisation.
- As two of the focus group members had to leave early, this meant that it was impossible to establish whether there was a complete consensus with regard to the topics covered in the later stages of the discussion.

Quantitative Research

Presenting quantitative findings can feel like a hard slog and, on many occasions, there is simply no exciting way of discussing the responses to different questions and the relationships between different variables. The best you may be able to do is to provide a variety of forms of presentation. If you have ever read a report where all the data is provided as pie charts, you will know what a tedious experience this can be! However, even more important than variety is that the method of presenting each finding is appropriate to the nature of the data.

The different methods of analysing quantitative data in SPSS were discussed in Chapter 11. Sometimes SPSS tables can be copied and pasted into your output, with some brief commentary added. On other occasions, it may be more appropriate to present the data in an alternative form.

Presenting individual variables

You will typically begin the findings section by discussing individual variables. One way of doing this is to present a simple narrative, which tends to be most effective when there are few possible answers to a question, such as a yes/no option, for example:

> Of the 120 respondents, 44 (36.7%) said that they had seen fly tipping taking place, 73 (60.8%) that they had not and 3 (2.5%) did not answer the question.

There are two points to note here:

1 I have given the percentages to one decimal place which is as much as is normally needed, even though this sometimes results in the percentages adding up to slightly more or less than 100.
2 Chapter 11 discussed the difference between the percentage and the valid percentage. An alternative, and slightly more helpful, way of presenting the results using the valid percentage is:

Of the 117 respondents who answered the question, 44 (37.6%) said that they had seen fly tipping taking place and 73 (62.4%) that they had not.

Where there are larger numbers of answers to a question, a frequency table may be the most effective method of presentation. In the case of ordinal variables in particular, it is sometimes appropriate just to copy and paste these tables from SPSS. An example – taken from a survey discussed in Chapter 11 where I asked students about their feelings of safety and other matters – is presented in Table 13.1.

Table 13.1 SPSS frequency table for question about safety around home during hours of darkness

Feelings of safety around place lived during hours of darkness

		Frequency	Percent	Valid Percent	Cumulative Percent
Valid	Not at all safe	2	2.1	2.1	2.1
	Not very safe	16	16.7	16.7	18.8
	Quite safe	49	51.0	51.0	69.8
	Very safe	29	30.2	30.2	100.0
	Total	96	100.0	100.0	

(Reprint courtesy of International Business Machines Corporation, © International Business Machines Corporation)

The reason that this form of presentation is particularly helpful for ordinal variables is that it is with these types of variables that the cumulative percentage function is likely to be most helpful, enabling you to make statements such as:

'Only 18.8% of respondents said that they felt "not very safe" or "not at all safe" around the place that they lived during the hours of darkness'; or

'81.2% of respondents said that they felt "quite safe" or "very safe" around the place that they lived during the hours of darkness.'

However, directly transferring a frequency table from SPSS is less likely to be helpful in the case of a nominal variable, where we are used to seeing the most frequently given answer listed first and the least frequently given answer listed last. The SPSS table is unhelpful here because:

1   SPSS orders answers in a different way, with the answer that was given the value label 1 appearing first, followed by the answer that was given the value label 2, etc.
2   The cumulative frequency function is unlikely to be helpful where similar answers are not grouped together.

Table 13.2 provides an example of an SPSS frequency table which would be particularly inappropriate to simply copy and paste into a dissertation or research report. Again, it is taken from my student survey.

Table 13.2 Whether reported crime(s) of which victim (SPSS version)

Whether reported crime(s) of which victim				
	Frequency	Percent	Valid Percent	Cumulative Percent
Valid	19	19.8	42.2	42.2
Yes, reported all of the crimes where I was a victim	8	8.3	17.8	60.0
Reported some crimes and not others	4	4.2	8.9	68.9
No, reported none of the crimes where I was a victim	14	14.6	31.1	100.0
Total	45	46.9	100.0	
Missing not applicable	51	53.1		
Total	96	100.0		

(Reprint courtesy of International Business Machines Corporation, © International Business Machines Corporation)

This table suffers from both weaknesses listed above, i.e. the cumulative percentage column tells us very little that is useful and the most frequently given answer does not appear at the top of the table. It also highlights another difficulty that frequently occurs when reporting quantitative data – how to deal with those who give no answer at all (rather than choosing the 'don't know' or 'not applicable' option). You will see from the first row of the table that there were 19 respondents who did not answer this question. In this case, I was able to look at the rest of the data provided by these 19 respondents and saw that none of them had been victims of crime. So they could be added to those who had chosen the 'not applicable' option.

To further enhance the helpfulness of the frequency table, I removed the cumulative percent and the valid percent columns and instead added a new column with a manual calculation, which gave each answer as a percentage of those who had been a victim of crime (i.e. excluding those for whom the question was not applicable because they had not been victims). The re-writing provided a much clearer view as to what was happening, as is shown in Table 13.3.

Table 13.3   Whether reported crime(s) of which victim (word version)

Response	Frequency	Percentage of all respondents	Percentage of respondents who had been victims
No, reported none of them	14	14.6%	53.8%
Yes, reported all of them	8	8.3%	30.8%
Reported some crimes and not others	4	4.2%	15.4%
Not applicable – have not been a victim	70	72.9%	
Total	96	100%	100%

Charts are another option for presenting the results from individual variables – it is important to think about the different options and to choose the chart that shows what is going on with a variable most clearly. Pie charts are particularly effective if you wish to show that there is a dominant response to any question. For example, if I wished to emphasise the point that less than a quarter of the students I surveyed had downloaded the university's security app onto their mobile telephone, I could write this in the text and then illustrate the point by using a pie chart:

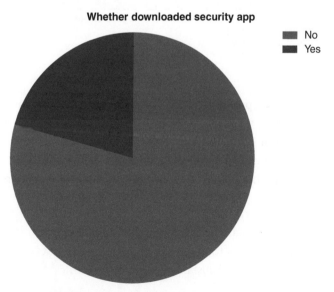

(Reprint courtesy of International Business Machines Corporation, © International Business Machines Corporation)

In contrast, a bar chart may be particularly helpful where there are a number of possible answers to a question and you want to give the reader a quick visual indication of the frequency with which these options were chosen. A question as to how students self-classified in relation to alcohol could be reported in the following manner:

When students were asked to classify themselves according to alcholol consumption, the most frequently chosen option was an occasional drinker. The second most popular classification was a binge drinker, narrowly ahead of a non-drinker, with regular drinker being the least frequently chosen option, as is shown by the bar chart below:

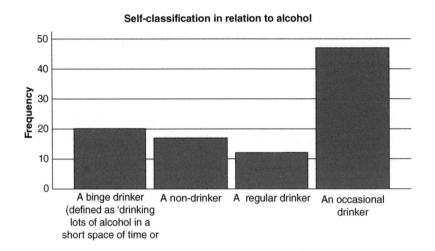

Self-classification in relation to alcohol

(This bar chart has been produced using the Frequencies command, as discussed in Chapter 11. More attractive versions of charts, without the title at both top and bottom, can be produced in SPSS or Word.)

When dealing with Scale variables, and using measures such as the Mean and the Median, there is often little option other than to describe the results in a narrative, for example:

Students were asked, in a typical week, how many crimes they heard about in the city through the news media. The mean figure was 1.7, but the median was 0, suggesting that most students took little interest in such reports but there were some who were hearing about substantial numbers of crimes.

Discussing relationships between variables

As was discussed in Chapter 11, the analysis of individual variables is usually followed by an examination of the relationships between variables. This order is often reflected in the way that students write about their findings, although it may well enhance your discussion if you feel confident to interweave the two elements.

Crosstables can often be copied across from SPSS directly and should be accompanied by a commentary pointing out what they demonstrate, for example:

Table 13.4

Whether downloaded security app * gender identity Crosstabulation						
			gender identity			
			Female	Male	Other	Total
Whether downloaded security app	No	Count	53	22	1	76
		% within gender identity	76.8%	84.6%	100.0%	79.2%
	Yes	Count	16	4	0	20
		% within gender identity	23.2%	15.4%	0.0%	20.8%
Total		Count	69	26	1	96
		% within gender identity	100.0%	100.0%	100.0%	100.0%

(Reprint courtesy of International Business Machines Corporation, © International Business Machines Corporation)

The crosstable shows that a higher percentage of women (23.2%) than men (15.4%) had downloaded the security app, although the figures were low for both. The one respondent who identified their gender as 'other' had not downloaded the app.

The above example illustrates a point that you should be cautious about when using crosstables. If anyone were to know which respondent had classified their gender as 'other', they would also know that this person did not have the security app downloaded to their mobile – a clear breach of confidentiality. In this case, I decided that this was not a risk because the invitation to complete the online questionnaire had gone out to such a large number of students, by such diverse means, that it was highly unlikely that anyone would be able to identify the one respondent whose data appeared in the 'other' column. However, this is an important factor to consider when collecting data from a smaller and more tightly defined group: if you are at a university where the large majority of students are White, and you ask 150 people on your course to complete a questionnaire, you may find that there is only one (easily identifiable) student who classifies their ethnic origin as 'Black: African'. In this case, crosstables with ethnicity in the columns would be inappropriate – a major challenge for presenting data.

Another challenge when using crosstables is knowing which to present, when there is only space in your output for a limited number. A balance must be struck between showing those that represent the most striking findings, usually involving the strongest relationships between variables, while making clear that many others were created that did not tell such a clear story. I tried to strike this balance when writing a section of my PhD where I compared young homeless people who were lone parents (all of them women) with other young homeless people who did not have dependent children. An extract from this section appears in Textbox 13.3:

Textbox 13.3

PhD extract comparing young homeless lone parents with other young homeless people

The idea that young lone parents are a particularly problematic or deviant group found no support within the data – indeed, there was evidence to suggest that they were less likely to have experienced some social problems than the remainder of the sample. They were less likely to have ever tried drugs, although the difference was not so noticeable when considering the women only. None of the lone parents were taking drugs at the time of the first interview. One finding that was unambiguous was that respondents with children were less likely to have been in trouble with the police. This finding is particularly well illustrated by considering the data for young women only:

Table 13.5

		Number of children living with you		Total
		None	One or more	
Been in trouble with the police	Yes	18 (30.5%)	0 (0%)	18
	No	41 (69.5%)	11 (91.7%)	52
	Not stated	0	1 (8.3%)	1
Total		59	12	71

When thinking about Scale variables, many of the methods of presentation (e.g. Scatterplots) are associated with more advanced statistics, so it is often most appropriate to use a simple narrative or to construct your own table. For example, in the study of student safety and other matters, I asked the students to mark out of 10 how influential several factors were in their decision to apply to Northumbria University. The resulting data could most effectively be presented as a table, with the factor with the highest mean score at the top and the one with the lowest mean score at the bottom, as is shown in Table 13.6.

Table 13.6   Possible Reasons for Choosing Northumbria University

Possible reason for choosing Northumbria	Mean mark out of 10
Liked the course I am studying	8.4
Had the grades or thought I could achieve them	7.0
Newcastle city centre location	6.7
Good reputation	6.7
Seemed friendly	6.6
Close to home	5.5
Open day good	4.7
Felt that there were people like me there	4.7
Parents or carers thought that I should go there	3.6
Recommendation of family member or friend	3.5

A possible further piece of analysis involving these marks out of 10 would be to look for gender differences using the Compare Means function. If I only wanted to do this for one of the factors, I might write up the results like this:

> Female respondents gave a higher mark out of 10 (6.9) for the importance of the city centre location as a reason for choosing Northumbria than male respondents (6.1), with the one respondent who classified their gender identity as 'other' giving a mark of 10.

However, if I wished to examine gender differences for every factor, I would add extra columns to Table 13.6, i.e. 'Mean mark out of 10 (males)', 'Mean mark out of 10 (females)' and 'Mean mark out of 10 (other)'.

Finally, correlations can only be reported in narrative form. It is important to say which correlation was used, the interpretation of either a positive or a negative correlation and the strength indicated by the value of the correlation, for example:

> A Spearman's rho correlation between a respondent's age and their feelings of safety around the place they lived during darkness gave a value of −2.1. The values given to the feelings of safety variable (1: very safe; 2: quite safe; 3: not very safe; 4: not at all safe) meant that lower values were associated with greater feelings of safety. So the negative correlation meant that older respondents tended to feel safer. However, the small correlation figure indicated that this was a weak relationship.

Qualitative Research

When considering research output for qualitative findings, it is important to remember that there is no 'correct' way of writing about them that is better than all others (Richards, 2009: 195). The findings section will usually incorporate a discussion of broad trends or themes, individual examples and quotations, but this can vary according to the nature of the data. The most important point is that the discussion conveys clearly and accurately to the reader what you found in the data.

When discussing broad trends or themes, there is a slightly frustrating tradition in qualitative research of rarely referring to numbers. Although analysis inevitably involves some counting – you need to know how many respondents discuss an issue in order to make a judgement as to whether it should be considered a theme – the numbers involved are rarely referred to in the research output. One example is provided by Nguyen and Le's (2021: 133) study of the perceptions of human trafficking among police officers and non-governmental organisations in Vietnam:

> The findings identify that a portion of police working in some of the mountainous provinces of Vietnam reported that some ethnic minorities become victims of sex trafficking since they are deceived when migrating to China searching for seasonal jobs ... Some interviewees considered this migration a habit or a custom of local citizens, especially ethnic minorities, to earn more money ... Only a small number of respondents indicated that this problem also happens in the mountainous districts of Nghe An ....

This quotation suggests approximate and varying quantities of respondents without giving specific numbers:

- 'A portion of police' suggests that a minority of police officers expressed this view.
- 'Some interviewees' also suggests a minority: I think that 'some' implies less than 'a portion', but others might disagree.
- 'Only a small number' clearly is less than 'a portion' or 'some'.

It is an important task to find your own terms to indicate approximate numbers and to decide where the boundaries between them lie. You may, for example, find yourself needing to decide at what figure 'few' respondents becomes 'some' respondents or 'several' respondents becomes 'many'.

Identifying trends within the data is important but, if qualitative researchers were only to do this, their findings would be like those of quantitative studies, but with fewer respondents. Instead, the interest of the qualitative researcher in the perspectives of individuals should be reflected in the research output. Broader trends can often be effectively illustrated by using individual examples and direct quotations.

The use of examples and quotations raises a tricky issue around the deployment of pseudonyms. This is something that I have often avoided when writing about interview-based research, instead describing people as 'respondents' or 'participants'. Where relevant, I have also included characteristics, for example: *a female respondent expressed concern over the potential for sexual assault on a darkened dance floor*; or *one of the younger respondents felt that they were looked at suspiciously by passers-by when they spoke with a group of friends outside the shops*.

Some of my colleagues feel that such an approach depersonalises people and puts a distance between the researcher and the respondents. They prefer to adopt pseudonyms, but such an approach should be used carefully. In the interviews with police officers discussed in Chapter 12 and later in this chapter, I asked all the officers what pseudonym they would like to be known as. This did not present any difficulty with potential identification as the ethnic origin of all was 'White: British', as was the case for most of their colleagues. However, if (for example) I had interviewed an Asian British officer who had requested the pseudonym Jawed this would have presented me with a difficulty: using this name could have made the officer easily identifiable, but using a name more often associated with White people (e.g. John) could have been both misleading and insulting. So, choosing pseudonyms that are culturally appropriate, while also protecting the identity of respondents, can be difficult.

Using individual examples

Individual examples can show how a theme is manifested in the case of one respondent. They are different from case studies, which are an approach to a whole research project, as was discussed in Chapter 5. The extent of information provided in any example can vary considerably: sometimes it can involve giving a brief account of all or part of a respondent's life; in other cases there can be a detailed description of their point of view. There are several reasons why research output might include detailed information about an individual or their perspective:

1   To illustrate or explain an element of the researcher's discussion of the findings. For example, Sandberg et al. (2021), in their study of mothering practices and identities among incarcerated women in Mexico, use an example to illustrate that the abuse that many had experienced as children and/or teenagers was linked to issues of family honour:

… one participant's (Ximena, aged 36) problems began when she ran away from home at the age of 14 and began using illegal drugs on the streets. The events that triggered her to run away from home was her exclusion from the family and the abuse that she was subjected to by her father after she was discovered kissing a boyfriend.

2   To emphasise an argument advanced by the researcher. Pells (2011: 599–600) supports her argument that a siege mentality exists in post-genocide Rwanda by using the case of Sylvie. Sylvie's one-year-old nephew died suddenly during the night and, while there was no evidence to corroborate the claim, she and her family believed that the baby had been poisoned – poisoning being thought to be the favoured method of murder in the village.

3   To present contrasting experiences or perspectives. An example is provided later in this chapter, in Textbox 13.4.

Using quotations

Most qualitative studies make use of quotations because they provide a direct connection between the reader and the research respondent (Morgan, 2010: 718). However, important decisions must be reached about where to include quotations and which ones to choose. This is something that many students find difficult; a common mistake is to write about findings using too many quotations that are held together loosely by a very brief commentary on the part of the writer. Quotations should be interspersed with your own discussion of the findings.

Boeije (2010: 201) suggests that a quotation should only be used once, even when it illustrates several points, and that a point should only ever be illustrated by one or two quotations. There is no set length for an effective quotation. You should use as few words as possible: sometimes a word or phrase is sufficient, but on other occasions a quite substantial section of text is needed to convey meaning effectively.

You should always be clear in your own mind why a quotation is being included in the discussion of your findings. There are several possible reasons, some of which are similar to reasons for discussing individual cases:

1   You may not be able to effectively re-phrase or summarise what was said. So, for example, Gadd et al. (2019: 1043) describe the account that one perpetrator gave of a relationship marked by domestic violence, including some of his own phrasing:

> Wayne, by contrast, only recalled one assault[,] explaining they 'didn't argue a lot' partly because his 'mind wasn't there'.

2   A point may need explaining. Goddard and Myers (2011: 560) describe the method by which a school for excluded young people in the USA used dispute resolution to overcome arguments. To explain what is meant by dispute resolution, an educator from the school is quoted:

We tell the students that you need to sit down and tell the person that committed the crime or did harm to the community what it is they did wrong and how you feel about it. We go through hard dialogue …

3   One or more quotations may illustrate particularly effectively a point that is being made. Martel et al. (2011: 243) discuss the programmes provided to Aboriginal offenders in Canadian prisons to encourage them to stop offending by reminding them of their cultural heritage. The hostility of Aboriginal staff to the involvement of non-Aboriginal people in delivering such programmes is illustrated with a quotation:

It's non Natives giving programmes on how to be a Native … showing us how to be a Native. How would they understand these concepts?

4   Contrasts between respondents may be effectively highlighted (see Textbox 13.4 below).

Good use of individual examples and quotations

To provide a further example of how individual cases and quotations might be used to illustrate an argument, we will return to the analysis of the qualitative interviews with police officers that was undertaken in Chapter 12. I showed there how the long-term ambition of Jane to become a police officer contrasted with the more pragmatic reasons that Kevin and Jack had for taking up this career. This proved to be the pattern among all the respondents, with most having pragmatic reasons for joining the police, compared to a minority having had a long-term ambition to be officers. Textbox 13.4 shows how this might be written into a findings section, using Jane and Kevin as contrasting individual examples and including quotations from both of them to illustrate the differences.

Textbox 13.4

Section from findings section about motivation to become a police officer

For most of the police officers interviewed, the job had not been a long-term ambition but something that they had chosen as an adult. This was often the result of another job or career path proving unsatisfactory and policing providing a more attractive alternative. As Kevin put it: 'My previous job was office-based and although it was fine, it was okay, I could tell at that point that it wasn't something I really wanted to do for the rest of my life …'.

He then saw that the police were recruiting, felt that he had the qualities that they were asking for, and decided that a job that offered excitement and the chance to work outside provided a better alternative to his current role.

(Continued)

In contrast, the minority for who policing was their first career choice had experienced this ambition from an early age. For example, Jane said:

> I think I was pretty sure I wanted to be one [a police officer] when I was probably still in primary school, probably about eight or nine years old, my mam spent a lot of time and effort trying to persuade me not to. So, I don't think I fully committed myself to it until I was probably about 14–16.

The jobs that she took prior to policing all had an element of customer service and were deliberately chosen to provide relevant experience for her policing application.

Bad use of individual examples and quotations

One danger of using quotations is that the researcher will simply choose those that best support their arguments (Silverman, 2007: 61) or reflect their initial expectations (Schmidt, 2004: 255). Another danger is that a respondent's views will be misrepresented through a quotation. Again, referring back to Chapter 12 (specifically the section on discourse analysis), Jack said of people with mental health problems:

> Mental health is a real shame, because it's never going to go away, and we still carry the can for – and it's nobody's fault – for the lack of funding in mental health services. We'll always be involved. We have to be involved, and it's a shame, because we could make more of a difference if we could focus on vulnerability and reducing crime. We can turn up if they have a knife at their throat and disarm them, but then we need to hand it over to a professional. But we don't because there's no one to hand it over to … I'm not saying we walk away, this person needs help, but we could be out there doing what we're supposed to do, which would be to patrol the streets to prevent crime. But that doesn't happen, unfortunately; we end up sitting with a person who needs help and we can't give them the help, so everyone gets frustrated.

It would be a misrepresentation of Jack's views to use him as an example and quote him in the following manner:

> Many of the police officers felt negatively about tasks that they were required to do that they felt were not appropriate to their role. For example, Jack spoke about sitting with a person with mental health problems when he could be 'doing what we're supposed to do, which would be to patrol the streets to prevent crime'.

By failing to acknowledge all that Jack said about the importance of people with mental health problems receiving the support that they need, writing in this way would wrongly imply that he regarded the needs of people with mental health problems as unimportant.

Presenting focus group data

While much of the advice given above can be applied to reporting focus group data, there is also some distinctive good practice that applies to this type of data. Here the creation of pseudonyms is essential to report interactions effectively and to demonstrate how the views of individuals develop during the discussion. If the cultural factors raised above mean that choosing names is problematic, an alternative is to describe people as Participant A, Participant B, etc.

It was suggested in Chapter 12 that care must be taken when assuming that there is a consensus between focus group members, and that this care should be reflected in reporting the findings. You should state how many people positively agree with a point of view when suggesting that it represented a common opinion.

Another key question is how to use quotations in a manner that captures the nature of interactions. Some authors writing about focus groups suggest that it is essential to quote full exchanges rather than individual responses. However, Morgan (2010: 719–721) argues that this approach is, in many cases, inefficient and that a quotation from a focus group can be either introduced or followed by a summary of other relevant contributions.

I applied Morgan's advice when writing about the online focus group that was discussed in Chapter 12, where my colleagues discussed anti-social behaviour by young people on the Tyne and Wear Metro. My report of the findings in relation to the section of the transcript is shown in Textbox 13.5.

Textbox 13.5

Section from a focus group findings section

Two respondents (Leon and Trevor) suggested that the problems with anti-social behaviour were most common when several young people were gathered together, with Trevor going so far as to say that 'It is always when they are in groups'. However, he then noted an exception that young people who were under the influence of drugs or alcohol could behave anti-socially when they were alone; Evelyn supported this view by

(Continued)

---

recalling the actions of a young individual 'who was off his face'. Naomi was prepared to offer the mitigation that the behaviour was often 'kids being kids' and Leon noted that young people had behaved similarly during his own adolescence. However, Trevor contested this view, arguing that: 'it's much more severe than "kids being kids". It's social deviance, creating fear of victimisation amongst commuters'.

He held to this view, even when asked by Leon how much of the behaviour in question should actually be defined as anti-social.

Evelyn discussed confronting a young person who was behaving anti-socially, but Leon suggested it was rare for anyone to do this.

If you have conducted one or more focus groups, your report of the findings may look a bit different to the one above for two reasons:

1   You may have conducted your group(s) face to face, in which case the contributions – and therefore the quotations – are likely to be longer.
2   You may have more members in your focus group(s), and the pattern of agreement/disagreement may be more complicated, meaning that the task of ensuring that all participants' views are represented in the findings section is a more complex one.

Citing Literature in the Findings Section

There are occasions when literature should be cited in the findings section of your research output if there is a very clear and specific link between a particular finding and previous published work. For example, Sheard (2011) undertook research into women's participation in the night-time economy, their consumption of alcohol and their fear of violence. When discussing her own findings about concerns over substances being added to drinks, she makes a brief reference to a previous study:

> … some women would consume their drink in one go or considerably faster than they would ordinarily have chosen to do rather than leaving their drink unattended … This issue is reported in Burgess et al. (2009) whereby a participant had heard from friends that it was recommended to drink 'as fast as possible' … (Sheard, 2011: 628)

However, more substantial links between the existing literature and the researcher's own study are usually made in the conclusion.

Your Final Output: The Conclusion

The section of the research output that students often find most difficult to write is the conclusion. It is usually the section that is written last, at a time when you may be tired and short of time. However, as it is also the last section of the output that will be read, it is crucial that it provides a clear message about the implications of the research and shows how your findings contribute to the debates that appear in the literature. This is a skill that many students find difficult to learn. Dissertations are frequently submitted that include a good account of the literature and a good discussion of the research findings, but do not make effective links between these two elements in the conclusion.

A good conclusion will include some reflection on the body of theory in which the research has been located and on previous research findings in similar areas. Some students are nervous about suggesting that their research contradicts – or provides a different perspective to – existing published work, but it is important to do this where appropriate: this is part of the process of academic debate. As an example, the study of racist offenders by Ray et al. (2004), which was referred to above, acknowledged the value of existing theory about motivation for racist offending but also suggested that this theory could be developed further:

> Many of the findings of our research resemble those of others (Hewitt, 1996; Sibbitt, 1997; Webster, 1999): for instance that racist violence rarely conforms to the image of classic hate crime, that those who perpetrate it are likely also to be involved in other types of violence and criminality, and that the racist sentiments they hold are widely shared in their local communities. But we have tried to develop a way of understanding such violence that stresses its deep emotional roots in alienation, shame and rage. (Ray et al., 2004: 364)

Of course, you should also acknowledge when your research supports existing theory or previous research findings. You may also be faced with the situation where your conclusion cannot simply agree or disagree with previous work: the contribution that your study makes to understanding your chosen subject area may be a complex one. For example, Adriaenssens and Hendrickx (2011) used their data collected in Brussels to examine two perspectives in relation to begging: a popular perspective that sees it as a lucrative activity organised by criminal gangs and an alternative perspective that sees it as an activity to provide the means to live. In the case of the Roma beggars studied, the authors were able to conclude that the popular perspective was incorrect, and that begging was a means to maintaining existence. However, they were not able to reach such a clear conclusion in the case of indigenous people, describing their results as 'inconclusive' (Adriaenssens and Hendrickx, 2011: 36).

Recommendations

It is sometimes appropriate to include practical recommendations as part of a conclusion. In the case of research reports, these can be so important that they form a section of their own. However, in the case of other forms of output such as dissertations, the decision as to whether it is appropriate to make practical recommendations will depend on the nature of the subject studied. Recommendations would be unlikely to arise from a piece of research into penal populism which concluded that public and media pressure tended to lead to harsher sentencing policies in the aftermath of high-profile crimes against children. In contrast, if a student were to undertake a case study piece of research in which they applied control theory to the difficulties of repeated vandalism to lifts and stairways in a block of flats, their conclusion might be in two parts: they might reflect on the helpfulness of control theory for understanding these crimes but also make practical recommendations, for example that CCTV should be installed in the block.

While policy recommendations are much more appropriate for some forms of research than others, recommendations for further research can be made across a wide range of studies. If your output begins with a discussion of what was known about a subject prior to your own work, and continues by considering how your findings contribute to knowledge of the subject, a logical next step is to indicate how future research could develop knowledge further. The word 'recommendation' does not need to be used specifically: you simply need to indicate how knowledge and understanding could be further advanced. To take an example, Roskin-Frazee (2020) analysed anti-sexual violence policies across 80 universities in Australia, Canada, the United Kingdom and the USA. She concluded that, despite women with marginalised identities being particularly likely to experience sexual violence, polices often failed to address their specific needs for protection against this form of crime. In addition, she identified several questions that could helpfully be addressed by further research, including whether the shortcomings identified in policies were shared throughout the world, what training could make staff more aware of the specific needs of women with marginalised identities, and how the limitations of policies impacted on the experiences of survivors of sexual violence from marginalised groups (Roskin-Frazee, 2020: 20–21).

Textbox 13.6

What is the mistake? Writing a conclusion

Try to identify the mistake(s) that a researcher has made here and then have a look at the Appendix to see whether your view is the same as mine.

(Continued)

An undergraduate student writes the following conclusion to their dissertation:

The research examined the views among members of the New Vale Labour Party of the blanket ban on sending books to prisoners. This ban was implemented as part of an attack on the perceived 'perks' of prison that was introduced by then Justice Secretary Chris Grayling in 2013. It was abandoned in 2014 after it was ruled to be illegal.

Respondents were unclear about the reasons for introducing the ban but were universally critical of it. The main theme of their responses was the need to educate prisoners to give them a better chance of finding work when they left prison, so reducing their risk of committing further crime. Some respondents discussed the poor education of prisoners, and the difficult backgrounds that many came from, and expressed the view that prisons should be places that seek to tackle social and economic disadvantage. There were also criticisms of Chris Grayling, who was viewed by many as having been a particularly incompetent minister.

It is recommended that everything possible is done to encourage reading in prisons and that each prison is set a target of having three books available for reading per prisoner. It is further recommended that Chris Grayling is given no further Ministerial posts.

Tips for Writing an Extended Piece of Work

I am assuming that many readers of this book will be incorporating their research into an undergraduate dissertation and that this will be the longest document that they have ever written. So, it is appropriate that I offer six tips, based on my experience and those of many students and colleagues, as to how to manage the writing process in order to achieve the best possible outcome:

1   At the risk of stating the obvious, plan your time carefully and make sure that you have enough time for writing the conclusion in particular. There are some people who are lucky enough to be able to write very quickly and still produce a coherent piece of work – I am not one of them and the likelihood is that you are not either!

2   Find the method of writing that is most productive for you. Some of my colleagues need a substantial chunk of time to be able to write effectively, so try to put blocks

of several hours into their schedule. However, I find it difficult to concentrate for that long, and work most effectively in shorter bursts, so instead look to include as many periods of 30–90 minutes as possible in my plans. You should work out what is best for you and try to schedule your writing time accordingly.

3   You should also work out the time of day when you work best and use this time for your most difficult pieces of writing, for example the ones where you have the most complex argument to put together. Less productive times of day can be used for less demanding tasks such as writing more descriptive sections of your work, checking references, ensuring that headings are used consistently, etc.

4   Save the different drafts of your work but choose your filenames carefully so that you do not get them confused. We have all had the experience of including some material in our first draft, deleting it from the second draft, and then realising that we need it again for the third! One of my students suggested emailing drafts to yourself, which seems a good way of ensuring that you can find them when you need to.

5   Many of us, when we complete our work, look back and see very few of the sentences that were used in our first draft. Your ideas are likely to become clearer as you get them typed into a document. Getting started and getting a first draft down is often the most difficult stage of writing – editing and refining ideas that are already there can feel much easier.

6   Linked to the last point, it is good to plan the structure of your work before you start writing, but quite natural for this plan to change as you progress. The experience of writing a section into one chapter, and then realising that it fits better in another, is a very common one. There is a balance to be struck between trying to write in a systematic way, according to a plan, and being prepared to adapt as you gain new insights while you are writing.

Key points for your own research

- At all times, keep in mind what you are trying to achieve through your output. Ensure that everything that you write contributes to your overall aims and to 'telling the story'.
- Unless you are writing a systematic literature review, your discussion of the existing literature should be arranged thematically, developing a critical argument. You should demonstrate how your research fits into the body of knowledge about your chosen topic. It is essential to discard sources, or mention them only briefly, if they are not central to your argument.
- The methodology section should explain and justify the key decisions that were made in the research process, citing the research methods literature. The topics covered in this section are likely to be similar to those that were covered in your research

proposal. It is a strength rather than a weakness to acknowledge the limitations of your methodology and to discuss how your plan had to be adapted in the light of difficulties.

- When writing about quantitative data, you should choose the form of presentation that is most appropriate for each individual variable and try to include some variety. Crosstables will usually be the most appropriate method of presenting relationships between nominal variables, while correlations (carefully explained) are often effective in discussing the relationships between ordinal and scale variables. It is important to acknowledge that relationships between variables can only be discussed selectively and also to provide an overview of the complete picture (e.g. to discuss the areas where there were major gender differences, but also areas where no such differences were found).

- If you have conducted qualitative research, your findings section will usually incorporate discussion of broad trends, individual examples and quotations. You should be clear as to why specific examples and quotations have been chosen. Two dangers to avoid are writing about qualitative findings as though they were quantitative – only identifying majority views or indicating how many respondents reported a particular experience – or depending too heavily on quotations, with insufficient commentary of your own to support them.

- The conclusion section should make explicit the links between your own findings and what is already known about the subject area through the literature. It should therefore demonstrate that the work that you have produced is a single entity, all designed to answer the same question(s) or achieve the same objective(s). If you have examined a practical issue, it is often relevant to include recommendations for policymakers or others. For other topics, recommendations of this nature may be inappropriate, but most types of study lend themselves to suggestions for further research.

Key points when reading other people's research

- Consider whether the literature review sets the scene for the research: does it demonstrate why the research was necessary and how it contributes to what is already known about the subject?

- Assess whether the methodology section provides a clear rationale for the chosen approach, but also acknowledges its limitations.

- It can be difficult to determine whether someone else has written about their research in a fair and unbiased way. However, think about what is not being said: has the writer given you an overview of their findings? If they have chosen to concentrate on a small part of the data, have they given a reason for this selection?

(Continued)

- Consider whether the conclusion follows the issues that were identified in the literature, methodology and findings.
- If the author has made recommendations – either practical or for further research – consider whether these arise logically from the findings that they have discussed.

Further reading

For a practical guide to finding, evaluating and writing about sources of literature, I recommend:

Deane, M. (2010) *Academic Research, Writing and Referencing*. Harlow: Pearson Education.

There is a helpful section on writing about qualitative data (including mistakes to avoid) in:

Richards, L. (2014) *Handling Qualitative Data*, 3rd edn. London: Sage (1st edn 2005).

For a discussion that incorporates issues of structure and style, but also practical questions such as finding the best time of day at which to write, see:

Henn, M., Weinstein, M. and Foard, N. (2009) *A Critical Introduction to Social Research*, 2nd edn. London: Sage (1st edn 2006).

There are also plenty of practical tips, such as how to get started with writing, in a clip with the title *Writing-up Qualitative Research*, which is on YouTube at:

www.youtube.com/watch?v=IFj2ucSP2jc

For a more advanced discussion of the presentation of qualitative findings, suitable for a student writing a Master's dissertation or a thesis, I recommend:

Halliday, A. (2016) *Doing and Writing Qualitative Research*, 3rd edn. London: Sage (1st edn 2002).

For an innovative and engaging way of presenting research findings, see:

Griffin, N. S. (2020) 'Spycops comic', *The Sociological Review*, 6 May [Online] (http://thesociologicalreview.org/magazine/may-2020/visual-sociology/spycops-comic).

However, please check carefully with your supervisor before deciding to produce output in this form!

14

EPILOGUE

It was noted in Chapter 1 that there has been research conducted in the area of crime that has brought about lasting change to the manner in which the issue is understood and responded to. Making the world a better place, or at least one that is better understood, should be the aim of any researcher in this area.

However, it is important to be realistic about the impact of research and to acknowledge that the outcomes are rarely exactly those that the researcher hoped for. One reason for this is that research findings can be interpreted in different ways. For example, advocates of a more rehabilitative approach to prison can point to the experience of Norway, where (as was noted in Chapter 4) there is an approach to imprisonment which seems extraordinarily relaxed by UK standards and where re-offending rates are far below the European average (www.bbc.co.uk/news/stories-48885846). However, the research findings that compare re-offending rates between countries cannot 'prove' that it is the nature of the prison system that is responsible for the low figure in Norway. A large range of other factors, such as the employment and housing opportunities that are available to those who are released, may contribute to this outcome.

In addition, and particularly pertinent to prison research, practical and political factors can limit the extent to which research is adopted into policy. The Norwegian prison system spends approximately twice as much per prisoner as is the case in the UK, and it is highly unlikely that the public would tolerate this increase in spending, or a move towards a regime with so much emphasis on rehabilitation and so little on punishment. Possibly the most famous example of politics interfering in the interpretation of research (which was discussed in Chapter 3) occurred when the then Home Secretary Michael Howard claimed in 1993 that 'prison works'. Howard made very selective use of research data to support his claim, attracting criticism from those who collected the data in question (Burnett and Maruna, 2004: 392). After reading this book, I am confident that you will be able adopt a more critical stance to the claims that are made by politicians in relation to research findings.

It is not only academic researchers who can find that their efforts to establish and promote the truth through research are thwarted. In 2015 Leicestershire Police introduced a pilot scheme, with many similarities to a classic experimental design (see Chapter 5), in relation to burglaries which did not involve vulnerable victims and were not linked to other crimes. Those burglaries reported at odd-numbered houses were not attended by crime scene investigators, while those at even-numbered houses continued to be examined forensically. The pilot was based on internal police research which showed that, of 1,172 attempted burglary scenes, only 33 provided forensic evidence that led to suspects being identified. At a time when police budgets were being reduced, the pilot could have provided important data to demonstrate whether forensic examinations had any impact on conviction rates for burglary, or whether they could be cut without any detrimental impact on the public. However, the evaluation of the pilot was never forthcoming because, once knowledge about the scheme became public, it was criticised by a wide range of parties: the Police and Crime Commissioner for the area, a local Neighbourhood Watch scheme, Victim Support and the local MP (www.bbc.co.uk/news/uk-england-leicestershire-33788264).

Your own research is very unlikely to be as high profile as the examples given here but you must be aware that your findings – no matter how useful or important – may not result in the action, or the change to public understanding, that you had hoped for. This is not to discourage you from doing your own study: the reason for writing this book is that I believe that research about crime can improve the world and that you can be part of that improvement. You may only be able to conduct a small study because of the time and resources available to you. However, if you conduct your research according to the good methodological practice described in this book, you will have the satisfaction of knowing that there is a small part of the world of knowledge about crime that you have created.

GLOSSARY

Academic sources – these are the types of books and journal articles that are usually written by lecturers and include a list of references at the end.

Access – this refers to the researcher's ability to find the data that they need, most typically by being able to approach the people that they wish to complete questionnaires, to take part in interviews or to participate in focus groups.

Action research – as its name implies, this is research which is very focused on bringing about positive, practical change. It is often associated with participatory approaches (see below).

Analyse – to analyse is to break something down to its component parts. In the case of literature, it means looking at the structure of what is written and establishing the concepts, assumptions and evidence that underlie it. In the case of qualitative or quantitative data, it means explaining what is going on by examining the different elements in the data and the relationship between these elements.

Anonymous, anonymity – participants in research are anonymous when the researcher does not know who has participated in the research or what information they have given. This can usually only apply when specific methods of data collection are used such as online or postal surveys. However, the presentation of results anonymously is the norm in all forms of research: no one who is reading the output should be able to determine who any of the participants were.

Average – this is the term that can be used to refer to what is typical in quantitative data. It is often seen as being the same as the mean, although the median is another method of measuring the centre of a dataset (both of these terms are defined below).

Bias – this may occur when a researcher allows their work to become too subjective and so conducts it in a way that makes a particular outcome more likely.

Biographical interview – see life history interview.

Bivariate – bivariate analysis examines the relationship between two variables, e.g. gender and whether someone has been convicted of a crime.

Case – a case is a unit from which data is collected. This can take a range of forms, such as a document or television programme, but is usually a person.

Case study – a case study is an example (e.g. one person or one city) that is examined in detail to illustrate particular themes or processes. One piece of research may include several case studies.

Category – this is a heading under which different sections of data can be placed for the purpose of analysis. It may be divided into sub-categories.

Causality, causation – this means establishing that one factor (the independent variable) has an impact on another (the dependent variable). For example, researchers working in crime prevention have been keen to establish whether changes such as improving street lighting (the independent variable) have an impact on the level of crime (the dependent variable).

Cell – the individual 'boxes' in a crosstable are referred to as cells. They show the number of cases that fit with the value in both the row and the column. Cells can also include percentages, if these are asked for.

Cite – to cite is to refer to what is said, either within your dataset or in the literature, without directly using the words of the speaker/writer.

Classic experimental design – this is a quantitative research design where an experimental group is compared to a control group. The experimental group receives an intervention, while the control group does not, and changes in the two are compared.

Closed question – a question, usually included as part of a survey, where respondents must choose from pre-set options. So, for example, the question might be *What do you think should be the primary purpose of prison?* and the options could be 'incapacitation', 'retribution', 'deterrence', 'rehabilitation' or 'other'.

Codes – a system of abbreviations, numbers, words or short phrases (or any combination of these), typically written by the side of transcripts, that identifies a feature of the data.

Computer Assisted Qualitative Data Analysis (CAQDAS) – this is the term used for several pieces of software (most notably NVivo) that can assist in the analysis of qualitative data.

Concept, conceptual – an underlying idea in literature or data. A qualitative researcher may find a concept in their data which is not referred to directly by respondents, but appears to be part of their thinking.

Confidentiality – confidentiality means the researcher only using information about a participant in a manner that the participant has agreed to. So a participant may give an answer in an interview (for example) that they later ask to be removed from the dataset.

Consensus – consensus is established when two or more people are in broad agreement.

Consent – see informed consent.

Constant comparative method – a method of analysing qualitative data that begins by looking for similarities and differences between the first two cases, then adds more cases to the analysis, one by one.

Content analysis – a method of measuring what is said, written and/or displayed visually, which is usually based on counting the number of times that elements occur.

Contextualism – this is an underlying principle of qualitative research which is based on understanding the broader situation in which data is collected.

Control group – see classic experimental design.

Correlation – there is a correlation between two variables when the value of one tends to increase as the other increases, or tends to decrease as the other increases. However, this does not necessarily mean that one variable 'causes' the other to change.

Covert observation – this is a form of observation in which the research participants do not realise that they are being observed. It presents major ethical challenges.

Crime Survey of England and Wales – this is the annual survey which asks people about their experiences as victims of crime, and from which crime statistics are often drawn. It was formerly known as the British Crime Survey.

Criteria – the conditions which must be satisfied, e.g. for someone to be included in a sample or for data to be placed in a particular category.

Critical research, critical analysis, critical methodologies – an approach to research that takes as its starting point an assumption that there are unequal and unjust power structures within society. The aim is to expose these power structures and their impact.

Cross-sectional research – research where data is collected at only one time point.

Crosstable – a method of presentation of quantitative data in which one variable is placed in the columns and one in the rows. A third variable can also be added for a three-dimensional crosstable.

Cumulative percentage – this is usually used with ordinal variables and refers to the percentage of respondents giving this answer and previous answers. So if 10% strongly agree with a statement and 30% agree, the cumulative percentage shows that 40% either strongly agree or agree.

Data, dataset – data can consist of a wide range of information collected by the researcher, including records of interviews, focus groups, questionnaire responses and documents. When all the different pieces of data are put together – e.g. transcripts of interviews with 15 people, 150 questionnaires or eight documentaries on drug trafficking – this is referred to as a dataset. There is a distinction between empirical data, which is collected directly from people (e.g. through interviews), and other forms of data (e.g. visual images).

Data analysis – in the case of quantitative data, this usually means examining individual variables before moving on to the more complex task of analysing relationships between variables. There is a less clearly defined process for qualitative data, but it involves examining, comparing, pulling apart and putting back together different pieces of data, in order to draw conclusions about overall trends, themes and issues within the dataset.

Data collection – this is the process by which empirical data is created by the researcher through conducting focus groups, distributing questionnaires, etc.

Deductive research – this form of research takes as its starting point what is already known about the topic in question. The researcher then considers how they can add to this body of knowledge through research that addresses a particular research questions or tests a specific hypothesis.

Dependent variable – this is a variable that is influenced by one or several independent variable(s), e.g. the level of fear of crime that someone feels is a dependent variable, which may be influenced by independent variables such as the number of times they have been a victim of crime.

Descriptive research question – see research question.

Descriptive statistics – these are statistics that explain what is going on in a dataset, e.g. the mean of an individual variable.

Discourse analysis – a form of analysis that focuses particularly on the words used in written text and speech, considering how meaning is constructed through the language that is used.

Documents, documentary analysis – many types of document (e.g. maps) can be analysed for research purposes but the focus tends to be on analysing written texts that can take a very wide variety of forms, e.g. letters, diaries, annual reports, reports of inspectorates and political manifestos.

Empirical data – see data, dataset.

Ethics – these are the values that are felt to determine whether social research is bringing about some good for the wider world. Often, the focus is on what is considered unethical, e.g. observing people without their consent, rather than on ensuring ethical practice, e.g. ensuring that all participants give informed consent, as far as is reasonably practical. All university-based research now needs to go through a process of ethical approval and is usually considered by an ethics committee.

Ethnography – this form of research focuses on the culture or everyday activities within a setting or group.

Ethogenics – this qualitative research principle involves considering events as part of a sequence, e.g. examining the set of circumstances that led to a fight breaking out in a pub.

Evaluation – this involves making a judgement as to whether something is good or bad, accurate or inaccurate. For example, the accuracy of a claim that crime is committed mainly by men could be evaluated either by examining the literature on this topic or by the collection of some original data.

Experimental group – see classic experimental design.

Explanatory research question – see research question.

Factorial research design – this is a method of planning research which seeks to establish the impact of one independent variable on a dependent variable, e.g. the impact of ethnicity on the likelihood of being stopped and searched.

Field – the area from which a researcher collects data is sometimes referred to as the field, particularly when conducting ethnographic research.

Finding – a finding is one outcome of a piece of research, i.e. one piece of information that a researcher has 'discovered'.

Fixed research designs – these designs involve the researcher making a very detailed and specific plan for their research and keeping closely to it through the research process (although some degree of variation is almost inevitable). They are typically used in quantitative studies.

Flexible research designs – these designs are typically used in qualitative research and allow the researcher to vary their plan as issues arise in the research, e.g. to add new topics to interview guides as their importance becomes clear.

Focus group – a group of typically 6–8 people who come together for a 'focused' discussion on a topic of interest to the researcher.

Frequencies – the number of times that something appears during research, e.g. the number of people who answer 'yes' to a particular question on a questionnaire.

Gatekeeper – someone who controls access to potential respondents to research. For example, the manager of a refuge would be the gatekeeper who could agree that a researcher could ask people who had experienced domestic violence if they were willing to be interviewed.

Generalisation – this is a principle underlying much quantitative research and refers to the application of findings beyond the site of data collection. It typically means the ability to apply survey findings taken from a random sample to a broader population.

Grounded theory – a specific form of inductive approach which seeks to collect and analyse data, then build theory, at the earliest opportunity.

Hypothesis – a statement which a researcher seeks to establish as true or false through deductive (usually quantitative) research.

Independent variable – this is a variable that has an impact on another, dependent variable. So, for example, the neighbourhood that someone lives in is an independent variable that has an impact on the dependent variable of their likelihood of being a victim of crime.

Individual example – an individual example can be used when writing about qualitative research findings to demonstrate the practical application of a concept or idea to one particular person or setting.

Individualism – surprisingly, perhaps, this is an underlying principle of quantitative research: the researcher is interested in the aggregate of individual responses (e.g. 42% of respondents strongly agreed with the statement) rather than considering relationships between respondents.

Inductive research – this is a form of research that begins with collecting and analysing data (and possibly building theory) before considering how the research fits with the wider literature on the subject. There is no specific research question, although there may be broad research objectives, and the researcher has the flexibility to direct the research in whatever way the data dictates.

Inferential statistics – these statistics are used to assess the likelihood that a pattern seen in a random sample will also be seen in a population.

Informed consent – consent is informed when someone who agrees to take part in research knows in detail what is likely to be involved in their participation.

Insider – a researcher is an insider when they are part of the group or situation which is the subject of their research.

Interpretation – this is a key task in qualitative research: the researcher must consider the meaning of the actions and/ or words of the respondent and how this meaning is relevant to the issue that is being examined. This is inevitably a subjective task, but the researcher must be careful that subjectivity does not become bias (see above).

Interpretivism – this is an approach to research, closely tied to qualitative methodology, which sees the world as being socially constructed, with every individual having a different perspective. It is these perspectives that are studied rather than seeking to find an 'objective' reality.

Intervening variable – a variable which provides an alternative explanation for the apparent impact of an independent variable on a dependent variable. So, for example, looking at the number of burglaries of student houses over the Christmas and New Year period might lead a researcher to conclude that times of celebration (the independent variable) have an impact on burglary levels (the dependent variable). However, the intervening variable is student term times – burglars know that certain properties are unlikely to be occupied during university holidays.

Interview – a method of collecting data through a one-to-one interaction which consists largely of the researcher asking questions and the respondent answering them.

Interview guide – in qualitative research, the interview guide provides the researcher with a list of topics to ensure that they cover, or possibly specific questions to ask, and some possible follow-up questions (or probes). However, it is important to remember that qualitative interviews allow the researcher to ask 'new' questions as the respondent introduces topics to the discussion. In quantitative research, the guide is used very differently and takes a structured form, specifying quite rigidly the wording of questions and the order in which they should be asked.

Journal – a record of events and thoughts about these events, kept by a respondent, which becomes research data.

Life history interview – a form of qualitative interview, possibly supported by documents, where the focus is on process;

the respondent is asked to discuss their life, or a specific part of it, in detail.

Literature review – the process of thoroughly searching through existing published (and sometimes unpublished) material on the researcher's chosen subject and similar subjects.

Longitudinal – research is longitudinal when it involves collecting data from two time periods. A prospective longitudinal study involves collecting data from respondents and then returning to collect further data at a later point. A retrospective longitudinal study involves asking respondents about their current situation and then asking them to recall their situation at some specified point in the past.

Mean – the mean is calculated by adding together all the values of a scale variable (see below) and dividing by the number of values. Like the median, it is one method of finding a typical or central value.

Measurement – an idea primarily associated with quantitative research and involving the representation of social phenomena in the form of numbers.

Median – like the mean, the median is a measure of the typical or central value of a scale variable (see below). It is found by listing the values from the highest to the lowest and taking the one that is in the middle.

Methodology – the large philosophical decisions which are made about how to conduct a research project, such as whether to use an inductive or deductive approach and whether to use a quantitative or qualitative approach.

Methods – the more practical, smaller-scale decisions that are made about research such as how to choose the sample and how to collect the data.

Mixed methods – an approach to research that uses elements of both quantitative and qualitative methodology, treating the two approaches as equal.

Moderator (of focus groups) – the person, usually the researcher, whose job it is to guide the focus group discussion, typically with some planned and some unplanned questions, and ensure that appropriate contributions are made by all group members.

Multivariate research design – a research design that seeks to establish the impact of several independent variables on one or more dependent variables, e.g. the impact of several crime prevention measures on the level of crime.

Narrative analysis – analysis of the accounts that people give, which seeks to understand how they make sense of their experiences.

Naturalism – an underlying principle of qualitative methodology suggesting that research should take place in as 'natural' an environment as possible, rather than the artificial environment created by completing a questionnaire, for example.

Netnography – a specialist form of ethnography (see above) which takes place online.

Nominal variable – a variable where any numbers attributed to the different values have no meaning but are simply labels. So, for example, there is a convention for a yes/no question of labelling 'yes' as 1 and 'no' as 2. However, it would make no difference if 'yes' were labelled as 7 and 'no' as 12.

Non-participant observation – a form of observation where the researcher does not take part in the situation they are studying but looks in from the outside.

Observation – a form of data collection that involves watching and listening to people, and recording what is said and done.

Open question – a question where there are no pre-set options for the respondent to choose from, but they answer 'in their own words', e.g. *Why do you think some people who are already on high incomes seek to increase their income further through fraud?*

Ordinal variable – a variable where the possible values are in a clear order and are numbered accordingly. For example, respondents can 'strongly agree' (1), 'agree' (2), 'neither agree nor disagree' (3), 'disagree' (4) or 'strongly disagree' (5) with a statement. In this example, lower numbers mean greater levels of agreement.

Output – most forms of research result in some sort of document (e.g. a dissertation, research report or journal article) which records the findings – this can be referred to as the research output.

Outsider – a researcher is an outsider when they are not part of the group or situation which is the subject of their research.

Overt observation – a form of observation where those involved know that they are being observed.

Panel design – a research design where a group is measured for some characteristic, attitude or opinion before and after an intervention. It is like a classic experimental design (see above), only without a control group.

Participant – people who take part in research are often referred to as participants.

Participant observation – a form of observation where the researcher takes part in the situation that they are studying.

Participatory action research, participatory appraisal, participatory research design – these are approaches to research that seek to give more power to those taking part in the research and less power to the researcher.

Perspective – the way that life, or one specific aspect of it, looks to an individual or group (this tends to be a concern of the qualitative researcher).

Pilot study – this takes the form of a 'practice' or 'trial run' before the main data collection and analysis and can be invaluable for identifying potential problems that may affect the research.

Population – any clearly defined group of people (e.g. everybody living in the UK, everybody who took part in the 2016 London Marathon) can be described as a population; a sample may be selected from this population.

Positionality – it is important for the researcher to consider their own 'position' in relation to the participants/respondents and the data because this may affect the data collection and analysis. For example, a volunteer at a Youth Offending Service, who collects data from the young people they are working with, should consider carefully how their position of power may affect the data collection and how their own opinions about the young people may affect the analysis.

Positivism – a philosophy that asserts that there is an objective reality, independent of the perspective of any individual, that the researcher should seek to reveal.

Probe – a follow-up to a main question that can be used when conducting interviews or collecting data from focus groups. A probe can be planned (e.g. 'ask about witnessing assaults on a night out if not previously mentioned') or unplanned, where the researcher responds to an issue that is raised by the respondent.

Pseudonym – a name that is given to a respondent when writing up research to disguise their identity.

Purposive sample – a method of selecting respondents, usually used in qualitative studies, which involves the researcher making a judgement as to who it would be most appropriate to collect data from.

Qualitative interview – this is a form of research interview where the focus is on allowing the respondent to talk about the issues that are of most importance to them, with limited guidance from the interviewer. Life history, semi-structured and unstructured interviews are all forms of qualitative interview.

Qualitative research – research that focuses on understanding the perspective of others, often based on collecting detailed data from relatively small numbers of respondents.

Quantitative research – research that seeks to identify broad trends, measure concepts numerically and find causal relationships between them. It often involves undertaking surveys of large numbers of people, with data collected through questionnaires or structured interviews.

Quasi-experimental design – a research design that involved dividing respondents into two groups based on outcomes (e.g. 'successes' and 'failures'), then seeking to identify the common characteristics of each group.

Quasi-panel design – a research design that involves collecting data from one group of people at one point in time, and another group of people at a second point in time, then comparing the data from the two groups.

Questionnaire – this is a common form of data collection in surveys (see below). Questionnaires can be sent by post, email or mobile phone, but most commonly by a link to an online program.

Quotation, quote – a statement taken directly, word for word, from a literature source or from an interview/focus group respondent.

Random sample – this is a method of choosing respondents that involves a random element to ensure that the researcher has no control of who is included in the sample. Each member of the sampling frame (see below) has an equal chance of being selected.

Rapport – a comfortable, trusting relationship between researcher and respondent that facilitates the respondent discussing issues in an uninhibited manner.

Recommendation – a suggestion for practical action or further research in response to research findings, usually included near the end of a piece of research output.

Reflexivity – the process by which a researcher evaluates the influence of their own role on the research process and on the outcomes of the research.

Replication – this is an underlying principle of quantitative research, meaning that research should be capable of being reproduced and achieving a similar result again.

Research design – the plan that is put in place for the research to ensure that it answers the research question(s) or meets the research objectives, incorporating areas such as sampling, data collection and data analysis.

Research objective – a broad goal to be pursued by a piece of research. Inductive studies often have several research objectives.

Research output – see output.

Research proposal – this is a document that is put together before a piece of research begins, specifying how it is to be conducted.

Research question – a specific question that a piece of research seeks to answer (and that it is feasible for the research to answer). Deductive studies tend to have one or more research questions. Explanatory research questions seek to explain relationships between different phenomena. Descriptive research questions seek to provide a clear picture of a particular social setting.

Research report – this is a form of research output that is often written for a specific organisation, focusing on the practical implications of research findings.

Respondent – a term that is used for someone who contributes data to a research project, e.g. by being interviewed or taking part in a focus group discussion.

Response – the way a respondent reacts to what is asked of them in the research, e.g. the answer that they give to a question or the contribution that they make to a focus group.

Response rate – this is the percentage of people who take part in research after being asked. It is particularly important for surveys to achieve as high a response rate as possible.

Retrospective panel design – a research design where a group of people are asked about their characteristics, attitudes and/or opinions at the present time, then asked to recall these characteristics, attitudes and/or opinions at some point in the past, to see how they have changed with time.

Sample, sampling – sampling is the process of selecting some potential respondents, but not others, from a sampling frame (see below) to take part in research. Samples can also be chosen that do not involve people, e.g. some newspapers but not others can be selected for analysis.

Sampling frame – this is the list of all the elements (usually people) from which a sample is to be selected. It is often the same as the population (see above).

Scale variables – these are variables where the values are 'real numbers', e.g. someone's age is 25, the number of full-time jobs they have held is three, they have been a victim of crime five times in their life, etc. Scale is the term used in SPSS for this type of variable, although you may see other, more precise terms – particularly 'interval' and 'ratio' – used in statistics textbooks.

Secondary analysis – the further analysis of data that was originally collected by another researcher and analysed for a different purpose to your own. This type of research is most commonly undertaken with quantitative datasets in SPSS or similar programs, but is also possible with qualitative data such as interview transcripts.

Semi-structured interview – this is a form of qualitative interview where the researcher must cover certain topics with,

or ask certain questions of, all respondents. However, it is also very important that they ask individualised questions to follow up issues and ideas that are identified as important by the respondent.

Snowball samples – these samples are often chosen for hidden groups, with sample members asked if they can find other people with similar characteristics to take part in the research.

SPSS (Statistical Package for the Social Sciences) – this is the main statistical software used within the social sciences in universities. It has a wide range of functions.

Statistics – the outcome of bringing data together in large quantities.

Structural analysis – in the case of documents and films/television programmes, this is an approach that concentrates on the aims of the creators of the material and how the material is put together to meet these aims.

Structural narrative analysis – this is usually used with interview and focus group data. It concentrates on the mechanisms by which the speaker seeks to make their narrative more persuasive.

Structured interview – this is the form of interview associated with quantitative research, where the same questions are asked of all respondents, with some variations based on their answers to previous questions. Structured interviews can be undertaken face to face or by telephone. The majority of questions are usually closed.

Subjective – a decision is subjective when the researcher is required to use their own judgement to determine which of two or more alternatives is most appropriate. All research involves subjective decision making, but there tends to be more of these kinds of decision in qualitative studies. The researcher must be careful not to allow their subjectivity to become bias (see above).

Survey – the survey is a method of collecting quantitative data by asking a population or sample a series of structured questions. Data is collected via a questionnaire or a structured interview.

Thematic analysis – an approach that seeks to identify commonalities, differences and patterns emerging from qualitative data.

Thematic narrative analysis – an approach that concentrates on the recurring ideas and concepts in a narrative.

Theme – an idea that can be seen running through several responses such as the satisfaction for police officers of seeing an offender convicted.

Theory, theoretical background, theoretical framework – a theory is a body of explanatory ideas that can be applied to a range of situations or social settings, helping to explain several phenomena.

Transcription, transcript – transcription is listening to an audio recording of an interview or a focus group discussion and reproducing it as a written or typed account, which is then referred to as a transcript.

Triangulation – the checking of findings from one method by using another method. So, for example, the findings from a large number of interviews might be triangulated by conducting a focus group, to determine whether similar issues emerge.

Unstructured interview – a form of qualitative interview that appears from the outside to operate like a conversation. The interviewer has a small number of questions to ask, or points to raise with, the respondent, and the remainder of the questions are unplanned follow-ups (or probes).

Valid percent – this is the percentage of respondents giving an answer to a particular question if the 'missing values' (i.e. those for whom the answer is 'don't know' or 'not applicable') are excluded.

Validity – the extent to which the outcomes of a piece of research accurately reflect the experiences, beliefs and values of the group or setting which is being explored.

Variable – this is something that varies between different respondents, e.g. gender, number of crimes committed, favourite word to describe the Home Secretary, etc. Quantitative datasets tend to be made up of large numbers of variables.

Vignettes – these are very short stories/accounts that can be used for the purposes of research. They are particularly useful for testing a respondent's reaction to a hypothetical situation.

APPENDIX:

WHAT IS THE MISTAKE?

Textbox 2.1 Grounded Theory

There is nothing wrong with the piece of research described here, except that the student has inaccurately described it as grounded theory. For the study to fit the model of grounded theory, she would need to begin by reading the reports and analysing the data that they provide. Once this data analysis was complete, she would then consider the middle-range theory that she had created and decide which body of existing theory to compare it with (which would probably be subcultural theory, given the importance that the reports attached to peer pressure).

In fact, the student has conducted a deductive study designed to answer the good research question: How helpful is strain theory in explaining the actions of young shop-lifters, based on the motivations discussed in the pre-sentence reports of the Youth Offending Service? The approach should not be described as grounded theory when it sets out to answer a specific research question.

Textbox 2.3 Cybercrime

The mistake here is that, although there are only six respondents, the student has reported the findings in a manner that reflects several of the underpinnings of quantitative methodology:

- Measurement – creating a mean 'score' for the number of times a password was reused.
- Individualism – counting the number of students who said that they did not take enough precautions and the fraction who had lost money to cybercrime at some point in their life.
- Generalisation – scaling up the results from this very small sample to estimate that one third of students across the university had lost money through cybercrime.

It would have been far more appropriate for the student to have undertaken and reported the interviews in a manner that satisfied principles of qualitative research, for example:

- Seeing through the eyes of others – seeking to understand how respondents viewed security precautions against cybercrime: e.g. did they feel they were unnecessary, were they worried about forgetting passwords, had they not made time to take precautions despite thinking they were important?
- Ethogenics – considering the 'sequence of events' for those respondents who had lost money due to cybercrime: e.g. were they trying to do something online for the first time, were they fooled by a convincing-sounding email, had they failed to update the security settings on their device?
- Contextualism – seeking to understand the environment in which students are living: e.g. is cyber security something that is discussed among students, is there pressure to engage in the latest activities online without thought for the possible security implications, would losing money to online fraud simply be a drop in the ocean to students who were accruing so much debt by being at university?

Textbox 3.3 Gun Control

The mistake here is that the student has only used one source, which has a particularly strong view on gun ownership. The National Rifle Association (NRA) describes itself as 'America's foremost defender of Second Amendment rights' (https://home.nra.org/about-the-nra). By this it means the second amendment to the constitution of the United States of America, which reads that: 'A well-regulated Militia, being necessary to the security of a free State, the right of the people to keep and bear Arms, shall not be infringed' (www.law.cornell.edu/wex/second_amendment). Such a source was inevitably going to be critical of proposals to introduce more gun control; the student should have acknowledged that they were citing the view of the NRA and balanced their view with at least one source that was supportive of the proposals. A much better version of the passage from the dissertation would have read as follows:

> During the race for the Democratic nomination for the 2020 US presidential election, Senator Cory Brooker made proposals to license guns and ban assault weapons. The proposals involved requiring people to apply for a gun licence in the same way that they applied for a passport, with the licence being valid for up to five years. Mr Booker said that he was 'sick and tired of hearing thoughts and prayers for communities that had been shattered by gun violence' (*New York Times*, 2019). The National Rifle Association attacked the plan, arguing

that Brooker had failed to define 'assault weapons', that he had not answered the question as to whether someone could ultimately be imprisoned for not surrendering their weapon and that similar proposals had been ruled illegal by the courts or had been ineffective in their implementation. For example, attempts to register all semi-automatic weapons in New York resulted in only 44,485 registrations, despite estimates that over 1 million such weapons were owned within the state (National Rifle Association, 2019).

(The full reference for *The New York Times* article is: *New York Times* (2019, 6th May) 'Cory Booker's gun control plan calls for national licensing program', www. nytimes.com/2019/05/06/us/politics/cory-booker-gun-control.html)

Textbox 3.4 The Gangs Matrix

Even before considering the claims made in the document, there are two factors that should cause alarm bells to ring for the student:

1   There is no author's name or date on the document. It seems reasonable to assume that it was written in 2021 because the people named were murdered in 2020. In addition, it was revealed that approximately 1,000 young men had been removed from the Gangs Matrix early in 2021 (Dodd, 2021), so this gives a likely date for the document. However, this should be clearly stated, rather than being a matter for investigation.
2   The use of emotive language – e.g. 'bleeding heart liberals' and 'young thugs' – is a warning that the document may be aimed at provoking emotions rather than presenting reasoned argument.

An examination of the claims made in the document confirm the weakness of the case being made:

1   The statistic of an increase of at least 10% in youth crime, gun crime and murder is presented without any source or any indication of the timeframe that it covers. Giving the names of those murdered does not demonstrate that there has been an increase in murders.
2   A brief investigation of the named murder victims shows that one, Sundeep Ghuman, was murdered in Her Majesty's Prison Belmarsh rather than on the streets of London.
3   No other evidence is cited to support any of the views expressed.

While it is appropriate to present both sides of an argument, the sources used to support each point of view must be of reasonable quality. A more appropriate source to use would have been the Metropolitan Police's own explanation of why the Gangs Matrix is a helpful tool: www.met.police.uk/police-forces/metropolitan-police/areas/about-us/about-the-met/gangs-violence-matrix

Textbox 4.1 Coming Out of Prison

Leaving aside the difficulties of drawing such broad and definitive conclusions from such a small sample, the main issue here is that the student has asked a factorial research question which their data is not adequate to answer. The data suggests that the dependent variable (whether the former prisoner rates themselves as being at high or low risk of re-offending) was affected by three of the independent variables:

- Age – the three youngest respondents assessed their risk as high.
- Addictions – the three respondents who had addictions to drugs and/or alcohol assessed their risk as high.
- Housing situation – the three respondents who were living in hostels assessed their risk as high.

In fact, length of sentence was the only independent variable that appeared to have no impact on the dependent variable.

The factorial research question could only have been answered by using a sample large enough to identify respondents who were similar in terms of other independent variables (e.g. age and addictions) and comparing those who were living in hostels with those who had other forms of accommodation. Given the data available to the student, it would have been more appropriate to set a multivariate research question, for example: Among recently released prisoners approaching the Bromsgrove Advice Centre in February 2020, which factors were linked to their self-assessed risk of re-offending?

Such a question could be answered by concluding that age, addictions and housing situation all appeared to be linked to this self-assessment, although it should be noted that there could be interactions between these factors, for example partners, parents and friends could refuse to accommodate a former prisoner on the grounds of their addictions.

Textbox 5.1 Domestic Violence Questionnaire

The researcher is wrong to assume that the change must have come about as a result of the Chief Constable's announcement. In the week beginning 16 March 2020, the government introduced major restrictions to people leaving their home because of the Covid-19 pandemic (www.bbc.co.uk/news/uk-scotland-51974969). As people left home less often, crime figures fell for many types of crime, for example burglary, vehicle crime and personal robbery. However, both police forces and charities reported increased requests for help from people experiencing domestic violence (www.theguardian.com/uk-news/2020/apr/15/in-uk-falls-sharply-since-start-of-coronavirus-lockdown). So it may have been Covid-19, rather than the Chief Constable's announcement, that was responsible for the increase in time spent dealing with domestic violence incidents.

For the researcher's argument to be effective, they would need to have taken a control group from another force where there had been no such announcement from the Chief Constable. If this other force showed no increase – or a smaller increase – in the time spent on domestic violence incidents, this would more strongly suggest that the Chief Constable's announcement had made an impact.

Textbox 5.4 Study of Rothbury

The student's only error is to describe the study as an ethnography. Ethnography is a study of the ordinary or the everyday – the seven days when Moat was at large around the village definitely do not fit with this description!

Textbox 6.2 Interviews with Vulnerable Respondents

One difficulty is that the researcher does not know whether the staff have assessed the second service user as being suitable for interview. Another is that the second service user has not gone through any process of having the research explained to them and giving their informed consent to take part. The mistake is therefore using the views of the second service user as data for the study.

As an aside, it is particularly difficult to collect data in an environment like a common room where you cannot guarantee that an interview will remain a one-to-one conversation. However, this may be the only safe option that is available. Where there is someone else present, you must make a judgement as to how far (if at all) your respondent is being influenced by them. If you feel that the second person has had a significant influence, you should exclude the entire interview from the data. This is extremely frustrating but is better than including data that does not accurately reflect your respondent's experiences or opinions.

Textbox 6.3 Metropolitan Police Research

The researcher reporting that officers occasionally prioritised contact with their families over their work is a step that breaches the principle of avoiding harm to respondents – senior staff might take action against the new officers in the light of this finding. This would not be such a danger if there had been a different method of recruitment but is extremely problematic when the most senior officer at the station knows the identity of the small number of people who are taking part in the research. Even worse, the use of a quotation with the word 'bairn' (a term used for a child in some parts of Scotland and the North East of England) breaks the principle of anonymity: there may only be one of the six officers who uses this term, meaning that they can be identified by the senior officer.

Textbox 7.4 Prisoner Research

There are two difficulties here. The first is with regard to access. While personal contacts can sometimes be a method of shortening the process of negotiating access, this is not the case with prisons, where any request for research to take place needs to go through Her Majesty's Prison and Probation Service as well as the governor of the prison in question. The student's approach presents risks for the prisoner, herself and her university.

The second difficulty is that the proposed sample for the research is not appropriate for the population which the student is seeking to understand. Open prisons have very different conditions to those of other prisons and the views of prisoners in such facilities cannot be generalised to those in more secure environments. In particular, there are likely to be far more opportunities for purposeful activity in open prisons (e.g. coming out of prison to volunteer in a charity shop) than elsewhere. So the student's findings can only be indicative of the opinions of prisoners in the most relaxed prison setting.

Textbox 8.1 Historic Crime Survey

The first difficulty here is an ethical one. It is highly unlikely that the student will gain approval from the ethics committee to collect empirical data on such a sensitive topic. The second difficulty relates to the mode of data collection: sheltered housing is for older people. While it would be incorrect to stereotype all older people as being unable to get online, it is true that they tend to be less comfortable with this method of communication than younger people, so an online survey is an inappropriate form of data collection.

Textbox 8.3 Legal Status of Cannabis Survey

The first question is unlikely to present difficulties. Age bands become more important the older respondents are likely to be, e.g. someone may be happier to choose a 50–60 age band than to give their age as 58. However, for a traditional student aged 18–21, who is distributing the questionnaire among their peers, a question about specific age is likely to be acceptable and to be answered truthfully.

All the other questions have clear problems:

Question 2 would now be expected to have an 'other' category and, if this option is chosen, a follow-up question where the respondent could identify their own gender.

Question 3 asks for information that is too precise. If a respondent had never smoked cannabis, or had only done so on one or two occasions, they would be able to give an exact number, but for more frequent users this would be impossible.

Question 4 has two difficulties. The first is that it assumes a degree of knowledge about the drug classification system and the difference between re-classification and legalisation. The second is that the re-classification option is not clear: it is possible (but unlikely) that a respondent could believe that cannabis should be re-classified from a class B drug to a class A drug, rather than to Class C.

Question 5 is a biased one for three reasons: the 'do you agree' format encourages respondents to answer 'yes', the phrase 'chill out' conjures up a positive picture of cannabis use, while the word 'fear' is one that creates negative associations with possible prosecution for cannabis use.

Question 6 is also biased because the phrase 'To what extent' implies that there has definitely been some level of overstatement. There is no option to say that the claims have been understated, only one option that suggests that the claims have been neither understated nor overstated, and four options which state that the claims have been overstated to different degrees. The question also assumes that respondents are aware of the claims that have been made about cannabis and mental health.

In addition, all the questions that ask for an opinion should include a 'don't know' option. An improved version of the survey is shown below.

Improved Version of the Legal Status of Cannabis Survey

1 What is your age?
2 What is your gender?

☐ *Male*

☐ *Female*

☐ *Other*

2a If you have answered 'Other', how would you classify your gender?

3 How would you identify yourself in relation to smoking cannabis?

☐ *Someone who has never smoked cannabis*

☐ *Someone who has smoked cannabis on a small number of occasions*

☐ *Someone who occasionally smokes cannabis*

☐ *Someone who frequently smokes cannabis*

☐ *Other*

3a If you have chosen 'Other', please say how you would classify yourself.

4 In the UK, some drugs are legal (e.g. paracetamol) while those that are illegal are categorised as class A (e.g. crack cocaine), class B (e.g. ketamine) or class C (e.g. anabolic steroids). Class A drugs carry the heaviest penalties for possession, supply and/or production; class C drugs carry the lightest penalties. Cannabis is currently classified as a class B drug. What do you think is the most appropriate legal status for cannabis?

☐ *Class A drug*

☐ *Class B drug*

☐ *Class C drug*

☐ *Legal drug*

☐ *Don't know*

5 In your opinion, should the police arrest people found in possession of cannabis for personal use?

☐ *Yes*

☐ *No*

☐ *Don't know*

6 The National Health Service website includes a comment that 'We do know that regular use of "street cannabis" – especially the very strong skunk kind of cannabis – can increases your risk of developing a psychotic illness, such as schizophrenia' (www.nhs.uk/news/mental-health/study-on-the-treatment-of-mental-health-conditions-using-medical-cannabis). Which of the statements below comes closest to your opinion on claims such as this?

☐ *They understate the mental health risks associated with taking cannabis*

☐ *They correctly represent the mental health risks associated with taking cannabis*

☐ *They overstate the mental health risks associated with taking cannabis*

☐ *Don't know*

Thank you for your help in completing this questionnaire.

Textbox 9.5 Training and Police Officers

The data that the student is collecting here requires personal narratives, which are much better elicited through one-to-one interviews than focus groups. There is no benefit to encouraging respondents to interact with each other in this scenario. If the research were to be conducted with current trainees, asking them to compare experiences and identify shared understandings of the training process, this would be an appropriate situation in which to collect data via one or more focus groups.

Textbox 9.6 Conducting a Focus Group

There are several difficulties here. Firstly, there is a power imbalance within the group, with probation officers holding considerable power over the offenders that they supervise. While the views of both groups on this topic could be highly relevant, they should be placed in separate focus groups to enable all to speak more freely. Conducting the focus groups in the probation service's offices highlights the power inequality, and the method of seeking to record the discussion means that large amounts of detail will be missed. It is essential that another venue is found, where the discussion can be recorded, although careful consideration will have to be given to personal safety issues.

The first question of the focus group discussion is unsuitable for several reasons. The introductory question should normally be an easy introduction to the discussion, leading into the more substantial questions once everyone is more comfortable with talking to each other. In addition, this question is too personal to be asked in a focus groups, where the focus should not be on the individual but on shared understandings. The instruction to ask the first question to each offender and their probation officer demonstrates that the discussion is being conducted as a group interview rather than a focus group, because it is unlikely to create discussion between group members. Even if the question were asked as part of an individual interview, it is too complex, ambiguously worded and irrelevant in the case of some types of offences, e.g. sex offences. It might be modified to appear on an interview guide as follows:

Please could you tell me about the offences that you have committed?

[For each acquisitive crime committed] Please could you tell me if one of the reasons for committing this offence was that you were short of money?

Textbox 10.2 Manifesto Analysis

The student does not acknowledge that political manifestos, perhaps more than any other type of document, are subjectively written and designed to persuade. Many critics of government policy offered alternative commentaries of the 2010–2015 period. For example, they argued that any reductions in police paperwork in no way compensated for the reduction in the number of police officers and that the supervision of released prisoners by the newly created Community Rehabilitation Companies was largely ineffective. There are occasions when it is entirely appropriate to undertake analysis of the documents produced by political parties, but it must be made clear in writing up this analysis that many of the claims are disputed.

Textbox 10.3 Analysis of a Television Programme

The difficulty here is that the student has failed to acknowledge the nature of the television programme. *Rough Justice* was concerned specifically with alleged miscarriages of justice, so the content focused on cases where there was a possibility that there had been a miscarriage, while ignoring those where a conviction was considered safe. It could not therefore be used to assess the number or proportion of actual/possible miscarriages, because these cases would always be the subject matter of 100% of the programmes. In addition, some of the cases were historic, so not relevant to the state of the criminal justice system around the time of the millennium.

A more useful form of analysis would be to focus on the most recent cases shown by the programme and to consider whether the factors that threw doubt on the convictions in these cases (e.g. doubts over the validity of forensic evidence) were different from those that had been key to notorious miscarriages of justice in the past (e.g. unreliable confessions made under duress and/or by people with mental health problems).

Textbox 11.6 Analysing a Single Variable

The student here has read from the wrong column. If he wants to know the percentage of respondents that have given the answer 'not very safe', he should read the figure of 22.9% from either the Percent or Valid Percent column (which are the same in this case, because there are no missing values). The figure of 26.0% is from the Cumulative Percent column and shows that 26.0% answered either 'not at all safe' or 'not very safe'.

Textbox 11.7 Analysing Relationships Between Variables

The statistical processes used here are inappropriate for the types of variables. The question as to whether a respondent has ever been arrested produces a nominal variable which should not be used in a Spearman's rho correlation. Useful data about the relationship between this variable and the score out of 10 given to the police could be provided by using the Compare Means command. This could show whether those respondents who had been arrested gave a different mean and median score out of 10 to those who had not been arrested.

Similarly, a crosstable is not the appropriate method for examining the relationship between the score out of 10 and the number of times a respondent has been arrested, as the table produced is likely to have very large numbers of cells and be impossible to draw conclusions from. Instead, as both variables are scale variables, correlation is the appropriate process to use to examine the relationship between them.

Textbox 12.5 First Attempt at Qualitative Analysis

There is only one 'What is the mistake?' exercise in this long chapter because there are so few 'right' or 'wrong' ways to do qualitative data analysis (unless they result in bias, as discussed in the chapter). However, the student discussed in this example made the common mistake of trying to follow all the advice that she had been given, and to use all the processes that had been recommended to her, without stopping to consider what would help her to understand her data better. It is unlikely that many researchers will find coding, the use of NVivo, making summaries and the constant comparative method all to be helpful, as is indicated by the student being left confused about her data. In addition, the student trying to use the three main forms of qualitative data analysis – thematic, narrative and discourse analysis – in one research project is asking a lot of herself as a new researcher. It would be better for her to decide what she wants from her data and to select one (or at most two) of these forms of analysis to try to achieve this.

Textbox 13.2 Writing a Methodology Section

The strength of this methodology section is that it identifies ethical issues that are pertinent to this particular research topic and explains how they were dealt with. However, there are also many weaknesses:

- There are no academic references to support any of the points that are made.
- There is no discussion of the choice of broad approach (usually quantitative in the case of questionnaire research), the choice of research design (cross-sectional when the data collection is at one point in time) or the choices that were made about data analysis. The reasons for making all these choices, and the limitations of them, should have been discussed.

- Only one advantage of collecting data via online questionnaires is identified (the anonymity that it provides) and none of the limitations of this approach. There could have been discussion, for example, of the difficulties that can arise when no explanation can be offered to a respondent who had misunderstood a question. Any examples of possible misunderstandings that arose during the research could have been discussed to illustrate this point.
- The reasons for adopting a snowball sampling strategy, such as being able to reach a larger number of potential participants, are not identified. In addition, there is no discussion of the disadvantages of such an approach, for example having no control over the sample's characteristics. The student could have discussed the characteristics of their sample to illustrate this point.
- When using a snowball sampling strategy, there is no way of knowing how many people have been invited to take part, so it is not possible to calculate a response rate. In any case, a response rate of 100% to a questionnaire seems highly unlikely.
- More generally, there is no discussion of any limitations of the methodology/methods used or any adjustments that had to be made to the original plans for the research.

Textbox 13.6 Writing a Conclusion

The main difficulty with this conclusion is that it focuses only on the research findings and not on any literature/theory or on the methods used. There could have been a brief discussion of the methods along the following lines:

> The research consisted of semi-structured interviews with a sample of eight members of New Vale Labour Party, which was selected purposively to ensure a range of views from the left, the centre and the right of the party.

The findings should also have been drawn together with the wider literature, which could have focused on the different purposes that prison seeks to serve. It could have been demonstrated that the ban on books was consistent with a traditional Conservative view of prisons existing primarily for the purpose of deterrence and retribution, while the views expressed by the Labour Party members were typical of their party's historic concern with rehabilitation. Links could also have been made between the views of the Labour Party members about the disadvantage faced by many prisoners and critical perspectives in Criminology, which see criminal justice as reinforcing structural social inequalities.

APPENDIX

While it is sometimes appropriate to make policy recommendations in a dissertation, even when it is unlikely that they will ever be adopted, these should not be of such a personal nature as to recommend who should (or should not) hold Ministerial posts.

REFERENCES

Adriaenssens, S. and Hendrickx, J. (2011) 'Street level informal economic activities: estimating the yield of begging in Brussels', *Urban Studies*, 48(1): 23–40.

Alexander, V. D. (2016) 'Analysing visual materials', in Gilbert, N. and Stoneman, P. (eds), *Researching Social Life*, 4th edn. London: Sage, pp. 501–518 (1st edn 1992).

Argyrous, G. (2011) *Statistics for Research*, 3rd edn. London: Sage (1st edn 2000).

Auerbach, C. F. and Silverstein, B. S. (2003) *Qualitative Data: An Introduction to Coding and Analysis*. New York: New York University Press.

Bacon, M., Loftus, B. and Rowe, M. (2020) 'Ethnography and the evocative world of policing (Part 1)', *Policing and Society*, 30(1): 1–10.

Banks, J. (2012) 'Edging your bets: advantage play, gambling, crime and victimisation', *Crime Media Culture*, 9(2): 171–187.

Barbour, R. (2007) *Doing Focus Groups*. London: Sage.

Barbour, R. (2008) *Introducing Qualitative Research*. London: Sage.

Barlow, C., Johnson, K., Walklate, S. and Humphreys, L. (2020) 'Putting coercive control into practice', *British Journal of Criminology*, 60(1): 160–179.

Berg, B. L. (2009) *Qualitative Research Methods for the Social Sciences*, 7th edn. Pearson International Edition. Boston: Pearson (1st edn 1989).

Blair, J., Czaja, R. F. and Blair, E. A. (2015) *Designing Surveys: A Guide to Decisions and Procedures*, 3rd edn. London: Sage (1st edn 1996).

Blaustein, J. (2016) 'Community policing from the "bottom up" in Sarajevo Canton', *Policing and Society*, 26(3): 246–269.

Blismas, N. G. and Dainty, A. R. J. (2003) 'Computer-aided qualitative data analysis: panacea or paradox?', *Building Research and Information*, 31(6): 455–463.

Bloor, M., Frankland, J., Thomas, M. and Robson, K. (2001) *Focus Groups in Social Research*. London: Sage.

Boeije, H. (2010) *Analysis in Qualitative Research*. London: Sage.

Bond, C. E. W. and Jeffries, S. (2014) 'Similar punishment? Comparing sentencing outcomes in domestic and non-domestic violence cases', *British Journal of Criminology*, 54: 849–872.

Bowling, B. (1993) 'Racial harassment and the process of victimisation', *British Journal of Criminology*, 33(2): 231–250.

Brain, T. (2010) *A History of Policing in England and Wales from 1974*. Oxford: Oxford University Press.

Brent, J. J. and Kraska, P. B. (2013) '"Fighting is the most real and honest thing": violence and the civilisation/barbarism dialect', *British Journal of Criminology*, 53: 357–377.

British Heart Foundation (2021) 'How has the smoking ban changed our health?' (www. bhf.org.uk/informationsupport/heart-matters-magazine/news/smoking-ban).

Brunton-Smith, I. and McCarthy, D. J. (2017) 'The effects of prisoner attachment to family on re-entry outcomes: a longitudinal assessment', *British Journal of Criminology*, 57(2): 463–482.

Bryman, A. (1988) *Quantity and Quality in Social Research*. London: Routledge.

Bryman, A. (2008) *Social Research Methods*, 3rd edn. Oxford: Oxford University Press (1st edn 2001).

Bryman, A. and Burgess, R. G. (1994) 'Developments in qualitative data analysis: an introduction', in Bryman, A. and Burgess, R. G. (eds), *Analysing Qualitative Data*. London: Routledge, pp. 1–17.

Buckle, A. and Farrington, D. P. (1984) 'An observational study of shoplifting', *British Journal of Criminology*, 24(1): 63–73.

Burgess, A., Donovan, P. and Moore, S. (2009) 'Embodying uncertainty? Understanding heightened risk perception of drink spiking' *British Journal of Criminology*, 49: 848–862.

Burnett, R. and Maruna, S. (2004) 'So "prison works" does it? The criminal careers of 130 men released from prison under Home Secretary, Michael Howard', *The Howard Journal of Crime and Justice*, 43(4): 390–404.

Butler, P. (2015) 'Troubled families scheme outcomes: miraculous success or pure fiction?', *The Guardian*, 22 June (www.theguardian.com/politics/2015/jun/22/ troubled-families-scheme-outcomes-miraculous-success-or-pure-fiction).

Cadwalladr, C. and Graham-Harrison, E. (2018) 'Revealed: 50 million Facebook profiles harvested for Cambridge Analytica in major data breach', *The Guardian*, 17 March (www.theguardian.com/news/2018/mar/17/cambridge-analytica-facebook-influence-us-election).

Carpenter, B., Tait, G., Quadrell, C. and Thompson, I. (2016) 'Investigating death: the emotional and cultural challenges for police', *Policing and Society*, 26(6): 698–712.

Case, S., Johnson, P., Manlow, D., Smith, R. and Williams, K. (2017) *Criminology*. Oxford: Oxford University Press.

Casey, L. (2012) *Listening to Troubled Families*. London: Department for Communities and Local Government (https://assets.publishing.service.gov.uk/government/uploads/ system/uploads/attachment_data/file/6151/2183663.pdf).

Charmaz, K. (2006) *Constructing Grounded Theory*. London: Sage.

Clough, P. and Nutbrown, C. (2012) *A Student's Guide to Methodology*. London: Sage.

REFERENCES

Coffee, A. (2006) 'Participant observation', in Jupp, V. (ed.), *The Sage Dictionary of Social Research Methods*. London: Sage, pp. 214–216.

Cohen, J. W. (1988) *Statistical Power Analysis for the Behavioural Sciences* (2nd end). Hillsdale, NJ: Lawrence Erlbaum Associates (1st edn, 1977).

Collison, M. (1996) 'In search of the high life: drugs, crimes, masculinities and consumption', *British Journal of Criminology*, 36(3): 428–444.

Cook, I. and Davies, P. (2017) 'Supporting victims and witnesses', in Harding, J. Davies, P. and Mair, G. (eds), *An Introduction to Criminal Justice*. London: Sage, pp. 388–404.

Coupe, R. T. (2016) 'Evaluating the effect of resources and solvability on burglary detection', *Policing and Society*, 26(5): 544–562.

Cox, P., Shore, H. and Godfrey, B. (2018) 'Using historical artefacts, records and resources in criminological research', in Davies, P. and Francis, P. (eds), *Doing Criminological Research*, 3rd edn. London: Sage, pp. 180–198 (1st edn 2000).

Coxon, P. and Valentine, T. (1997) 'The effects of age of eyewitnesses on the accuracy and suggestibility of their testimony', *Applied Cognitive Psychology*, 11: 415–430.

Crawford, A., Lewis, S. and Traynor, P. (2017) '"It ain't just what you do, it's (also) the way you do it": the role of procedural justice in the implementation of anti-social behavior interventions with young people', *European Journal of Criminal Policy and Research*, 23: 9–26.

Crewe, B. (2006) 'Prison drug dealing and the ethnographic lens', *The Howard Journal of Criminal Justice*, 45(4): 347–368.

Davies, P. (2006) 'Research design', in Jupp, V. (ed.), *The Sage Dictionary of Social Research Methods*. London: Sage, pp. 265–266.

Davies, P., Francis, P. and Jupp, V. (2011) 'Glossary', in Davies, P. Francis, P. and Jupp, V. (eds), *Doing Criminological Research*, 2nd edn. London: Sage, pp. 345–356 (1st edn 2000).

Davis, R. C., Taylor, B. and Lurigio, A. J. (1996) 'Adjusting to criminal victimisation: the correlates of post-crime distress', *Violence and Victims*, 11(1): 21–38.

Dawson, C. (2009) *Introduction to Research Methods*. Oxford: How to Books Limited.

Day, L., Bryson, C., White, C., Purdon, S., Bewley, H., Sala, L. K. and Portes, J. (2016) *National Evaluation of the Troubled Families Programme: Final Synthesis Report*. London: Department of Communities and Local Government.

Deakin, N. (1990) 'Mr. Murray's ark', in Lister, R. (ed.) (1996) *Charles Murray and the Underclass*. London: Institute of Economic Affairs, Health and Welfare Unit, pp. 75–80.

Dennis, N., Henriques, F. and Slaughter, C. (1969) *Coal is Our Life: An Analysis of a Yorkshire Mining Community*. London: Tavistock Publications.

De Vaus, D. (2002) *Surveys in Social Research*, 5th edn. London: Routledge (1st edn 1986).

Dobash, R. E. and Dobash, R. (1979) *Violence Against Wives: A Case Against the Hierarchy*. New York: Free Press.

Dodd, V. (2020) 'Crime in UK falls sharply since start of coronavirus lockdown', *The Guardian*, 15 April (www.theguardian.com/uk-news/2020/apr/15/in-uk-falls-sharply-since-start-of-coronavirus-lockdown).

Dodd, V. (2021) 'A thousand young, black men removed from Met gang violence prediction database', *The Guardian*, 3 February (www.theguardian.com/uk-news/2021/feb/03/a-thousand-young-black-men-removed-from-met-gang-violence-prediction-database).

Dufour, I. F., Richard, M. C. and Li, J. (2019) 'Theorizing from secondary qualitative data: a comparison of two data analysis methods', *Cogent Education*, 6(1).

Durkheim, E. (1952) *Suicide*. London: Routledge and Kegan Paul.

Elliott, J. (2005) *Using Narratives in Social Research: Qualitative and Quantitative Approaches*. London: Sage.

Elmquist, J., Hamel, J., Shorey, R. C., Labrecque, L., Ninnemann, A. and Stuart, G. L. (2014) 'Motivations for intimate partner violence in men and women arrested for domestic violence and court referred to batterer intervention programs', *Partner Abuse*, 5(4): 359–374.

Fagan, J., Piper, E. and Cheng, Y.-T. (1987) 'Contribution of victimisation to delinquency in inner cities', *Journal of Criminal Law and Criminology*, 78(3): 586–613.

Fallik, S. W. (2018) 'Detective effort: what contributes to arrests during retrospective criminal investigations?', *Policing and Society*, 28(9): 1084–1104.

Ferguson, A. G. (2017) 'Policing predictive policing', *Washington University Law Review*, 94(5): 1112–1189.

Fetterman, D. (1989) *Ethnography Step-by-Step*. London: Sage.

Field, F. (1990) 'Britain's underclass: countering the growth', in Lister, R. (ed.) (1996) *Charles Murray and the Underclass*. London: Institute of Economic Affairs Health and Welfare Unit, pp. 57–60.

Fielding, J. (2006) *Understanding Social Statistics*. London: Sage.

Finch, H. and Lewis, J. (2003) 'Focus groups', in Ritchie, J. and Lewis, J. (eds), *Qualitative Research Practice*. London: Sage.

Fitz-Gibbon, K. and O'Brien, W. (2017) 'The naming of child homicide offenders in England and Wales: the need for a change in law and practice', *British Journal of Criminology*, 57(5): 1061–1079.

Flick, U. (1998) *An Introduction to Qualitative Research*. London: Sage.

Flyvbjerg, B. (2006) 'Five misunderstandings about case study research', *Qualitative Inquiry*, 12(2): 219–245.

Fontana, A. and Frey, J. H. (2008) 'The interview: from neutral stance to political involvement', in Denzin, N. K. and Lincoln, Y. S. (eds), *Collecting and Interpreting Qualitative Materials*, 3rd edn. London: Sage, pp. 115–160 (1st edn 1998).

REFERENCES

Fontes, A. W. (2019) 'Portrait of a "real" *marero*: fantasy and falsehood in stories of gang violence', *Ethnography*, 20(3): 320–341.

Franzke, A. S., Bechmann, A., Zimmer, M. and Ess, C. M. (2020) *Internet Research: Ethical Guidelines 3.0*. Chicago: Association of Internet Researchers, (https://aoir.org/reports/ethics3.pdf).

Gadd, D., Henderson, J., Radcliffe, P., Stephens-Lewis, D., Johnson, A. and Gilchrist, G. (2019) 'The dynamics of domestic abuse and drug and alcohol dependency', *British Journal of Criminology*, 59(5): 1035–1053.

Garwood, J., Rogerson, M. and Pease, K. (2000) 'Sneaky measurement of crime and disorder', in Jupp, V., Davies, P. and Francis, P. (eds), *Doing Criminological Research*. London: Sage, pp. 157–168.

Gayle, D. (2019) 'Sean Rigg: five officers cleared of misconduct over death in custody', *The Guardian*, 1 March (www.theguardian.com/uk-news/2019/mar/01/sean-rigg-five-officers-cleared-of-misconduct-over-death-in-custody).

Gaywood, D., Bertram, T. and Pascal, C. (2020) 'Involving refugee children in research: emerging ethical and positioning issues', *European Early Childhood Research Journal*, 28(1): 149–162.

Gibson, W. J. and Brown, A. (2009) *Working with Qualitative Data*. London: Sage.

Gillham, B. (2005) *Research Interviewing: The Range of Techniques*. Maidenhead: Open University Press.

Glaser, B. and Strauss, A. L. (1967) *The Discovery of Grounded Theory: Strategies for Qualitative Research*. New York: Aldine de Gruyter.

Gorard, S. (2016) 'Damaging real lives through obstinacy: re-emphasising why significance testing is wrong', *Sociological Research Online*, 21(1).

Gottschalk, P. (2010) 'Crime-based survey instrument for police integrity measurement', *Policing: International Journal of Police Strategy and Management*, 33(1): 52–68.

Grbich, C. (2007) *Qualitative Data Analysis: An Introduction*. London: Sage.

Greco, L. (2006) 'Conversation analysis', in Jupp, V. (ed.), *The Sage Dictionary of Social Research Methods*. London: Sage.

Green, N. (2008) 'Formulating and refining a research question', in Gilbert, N. (ed.), *Researching Social Life*, 3rd edn. London: Sage (1st edn 1993).

Hales, J., Nevill, C., Pudney, S. and Tipping, S. (2006) *Longitudinal Analysis of the Offending, Crime and Justice Survey 2003–06*. London: Home Office Research Report 19.

Hall, N. (2013) *Hate Crime*, 2nd edn. Milton Park: Taylor and Francis (1st edn 2005).

Hall, S., Critcher, C., Jefferson, T., Clarke, J. and Roberts, B. (1978) *Policing the State: Mugging, the State and Law and Order*. Basingstoke: Macmillan.

Hammersley, M. (2018) 'What is ethnography? Can it survive? Should it?', *Ethnography and Education*, 13(1): 1–17.

Haney, C., Banks, C. and Zimbardo, P. (1981) 'A study of prisoners and guards in a simulated prison', in Potter, D., Anderson, J., Clarke, J., Coombes, P., Hall, J., Harris, L., Holloway, C. and Walton, T. (eds), *Society and the Social Sciences: An Introduction*. London: Routledge and Kegan Paul, pp. 181–199.

Harding, J. (2001) 'Success and failure in independent living among 16–17 year olds', PhD thesis, University of Newcastle upon Tyne.

Harding, J. (2004) *Making it Work: The Keys to Success for Young People Living Independently*. Bristol: Policy Press.

Harding, J. (2006) 'Grounded theory', in Jupp, V. (ed.), *The Sage Dictionary of Social Research Methods*. London: Sage, pp. 131–132.

Harding, J. (2019) *Qualitative Data Analysis from Start to Finish*, 2nd edn. London: Sage (1st edn 2013).

Heaton, J. (2004) *Reworking Qualitative Data*. London: Sage.

Henn, M., Weinstein, M. and Foard, N. (2009) *A Critical Introduction to Social Research*, 2nd edn. London: Sage (1st edn 2006).

Henne, K. and Troshynski, E. I. (2019) 'Intersectional criminologies for the contemporary moment: crucial questions of power, praxis and technologies of control', *Critical Criminology*, 27(1): 55–71.

Hennink, M., Hutter, I. and Bailey, A. (2011) *Qualitative Research Methods*. London: Sage.

Hera, G. (2017) 'The relationship between Roma and the police: a Roma perspective', *Policing and Society*, 27(4): 393–407.

Hesse-Biber, S. and Leavy, P. (2011) *The Practice of Qualitative Research*, 2nd edn. Thousand Oaks, CA: Sage (1st edn 2006).

Hewitt, R. (1996) *Routes of Racism*. Stoke-on-Trent: Trentham Books.

Hirtenfelder, C. (2016) 'Masking over ambiguity: suburban Johannesburg police reservists and the uniform fetish', *Policing and Society*, 26(6): 659–679.

HM Government (2016) *Ending Violence Against Women and Girls Strategy 2016–2020* (https://assets.publishing.service.gov.uk/government/uploads/system/uploads/attachment_data/file/522166/VAWG_Strategy_FINAL_PUBLICATION_MASTER_vRB.PDF).

HM Government (2019) *Transforming the Response to Domestic Abuse: Consultation and Draft Bill* (https://assets.publishing.service.gov.uk/government/uploads/ system/uploads/attachment_data/file/772202/CCS1218158068-Web_Accessible.pdf).

HM Inspectorate of Prisons for England and Wales (2018) *Annual Report 2017–18*, HC1245 (https://assets.publishing.service.gov.uk/government/uploads/system/uploads/attachment_data/file/761589/hmi-prisons-annual-report-2017-18-revised-web.pdf).

HM Prison and Probation Service (2019) *Prison Drug Strategy* (https://assets.publishing.service.gov.uk/government/uploads/system/uploads/attachment_data/file/792125/prison-drugs-strategy.pdf).

Holdaway, S. (1983) *Inside the British Police: A Force at Work*. Oxford: Blackwell.

Homan, R. (1991) *The Ethics of Social Research*. London: Longman.

Home Office (2019) *Crimes Against Businesses: Findings from the 2018 Commercial Victimisation Survey. Statistical Bulletin 17/19* (https://assets.publishing.service.gov.uk/government/uploads/system/uploads/attachment_data/file/829399/crime-against-businesses-2018-hosb1719.pdf).

Hope, T. (2015) *We Need a Different Crime Survey*. London: Centre for Crime and Justice Studies.

House of Commons Home Affairs Committee (2013) *Independent Police Complaints Commission, Eleventh Report of Session 2012–13, HC494*. London: House of Commons.

Humphreys, L. (1970) *Tearoom Trade*. London: Gerald Duckworth and Co Ltd.

Huq, A. Z., Jackson, J. and Trinkner, R. (2017) 'Legitimating practices: revisiting the predicates of police legitimacy', *British Journal of Criminology*, 57(5): 1101–1122.

Hutton, A., Whitehead, D. and Ullah, S. (2017) 'Can positive faith-based encounters influence Australian young people's drinking behaviours?', *Health Education Journal*, 76(4): 423–431.

ICAR (Information Centre about Asylum Seekers and Refugees in the UK) (2004) *Media Image, Community Impact*. London: Kings College.

Ilan, J. (2019) 'Cultural criminology: the time is now', *Critical Criminology*, 27(1): 5–20.

Irving, A. (2018) 'Homelessness pathways and capabilities: a study of the lived experiences of the hidden homeless in private hostels in Newcastle-upon-Tyne', Doctoral thesis, Northumbria University.

Irving, A. and Laing, M. (2013) *PEER: Exploring the Lives of Sex Workers in Tyne and Wear* (http://nrl.northumbria.ac.uk/11674/2/PEER_finalreport.pdf).

James, E. (2003) *A Life Inside: A Prisoner's Notebook*. London: Atlantic Books.

Johnsen, S., May, J. and Cloke, P. (2008) 'Imag(in)ing "homeless places": using auto-photography to (re)examine the geographies of homelessness', *Area*, 40(2): 194–207.

Jolicoeur, J. R. and Grant, E. (2018) 'Form seeking function: an exploratory content analysis evaluation of the imagery contained in law enforcement agency police officer recruitment brochures', *The Police Journal: Theory, Practice and Principles*, 91(4): 339–355.

Jordan, J., Lynch, U., Moutray, M., O'Hagan, M. T., Orr, J., Peake, S. and Power, J. (2007) 'Using focus groups to research sensitive issues: insights from group interviews on nursing in the Northern Ireland "Troubles"', *International Journal of Qualitative Methods*, 6(4): 1–19.

Josselson, R. (2011) 'Narrative research', in Wertz, F. J., Charmaz, K., McMullen, L. M., Josselson, R., Anderson, R. and McSpadden, E. (2011) *Five Ways of Doing Qualitative Analysis*. New York: The Guilford Press, pp. 224–242.

Jowett, A., Peel, E. and Shaw, R. L. (2011) 'Online interviewing in psychology: reflections on the process', *Qualitative Research in Psychology*, 8(4): 354–369.

Junger-Tas, J. and Marshall, I. H. (1999) 'The self-report methodology in crime research', *Crime and Justice*, 25: 291–367.

Jupp, V. (2006) 'Validity', in Jupp, V. (ed.), *The Sage Dictionary of Social Research Methods*. London: Sage.

Kantar Public (2017a) *2015–16 Crime Survey for England and Wales Technical Report – Volume 1*. London: Office for National Statistics.

Kantar Public (2017b) *2017–18 Crime Survey for England and Wales Questionnaire (from April 2017)*. London: Office for National Statistics.

Kavanaugh, P. R. and Anderson, T. L. (2017) 'Neoliberal governance and the homogenization of substance use and risk in night-time leisure scenes', *British Journal of Criminology*, 57(2): 483–501.

Kemp, P. A., Neale, J. and Robertson, M. (2006) 'Homelessness among problem drug users: prevalence, risk factors and trigger events', *Health and Social Care in the Community*, 14(4): 319–328.

King, N. and Horrocks, C. (2010) *Interviews in Qualitative Research*. London: Sage.

Kite, J. and Phongsavan, P. (2017) 'Insights for conducting real-time focus groups online using a web conferencing service', *F1000 Res*, 6: 122. (www.ncbi.nlm.nih.gov/pmc/articles/PMC5527981).

Kozinets, R. V. (2020) *Netnography: The Essential Guide to Qualitative Social Media Research*. London: Sage.

Krueger, R. A. (1998) *Analysing and Reporting Focus Group Results*. London: Sage.

Kvale, S. (1996) *Interview Views: An Introduction to Qualitative Research Interviewing*. Thousand Oaks, CA: Sage.

Lauritsen, J., Sampson, R. and Laub, J. (1991) 'The link between offending and victimisation among adolescents', *Criminology*, 29(2): 265–292.

Lea, J. (2000) 'The MacPherson report and the question of institutional racism', *Howard Journal*, 39(3): 219–233.

Leerkes, A., Martinez, R. and Groeneveld, P. (2019) 'Minority paradoxes: ethnic differences in self-reporting offending and official crime statistics', *British Journal of Criminology*, 59(1): 166–187.

Legard, R., Keegan, J. and Ward, K. (2003) 'In-depth interviews', in Richie, J. and Lewis, J. (eds), *Qualitative Research Practice*. London: Sage, pp. 139–168.

Levitas, R. (2012) 'Troubled families report contains more anecdote than evidence', Letters to *The Guardian*, 19 July (www.theguardian.com/society/2012/jul/19/troubled-families-report-anecdote-evidence).

Lewis, S. (2006) 'Minority ethnic experiences of probation supervision and programmes', in Lewis, S., Raynor, P., Smith, D. and Wardak, A. (eds), *Race and Probation*. Cullompton: Willan Publishing.

Lewis, S., Crawford, A. and Traynor, P. (2017) 'Nipping crime in the bud: the use of antisocial behaviour interventions with young people in England and Wales', *British Journal of Criminology*, 57: 1230–1248.

Liamputtong, P. (2011) *Focus Group Methodology*. London: Sage.

Lissaman, C. (2011) 'Birmingham Six "were in the wrong place at the wrong time"', BBC News, 14 March (www.bbc.co.uk/news/uk-england-12664938).

Lo Iacono, V., Symonds, P. and Brown, D. H. K. (2016) 'Skype as a tool for qualitative research interviews', *Sociological Research Online*, 21(2): 103–117.

Lopes, A. (2006) 'Participatory action research', in Jupp, V. (ed.), *The Sage Dictionary of Social Research Methods*. London: Sage, pp. 216–217.

MacDonald, A. (2016) *The Nuremberg Trials: The Nazis Brought to Justice*. London: Arcturus Publishing Limited.

MacQueen, S. and Norris, P. A. (2016) 'Police awareness and involvement in cases of domestic and partner abuse', *Policing and Society*, 26(1): 55–76.

Maguire, E. R., Johnson, D., Kuhns, J. B. and Apostolos, R. (2019) 'The effects of community policing on fear of crime and perceived safety: findings from a pilot project in Trinidad and Tobago', *Policing and Society*, 29(5): 491–590.

Maguire, M. and McVie, S. (2017) 'Crime data and criminal statistics: a critical reflection', in Liebling, A., Maruna, S. and McAra, L. (eds), *The Oxford Handbook of Criminology*, 6th edn. Oxford: Oxford University Press, pp. 163–189 (1st edn 1994).

Mandracchia, J. T. and Smith, P. N. (2015) 'The interpersonal theory of suicide applied to male prisoners', *Suicide and Life Threatening Behaviour*, 45(3): 293–301.

Martel, J., Brassard, R. and Jaccoud, M. (2011) 'When two worlds collide: Aboriginal risk management in Canadian corrections', *British Journal of Criminology*, 51(2): 235–255.

Mayock, P. and Sheridan, S. (2012) *Migrant Women and Homelessness: Key Findings from a Biographical Study of Homeless Women in Ireland*. Women and Homelessness in Ireland, Research Paper 1. Dublin: School of Social Work and Social Policy and Children's Research Centre, Trinity College Dublin.

Mayor of London Office for Policing and Crime (2018) *Review of the Metropolitan Police Service Gangs Matrix* (www.london.gov.uk/sites/default/files/gangs_matrix_review_-_final.pdf).

McMullen, L. M. (2011) 'A discursive analysis of Teresa's protocol', in Wertz, F. J., Charmaz, K., McMullen, L. M., Josselson, R., Anderson, R. and McSpadden, E. (eds), *Five Ways of Doing Qualitative Analysis*. New York: The Guilford Press, pp. 205–223.

Mead, M. (1943) *Coming of Age in Samoa: A Study of Adolescence and Sex in Primitive Societies*. Harmondsworth: Penguin.

Menting, B., Lammers, B., Ruiter, S. and Bernasco, W. (2020) 'The influence of activity space and visiting frequency on crime location choice: findings from an online self-report survey', *British Journal of Criminology*, 60(2): 303–322.

Mercan, B. A. (2018) 'The making of the professional criminal in Turkey', *Ethnography*, 21(1): 92–112.

Miles, M. B. and Huberman, M. (1994) *Qualitative Data Analysis*, 2nd edn. London: Sage (1st edn 1984).

Miles-Johnson, T. (2016) 'Perceptions of group value: how Australian transgender people view policing', *Policing and Society*, 26(6): 605–626.

Miller, J. and Glassner, B. (2011) 'The "inside" and the "outside": finding realities in interviews', in Silverman, D. (ed.), *Qualitative Research*, 3rd edn. Thousand Oaks, CA: Sage, pp. 131–148 (1st edn 1997).

Ministry of Justice, New Zealand (2014) *Public Perceptions of Crime and the Criminal Justice System Survey – 2014 Results*. Wellington, New Zealand: Ministry of Justice.

Mitchell, B. and Roberts, J. V. (2012) 'Sentencing for murder: exploring public knowledge and public opinion in England and Wales', *British Journal of Criminology*, 52(1): 141–158.

Mohdin, A. (2018) 'Top film-makers back penguin intervention on Attenborough show', *The Guardian*, 19 November (www.theguardian.com/tv-and-radio/2018/nov/19/top-filmmakers-back-penguin-intervention-on-attenborough-show).

Moore, S. E. H. (2014) *Crime and the Media*. Basingstoke: Palgrave Macmillan.

Morgan, D. L. (2010) 'Reconsidering the role of interaction in analyzing and reporting focus group data', *Qualitative Health Research*, 20(5): 718–722.

Moses, J. M. and Knutsen, T. L. (2007) *Ways of Knowing: Competing Methodologies in Social and Political Research*. Basingstoke: Palgrave Macmillan.

Muncie, J. (2006) 'Discourse analysis', in Jupp, V. (ed.), *The Sage Dictionary of Social Research Methods*. London: Sage, pp. 74–76.

Munoz, J., Anduiza, E. and Gallego, A. (2016) 'Why do voters forgive corrupt mayors? Implicit exchange, credibility of information and clean alternatives', *Local Government Studies*, 42(4): 598–615.

Murphy, K. and Harris, N. (2007) 'Shaming, shame and recidivism: a test of reintegrative shaming theory in the white-collar crime context', *British Journal of Criminology*, 47: 900–917.

Murray, C. (1990) 'The emerging British underclass', in Lister, R. (ed.) (1996) *Charles Murray and the Underclass*. London: Institute of Economic Affairs, Health and Welfare Unit, pp. 23–53.

REFERENCES

Murray, C. E., Davis, J., Lin, R., Graves, K., Colbert, R., Fryer, M., Mason, A. and Thigpen, B. (2016) 'Domestic violence training experiences and needs among mental health professionals: implications from a statewide survey', *Violence and Victims*, 31(5): 901–920.

Murthy, D. (2008) 'Digital ethnography: an examination of new technologies for social research', *Sociology*, 45(5): 837–855.

Myers, L. P. (2019) *Insider Research: Ethics, Professionalism and Positionality*, paper presented at the 2019 British Accounting and Finance Association (BAFA) Accounting Education Conference, University of Birmingham.

Neuendorf, K. (2017) *The Content Analysis Guidebook*, 2nd edn. London: Sage (1st edn 2002).

Newburn, T. and Stanko, E. A. (1994) 'When men are victims', in Newburn, T. and Stanko, E. A. (eds), *Just Boys Doing Business? Men, Masculinities and Crime*. Abingdon: Routledge.

Newburn, T., Shiner, M. and Hayman, S. (2004) 'Race, crime and injustice?', *British Journal of Criminology*, 44: 677–694.

Nguyen, O. and Le, T. (2021) 'Perceptions of governmental and non-governmental actors of human trafficking victims: the case of Vietnam', *International Journal for Crime, Justice and Social Democracy*, 9(4): 127–139.

Nicholson, J. and McCusker, S. (2016) 'Damaging the case for improving social science methodology through misrepresentation: re-asserting confidence in hypothesis testing as a valid scientific process', *Sociological Research Online*, 21(2).

Nix, J., Pickett, J. T., Beek, H. and Alpert, G. P. (2019) 'Police research, officer surveys and response rates', *Policing and Society*, 29(5): 530–550.

Oates, C. (2000) 'The use of focus groups in social science research', in Burton, D. (ed.), *Research Training for Social Scientists*. London: Sage, pp. 186–195.

Office for National Statistics (2018) *Domestic Abuse in England and Wales: Year Ending March 2018*. London: Office for National Statistics.

Oliver, P. (2012) *Succeeding with Your Literature Review: A Handbook for Students*. Maidenhead: Open University Press

Onifade, D. (2002) *The Experience of Black/Minority Ethnic Police Officers, Support Staff, Special Constables and Resigners in Scotland*. Edinburgh: Scottish Executive, Central Research Unit.

Onwuegbuzie, A. J., Dickinson, W. B., Leech, N. L. and Zoran, A. G. (2009) 'A qualitative framework for collecting and analyzing data in focus group research', *International Journal of Qualitative Methods*, 8(3): 1–21.

Oppenheim, A. (1992) *Questionnaire Design, Interviewing and Attitude Measurement*. London: Continuum.

Osborne, S. (2018) *Crime Against Businesses: Findings from the 2017 Commercial Victimisation Survey, Home Office Statistical Bulletin 07/18*. London: Home Office.

Osborne, T. and Rose, N. (1999) 'Do the social sciences create phenomena? The example of public opinion research', *British Journal of Sociology*, 50(3): 367–396.

Pain, R. and Francis, P. (2003) 'Reflections on participatory research', *Area*, 35(1): 46–54.

Pain, R. and Francis, P. (2004) 'Living with crime: spaces of risk for homeless people', *Children's Geographies*, 2(1): 95–110.

Pallant, J. (2001) *SPSS Survival Manual*. Buckingham: Open University Press.

Pallister, D. (2007) 'Solicitor wrongly jailed for killing sons died from excess alcohol', *The Guardian*, 8 November (www.theguardian.com/society/2007/nov/08/childrens).

Patrick, J. (1973) *A Glasgow Gang Observed*. London: Eyre Methuen.

Patton, M. (1990) *Qualitative Evaluation and Research Methods*. Beverly Hills, CA: Sage.

Patton, M. Q. (2002) *Qualitative Research and Evaluation Methods*. London: Sage.

Pearce, G., Thøgersen-Ntoumani, C. and Duda, J. L. (2014) 'The development of synchronous text-based instant messaging as an online interviewing tool', *International Journal of Social Research Methodology*, 17(6): 677–692.

Pells, K. (2011) 'Keep going despite everything: legacies of genocide for Rwanda's children and youth', *International Journal of Sociology and Social Policy*, 31(9/10): 594–606.

Phillips, C. and Bowling, B. (2017) 'Ethnicities, racism, crime and criminal justice', in Liebling, A., Maruna, S. and McAra, L. (eds), *The Oxford Handbook of Criminology*, 6th edn. Oxford: Oxford University Press, pp. 190–212 (1st edn 1994).

Poysner, S., Nurse, A. and Milne, R. (2018) *Miscarriages of Justice: Causes, Consequences and Remedies*. Bristol: Policy Press.

Pryke, S. (2004) '"Some of our people can be the most difficult": reflections on difficult interviews', *Sociological Research Online*, 9(1).

Ramesh, R. (2012) 'Poor families, poor research: Eric Pickles' flawed recasting of society', *The Guardian*, 12 June (www.theguardian.com/politics/2012/jun/11/eric-pickles-payment-by-results).

Ramshaw, P. (2012) 'Community policing and lateral career paths', *Policing Practice and Research: An International Journal*, 14(6): 464–477.

Ranasinghe, P. (2017) 'Rethinking the place of crime in police patrol: a re-reading of classic police ethnographies', *British Journal of Criminology*, 57: 867–884.

Ratcliffe, J. H. (2016) 'Central American police perception of street gang characteristics', *Policing and Society*, 26(3): 291–311.

Ray, L., Smith, D. and Wastell, L. (2004) 'Shame, rage and racist violence', *British Journal of Criminology*, 44: 350–368.

Raymen, T. (2017) 'The paradox of parkour: an exploration of the deviant-leisure nexus in late-capitalist urban space', Doctoral thesis, University of Durham.

Reason, P. and Bradbury, H. (2006) 'Introduction: inquiry and participation in search of a world worthy of human aspiration', in Reason, P. and Bradbury, H. (eds), *Handbook of Action Research*, 2nd edn. London: Sage, pp. 1–14 (1st edn 2001).

Retzinger, S. M. (1991) *Violent Emotions: Shame and Rage in Marital Quarrels*. Thousand Oaks, CA: Sage.

Richards, L. (2009) *Handling Qualitative Data*, 2nd edn. London: Sage (1st edn 2005).

Risdaneva (2018) 'A critical discourse analysis of women's portrayal in news reporting on sexual violence', *Studies in English Language and Education*, 5(1): 126–136.

Rivlin, A., Fazel, S., Marzano, L. and Hawton, K. (2013) 'The suicidal process in male prisoners making near-lethal suicide attempts', *Psychology, Crime and Law*, 19(4): 305–327.

Robinson, A. (2011) 'Giving voice and taking pictures: participatory documentary and visual research', *People, Place and Policy Online*, 5(3): 115–134.

Robson, C. (2002) *Real World Research* (2nd edn). Oxford: Blackwell (1st edn 1993).

Robson, C. (2011) *Real World Research*. Chichester: John Wiley and Sons Limited.

Rock, P. (2017) 'The foundations of sociological theories of crime', in Liebling, A., Maruna, S. and McAra, L. (eds), *The Oxford Handbook of Criminology*, 6th edn. Oxford: Oxford University Press, pp. 21–56 (1st edn 1994).

Rodriguez, J. A., Santiago, N. P., Birkbeck, C. H., Crespo, F. and Morillo, S. (2017) 'Internationalising the study of gang membership: validation issues from Latin America', *British Journal of Criminology*, 57: 1165–1184.

Roh, S., Kwak, D. H. and Kim, E. (2013) 'Community policing and fear of crime in Seoul: a test of competing models', *Policing: An International Journal of Police Strategies & Management*, 36(1): 199–222.

Roskin-Frazee, A. (2020) 'Protection for marginalized women in university sexual violence policies', *International Journal for Crime, Justice and Social Democracy*, 9(1): 13–30.

Rothe, D. and Steinmetz, K. F. (2013) 'The case of Bradley Manning: state victimisation, realpolitik and Wikileaks', *Contemporary Justice Review*, 16(2): 280–292.

Roulston, K. (2010) *Reflective Interviewing: A Guide to Theory and Practice*. London: Sage.

Roulstone, A. and Mason-Bish, H. (2013) *Disability, Hate Crime and Violence*. Abingdon, Oxon: Routledge.

Rowe, M. (2007) 'Tripping over molehills: ethics and the ethnography of police work', *International Journal of Social Research Methodology*, 10(1): 37–48.

Rowlingson, K. and McKay, S. (2005) *Attitudes to Inheritance in Britain*. York: Joseph Rowntree Foundation.

Rudestam, K. E. and Newton, R. R. (2007) *Surviving Your Dissertation: A Comprehensive Guide to Content and Process*. London: Sage.

Ryan, J., Roman, N. V. and Rich, E. (2015) 'Original contributions. Perceived childhood exposure to domestic violence: the risk for adult revictimisation', *African Safety Promotion*, 13(2): 1–16.

Sandberg, S., Agoff, C. and Fondevila, G. (2021) 'Doing marginalized motherhood: identities and practices among incarcerated women in Mexico', *International Journal for Crime, Justice and Social Democracy*, 10(1): 15–29.

Sanders, C. and Sheptycki, J. (2017) 'Policing, crime and "big data": towards a critique of the moral economy of stochastic governance', *Crime, Law and Social Change*, 68(1–2): 1–15.

Sapsford, R. (2006) 'Methodology', in Jupp, V. (ed.), *The Sage Dictionary of Social Research Methods*. London: Sage, pp. 175–177.

Saunders, D. and Vanstone, M. (2010) 'Rehabilitation as presented in British film: shining a light on desistance from crime?', *The Howard Journal of Criminal Justice*, 49(4): 375–393.

Scarman, L. G. (1982) *The Scarman Report: The Brixton Disorders 10–12 April 1981: Report of an Inquiry*. Harmondsworth: Penguin.

Schmidt, D. (2004) 'The analysis of semi-structured interviews', in Flick, U., Von Kardoff, E. and Steinke, I., (eds), *A Companion to Qualitative Research*. London: Sage.

Semmens, N. (2011) 'Methodological approaches to criminological research', in Davies, P., Francis, P. and Jupp, V. (eds), *Doing Criminological Research*, 2nd edn. London: Sage, pp. 54–77 (1st edn 2000).

Sharkey, J. (2010) 'Does overcrowding in prisons exacerbate the risk of suicide among women prisoners?' *Howard Journal of Criminal Justice*, 49(2): 111–124.

Shaw, D. (2020) 'UK's 2021 census could be the last, statistics chief reveals', BBC News (www.bbc.co.uk/news/uk-51468919).

Sheard, L. (2011) '"Anything could have happened": women, the night-time economy, alcohol and drink spiking', *Sociology*, 45(4): 619–633.

Shortland, A. and Varese, F. (2014) 'The protector's choice: an application of protection theory to Somali piracy', *British Journal of Criminology*, 54: 741–764.

Sibbitt, R. (1997) *The Perpetrators of Racial Harassment and Racial Violence*. Home Office Research Study 176. London: Home Office.

Siddique, H. (2012) 'Antisocial behaviour: Eric Pickles insists troubled families are not victims', *The Guardian*, 11 June (www.theguardian.com/society/2012/jun/11/antisocial-behaviour-eric-pickles-victims).

Silverman, D. (2006) *Interpreting Qualitative Data*, 3rd edn. London: Sage (1st edn 1993).

Silverman, D. (2007) *A Very Short, Fairly Interesting and Reasonably Cheap Book About Qualitative Research*. London: Sage.

Singer, S. (1981) 'Homogeneous victim-offender populations: a review and some research implications', *Journal of Criminal Law and Criminology*, 72(2): 779–788.

REFERENCES

Sleath, E. and Brown, S. (2019) 'Staff and offender perspectives on Integrated Offender Management and the impact of its introduction on arrests and risk of reoffending in one police force region', *Policing and Society*, 29(5): 511–529.

Smith, D. (2009) 'Quarter of men in South Africa admit rape, survey finds', *The Guardian*, 17 June (www.theguardian.com/world/2009/jun/17/south-africa-rape-survey).

Smith, D. (2010) 'One in three South African men admit to rape, survey finds', *The Guardian*, 25 November (www.theguardian.com/world/2010/nov/25/south-african-rape-survey).

So-kum Tang, C., Wong, D., Cheung, F. M. C. and Lee, A. (2000) 'Exploring how Chinese define violence against women: a focus group study in Hong Kong', *Women's Studies International Forum*, 23(2): 197–209.

Sollund, R. A. and Runhovde, S. R. (2020) 'Responses to wildlife crime in post-colonial times: Who fares best?', *British Journal of Criminology*, 60(4): 1014–1033.

Sosa, V., Bichler, G. and Quintero, L. (2019) 'Yelping about a good time: casino popularity and crime', *Criminal Justice Studies*, 32(2): 140–164.

Spicer, N. (2012) 'Combining qualitative and quantitative methods', in Seale, C. (ed.), *Researching Society and Culture*. London: Sage, pp. 479–494.

Spreckelsen, T. F. and Van der Horst, M. (2016) 'Is banning significance testing the best way to improve applied social science research? Questions on Gorard (2016)', *Sociological Research Online*, 21(3).

Steinke, I. (2004) 'Quality criteria in qualitative research', in Flick, U., von Kardoff, E. and Steinke, I. (eds), *A Companion to Qualitative Research*. London: Sage, pp. 184–190.

Stith, S. M. (1990) 'Police response to domestic violence: the influence of individual and familial factors', *Violence and Victims*, 5(1): 37–49.

Strobl, S. (2016) 'Policing in the Eastern Province of Saudi Arabia: understanding the role of sectarian history and politics', *Policing and Society*, 26(5): 544–562.

Sue, V. M. and Ritter, L. A. (2012) *Conducting Online Surveys*. London: Sage.

Sung, H., Delgado, S., Peña, D. and Paladino, A. (2016) 'Surveillance without protection: policing undocumented migrant workers in an American suburb', *British Journal of Criminology*, 56(5): 877–897.

Telep, C. W. and Somers, L. G. (2019) 'Examining police officer definitions of evidence-based policing: are we speaking the same language?', *Policing and Society*, 29(2): 171–187.

Thompson, P. (2003) 'Towards ethical practice in the use of archived transcribed interviews: a response', *International Journal of Social Research Methodology, Theory and Practice*, 6(4): 347–355.

Ugelvik, T. (2016) 'Prisons as welfare institutions?', in Jewkes, Y., Bennett, J. and Crewe, B. (eds), *Handbook on Prisons*, 2nd edn. London: Sage, pp. 388–402 (1st edn 2007).

Urbanik, M. M., Thompson, S. K. and Bucerius, S. M. (2017) '"Before there was danger but there was rules. And safety in those rules": effects of neighbourhood redevelopment on criminal structures', *British Journal of Criminology*, 57(2): 422–440.

Van Maanen, J. (1983) 'The boss: the American police sergeant', in Punch, M. (ed.), *Control in the Police Organisation*. Cambridge, MA: MIT Press, pp. 275–317.

Vollum, S. and Longmire, D. R. (2007) 'Covictims of capital murder: statements of victims' family members and friends at the time of execution', *Violence and Victims*, 22(5): 601–619.

Waddington, P. A. J. (1994) *Liberty and Order: Public Policing in a Capital City*. Milton Park: Taylor and Francis.

Waddington, P. A. J., Stenson, K. and Don, D. (2004) 'In proportion: race, and police stop and search', *British Journal of Criminology*, 44: 889–914.

Waddington, P. A. J., Williams, K., Wright, M. and Newburn, T. (2015) 'Dissension in public evaluations of the police', *Policing and Society*, 25(2): 212–235.

Wakefield, A. (2018) 'Undertaking a criminological literature review', in Davies, P. and Francis, P. (eds), *Doing Criminological Research*, 3rd edn. London: Sage, pp. 67–92 (1st edn 2000).

Walker, P. (2019) 'Was Boris Johnson as successful as London mayor as he claims?', *The Guardian*, 12 June (www.theguardian.com/politics/2019/jun/12/was-boris-johnson-as-successful-as-london-mayor-as-he-claims).

Walklate, S. and Mythen, G. (2016) 'Fractured lives, splintered knowledge: making criminological sense of the January, 2015 terrorist attacks in Paris', *Critical Criminology*, 24: 333–346.

Wall, S. (2008) 'Easier said than done: writing an autoethnography', *International Journal of Qualitative Methods*, 7(1).

Webster, C. (1999) *Inverting Racism*, paper presented to the British Criminology Conference, Liverpool.

Wells, A. (2018) 'Why the polls were wrong in 2017', blog post, 7 June (http://ukpollingreport.co.uk/blog/archives/date/2018/06).

Werth, R. (2017) 'Individualising risk: moral judgement, professional knowledge and affect in parole evaluations', *British Journal of Criminology*, 57(4): 808–827.

Wertz, F. J., Charmaz, K., McMullen, L. M., Josselson, R., Anderson, R. and McSpadden, E. (2011) *Five Ways of Doing Qualitative Analysis*. New York: The Guilford Press.

Westera, N. J., Kebbell, M. B., Milne, B. and Green, T. (2016) 'Towards a more effective detective', *Policing and Society*, 26(1): 1–17.

Whowell, M. (2009) 'Inappropriate sexualities? The practice, performance and regulation of male sex work in Manchester', PhD thesis, University of Loughborough.

REFERENCES

Whyte, W. F. (1955) *Street Corner Society*. Chicago: University of Chicago Press.

Wilkinson, S. (2011) 'Analysing focus group data', in Silverman, D. (ed.), *Qualitative Research*, 3rd edn. London: Sage, pp. 168–184 (1st edn 1997).

World Health Organization (2007) *Preventing Suicide in Jails and Prisons*. Geneva: World Health Organization.

Wu, Y. (2014) 'Race/ethnicity and perceptions of the police: a comparison of White, Black, Asian and Hispanic Americans', *Policing and Society*, 24(2): 135–157.

Yates, K. (2019) *The Maths of Life and Death*. London: Quercus Editions Ltd.

Yin, R. K. (2003) *Case Study Research*, 3rd edn. London: Sage.

Yin, R. K. (2011) *Qualitative Research from Start to Finish*. New York: The Guilford Press.

Young, M. (1991) *An Inside Job: Policing and Police Culture in Britain*. Oxford: Clarendon Press.

Young, M. and Willmott, P. (1957) *Family and Kinship in East London*. London: Routledge and Kegan Paul.

Yuille, J. C. and Tollestrup, P. A. (1990) 'Some effects of alcohol on eyewitness memory', *Journal of Applied Psychology*, 75(3): 268–273.

Zilberg, E. (2011) *Spaces of Detention: The Making of a Transnational Gang Crisis Between Los Angeles and San Salvador*. Durham, NC: Duke University Press.

INDEX

This index is in word-by-word alphabetical order. The letter "b" after a page number indicates bibliographical information in a "Further reading" section.